Charter Conflicts
What Is Parliament's Role?

Although the Canadian Charter of Rights and Freedoms is twenty years old, little is known about how it affects those who wield power, what influence it has on legislative decision, or to what extent the government believes it should be constrained by Charter concerns. For most laws Parliament has the final word on how social policy is balanced against protected rights. Thus the extent to which legislation is sensitive towards rights depends on how those who develop, propose, and assess policy view the Charter. How influential are governmental legal advisers? How risk-averse or risk-tolerant are government ministers when pursuing legislative goals that may result in Charter challenges? How capable is Parliament in requiring government to justify and explain legislative choices that may impair rights?

In *Charter Conflicts* Janet Hiebert examines these questions while analysing the Charter's influence on controversial legislative decisions such as social benefits for lesbians and gay men, the regulation of tobacco advertising, the rules of evidence for sexual assault trials, the use of DNA for law-enforcement purposes, and the rules for police searches of private residences. She questions the broadly held assumption that only courts are capable of respecting rights, arguing that Parliament shares responsibility with the judiciary for resolving Charter conflicts. She views the Charter's significance less in terms of the judiciary overruling Parliament than in the incentives and pressures it provides for public and political officials to satisfy themselves that legislation is consistent with protected rights.

JANET L. HIEBERT is associate professor in the Department of Political Studies, Queen's University.

Charter Conflicts

What Is Parliament's Role?

JANET L. HIEBERT

McGill-Queen's University Press
Montreal & Kingston · London · Ithaca

ISBN 0-7735-2399-5 (cloth)
ISBN 0-7735-2408-8 (paper)

Legal deposit second quarter 2002
Bibliothèque nationale du Québec

Printed in Canada on acid-free paper

This book has been funded with the help of the Institute
for Research on Public Policy. Founded in 1972,
IRPP is an independent, national, nonprofit
organization. IRPP seeks to improve public policy in
Canada by generating research, providing insight, and
sparking debate that will contribute to the public-policy
decision-making process and strengthen the quality of
the public-policy decisions made by Canadian
governments, citizens, institutions, and organizations.

McGill-Queen's University Press acknowledges the
financial support of the Government of Canada through
the Book Publishing Industry Development Program
(BPIDP) for its publishing activities. We also acknowledge
the support of the Canada Council for the Arts for our
publishing program.

**National Library of Canada Cataloguing in Publication
Data**

Hiebert, Janet, 1960–
    Charter conflicts: what is Parliament's role?
    Includes bibliographical references and index.
    ISBN 0-7735-2399-5 (bound). – ISBN 0-7735-2408-8 (pbk.)
    1. Canada. Canadian Charter of Rights and Freedoms.
    2. Civil rights – Canada. 3. Legislative power – Canada.
    I. Title.
    KE4381.5.H53 2002   342.71'085   C2002-90028-9

This book was typeset by Dynagram Inc. in 10/12 Baskerville.

Contents

Acknowledgments

Research for this book began as a comparative project to determine whether different social-policy outcomes emanate from political systems that assign courts a more authoritative role to interpret rights than from those that rely more heavily on political judgment. Early in the research process, however, I recognized the necessity for a more thorough understanding of how the Canadian Charter of Rights and Freedoms has influenced social-policy decisions before I could engage in meaningful comparative assessments.

I have published two papers drawn from earlier stages of this research. One is "Wrestling with Rights: Judges, Parliament and the Making of Social Policy," published by the Institute for Research on Public Policy (IRPP) in *Choices*, 5:3 (1999). I benefited enormously from the comments and advice from co-editors Peter Russell and Paul Howe. The second paper, "A Relational Approach to Constitutional Interpretation: Shared Legislative and Judicial Responsibilities," was published in *Journal of Canadian Studies* 35:5 (2001). I wish to thank the editors and anonymous reviewers for their helpful suggestions.

I am grateful as well to the Social Sciences and Humanities Research Council of Canada for funding, and to assistance from Queen's University in the form of the Chancellor's Research Award. I would also like to thank IRPP for its support of this project. Finally, I am indebted to many colleagues who have helped me refine my thinking about judicial and political responsibilities under the

Charter. Special thanks to Ed Broadbent, Rainer Knopff, John McLean, Nazeer Patel, Victor Perton, Kent Roach, Cheryl Saunders, Ned Franks, Miriam Smith, and George Thomson. I would also like to acknowledge the valuable research assistance of Jessica Marchand, Laura MacInnis, and Gerard Horgan. Above all, my greatest debt is to Wayne Hiebert for his unwavering support.

Introduction

Currently, Canada's political culture is being transformed by a focus on human rights that is influencing how governments assess their legislative initiatives and how the public and courts evaluate these in turn. This trend, with human rights seen as critical standards for evaluating the merits of state actions, reflects an international sensitivity of the post-Second World War era. But the emphasis on rights claiming in Canada has increased dramatically since the introduction of the Canadian Charter of Rights and Freedoms in 1982. The Charter introduced a profound change to the nation's governing principles. It sets out protected rights of the members of the polity, empowers individuals to ask courts to review state actions to determine whether protected rights are violated, and authorizes judges to review the validity of legislative and executive decisions and to grant remedies.

Not surprisingly, the Charter has generated substantial public, media, and scholarly interest in the changes it has introduced to the judiciary's role. While the Charter's effects on the judiciary are certainly significant, and rightly the subject of spirited debate, judicial rulings tell only a partial story of the political consequences of adopting a bill of rights. The present book examines the Charter's influence on legislative decisions. This focus is important for several reasons. First, the Charter has changed the political environment and climate of governing and is influencing legislative choices at all stages of the policy process. Governments incur Charter-inspired constraints in how they define legislative priorities or pursue policy objectives, even when legislation is thought to represent a compelling public interest. These constraints arise not only from judicial rulings but also from the assumptions and expectations of individuals and interest groups, public servants, and political representatives who have different views on how the Charter does, and should, alter legislative responsibility.

Second, legislation often represents a final and authoritative decision about how to balance social objectives with protected rights. Only a fraction of legislative initiatives will ever be subject to Charter litigation. For the majority of issues, Parliament retains a hegemonic position to define the scope and parameters of legislation. Thus, whether and how the Charter constrains or influences the use of state power depends heavily on how those who develop, propose, and assess policy initiatives view their responsibilities under the Charter. For example, does the government believe it should be constrained by Charter concerns? How influential are the government's legal advisers? How risk-averse or risk-tolerant are government ministers when pursuing legislative goals that are likely to result in Charter litigation? How capable is Parliament in requiring government to justify and explain legislative choices that may impair rights? These are important questions for a full understanding of the political consequences of adopting the Charter.

Third, judgment about whether the Charter is improving or harming the polity is closely linked to how it affects political behaviour. Two divergent views have emerged about how the Charter will influence legislative decisions. One view, which is pessimistic about the purported advantages of a bill of rights, considers the Charter as offering convenient refuge for politicians to avoid difficult political and moral decisions.[1] Elected representatives can insulate themselves from criticism, and political parties can protect their internal cohesion, by ignoring controversial and divisive issues and claiming that because these conflicts involve rights, they should be treated as legal issues rather than political ones. Thus, the expectation is for political inaction. Political leaders will avoid controversial issues and, by implication, will not try to influence judicial opinion about how to interpret the Charter or reconcile Charter conflicts.

A more optimistic view of the Charter's effects on political behaviour suggests that Parliament will become a party to a salutary dialogue on how to reconcile social conflicts involving rights. This explanation suggests that the Charter need not frustrate legislative agendas. The Supreme Court rarely rules that a legislative objective itself is inconsistent with the Charter and therefore cannot be pursued. Instead, judicial concerns tend to focus on the reasonableness with which legislative objectives are pursued. This provides Parliament the opportunity to revise legislation to respond to judicial concerns. Thus, Parliament is not impeded from undertaking legislative initiatives. It simply has to give more sensitivity and thought to their implementation. This optimistic view envisages the Charter as facilitating a healthy dialogue about "how best to reconcile the individualistic values of the *Charter* with the accomplishment of social and economic policies for the benefit of the community as a whole."[2]

Fourth, understanding how the Charter affects legislative decisions may influence public perceptions of Parliament's role with respect to resolving Charter conflicts. The criteria for evaluating the justification of legislation under the Charter are both open-ended and subject to philosophical disagreements. The possibility that reasonable people may differ about how to resolve Charter conflicts leads some to question whether courts should have the final word on such controversial issues. Yet others believe that only courts can validly resolve Charter conflicts. Greater awareness of the role and effects of Charter considerations in legislative decision making may influence these opinions. The Canadian constitution provides a mechanism for resolving the most extreme forms of Charter disagreements – the legislative override (or notwithstanding clause) in section 33. This controversial clause allows Parliament and the provincial legislatures to set aside a judicial finding under the Charter, with some important exceptions.[3] Public opinion is generally critical of the override and, for this reason, governments are generally reluctant to invoke it. This scepticism may be well founded if Parliament does not pay due regard to Charter values when developing legislation. Yet if legislative decisions are based on careful consideration of how best to balance conflicting rights and values, and the judiciary nevertheless invalidates these decisions, the override might have greater public acceptance.

Judgment about how the Charter should guide or constrain legislative objectives often generates varied responses. Judges, legal advisers, policy advisers, governmental ministers, and parliamentarians are all grappling, in their different ways and from their particular vantage points, with difficult normative and practical issues that arise from Canada's decision to utilize a bill of rights to evaluate the merits of legislative decisions and other state actions. For this reason, assessing how the Charter is affecting legislative choices must be situated within a broad context that considers the importance of and relationship among judicial, bureaucratic, governmental, and parliamentary judgments about whether legislation is consistent with Charter values.

This study's analysis of the Charter's influence on legislative decisions is based on five case studies involving significant Charter conflicts, stemming either from judicial disagreement with legislation or from legislative disagreement with judicial interpretations of how the Charter changes the common law. These were selected after an examination of parliamentary records of debate (particularly at the committee stage where Charter concerns figure more prominently), discussions with relevant public and political officials to identify policy issues that reveal significant differences between political and legal judgments, and assessments of Supreme Court rulings that clearly conflicted with legislation or, in the case of a Charter-inspired change to a common law rule, prompted legislative reaction. Legislative decisions were evaluated with reference to the following sources: government publications; interviews with relevant public officials; the records of deliberation in parliamentary committees, which involve testimony from public officials and concerned individuals and groups; proceedings of Parliament as a whole; and media reports. Most of these decisions were made at the federal level, which combines a systematic process for evaluating the Charter implications of legislation with parliamentary committees charged with the responsibility for scrutinizing the constitutional implications of bills. Important exceptions to this federal focus are provincial responses to judicial rulings on equality rights affecting lesbians and gay men.

Although the focus of this book is empirical, a qualitative assessment of the Charter's influence on legislative decisions, a distinct normative perspective informs the analysis. Throughout, I argue that Parliament shares responsibility with the judiciary for determining how the Charter should direct social conflicts. In putting forth this position, I am arguing contrary to a tendency in scholarly analysis to accept a judicial-centric approach for resolving Charter conflicts. My perspective does not arise from scepticism about the salutary merits of the Charter, distrust of the judiciary, or criticism that its approach has generally been too activist. My focus and concerns are directed more towards Parliament. They are influenced by the adverse implications for governing that may stem from an excessive reliance on judicial wisdom to resolve contentious social conflicts.

Judicial perspectives provide important and salutary insights into whether legislative goals conflict with the Charter's normative values or have unintentional consequences that unnecessarily or unduly restrict rights. But, despite their importance, judicial insights do not negate governmental responsibility to define what kinds of programs and services are needed for the public interest or to determine the best way to pursue complex social policies.

A judicial-centric approach to the Charter rests on the idea that only judges are capable of resolving social conflicts involving rights in a principled manner. Yet many Charter conflicts are amenable to more than a singular, reasonable answer. Parliament and courts are situated differently, in relation to Charter conflicts. Their respective judgments will be influenced by these different points of reference, by the distinct institutional characteristics they possess, and by the specific responsibilities that characterize their roles. In reviewing rights conflicts, judges enjoy more liberty from political and social pressures, and for this reason they may have more freedom to identify when legislative decisions impose unwarranted or undue restrictions on fundamental rights. Judges, however, are not charged with the broader responsibility to identify social problems or decide how best to address these. When it comes to determining the best way to pursue legislative objectives that are considered important enough to restrict rights – where these objectives are consistent with a free and democratic society – representative institutions have distinct advantages in their access to extensive resources and the policy expertise necessary for prudent and responsible policy decisions. To assume that only judges can resolve Charter conflicts is not healthy for the polity, because it diminishes political responsibility to pursue important policy goals and may lead to the unnecessary use of non-ambitious or ineffective means to pursue these objectives.

Parliament and the judiciary may have different assessments about how Charter conflicts should be resolved. But different judgments do not necessarily mean that judicial opinion represents the only justifiable or reasonable resolution of a Charter conflict. Nor does the possibility of disagreement necessarily threaten political stability or create constitutional stalemate. Both parliamentary and judicial opinions may change after the reasons for the other's differing judgment are considered. Where this does not occur, the legislative override allows for the resolution of most disagreements, by temporarily setting aside the effects of a judicial ruling. The substantial controversy that appropriately surrounds this clause should ensure its use only upon strong political conviction that this contrary judgment is justified and will withstand political and public scrutiny.

The Charter's influence on legislative decisions begins early in the policy process. The potential consequences associated with the nullification of legislation on Charter grounds enhance the importance of legal evaluations in the formative stages of policy as well as in the drafting of legislation. Chapter 1 discusses the process adopted at the federal level for evaluating government bills for their consistency with the Charter. Despite the systematic nature of Charter evaluations on behalf of the government, Parliament itself is poorly situated to assess whether legislative choices are justifiable and defensible from a Charter perspective. Executive dominance and insufficient resources have at times placed Parliament in an unenviable position of passing legislation while failing to comprehend fully the significance or magnitude of Charter conflicts. The chapter discusses this tension between these processes of internal/executive and external/parliamentary evaluation.

The Charter's change to governing principles has generated strong reaction. Political and legal scholars have actively debated the proper role of the courts and the consequences of judicial review for principles of democratic governance. The democratic legitimacy of judicial review is an enduring issue in liberal-democratic polities, particularly where the judiciary has been given responsibility to review constitutional principles and the power to set aside the legislative decisions of those who are democratically elected. Chapter 2 discusses the Canadian version of this debate. Both those who are enthusiastic about the Charter as well as those who are sceptical about its value tend to delineate their version of the appropriate judicial role to correspond with their particular democratic claims. The former argues that a robust interpretation of rights is required to enhance democracy, to realize the substantive conditions for citizens' meaningful engagement in the polity. Judicial review protects the very rules and conditions that are necessary for citizens to function equitably, which otherwise may be eroded by Parliament or by others exercising power on behalf of the state. In contrast, those who are sceptical about a bill of rights conceive of judicial review as being inherently in tension with democracy. They regard the appropriate judicial role as being guided by a strict interpretation of Charter provisions; any more interventionist role would be inconsistent with the democratic principle that those who are democratically accountable make policy choices. Participants in this debate share few assumptions in common on issues that are central to assessing the relationship between the judiciary and Parliament, such as the normative role of the state and how rights relate to other principles of governance.

Chapter 3 offers an alternative to the extreme positions that dominate this debate. Rather than focusing so heavily on the judiciary, I suggest the need to look more closely at Parliament's role in rendering constitutional judgment. In contemplating a significant role for parliamentary constitutional judgment, I am not offering a defence for legislative decisions, regardless of their implications for protected rights. The Charter establishes the polity's commitment to a set of normative values that should be respected in the course of governing. Yet, at the same time, representative institutions should contribute to the interpretation of these fundamental values and should not renege on their responsibility to make responsible policy decisions. Thus, governing under the Charter requires critical reflection on how best to reconcile compelling legislative purposes with Charter values. It also requires that Parliament is satisfied that its decisions are appropriate and justified.

Admittedly, this vision of shared responsibility for the reconciliation of legislative objectives and Charter values is very much an ideal rather than a general description of existing practices. Not all legislative responses can be described, by any stretch of the imagination, as thoughtful or principled attempts to reconcile Charter conflicts. Nevertheless, this ideal is worth pursuit. The normative goal is not that Parliament should aspire to ensure that legislation anticipates or replicates all judicial concerns, any more than it is to encourage judicial deference towards Parliament's judgment without regard for how legislation affects rights. Rather, it is for each body to satisfy itself that its judgment respects Charter values, particularly when faced with the reasons for the other's contrary judgment. I contemplate the Charter's contribution to the polity more in terms of compelling critical reflection by all institutions of governance – on how the normative principles should affect their judgment – than in terms of the judiciary simply correcting the "wrong" decisions of Parliament.

Chapters 4 through 8 examine policy disagreements between Parliament and the Supreme Court. The first of these, discussed in Chapter 4, analyses the political response to a controversial judicial ruling on tobacco advertising. Those who are sceptical about the benefits of a bill of rights can hardly find a better example of how a bill of rights can operate to distort legislative objectives than the Supreme Court's 1995 ruling in *RJR-MacDonald Inc.* and Parliament's response. This Supreme Court decision overturned federal legislation that sought to discourage young people from becoming smokers. Parliament responded meekly, with revised legislation that put more emphasis on the Supreme Court's concerns to protect the rights of the tobacco industry than on Parliament's original concern to shield children from the manipulative effects of tobacco advertising. More than any other policy examined in this book, the political response to this negative court ruling reinforces the concern that legislative objectives in the public interest may be compromised under the Charter even when fundamental human rights are not at jeopardy.

Chapter 5 provides evidence of far more assertive legislative responses to contrary judicial judgments. Two Supreme Court rulings – one nullified legislation that restricted the kind of evidence that could be introduced in sexual assault trials, and the other changed a common law rule to allow extreme intoxication to be used in defence of sexual assault charges – exposed serious disagreement between judicial and parliamentary perspectives. Parliamentary concerns to protect women, who disproportionately are the victims of sexual assault, clashed with the judiciary's emphasis on the right of the accused to a fair trial. Troubled that these rulings would alter critical assumptions for sexual assault trials, Parliament decided upon a response that expressed different assumptions about how Charter considerations should guide legal rules for sexual assault trials. Some may question the validity of a parliamentary approach that diverges substantially from judicial opinion. Yet what is significant about Parliament's reaction is that, despite strong disagreement with judicial assumptions, legislative responses did not reflect disregard for the Charter or the triumph of partisan or other self-serving interests over rights-based principles. Rather, these legislative initiatives revealed deliberate and conscious intent to influence the prevailing normative and legal assumptions for sexual-assault trials, as well as to alert the judiciary to an alternative interpretation of the Charter – one that situates the fairness of the trial process in a broader context of respect for other Charter rights (privacy and equality).

Chapter 6 demonstrates the difficulty of exercising careful judgment when jurisprudence is unsettled and incomplete and when political opinion is divided on the relevance and merits of Charter arguments. At issue were legislative initiatives to compel criminal suspects to provide samples for DNA analysis for law-enforcement purposes. Enormous challenges arise when attempting to reconcile law-enforcement objectives with possible violations of rights. But the tone of the debate in this instance was not conducive for making Charter-sensitive decisions. Opposition members emphasized the need for law and order while paying insufficient attention to privacy and other Charter values. Government members responded with blanket claims about Charter constraints, without arguing the merits of their policy position. This form of argument, not surprisingly, did little to persuade opponents to accept that Charter sensitivity appropriately constrains Parliament's decisions.

Chapter 7 focuses on how an unanticipated change to a common law rule may necessitate a quick political response, and raises serious questions about whether the Supreme Court has sufficient understanding of the time-frame required for responsible legislative judgment. In May 1997 the Supreme Court, by the narrowest of margins, reversed itself on the validity of a common law rule that had allowed police, under certain conditions, to enter a home without a warrant to arrest a suspect. The government was concerned that the decision might compromise public safety in extreme incidents, such as domestic violence, because police might need to enter a dwelling immediately, before being able to obtain a warrant. Complicating the government's ability to proceed quickly with new legislation was the need for substantial consultation with the provinces. Legislation was rushed so quickly through Parliament that some members worried about the consequences of insufficient scrutiny of legislation that might have serious Charter implications.

Chapter 8 examines federal and provincial legislative responses to judicial decisions involving the equality claims of lesbians and gay men. Lesbians and gay men have been successful in achieving a profound change in how legislative discrimination is viewed. The Supreme Court has agreed with many of their claims and has issued a strong message, applicable to all governments, that legislative concern about costs and traditional assumptions of the family do not justify unfair or discriminatory distinctions in social policy. Thus, these rulings have cast doubt on the constitutional validity of a broad range of federal and provincial legislation, while also challenging hegemonic social norms about the family. They have generated more controversy and political resistance than any other Charter conflict examined here. Nevertheless, at the time of writing, six provinces and the federal government have enacted comprehensive legislative reforms. Those governments that have yet to respond to judicial rulings have little reason to doubt the significance of what can only be characterized as a new legal paradigm of equality rights. Continued delay may have significant consequences. The Supreme Court is indicating that its patience with legislative inaction is wearing thin and prolonged legislative inaction may result in the court assuming a more activist posture in proffering remedies.

Chapter 9 considers the reform potential of the Charter by reflecting upon the claims of Charter sceptics. These sceptics hold either that the Charter is unnecessary or that, alternatively, it will be ineffective. The judiciary will not be able to compel political compliance for rulings that diverge substantially from societal consensus about fundamental values, and, in instances where this consensus exists, the Charter is not necessary because citizens will not abide by decisions that are contrary to their fundamental values. If correct, this argument would discourage lesbians and gay men from expecting that they could use the Charter to advance their reform objectives. Yet, as noted, despite the large gap that initially separated judicial rulings and legislative assumptions about the merits of legislative discrimination against same-sex partners, governments have shown considerable compliance in their responses to Supreme Court rulings in this area – a fact that contradicts the expectations of the sceptics. The explanation for this rests, in large part, on the dynamic role the Charter is playing in changing the assumptions and expectations of the polity.

The Charter's significance arises from the authority and incentives it provides for critical reflection upon whether the values it embodies are actually being respected in legislative choices. As part of a new constitutional paradigm, the Charter is altering assumptions about the judiciary's role in protecting rights and preventing discrimination, influencing interest-group behaviour, and shaping political responses to rights claiming, particularly where these claims are upheld by the judiciary. The juxtaposition of judicial and political judgment on the equality claims of lesbians and gay men suggests the need to revise the sceptical view of a bill of rights. It further suggests that we take into account the Charter's influence in compelling those in positions of political power to re-examine existing policies in the light of normative values widely agreed upon in society at large.

Charter Conflicts

1 Political Scrutiny of Charter Conflicts

The idea of codifying rights and empowering courts to interpret them indicates more confidence in judicial than political resolutions to rights conflicts. Yet judicial review creates serious tensions for parliamentary systems that emphasize the sovereignty of Parliament's judgment as an essential constitutional principle. This tension likely explains why the American approach of giving courts final authority to interpret rights has not been the model of choice for a number of mature parliamentary systems which, while pursuing new ways to ensure that principles of rights have more prominence in legislative decision making, are reluctant to abandon reliance on Parliament's judgment.

By the standards of today's more litigious culture, the emphasis on parliamentary judgment to protect rights may seem odd and even incomprehensible. This is particularly the case for those who have been lured by the calls of some scholars of American constitutionalism to conceive of rights as trumping political decisions and of judicial determination as final and superior to political judgment.[1] Yet, perhaps as testimony to the formative influence of and confidence in this parliamentary heritage, several of the older parliamentary nations have continued to rely on Parliament's judgment while simultaneously trying to respond to international pressures to increase the sensitivity accorded rights in legislative decisions. In 1960 Canada introduced a statutory bill of rights intended to increase the role and prominence of rights in legislative decision making. Thirty years later New Zealand adopted a similar approach,[2] followed by Britain in 1998.[3] In adopting a bill of rights, all three countries were guided by the principle that, whatever salutary influence might result from judicial review, Parliament would exercise ultimate judgment about the resolution of rights conflicts. Australia has also decided to retain Parliament's authority on issues of rights. Instead of a bill of rights, it has chosen, among other methods, to rely on parliamentary committees to evaluate proposed legislation for consistency with rights and issues of fundamental justice.[4] Canada's decision to entrench the Charter of Rights in Freedoms in the constitution in 1982, with a new judicial power to nullify legislation that is inconsistent with the Charter, may be viewed as an abandonment of this reliance on Parliament. But this view underestimates the continued importance and potential influence of Parliament's judgment for resolving Charter conflicts.

My central argument – that Parliament shares responsibility for interpreting the Charter – is derived from concern about the implications for government of Parliament failing to exercise careful judgment about how Charter values should guide and influence legislative decisions. In appealing for an increased parliamentary role in the resolution of Charter conflicts, I take my inspiration from the expectations initially associated with the Canadian Bill of Rights, enacted more than forty years ago. The ideal at the heart of this measure was to increase the saliency of rights in political decision making, an ideal that rested on the dynamic possibility of utilizing a framework of rights to evaluate legislative proposals before and after they were introduced into Parliament. The assumption was that from more careful political scrutiny would come more sensitive legislation.

While the Bill of Rights never fully realized the hopes of its advocates, the Charter has greater potential to encourage political scrutiny of legislative choices. This potential comes from the threat that judicial review poses for abrupt changes to legislative objectives, because legislation may be nullified if deemed inconsistent with Charter values. Judicially induced pressures have compelled governments to take steps to try and address Charter inconsistencies in proposed legislation. The consequences of having legislation nullified, and the implications of not exerting influence on how the judiciary reconciles Charter conflicts, may also force Parliament to become a more important partner in constitutional judgment.

THE CANADIAN BILL OF RIGHTS: PROMOTING POLITICAL SCRUTINY

The Canadian Bill of Rights led to ambivalence and confusion on the part of the judiciary.[5] However, what was innovative about the bill was the way it attempted to infuse political decision making at the federal level with greater sensitivity to rights.[6] Its salutary benefits were expected to arise largely from the impetus it provided government to give effect to rights principles when developing legislation, encouraged by subsequent scrutiny by Parliament. Under this arrangement, the justice minister was required to examine all bills introduced into the House[7] and report any inconsistencies with the Bill of Rights, as provided in the following regulation:[8] "Where any of the provisions of any Bill ... are ascertained by the Minister to be inconsistent with the purposes and provisions of the *Canadian Bill of Rights*, the Minister shall make a report in writing of the inconsistency and shall cause such report to be deposited with the Clerk of the House of Commons ... at the earliest convenient opportunity."[9]

The expectation that the strength of the Bill of Rights would rest largely on this combination of self-scrutiny undertaken on behalf of the minister of justice and parliamentary evaluation prompted questions about whether the reporting requirement was adequate. Opposition members queried whether or not sufficient pressure would be placed on the government to conduct this self-audit. In 1958 the proposed reporting responsibility was altered from one that required the minister to "ensure" that all future regulations and bills were in accordance with the Bill of Rights to a lesser standard of having to "ascertain" that they were consistent. In response to concerns about the change, then Justice Minister E.D. Fulton suggested that, if the minister of justice were required to "ensure" the consistency of all bills and regulations, this would represent dictatorial powers. Under the wording as enacted, the justice minister would instead be required to advise the cabinet and Parliament of any inconsistency, which would ultimately decide whether to accept or override that advice.[10]

Despite this less encompassing reporting obligation, considerable optimism existed that it would nevertheless encourage government to ensure that bills were consistent with rights. A former deputy minister of justice, Elmer Driedger, believed that the reporting requirement, found in section 3 of the Bill of Rights, would be effective because if a bill was considered by Justice officials to violate the Bill of Rights, the offending provision would in all probability be "immediately rejected." Otherwise, if cabinet decided to proceed with legislative activity that was patently inconsistent with rights, the minister of justice would likely resign before being placed in the position of having to report this to Parliament.[11] From Driedger's perspective, no government could "politically afford to put itself in a position in which the Minister of Justice would resign over the issue or make an adverse report against the Government in the House of Commons as required."[12]

Driedger's optimism about the effectiveness of political scrutiny was enhanced by his interpretation of the effects of another aspect of the Bill of Rights, the notwithstanding provision of section 2. Under this provision, if a government is intent on pursuing a course of action that is patently in violation of a right, it must declare that the legislation will operate notwithstanding the Canadian Bill of Rights. Without this declaration, courts are obliged to interpret the legislation in a manner that does not abrogate, abridge, or infringe the rights or freedoms in the Bill of Rights. Driedger assumed that anticipation of the inevitable criticism that would accompany use of this power (both in and beyond Parliament) would discourage any government from introducing a bill that depended upon the notwithstanding provision. In his view, no government "would be so foolish or stupid as to submit to Parliament a bill obviously in conflict with the Bill of Rights." To do so, he believed, would give opposition parties grounds for moving an amendment "which, as a matter of simple politics, the government would have to accept."[13] Consequently, he was of the view that a bill requiring a reference to the section 2 notwithstanding clause had almost no chance of becoming law.[14] In short, Driedger was confident that the effects of a political interest in not having to report to Parliament that a bill was inconsistent with the Bill of Rights, combined with the political necessity not to attract criticism by relying on the notwithstanding provision, would be ample insurance that the government would comply with the Bill of Rights.

Another informed commentator, Walter Tarnopolsky, recognized that the Bill of Rights would derive much of its efficacy from the internal pressure on government to avoid having to report to Parliament that a bill or regulation is inconsistent with rights. Tarnopolsky was not quite as confident in this respect as Driedger, yet he was hopeful that Parliament would play an important scrutiny role and, failing that, the judiciary would.[15]

On only one occasion did the minister of justice make a report to Parliament under section 3 of the Bill of Rights.[16] Yet opposition members sometimes identified possible conflicts between governmental bills and the Bill of Rights and questioned why the justice minister had not reported these to Parliament.[17] Despite these observations, the reporting obligation made no appreciable difference in the general sensitivity of legislative debate to issues of rights.

With regard to the pre-Charter era, it is difficult to assess the effects of the internal form of scrutiny on legislative proposals before their introduction into the House of Commons. Today, however, Justice officials suggest that the vetting process was far less vigorous prior to 1982 than now occurs under the Charter. An important reason for this is that legislation that deviated from the Bill of Rights would not suffer the consequences of judicial nullification because of its inconsistency. The threat of embarrassment in Parliament, or in the public from the attention that parliamentary scrutiny might bring to the government, was not likely significant enough to encourage serious change in policy deliberation at the stage of legislative development.

In hindsight, an obvious difficulty with Driedger's assumption about the effectiveness of executive scrutiny is the extent to which he understated the potential for disagreement about whether or not a bill is consistent with protected rights. His position was that disagreements would arise over the issue of intent – whether or not the government chooses to comply with the Bill of Rights – as distinct from conflicting interpretations of whether rights were restricted unduly. A more serious error was the expectation that these procedures would seriously alter the political behaviour of the executive and Parliament. Effective political scrutiny under the Bill of Rights required rigorous audits of proposed legislation; a willingness of the minister of justice to compel other ministers to revise bills, sometimes to the detriment of their political objectives as originally conceived; and a capacity or inclination by Parliament to evaluate bills from a perspective or rights.

POLITICAL SCRUTINY UNDER THE CHARTER

The federal minister of justice has a similar statutory reporting requirement under the Charter. This requirement, provided in section 4.1 of the Department of Justice Act, obliges the minister to certify that bills have been assessed in light of the Charter and, when inconsistent with its purposes and provisions, report this fact to Parliament.

The Charter of Rights and Freedoms is a very different rights instrument than the Bill of Rights. The constitutional status of the Charter increases the relevance of political evaluation of bills because new consequences arise from inconsistencies between legislation and protected rights. Courts are empowered not only to review legislation but also to grant remedies for breaches, which may include the nullification of legislation in whole or in part. Those who review bills indicate that the bureaucratic culture has changed significantly; more robust sensitivity now exists for how legislation affects rights. A dynamic and evolving jurisprudence, the knowledge that the courts are willing to invalidate legislation, and the recognition that both the purposes and the effects of legislation can be impugned have combined to encourage more rigorous and systematic scrutiny of bills.

The increased consequences for a government's agenda if legislation is nullified for being inconsistent with protected rights has enhanced the prominence of the Department of Justice. The Human

Rights Law Section was established in 1982 to review existing legislation, identify Charter conflicts, bring statutes into conformity with
the Charter, and provide ongoing advice on Charter issues. The latter task involves analysing the legal implications of policy proposals
and systematically assessing whether government bills comply with
the Charter.

The nature of this internal evaluation process and its influence on
policy decisions are difficult to assess. Those in the Department of Justice whose job it is to identify Charter concerns and give advice are reluctant to speak frankly about the specific policies that raise Charter
difficulties, the exact nature of the advice given, and the response of
department and political officials to that advice. The secretive nature
of this exercise is protected by confidentiality requirements of lawyers
working within the Department of Justice, by a lack of public access to
the relevant paper trails, and by cabinet secrecy. Yet, despite the secretive nature of the process, interviews with a number of former and
current Justice lawyers, who are willing to speak generally and anony-
mously, occasional policy statements or background papers released by
the department, and testimony of Justice lawyers who appear before
parliamentary committees allow for the following observations.

The department has responsibility for drafting all government bills.
Before this takes place, however, the sponsoring minister must submit
to cabinet a memorandum setting forth the objectives and implications of the proposal, including any Charter concerns. The awareness
that Charter difficulties will be noted, along with their implications for
the viability of the policy in terms of judicial review, places pressure on
departments to work with Justice officials to address Charter concerns
before the memorandum is submitted.

Justice lawyers have adopted an approach for reviewing bills based
on a risk-assessment of the degree of difficulty in justifying legislation
under the Charter. Risk-assessments are undertaken on a continuum
from minimal, significant, substantial, and serious to unacceptable, the
latter category representing the near-certainty that courts will invalidate the legislative action. At times, Justice officials have been asked to
put their assessment into numerical terms: evaluating whether legislation has a 60 per cent chance of surviving as opposed to a lesser
chance, or indicating where the degree of risk lies on a scale of 1–10.
They are reluctant, however, to offer advice in these quantitative terms.
While it can be difficult to distinguish between significant, substantial,
or serious risks, assessments continue to be framed qualitatively.

The Supreme Court has almost certainly influenced the approach
taken to evaluating bills. The Charter's structure and, in particular, its inclusion of a general limitation clause in section 1 has encouraged the

court to adopt a two-stage approach to judicial review: 1) does the rights claim have constitutional protection and is it infringed?; if so, 2) is the restriction reasonable? The Charter states explicitly in section 1 that rights can be subject to "such reasonable limits prescribed by law as can be demonstrably justified in a free and democratic society." It is largely with reference to this second stage that risk-assessments occur, particularly for those rights and freedoms that do not contain any internal reference to reasonableness.

Moreover, the willingness of the Supreme Court to nullify legislation deemed inconsistent with the Charter has had an important effect both on the process of vetting bills and on the influence Justice officials exert on other departments and ministers. The first time the federal government was called on to defend legislation on Charter grounds, it tried to minimize the Charter's effects by claiming that the legislation should be upheld by virtue of the mere presence in the Charter of the limitation clause in section 1.[18] Had the court accepted that neither evidence nor sound arguments are required to justify legislation, this would have seriously constrained the Charter's effects. But the court made it clear in this case, and in others to follow, that government had the burden of persuading courts about the reasonableness of its actions (as opposed to litigants assuming the onerous burden of having to convince courts that legislation is unreasonable). These rulings have encouraged a more rigorous approach to internal scrutiny than existed under the Bill of Rights.

Initially, some public officials were resentful of what they considered to be unwelcome interference by Justice lawyers into other departments' responsibilities. The Department of Justice has been accused both of having unnecessary sensitivity towards rights concerns and of using the department's advisory role to increase the extent of its influence. These early conflicts have been alleviated, to a considerable extent, by a greater awareness on the part of public officials that they cannot escape Charter scrutiny. As jurisprudence has evolved, the Supreme Court has made clear its willingness to nullify legislative provisions that conflict with Charter values. Early Supreme Court decisions such as *Singh v. Minister of Employment and Immigration*,[19] *Schachter v. Canada*,[20] *R. v. Oakes*,[21] and *Hunter et al. v. Southam*[22] had considerable influence on bureaucratic culture, which became more receptive, or at least more resigned, to the department of Justice's role in assessing bills and advising on Charter issues. These decisions underscored the magnitude of the Charter's implications for governing. In particular, they conveyed to departments the message that governments would have the burden of proof for demonstrating the reasonableness of their actions and that, if courts declare legislation invalid or grant other remedies, these judicial decisions could have substantial policy and fiscal implications.

The Human Rights Law Section has sought to convince other departments to seek Charter advice as early as possible in the process of developing policy. Justice lawyers believe that Charter assessments done early help identify ways of accomplishing legislative objectives in a manner that is more likely both to survive a Charter challenge and to minimize disruption in attaining the policy goal. Another perceived advantage of thinking about Charter implications sooner is to anticipate possible Charter challenges and consciously develop a legislative record for addressing judicial concerns. This record may include policy objectives, consultations with interested groups, social-science data, the experiences of other jurisdictions with similar legislative initiatives, and testimony before parliamentary committees by experts and interest groups. Another form of anticipating judicial review is the increased use of legislative preambles, which state the objectives and assumptions underlying the legislation.

This sensitivity to the Charter does not mean that policies are forsaken because they incur serious Charter risks. The threshold for accepting whether a bill complies with the Charter, and therefore does not require a report to Parliament, is whether or not a credible Charter argument can be made. When less risky ways to accomplish policy objectives cannot be identified, cabinet ultimately will be required to render a political judgment about whether to proceed. However, the context in which this judgment is made gives rise to obvious tension between the justice minister's statutory obligation to report to Parliament, if a bill is inconsistent with the Charter, and an emerging political culture that assumes that no report should be made. Thus, the prevailing assumption is that government should not pursue legislation that is considered to be so patently inconsistent with the Charter that it would require the justice minister to report to Parliament. Before reaching this stage, the bill should be either amended or withdrawn. This political presumption against a report to Parliament creates strong incentives to find ways of pursuing legislative objectives in a manner that incurs lower Charter risks. It puts pressure on the minister of justice, who also serves as the attorney general, to convince his or her colleagues of the need to amend policies so that a credible Charter argument can be made. If the government is intent on pursuing a course of action for which the justice minister concludes that no credible Charter argument can be made, the minister will likely feel compelled to resign. To date, these conflicts have been resolved to the satisfaction of the justice minister, at least to the extent that no minister has yet concluded that it is necessary to report to Parliament or resign for this reason.

Yet it is important to note that the evaluation and reporting responsibilities undertaken by and on behalf of the minister of justice enhance an already existing tension in the responsibilities he or she assumes in the dual role of justice minister and attorney general. This tension arises because of a potential conflict the minister may face in guarding the public interest and serving in cabinet – that is, the cabinet may be committed to a course of action that may conflict with the public interest.[23] Exactly how often these conflicts occur or how they are resolved is confidential. Informed sources, however, indicate that occasional "wing-ding" fights have occurred in the cabinet room.

A question that arises is how influential is the justice minister within cabinet? Donald Savoie has studied changing power relations in Ottawa between political actors who constitute the centre of government in Canada: senior officials within the Privy Council Office, the Prime Minister's Office, the Department of Finance, and the Treasury Board Secretariat. Savoie argues that an increased concentration of power has shifted away from cabinet and cabinet committees to the prime minister and senior advisers.[24] An implication of Savoie's analysis is that this concentration of power in the office of the prime minister may affect the extent to which a justice minister will be able to convince others, and in particular the prime minister, that changes to bills are necessary to address Charter concerns. This task may be particularly difficult if these changes are inconsistent with the prime minister's objectives.

A serious shortcoming in Savoie's analysis, however, is that he does not address whether and how judgment about the Charter affects power relations. As James Kelly suggests, Savoie's analysis of power does not take into consideration the significance of bureaucratic judgments on Charter issues. Kelly argues that, because the Department of Justice has a monopoly on providing Charter advice to the government, its influence is stronger than other departments.[25] Moreover, a shift in the department's focus, from amending perceived conflicts in existing legislation to a more activist position of providing technical and substantive review of the activities of other departments, has contributed to the department assuming an "executive-support" role. This shift in focus has been sufficient to admit the department into the centre of government because of the department's influence on policy development.[26] Indeed, the department itself characterizes its role of assessing the implications of policy from a Charter perspective as being analogous to that of a central agency.[27]

While the justice minister almost certainly has considerable influence in cabinet, because of the consequences for the government's
agenda of pursuing a policy that has unnecessarily high levels of risk,
he or she must be prudent in deciding when and how to exercise this
influence. Other ministers will have a strong commitment to their department's policies and may not be easily convinced about the need or
value of modifying or withdrawing proposals. Consequently, the minister of justice must save the ultimate recourses of the office in this area,
a warning of the need for a report to Parliament or the even stronger
threat of resignation, for those rare circumstances when other forms
of influence and pressure are not successful and where the minister
believes emphatically that a credible Charter argument cannot be
made.

Since no report of Charter incompatibility has yet been, or is likely
to be, made to Parliament, some might understandably interpret the
influence and rigour of Charter advice and scrutiny with scepticism.
Peter Russell, commenting on the earlier process of executive scrutiny that occurred under the Bill of Rights, expresses doubt about the
effectiveness of relying on an approach that is tantamount to the executive checking itself.[28] David Kinley similarly lacks confidence that
any internal process will prevent abuses of rights because, in the absence of representation of extra-governmental opinions, insufficient
pressure may be placed on Justice officials to do otherwise than endorse any government-sponsored legislative provision coming before
it.[29] Although the secretive and confidential nature of the process for
evaluating proposed legislation make it difficult to assess whether
this scepticism is appropriate or misplaced, a more complete explanation for the absence of reports to Parliament likely contains the
following elements.

First, the Charter has helped to facilitate a political culture within
the bureaucracy and government that is reluctant to be, or appear to
be, indifferent or insensitive towards the Charter. One manifestation
of this culture is the view that the integrity of the Charter, as a statement of fundamental constitutional values, would be undermined if
the government purposely pursued a course of action considered by
its own justice minister to be unreasonable under the Charter. From
a pragmatic standpoint, legislation requiring a report to Parliament
would be in an extremely precarious position, vulnerable both to political embarrassment and to successful Charter challenge. Opposition parties would robustly criticize the government for pursuing a
course of action that its own justice minister believes to be patently
unconstitutional. Furthermore, litigants would readily argue that the
legislation should not be upheld because even the government rec-

ognizes that it violates the constitution in a manner that cannot be considered reasonable or justifiable. It is difficult to imagine that the Supreme Court would be prepared to uphold legislation as a justifiable infringement of the Charter when the justice minister has admitted such a profound inconsistency.

A political culture premised on not reporting has interesting implications for government if it wishes to pursue legislation that is clearly inconsistent with the Charter or leading Supreme Court precedents. It suggests that the only political option in such circumstances is to enact the legislative override. While the override overcomes the difficulty of courts overturning legislation, it is as susceptible to political difficulty as is a report to Parliament.

Second, this threshold for not having to report to Parliament is wide enough to permit a high degree of perceived Charter risk, thus minimizing the circumstances in which judgment precludes a credible argument being made. Unless a bill is patently inconsistent with the purposes of the Charter, it can likely be subsumed under this criterion. The Charter itself, and how it has been interpreted, have contributed to the breadth of this threshold. Questions regarding what values are consistent with a free and democratic society, which is the normative framework for evaluating limits on rights, will invoke differences of opinion among reasonable people.[30] The Supreme Court has declared that these are not universal standards but that the Charter's structure, with its inclusion of limitation and override clauses, provides a unique context for evaluating the justification of legislative policies that differentiates assessments of reasonableness in Canada from other jurisdictions.[31] Furthermore, issues relating to a policy's reasonableness, evaluated against a changing and evolving jurisprudence around interpretations of proportionality criteria, are also subject to differences of opinion, both within the Supreme Court and among political and public officials. Thus, the justice minister's philosophical views and approach to Charter conflicts will influence judgment about whether a credible Charter argument can be made. This standard, therefore, also allows for broad discretion when determining how much Charter risk a government wishes to incur.

The Charter's effects on how policies are assessed and analysed before they are introduced to Parliament may not be visible. Its influence, however, has been both systemic and systematic and has changed the political environment in which policies are conceptualized and drafted. Bureaucratic scrutiny and the justice minister's obligation to report to Parliament ensure that the Charter receives significant consideration before legislation is put forward.

PARLIAMENTARY EVALUATION

Few would expect that executive scrutiny should guarantee there will not be subsequent Charter litigation. If all legislative objectives were forsaken, because of the possibility that someone would litigate under the Charter, this would have a debilitating and chilling effect on governing. Yet the absence of reports has serious implications for Parliament. Parliament may have little insight into why the minister of justice has decided that proposed legislation is consistent with the Charter. Moreover, Parliament may be unaware, in many circumstances, of the degree of Charter risk that may be incurred when passing legislation. The possibility that legislation could be nullified makes this lack of comprehension particularly worrisome.

It is virtually impossible for Parliament (or, for that matter, courts or any individual or group beyond cabinet and the Department of Justice) to ascertain the quality and influence of the process of evaluating government bills. This is due to the secrecy and confidentiality that govern the executive Charter-vetting process.

Some may not find this situation troubling. If the process of internal evaluation is not sufficient, the judiciary will recognize and remedy the deficiencies; it will invalidate offending legislation. But this response is not persuasive. First, not all legislative decisions will be subject to litigation. Thus, the majority of legislative acts will represent a final and authoritative judgment about how to balance rights, values, interests, and other policy perspectives. An important reason why government and Parliament should reflect on Charter concerns at the time of legislative consideration and debate is to ensure that Charter values are respected in the course of governing. Otherwise, if responsibility to ensure that legislative decisions are consistent with Charter values is ignored, the Charter's normative values may not be respected where litigation does not arise. Moreover, this would place undue responsibility on citizens and courts. As Brian Slattery argues:

Only a selection of laws can ever by effectively subjected to judicial review, which, in any case, is a lengthy and expensive process. Courts have only a limited capacity to assess the correctness of governmental decisions on crucial aspects of public policy and so (quite properly in many instances) may feel constrained to defer to the wisdom of the government on these points. It follows that for a government to adopt the attitude of "pass now, justify in court later" would not only be an abdication of its *Charter* responsibilities, but in fact would undermine the foundations of judicial respect for the decisions of coordinate branches of government.[32]

Second, to conceive of the resolution of rights conflicts as the exclusive responsibility of courts does not give sufficient consideration either to the philosophical nature of such conflicts or to the fact that valid differences of opinion will exist on the uses of state power to redress social problems. If the possibility of reasonable difference justifies doubt that judges have the only relevant opinions on how to reconcile conflicting values, then even stronger doubt should arise from relying so heavily on the judgment of a small number of governmental lawyers and the minister of justice. I have no reason to assume that Justice officials are not rigorous or conscientious in their evaluation of legislation or that the minister of justice is unwilling or unable to persuade other ministers to respect Charter values. However, no matter how vigilantly a bill is scrutinized on behalf of the executive, political judgment is being made within a closed process that effectively shuts out Parliament. In the process, the possibility of any public record of the assumptions and reasons that influenced that judgment is foreclosed. Parliament and the public can at least read the Supreme Court's reasons and be in a position to examine, reflect upon, and react to its assumptions. But this is not an option with the process of internal review.

Although the government develops policies and introduces bills at an advanced stage of preparation and oversees the passage of these through Parliament, this does not negate Parliament's obligation to scrutinize the actions of government and to compel government to defend and justify its choices. Yet it is difficult to discuss this responsibility without acknowledging, at the outset, that Parliament is a weak institution that exercises little direct influence on policy. The government, historically, has dominated Parliament. Parliament is a body where the structure of power ensures that members, disciplined along party lines, assume a subordinate role. Moreover, issues are dealt with in an adversarial format which assumes that the resolution to multifaceted conflicts can be reduced to two viewpoints – in favour or opposed. At the same time, as Savoie's examination of political power in Ottawa reveals, concentration and centralization of power in the office of the prime minister has increased since the Trudeau era.[33] Parliament's power, in relative terms, is almost certainly weaker.[34] Its ability to compel substantive changes to a legislative agenda may hit an extremely resilient roadblock if the prime minister considers a particular bill a vital part of his or her legislative agenda.

Yet, while Parliament is weak, it is not inconsequential. The effects of its adversarial role, and of the attendant publicity surrounding the public airing of grievances and questions for the government, should not be discounted. Parliament itself may wield little direct leverage on the government, but the barrage of questioning to which the prime minister or other ministers may be exposed is reported in the media. Consequently, media coverage stimulates a broader public debate on the merits of a particular bill or the explanation tendered by the government. As Ned Franks suggests:

The important influence of parliament is not in its direct effect on legislation and policies. Rather, its influence is indirect. Parliament normally wields power through the deterrent effect of bad publicity. A government, to be successful, must anticipate criticism, and ensure that its policies, budgets, and proposals are defensible as a good balancing of special interests, and an expression of a public interest. The opposition will be quick to pounce on flaws and errors of omission and commission. The adversarial system thus puts strong inducements on a government to consult widely, deliberate carefully, and present well-thought-out policy proposals.[35]

Most bills that raise Charter concerns will be assessed by a standing committee in each chamber that focuses particular attention on consistency with the Charter. These two committees are the House of Commons Standing Committee on Justice and Legal Affairs (formerly known as Justice and Human Rights, and commonly called the Justice Committee) and the Standing Senate Committee on Legal and Constitutional Affairs. The committees usually hear from witnesses who present a range of opinions on Charter and other relevant issues.

Despite the relevance of Charter issues to the legitimate scope of their inquiries, these committees have indicated that they often lack adequate time and information to make informed judgments about the extent and nature of Charter concerns.[36] Requests for access to assessments that explain the government's assumptions about relevant Charter concerns have been denied,[37] leaving some committee members feeling compromised in their ability to assess the constitutional implications of bills. The knowledge that the government has not reported to Parliament a bill's inconsistency with the Charter may be puzzling in light of the testimony of individuals or groups raising what they consider to be serious Charter problems. As one member described the difficulties these committees encounter: "We find ourselves in a terrible position where we are asked to pass legislation in respect of which we do not have the resources to make a judgment as to whether [it is] in accordance with the Charter. We take the word of the Minister of Justice, but we never have an opportunity to find out to what extent that word is based on reality."[38]

Parliamentarians' attempts to understand why there has been no report to Parliament that rights are violated, despite witnesses' claims of serious potential Charter violations or similar concerns raised in the media, have led the committees to summon Justice lawyers for answers to Charter-related questions. But it is important to recognize that these officials are responsible to the government, not to Parliament, and that the committees do not have their own legal advisers to provide guidance on constitutional questions. Thus, the ability to hear from witnesses, particularly from non-governmental organizations that may raise objections or identify concerns that rights are unduly or unnecessarily infringed, often affords committees different perspectives than those provided by public officials.

The federal government has encountered, and will likely continue to encounter, an interesting dilemma when passing legislation that is susceptible to a Charter challenge. This dilemma focuses on how to treat Parliament. The lack of transparency that characterizes the internal process of evaluation may mean that the government has little choice but to focus on the public or parliamentary dimension to demonstrate that legislation was guided by principled judgment about the Charter. But Parliament's weakness may be a liability in terms of defending legislation that raises a potentially serious Charter conflict. In the absence of a fulsome parliamentary record, judges may be reluctant to accept the assurances of governmental lawyers that Charter concerns were fully considered. Alternatively, materials and evidence cobbled together after legislation has been passed, to support the government's claim that Charter issues were duly considered, may be discounted by judges if viewed as perfunctory.

Yet, if the government were to encourage a more robust parliamentary role, this would sit in tension with a government's inclination to dominate the parliamentary process. For example, more parliamentary hearings with broader public intervention could put the government on the defensive if witnesses criticized proposed legislation for conflicting with Charter principles. Witnesses may raise Charter concerns that are not duly addressed by government members and, in so doing, contribute to a record that is not supportive of a government's claim that legislation is justified.

Although the government does not generally advise Parliament about the degree of Charter risk that is associated with a particular bill, and it never reports that its proposed legislation is patently inconsistent with the Charter, there have been occasional instances when Parliament has been viewed as a chamber for debate about controversial policies that are likely to result in Charter litigation. The government has recognized the advantages, from a pragmatic perspective, of having more transparent parliamentary judgment to strengthen its anticipated legal claim that legislative restrictions on rights are justified. Good examples of this can be found in the government's handling of the rules for sexual assault trials and its legislative response to the Supreme Court's change of a common law rule that allowed extreme intoxication to be used as a defence to sexual assault charges, discussed in chapter 5. In both instances, the government consciously focused on Parliament as the venue for expressing philosophical differences from the court. These differences were recorded in a legislative preamble, constructed deliberately to support arguments about why the judiciary should consider the legislation as reflecting reasonable judgment about how to reconcile conflicting values. Parliament, therefore, played a substantial role in evaluating legislative proposals, proposing changes that were accepted, and hearing from witnesses who provided testimony that might be useful if the legislation was subsequently challenged.

The conscious use of parliamentary hearings suggests expectations of a linkage between parliamentary deliberation and success in litigation. But there is little reason why the government should be so selective in viewing Parliament as an important venue for expressing political judgment on Charter issues. The failed attempt to enhance parliamentary scrutiny under the Bill of Rights raises the obvious question of whether any similar intent can be more effective under the Charter. Many will understandably take the view that the weakness of Parliament is so ingrained that, in the face of decades of failure to introduce reforms, it is simply naive to expect Parliament to become more independent or more powerful vis-à-vis the government. Parliament's weakness, relative to the government, and the prevalence of strict party discipline certainly affect its ability to scrutinize legislation, which is one of the principal functions for which it is associated. Yet whether or not Parliament appreciates it, the very real possibility of judicial nullification of legislation that imposes an unnecessary or excessive restriction on a protected right mitigates, to some degree, the weakness Parliament might otherwise display in its scrutiny of government legislation. Suggestions to encourage more robust parliamentary scrutiny and to enhance parliamentarians' knowledge of the Charter risks associated with governmental bills will be offered in chapter 3.

CONCLUSIONS

It is extremely short-sighted to assume that the principal benefit of the Charter will arise from the judiciary's willingness to play a corrective role of recognizing and remedying violations of rights. This perspective suggests that, for Charter values to be effective, members of the polity will have to depend principally upon judicial review. But if this were true, it would greatly limit the scope of rights protection because only a small percentage of legislative actions will ever by reviewed by courts. The extent to which public and political officials respect Charter values will determine how robust the Charter's influence is on the majority of legislative outcomes.

An emphasis on Parliament as a venue for deliberation over rights relies on expectations first identified forty years ago but still unfulfilled. Nevertheless, conditions are now more conducive for their realization than under the *Bill of Rights*. These conditions result, in large part, from judicial insistence that governments justify restrictions on rights through evidence and argument.

2 The Legitimacy Debate

Before the Charter's adoption, Canada had become accustomed to a conservative judicial culture. With the exception of rare instances where some Supreme Court judges were provoked to find creative means to protect citizens from flagrant civil rights abuses by governments,[1] the general proposition that judges should query the merits of legislative choices was foreign to the judiciary's tradition and to its professional assumptions. For example, less than a decade before the introduction of the Charter, then Supreme Court justice Brian Dickson declined to comment on the merits of competing arguments in a labour dispute. His explanation was that he considered the resolution of competing social values to be an inherently "arbitrary" judgment and, as a result, best left to elected representatives. This reservation was perfectly consistent with the prevailing Canadian judicial culture of the period: "The submission that this court should weigh and determine the respective values of society of the right to property and the right to picket raises important and difficult political and socio-economic issues, the resolution of which must, by their very nature, be arbitrary and embody personal economic and social beliefs."[2]

The Supreme Court, however, no longer seems to be troubled by the kind of discretionary decision making that accompanies the arbitration of social and political conflicts. The court has acknowledged that the Charter has substantially changed its role and function in the political system. From its first few Charter cases, where it seemed almost anxious to dispel suggestions that a conservative judicial culture would or should carry over under the Charter, the court has gone out of its way to emphasize its new role as the "guardian of the Constitution."[3] Commentators differ on the extent and significance of this role, but what is beyond question is that under the Charter's influence the court no longer avoids the task of evaluating conflicting values that arise from legislative decisions. Former Supreme Court justice Bertha Wilson captures what appears to be a growing sentiment among judges – fatigue, from having to justify to critics the implications of judicial review. This is apparent in her statement: "We Didn't Volunteer." As Justice Wilson explains, Canadian political leaders, not the courts, decided to codify rights and give courts the responsibility to review legislative and executive action for compliance with the constitution. This was done with "full knowledge of the American experience and the criticism of the role of the courts in that society," including criticism by some of most eminent judges. Therefore, she argues, it is time for political commentators to stop portraying the court's role under the Charter as a colossal "power grab" because Canada's decision to entrench rights inevitably vaulted courts into the position of assuming this new "onerous responsibility."[4]

This change in the scope of judicial responsibilities has, not surprisingly, provoked considerable reflection and comment. Political and legal scholars have actively debated the proper role of the judiciary and the consequences of judicial review for principles of democratic governance. The democratic legitimacy of judicial review is an enduring issue in liberal-democratic polities where the judiciary has been given the responsibility to review constitutional principles and the power to set aside the legislative decisions of those who are democratically elected. Disagreement arises around any attempt to frame an appropriate standard for evaluating judicial review. But efforts to assess the relationship between democratic principles and judicial review under the Charter seem to be driving participants towards polar ends of the argument. The distance between contrary perspectives appears all the greater because different normative prescriptions are offered to central questions: What is the role of the state? How should rights principles be interpreted? How do these relate to other principles of governance? And how should the judiciary interpret its responsibility to give effect to fundamental rights and values?

Both supporters and critics of the Charter delineate versions of the appropriate judicial role that correspond with their particular democratic claims. The former group argues that a robust interpretation of rights is required to enhance democracy and to allow for the realization of substantive conditions for citizens' meaningful engagement in the polity. Judicial review, rather than restrict democratic principles, protects the very conditions that are necessary for citizens to function equitably. They conceive of these conditions as rights and argue that, absent robust judicial protection, rights will be eroded by Parliament or by others exercising power on behalf of the state.

In contrast, Charter critics perceive an inherent tension between judicial review and democracy. Some on the conservative end of the political continuum argue that judicial review should be guided by a strict interpretation of the Charter's provisions, to avoid any unnecessary interference with the will of the people, as expressed through the decisions of their political representatives. Others, who are sceptical about the benefits of the Charter, question the desirability of posing normative questions for the state in terms of individual rights, at least as embodied in legal liberalism. They are concerned that rights will be counter-productive for redressing need. Rights will be used by corporate and other powerful interests to constrain state actions necessary to address economic and social impediments to the fair and just treatment of citizens.

This focus on the legitimacy of judicial review has led Miriam Smith to argue that political scientists should leave behind their normative judgments and engage in empirical analysis of the Charter's effects. In Smith's view, the questions generated in the legitimacy debate, by both critics and supporters of the Charter, are basically uninteresting. Legitimacy questions revolve around normative issues that may be suited for law schools, but they do not address more pressing issues for political scientists. Smith argues that political scientists should focus on relationships between institutions and the power structures of society. She also criticizes commentary on the legitimacy issue for borrowing from theoretical approaches that are rooted in outdated pluralist assumptions.[5]

Smith may be correct in her criticism of the literature for failing to engage sufficiently in empirical analysis of the Charter's effects. Yet, despite her plea for an abandonment of normative judgments, it is difficult to understand how this is either possible or desirable. How one evaluates the role of the state, how Charter values are interpreted and applied to specific legislative circumstances, and how one envisages the responsibilities of Parliament or the judiciary to give effect to these values remain relevant questions for empirical analysis. These question, however, evoke necessary and inevitable normative judgments. Principles of rights are not freestanding or self-defining concepts. Instead, they require philosophical judgment to elicit their meaning and application for social and political conflicts. The subjective nature of these judgments and the discretionary nature of the legal rules that may underlie their interpretation make it difficult, if not artificial, to separate empirical analysis from normative judgment. Furthermore, as Samuel La Selva has argued, the Charter requires an understanding of the relationship between a theory of justice and a theory of federalism, which itself constitutes a normative exercise.[6]

My focus in this book is on how the Charter affects legislative decision making. In discussing the juxtaposition of legal and political judgments on the Charter's implications for governing, I wish to offer a different perspective on the relationship between the judiciary and representative institutions. This perspective reflects my unwillingness to accept the extreme positions generated by opposing commentators in the legitimacy debate. Thus, it is necessary to acknowledge the normative assumptions that influence my analysis. I will explain these by focusing first on why I am not persuaded by the claims made by those who occupy extreme positions in the legitimacy debate. I will then examine the metaphor of constitutional dialogue that has been offered as an alternative conception to a legitimacy-based argument.

EXTREME POSITIONS IN THE LEGITIMACY DEBATE

Fundamental-Rights Scholars

At one end of the legitimacy debate are those scholars who believe in judicial hegemony for resolving rights conflicts (I will refer to this view as the fundamental-rights position). What unites fundamental-rights scholars is their confidence that a skilful interpretation of the constitution will allow judges to come up with the correct answer to conflicts over rights, or at least a more persuasive answer. Certainly not all fundamental-rights scholars want to engage in the legitimacy debate or preface their normative assumptions about judicial hegemony in democratic terms.[7] Nevertheless, for many, an implicit assumption about democracy corresponds with their particular normative view of the judiciary's role: judicial involvement to protect rights provides the necessary conditions for citizens to be treated as equal members of the polity and thus is a prerequisite for democracy.[8]

Lorraine Weinrib is explicit on the connection between judicial review and democracy. Weinrib distinguishes between a constitutional and a legislative state in terms of whether rights have peremptory status. Canada, with the adoption of the Charter, has become a member of the former category. A constitutional state may respect the majoritarian process but recognizes that this is not an end in itself. Democracy requires an emphasis on constitutionalism because limitations must be placed on majority rule to respect basic human rights and values. Rather than impairing democracy, these restrictions ensure its full realization. In a legislative state, normative principles of liberal democracy remain vulnerable to legislative choices that may embody other priorities and preferences. Weinrib argues that Canada's transformation into a constitutional democracy "imposes the core principles of liberal democracy as supreme legal prescriptions on every exercise of state power, including the enactment of legislation."[9] With this transformation, which Weinrib characterizes as a revolution, the fundamental norms of liberal democracy take priority over majoritarian decisions: "The constitutional state ... respects the majoritarian process, but not as an end in itself. Its strongest commitment is to the enduring norms of liberal democracy, binding on all persons and institutions that wield public power. While legislation and legislative bodies retain high status and function, they are servants to, not masters of, these norms. Respect for citizens as free and equal members of the political community ranks as the prime organizing feature of the polity. Liberty, equality and human dignity act as restraints upon the majoritarian democratic machinery."[10]

Judicial review of constitutional rights ostensibly places a higher priority on principled resolutions than would be accorded by the bureaucracy or Parliament. Fundamental-rights scholars perceive legislative objectives as inherently in tension with rights. Legislative objectives, some argue, gain their inspiration not from rights but from majoritarian preferences or utilitarian considerations informed by costs and convenience. As a result, rights will be vulnerable without a bill of rights, which provides a valuable corrective instrument for unjust decisions that would otherwise occur. The Charter performs this function by requiring legislatures to demonstrate and justify the reasons for deviating from its principles. Weinrib concisely expresses this viewpoint:

Convenience, commonly held preferences and usage are repugnant not only to the rights-guaranteeing aspects of the Charter, but moreover to section 1 justification. Once admitted as grounds for limiting rights, these ever-present grounds will always triumph over rights guarantees: it is all or never. Interests specified as rights and freedoms are by definition granted at the expense of the collectivity, to the extent that a majoritarian measure of cost, convenience and custom prevails. Indeed, the primary purpose of constitutionalizing these interests is to give them protection from the majority's ability to infringe them without political cost.[11]

The above passage conveys three important tenets informing the argument frequently used to justify judicial hegemony for reconciling Charter conflicts. These are: 1) while courts protect rights, Parliament deviates from constitutional principles by restricting rights; 2) legislative restrictions on rights arise from discretionary policy concerns over costs, convenience, and other non-rights concerns; and 3) the supremacy of the constitution requires that judicial determinations of rights trump political judgments.

For many who believe that judicial review is necessary to protect rights adequately, qualms about this important judicial role are not directed at how Charter judgments will affect the role of Parliament. Instead, the focus centres on whether the courts will have the necessary fortitude to respect rights-based principles or resist pressures for deference towards legislative decisions. The vitality of the Charter is seen as dependent upon the legal remedies granted for violations of rights. These include the exclusion at trial of evidence obtained by police in a manner that conflicts with legal rights or the nullification of legislation for improperly infringing upon rights. Accordingly, the expected salutary benefits of the Charter relate directly to the robustness and vigour of the judiciary when articulating these principles, and the extent to which the court insists that these principles take precedence over contrary police actions or legislative decisions. As Weinrib argues, if rights remain susceptible to the "tides of the political marketplace, then the effect of the entrenchment of the Charter, like the enactment of the *Canadian Bill of Rights*, will be without legal meaning or institutional coherence."[12]

David Beatty argues the need for principles to triumph over expediency. He describes judicial responsibility under the Charter as being "derived objectively from the most basic principles and values which underlie the Charter."[13] This objective characterization of rights arises from his controversial suggestion that when a court fails to adopt the appropriate method of reasoning, which includes a principled approach to evaluating legislative limits on rights, judges "have themselves acted unconstitutionally."[14] Beatty's statement is contentious, however, because the judicial approach for evaluating legislative limits on rights is discretionary, arising not from the constitution itself but from judges' interpretation of section 1, the general limitation clause.

Weinrib recognizes that there may not be a single correct answer to resolve Charter conflicts. Nevertheless, she suggests that the Charter provides "a significant degree of guidance for judicial interpretation." This guidance is based on the Charter's respect for "individual conscience and equal human dignity" and its recognition that these "new rights" are subject only to "normatively justified limits, and an exceptional, qualified legislative override."[15]

The considerable optimism expressed about the Charter's salutary potential parallels the confidence many American legal scholars have in the judiciary's ability to distil enduring and binding legal principles from vague constitutional principles. This confidence stems from the conviction that judges are better equipped than legislators (institutionally, philosophically, and methodologically) for the task of expounding the meaning of rights and evaluating the legitimacy of state actions where rights are implicated.

The influence of American scholarly ideas, as they relate to the rights-based liberal ethic many associate with the Charter, is hardly surprising. The relative newness of the Charter, and uncertainty about how it will affect the practice of government and political culture, contrasts with the much older American tradition of judicial review on issues of rights. American judicial review has provided considerable opportunities to ponder the effects of judicial interpretations of rights. Furthermore, this American experience is already familiar to many Canadian scholars who have studied American legal debates either in Canada or in American graduate and law schools.

Ronald Dworkin epitomizes the confidence American scholars have in the rights-protecting skills of the judiciary. Dworkin is not greatly troubled by the alleged tension between judicial review and democratic principles. He argues that the constitutional establishment of individual legal rights beyond the ability of the legislature to compromise them does not subvert or compromise democracy. This apparent tension, he suggests, is in fact illusory because an important distinction exists between democracy and majority rule. For democracy to exist in a meaningful sense, people must be treated as equals. In his view, this is best accomplished when the conditions for achieving equality are conceived of as moral rights against the state: "Democracy means *legitimate* majority rule, which means that mere majoritarianism does not constitute democracy unless further conditions are met. It is controversial just what these conditions are. But *some* kind of constitutional structure that a majority cannot change is certainly a prerequisite to democracy. There must be embedded constitutional rules stipulating that a majority cannot abolish future elections, for example, or disenfranchise a minority."[16]

Dworkin believes that the American Bill of Rights rests on a particular liberal assumption: individuals have moral rights against the state. He predicates his theory on the egalitarian ideal that government must treat all its citizens as equals – political decisions and arrangements must display equal concern for the fate of all. Dworkin assigns judges a particularly important role in preserving these moral rights. He believes that the task of courts is fundamentally different from that of legislatures. The judiciary's task requires a fusion of moral and political philosophy.[17] Dworkin argues that a distinction exists between the strategies used by government to secure the general interest, as a matter of policy, and the rights of individuals, which are a matter of principle. The latter should be recognized as having primacy over the former.[18] Rights should "function as trump cards" against legislation that would impose some particular vision of the good on society as a whole.[19] As a result, judges should rest their judgment on arguments of political principle and, even in hard cases, should ensure that decisions reflect their best judgment of what the law requires. Dworkin's confidence in judges is exemplified by the fact that, even on rare occasions when judges are wrong, he considers society to be better served by asking judges to "reason intuitively or introspectively" about different conceptions of equality or other contested concepts than by subjecting these difficult decisions to the ordinary realm of legislative politics. To believe otherwise would be to suppose that the ordinary voter has better capacity to engage in moral argument than judges.[20] While he recognizes "idealization" in his characterization of the judiciary's ability to engage in moral reasoning, he nevertheless has confidence that a political society benefits from adding an institutionally structured debate over rights principles: "Judges are not trained as political philosophers, and are not necessarily impressive at it – though the decisions of the Supreme Court do contain some marvellously lucid and effective arguments of principle … I believe that adding to a political system a process that is institutionally structured as a debate over principle rather than a contest over power is nevertheless desirable, and that counts as a strong reason for allowing judicial interpretation of a fundamental constitution."[21]

Laurence Tribe, like Dworkin, believes in judges' superior ability to discern principled answers to rights conflicts. According to Tribe, judges have a unique capacity and commitment to engage in constitutional discourse that explains and justifies the judiciary's conclusions about the legitimacy of government authority. Indeed, it is a commitment that "only a dialogue-engaging institution, insulated from day-to-day political accountability but correspondingly burdened with oversight by professional peers and vigilant lay critics," can be expected to maintain.[22] Similarly, Owen Fiss characterizes the legislative role as having little to do with uncovering the meaning of constitutional values. Instead, legislators register the actual preferences of the people: "what they want and what they believe should be done." Judges, in contrast, are "ideologically committed [and] institutionally suited to search for the meaning of constitutional values."[23] This superior judicial capacity to protect rights arises not from any personal traits or knowledge but "from the definition of the office in which they find themselves and through which they exercise power," a definition that enables and even forces "the judge to be objective" when determining "the true meaning of the constitutional value."[24] Michael Perry has a particularly optimistic view of judicial review. He sees the virtue of the judicial role as facilitating a higher moral political culture. Courts can and should search for right answers to political and moral problems. They have more institutional competence to discover these than do legislatures, which, if and when they get around to confronting moral dilemmas, rely on established moral conventions and ignore the occasion for moral re-evaluation. This is because few values outrank elected politicians' interest in re-election.[25]

Difficulty with Claims for Judicial Hegemony

Judicial-centric views of constitutional interpretations, especially as applied to Charter analysis, epitomize the tendency to view the judiciary as the exclusive custodian of rights. Parliament, in contrast, is viewed as the deviant institution with regard to its rights-respecting capacity. Parliament's relationship to rights is not that of defender and interpreter; rather, its decisions, when different from judicial interpretations, are said to ignore or restrict rights.

To the extent that Parliament is constitutionally empowered to give an independent assessment of the scope or applicability of rights principles to social conflicts, as distinct from merely giving effect to judicial judgments, this power arises from the inclusion in the Charter of the legislative override. But using the override power is not viewed as a worthwhile contribution to constitutional judgment. This is because the override is broadly viewed as part of a "grubby" political compromise, devised in the final stages of constitutional negotiations to secure majority provincial support for the Charter. Many consider Parliament's ability to insist temporarily on the primacy of its judgment over judicial rulings, to be inconsistent with the purpose of a bill of rights.

Although many fundamental-rights scholars place more trust in courts than they do in Parliament, there is no guarantee that judicial opinion will necessarily be more supportive of rights than political judgment. Many Charter commentators may be overly influenced by perceptions that contemporary rulings have been more sympathetic to rights claims, particularly those of minorities or vulnerable groups, than popularly enacted legislation. Yet the philosophical nature of judgment about rights provides no reason to assume that judges' interpretations are more likely to be sympathetic to a particular rights claim than the judgment of elected representatives. As will be argued below, much depends on the nature of the rights claim. Judges are drawn from the sector of society that is among the least likely to be on the progressive side of politics. Courts, by their very nature, are conservative institutions that rule on disputes according to the dictates of the past: the reasoned application of previous generations of judge-made laws. As a result, they do not generally lead public opinion so much as adhere to the values and prejudices of the past.

The claim that judges possess the unique or singular qualification to define the meaning and scope of rights and resolve rights conflicts in a reasonable way gives insufficient attention to the philosophical character of judgments about rights. Judicial determinations of the scope of rights reflect normative views about the meaning of equality, liberty, or other equally subjective concepts; the precise meaning of which is subject to judicial, scholarly, and philosophical debate. The fact that so much political debate focuses on the composition of courts underscores the importance of the philosophical inclinations of judges who interpret constitutional principles that constrain state action. As Andrée Lajoie and Henry Quillinan suggest, the meaning of a constitution will change not only when judges change but also when judges change their minds.[26]

Over generations, fluidity in rights claims has had important implications for their interpretation and application to social practices and legislative policies. Societal values change and along with them the particular meaning of enduring rights principles such as equality and justice. Today, few can countenance an historic interpretation of equality to justify differential treatment of persons of different races. Increasing numbers now question the validity of differential treatment of heterosexuals and gay men or lesbians. While the shift in the interpretation and scope of rights may be necessary for rights principles to be recognizable and significant in a contemporary context, the very necessity of this change speaks against a timeless application of judicially defined principles. Newer or different perspectives will challenge views from the past by trying to show why these provide for more persuasive interpretations of the normative ideals reflected in constitutional principles. However, the constitutional evolution of and societal reception of new or altered rights claims may not occur simultaneously. The rightness or wrongness of different perspectives may be apparent only with the passage of time. But the very fact of having to reassess existing assumptions or earlier definitions of rights raises the serious question of why judges alone should have this philosophical responsibility. If we move away from the possibility that a right has an enduring and stable constitutional meaning, there is little reason to presume that at any moment in history or during any clash of values, courts alone can identify the best or even the most reasonable answer to a rights conflict.

By questioning the singularity of a correct judicial answer to rights conflicts, I do not intend to deny the legal component to the resolution of such conflicts. To make this suggestion would be foolish and patently in denial of the clear constitutional authority given courts to interpret the Charter and grant remedies where appropriate. Nor is my intent to deny that some interpretations may be more persuasive than others. What I am suggesting is that, although the judicial interpretation of a right has legal standing, rights conflicts are at heart philosophical and political. As one strays beyond the most basic beliefs that governments should not prevent the expression of critical opinions on social policy, that all individuals must be treated equally before the law, or that individuals should not be deprived of their liberty in an arbitrary fashion, differences of opinion exist on the proper scope of rights.[27]

But, if the content and scope of protected rights are not self-defining, nor are decisions about their application to specific legislative circumstances. Rights claims can seldom be viewed as an independent standard for critically evaluating state actions unless they are viewed at such a level of abstraction that their normative force in any particular circumstance cannot determine a definitive outcome. Judgment about the justification of legislative actions, where rights might be affected, is influenced by how the role of the state is conceived. For example, what are the responsibilities of the state when responding to power imbalances that accrue because of unequal distributions of resources or power? How active should the state be when trying to anticipate and redress societal harms? Perspectives on these issues will shape responses to questions that inevitably lead to differences of opinion, such as: Can the state prohibit nudity in public places? Is mandatory retirement valid? Can the amount of money that political parties spend in elections be regulated?

To claim that there is a correct answer to rights conflicts is to have little regard for the subjective qualities of interpreting and applying abstract philosophical principles to specific political conflicts. Moreover, it denies the likelihood of reasonable disagreements on how complex social objectives can best be achieved without imposing undue restrictions on fundamental rights. If rights conflicts allowed for singular or obviously superior answers, citizens would be justifiably troubled by the frequency of split judicial decisions. For, if a correct answer exists for such conflicts, what explains the regularity with which so many judges must be presumed to reach the "wrong" answer? Fortunately, citizens do not generally view a court as incompetent for failing to render a unanimous ruling. And for good reason.

The adoption of a bill of rights represents a deliberate decision to give the judiciary responsibility to assess the validity of state actions. But these assessments will almost certainly be conducted according to broad rights principles that inevitably require some degree of philo-

sophical elucidation. With this arises the likelihood of different interpretations of the scope of rights and their application to specific
legislative objectives. The possibility that a range of reasonable answers
exists is more persuasive than is the view that a single or best answer
will emerge from a principled interpretation of a bill of rights. But if
this is the case, why should it be assumed that the judiciary is the only
locus for resolving rights conflicts?

The possibility of a range of reasonable answers to rights-based conflicts leads Jeremy Waldron to puzzle over why so many legal commentators take such great comfort in judicial resolutions of such conflicts.[28]
A principal objection Waldron has with reliance on a bill of rights is
that, even though disagreements will invariably arise over the application of abstract philosophical principles to specific political conflicts,
these conflicts are nevertheless portrayed as if they are amenable to a
principled and singular resolution. Yet, as he argues, recognition of
persistent disagreements should be regarded "as one of the elementary
conditions of modern politics."[29]

To understand the importance and value of political judgment,
Waldron draws support from Kant's recognition that in the transition from moral to political philosophy it is necessary to be cogni-
zant of others not just as objects of moral concern or respect but as
"*other minds, other intellects, other agents of moral thought, coordinate and
competitive with our own.*"[30] This recognition leads to Waldron's acceptance of the concept of majoritarianism in representative institutions
as the best way to respect the fact that a singular view of justice does
not exist. He considers the majority principle not only as an "effective decision-procedure" but also as a "respectful one" since it takes
seriously the reality of differences of opinion about justice or the
common good: "Whatever the state of my confidence about the correctness of my own view, I must understand that politics exist, in
Arendt's words, because 'not man but men inhabit the earth and
form a world between them' – not one person but people – that
mine is not the only mind working on the problem in front of us,
that there are a number of distinct intelligences working on whatever issue we face, and that it is not unexpected, not unnatural, not
irrational to think that reasonable people would differ."[31]

Arguably, the claim for judicial hegemony in the face of philosophical disagreements about resolving rights conflicts pays too much hom-
age to the Platonic conception that the people need guardians for
issues of justice. Although not a conventional view, it is entirely possible to conceptualize rights-regarding procedures, including a bill of
rights, with no provision for judicial review, where an entirely different
institutional (and non lawyerly) body evaluates state actions for their

consistency with fundamental rights. Mark Tushnet has written a comprehensive critique of judicial review in the United States. His suggestion of imagining the possibility of living without judicial review has, not surprisingly, generated substantial response.[32]

The subjective and philosophical qualities associated with the interpretation and resolution of rights conflicts challenge the peremptory and objective character in which rights claims are so often cast. But the argument against judicial hegemony extends beyond the inevitability of philosophical disagreements about the meaning and scope of rights or the normative role of the state in recognizing and responding to rights claims. Critical analysis of the law is far too persuasive in demonstrating the discretionary nature of legal rules to accept the very assumptions upon which claims for judicial hegemony rely: that legal rules can be distilled as objective or coherent principles; that an appeal to these can identify the correct or best answer to resolve conflicts around rights; and that judges have distinct and superior qualities of reasoning with respect to distilling the essential meaning of rights. Critical analysis demonstrates the different ways in which judicial interpretations of rights rest on the meaning of legal rules derived from the values and assumptions of previous generations and current occupants of judicial authority.

Critical Legal Studies (CLS) scholars make it particularly difficult to accept that judicial review does, or ever could, represent an objective, non-discretionary, principled mode of reasoning. They argue that the judicial conception of the limited state – the foundation of a bill of rights in the liberal legal vision – necessarily makes judging an ideological task because no set of formal rules could possibly evolve from value-free interpretations.[33] Critical race scholars also make persuasive arguments demonstrating that legal rules and social norms are not neutral but stem from racial, social, and cultural assumptions.[34] Feminist legal critics emphasize the masculine orientation of these rules,[35] and scholars who examine how law affects lesbians and gay men demonstrate the reliance of these rules upon heterosexuality as the norm for social and sexual relationships.[36]

The possibility of a range of reasonable interpretations, as an inevitable consequence of judicial review, represents my principal disagreement with some fundamental-rights scholars. They justify judicial hegemony for resolving rights conflicts by claiming that the function of the court, when applying rights principles to broad social conflicts, involves skills, methods, or aptitudes unique to the judiciary. I disagree with this perspective. Judges may invoke legal rules to distinguish a particular circumstance from an earlier precedent. Nevertheless, working towards reasonable resolutions of rights conflicts involves philosophical and value-laden judgments that are not derived objectively from legal rules, from a specific form of analysis, or from particular skills that the judiciary alone possesses. Because the interpretation and application of legal rules depend on value choices, serious doubt arises about whether their discretionary quality can be distinguished from the discretionary character of other forms of judgment, including that which is undertaken by representative institutions.

Both the subjective nature of rights principles and the discretionary character of legal rules challenge the virtue of building a legal and political theory around claims that judges can singularly define the meaning of rights or how rights should be interpreted in the context of complex issues of social policy. My interpretation of the judicial role is also to be distinguished from the position of some proponents of liberal constitutionalism (discussed below), who believe that regard for a more textual or historical approach will significantly reduce the philosophical quality of judicial rulings.

The Other End of the Legitimacy Continuum: Charter Sceptics

Many Charter sceptics consider judicial review to be inherently in tension with democratic principles of representative government. Those who come from a CLS perspective, or share many of its assumptions, are suspicious of the virtues of casting progressive changes in terms of liberal arguments about rights, particularly since rights are generally thought to impose negative constraints on the state. For example, Allan Hutchinson believes that a better approach abandons framing political debates in Charter terms and instead relies on broader democratic conversation about the building of a good political community.[37] Other Charter sceptics, who do not reject liberalism but remain suspicious of judicial review, suggest that a narrow interpretation of rights and the confinement of judgments to the obvious or logical meaning of the constitutional text – an approach termed "interpretivism" – best addresses democratic concerns.[38] The focus here deals with the latter scholars, who have a conservative approach to social reform and who base their democratic concerns about the implications of judicial review on the following assumptions: a constitution that establishes the conditions for the exercise of government power and the separation of institutional powers provides the democratic foundation for a polity; a fundamental premise of democracy is that the political system is based on representative and accountable government; judicial review is inherently anti-democratic in that it is neither representative nor accountable; and the legitimate exercise of judicial review rests on its role to uphold the constitutional values as stated in the text or implied from the intent of the framers. Thus, when courts recognize rights claims that are not obviously or logically derived from the constitution, they themselves become involved in political causes.

Many Charter sceptics are critical of the courts' approach to the Charter, which they believe is characterized by judicial activism. Claims about the desirability of, or dangers implied from, judicial activism have structured much of the legal and political discussions critical of the Charter. Like any concept, judicial activism is subject to different interpretations. Peter Russell provides the definition of judicial activism used here: "judicial vigour in enforcing constitutional limitations on the other branches of government and a readiness to veto the policies of those branches of government on constitutional grounds."[39] This definition does not equate judicial activism with criticism, despite the fact that critics of judicial review often invoke "judicial activism" as if it were a self-contained and obvious critical statement. This descriptive rather than normative statement requires those with opinions on the issue to explain what it is about the nature of a judicial ruling that does or does not justify vetoing legislative or executive decisions to enforce constitutional norms.

Problems with using liberal constitutionalism to define judicial role
Some of the same commentators who argue that the judiciary should be guided by interpretivism when approaching the Charter also believe that liberal constitutionalism provides a useful standard for evaluating judicial decisions. The concept of constitutionalism is subject to different interpretations,[40] related in part to the period and version of civil society to which they apply. The struggle for personal freedom and escape from arbitrary political rule, which have been conspicuous features of the history of Western Europe and the United States since the sixteenth century, explains the endurance of constitutionalism in liberal-democratic theory.[41] For example, James Madison characterized the challenge to contain authority in a democratic state in the following terms:

"But what is government itself but the greatest of all reflections on human nature? If men were angels, no government would be necessary. If angels were to govern men, neither external nor internal controls on government would be necessary. In framing a government which is to be administered by men over men, the great difficulty lies in this: you must first enable the government to control the governed; and in the next place oblige it to control itself. A dependence on the people is, no doubt, the primary control on the government; but experience has taught mankind the necessity of auxiliary precautions."[42]

Two essential premises characterize liberal constitutionalism: limited government and the rule of law. Together these rules stipulate that governments exist only to serve "specified ends and properly function only according to specified rules."[43] Restrictions on government envisaged in liberal constitutionalism are consistent with a limited rather than expansive role for the state; they reflect negative rather than positive liberty and are associated with the absence of state intervention.

However, claims that democratic and constitutional norms require a limited judicial role, restricted to interpreting the meaning of the text to give effect to the drafters' intent, or to enforce the limited state, provide no more persuasive approaches to the Charter than do arguments for judicial hegemony. Reliance on interpretivism in conceiving of the judicial task is fraught with difficulties. A singular intent may not underlie rights provisions, intent is extremely difficult to determine, the values espoused by the framers may not address contemporary moral dilemmas, and the open-ended wording of many provisions does not provide adequate guidance to determine which values and circumstances should be protected or how conflicting rights should be reconciled.[44]

Furthermore, the liberal-constitutional emphasis on the limited state to regulate political power has roots in eighteenth- and nineteenth-century assumptions that have little resonance for a modern welfare state.[45] Some also consider it misguided to construct a contemporary theory of judicial review around the idea of liberal constitutionalism because this idea was heavily influenced by American concerns to insulate private property from self-interested public officials or from factional tyranny. A number of the individual rights provisions in the American constitution were intended to safeguard property by making governmental action difficult and by requiring agreement across branches of government to enable redistribution.[46] The problem of factions, so central to the Federalist Papers, was closely associated with the concern that private groups might try to redistribute resources from the wealthy to the poor. Thus, the structure of the American constitution and many of its individual rights provisions, which convey the idea of limited government, are intended to safeguard property.[47]

Rainer Knopff and F.L. Morton criticize the judiciary's record for the inconsistency between judicial activism and the dictates of liberal constitutionalism. They worry that judicial review has relinquished its traditional character as a conservative check on democratic change. In altering its function of defending traditional rights that are framed around the idea of limited government, the judiciary has come to be viewed as an instrument for implementing social and political reform.[48] This troubles Knopff and Morton, who believe that Canadian courts have insufficient regard for the separation of powers which, they argue, is implicit in respect for the principle of liberal constitutionalism.

The doctrine of separation of powers ensures that those who make the laws remain distinct from those with responsibility to interpret, apply, and enforce them. This provides incentives to establish general rather than particular rules to ensure that these rules are equally applicable to all. The theoretical idea is to allocate governmental powers to branches of government based on the relationship each has to the process of making and enforcing laws.[49] Although significant problems with lack of coherency arise from the blurring of institutional responsibilities,[50] and its particularly uneasy fit to a Westminster system with its fusion rather than separation of legislative and executive powers, Knopff and Morton believe that the concept is relevant for a parliamentary system: "This is an *issue*, rather than an automatic division of responsibilities, because the distinction between legal and political questions is often controversial. Such controversy lies at the heart of the legitimacy debate: Are Charter rights really legal entities suitable for judicial resolution, or do they pose political questions most appropriately settled by Parliament? Is judicial review of the Charter best understood as constitutional law or courtroom politics?"[51]

Christopher Manfredi similarly invokes liberal constitutionalism to assess judicial power. Manfredi argues that the principle of liberal constitutionalism requires that the positive law of a constitution binds judges. Consequently, judges should "enforce only those rights" that the constitution authorizes them to enforce. Although judicial review may be "an indispensable and key element of liberal constitutionalism," there is a fundamental paradox here and courts are at its centre. The paradox relates to the fact that judicial enforcement of rights may be necessary to protect liberal constitutionalism and yet risks destroying the most important right that citizens in liberal democracies possess: the right of self-government. The interference with the right of self-government occurs when the judicial role itself is not properly constrained by constitutional limits.[52] "If judicial review evolves such that political power in its judicial guise is limited only by a constitution whose meaning courts alone define, then judicial power is no longer itself constrained by constitutional limits."[53]

A central claim of liberal constitutionalism affirms the judiciary's responsibility to protect existing rights, not to create new ones. Citizens rather than judges have the responsibility to make the necessary constitutional changes should the constitution require adjustment.[54] The only acceptable constraints on the decisions of representative institutions, where these are duly enacted and consistent with the rule of law, are those that have been tacitly accepted by the polity in the form of agreed-on limitations as embodied in the actual text and intents of Charter provisions or their logical implications. However, when judges recognize rights claims that are not obviously or logically derived from the constitution, they themselves become implicated in political causes. Not only is this inconsistent with their proper role of preserving limited government, but such judicial intervention imposes unwarranted and undemocratic restraints on representative government. Manfredi claims that his argument is not a defence of majority rule for its own sake but a recognition of the moral judgment about fundamental values that a legislative majority has made.[55]

Knopff and Morton worry that judicial review will interfere with democratic responsibilities to make difficult choices between competing perspectives. Like Manfredi, they suggest that legitimacy concerns arise when courts go beyond their recognized role to settle specific constitutional disputes:

No one will challenge the legitimacy of appointed and politically independent judges settling concrete disputes, and the lawmaking incident to that function is likely to be accepted as long as it is seen as the unavoidable corollary of the primary adjudicative function, and is closely circumscribed by the adjudicative context. When the relationship between the two judicial functions is reversed, however, with the concrete case becoming a mere pretext for the authoritative declaration of what the law requires in circumstances extending well beyond the confines of the case, the problem of democratic legitimacy looms much larger.[56]

Their focus on liberal constitutionalism as the standard for judicial review leads Knopff and Morton to criticize the judiciary's recognition of the rights claims of equality-seeking groups who view Charter litigation as a way to achieve substantive outcomes different from what they could achieve in the representative realm of politics. Underlying their criticism of these groups is their assessment that much of what occurs around the rights claiming by equality-seeking groups is not about rights at all. By defining the valid role of judicial review in terms of upholding the principles of limited government, with its emphasis on negative liberty, Knopff and Morton equate substantive or outcome-oriented rights claims with "special interests" that they consider illegitimate subjects for judicial review. Judicial reception of these claims constrains or imposes affirmative obligations on Parliament beyond those which the people have agreed on. But it also undermines the ability of the democratic polity to resolve contentious and conflicting rights claims because the new language in which these equality objectives are articulated – rights – takes on peremptory qualities that make political compromises or accommodations for other concerns more difficult:

To entrench rights and thereby transfer the resolution of reasonable disagreements from legislatures to courts not only inflates rhetoric to unwarranted levels but also grants the policy preferences of courtroom victors an aura of coercive force and permanence that they do not deserve. Issues that should be subject to the ongoing flux of "government by discussion" are presented as beyond legitimate debate, with the partisans claiming the right to permanent victory. The result is to embitter politics and decrease the inclination of political opponents to treat each other as fellow citizens – that is, as members of a sovereign people.[57]

Knopff and Morton recognize that judicial review will entail some degree of interpretation, but they argue that a distinction can and should be drawn between necessary law-making and more excessive and undemocratic forms. The Supreme Court's willingness to interpret equality as protecting against discrimination on the basis of sexual orientation is used by Morton as an example of the court exceeding a reasonable and acceptable degree of law-making and of creating a right not derivative of the text and requirements of the Charter. Morton also criticizes the federal government for responding to judicial rulings that he believes fail to draw on the explicit requirements of the constitution. For example, in testimony before a federal parliamentary committee, he criticized the decision to extend social-policy benefits to same-sex couples, stating that the government should ignore the judicial decision since it was an "abuse of [the Supreme Court's] power."[58]

His criticism of the court's recognition that equality is implicated by the denial of benefits to same-sex partners is not persuasive, even from the traditionally conceived vantage point of liberal constitutionalism. Liberal constitutionalism, at its core, seeks to protect citizens from arbitrary state actions. Its focus is to prevent uses of state power, whether in granting benefits or imposing burdens, according to rules that are partial, rather than impartial, and particular, rather than general. Distinctions that are based on personal characteristics and that have no bearing on the reason for a legislative benefit, or that reflect arbitrary decisions which reflect bias or prejudice towards individuals or groups, are inconsistent with the classic purpose of liberal constitutionalism. For example, it is difficult to conceive how legislative distinctions that have been created to perpetuate a heterosexual norm can be viewed as anything but discrimination against the most basic understanding of equality: treating all citizens as equal subjects before and under the law and, as a corollary, having a legitimate expectation to the equal effects of laws. That people may differ in their moral or religious attitudes with respect to how they view homosexuality, or that the Charter does not explicitly state its intention to ban discrimination on the basis of sexual orientation, does not support a conclusion that this form of sexual discrimination should be thought of as any less than a first-order equality concern. Without a theory that would help clarify and distinguish an "acceptable" from an "excessive" degree of judicial law-making in defining the scope of equality, criticism of excessive law-making seems to correspond more to disagreement with particular judicial outcomes. However, even if a theory of equality or democracy is relied upon to distinguish between acceptable and excessive degrees of judicial law-making, rival theoretical approaches could argue that both equality and democracy necessitate inclusion and full participation of all members of society.

Those who argue that the logic of liberal constitutionalism requires a narrow judicial approach are no less guilty than are fundamental-rights scholars of failing to confront the discretionary quality of legal judgments, even when courts confine the interpretation of rights to the obvious or logical meaning of the constitution. This might seem a strange criticism for these critics to be presented with, particularly since their advocacy of a narrow interpretation of the Charter is defended as a way of preventing courts from erroneously or mischievously granting rights status to value-laden policy choices. Overlooked is that the rights associated with limited government depend upon the creation of legal rules to give expression to how liberalism conceives of the market/state/freedom relationship. Interpretations of this relationship, whether derived from the constitution or common law, are influenced by legal liberalism's ideological assumptions. Liberal assumptions portray the state as the only and inherent enemy of freedom, treat the capitalist marketplace as a natural creation, and do not acknowledge that, rather than being sustained by objective rules, legal liberalism represents a form of ideology. Yet, as CLS convincingly demonstrate, the essential liberal claim that a formal set of rights provides an intelligent way to regulate state actions is extremely problematic. Not only is there no deductive process by which judges can derive the correct legal answers from abstract concepts such as freedom or property, but empirical analysis of the evolution of the common law demonstrates that the breadth of changes to legal rules defies the non-value characterization of its development. Rather than viewing legal rules as neutral in their ability to promote freedom and liberty, they should be understood as a manifestation of legal choices that have facilitated some forms of action while restricting others.[59]

Critics of judicial activism present a seemingly paradoxical argument. They accept the legitimacy of judicial review to protect the rights they consider fundamental (those associated with limited government) but profess the illegitimacy of judicial review when it confers rights status upon policy or "special interest" claims (those not specifically entrenched in a bill of rights). Yet, if no set of formal legal rules could possibly evolve from value-free interpretations, this suggests that the rights recognized by liberal constitutionalism – limited government and the public/private distinction upon which limited government rests – are no less the product of judicial discretion than are other forms of rights recognition. Rights associated with limited government may come from an earlier ideological tradition than do claims of autonomy, dignity, and substantive equality, but their vintage alone does not render them objective or neutral.

Protection against arbitrary state and governmental powers, the relationship between the governors and the governed, and the legal obligations that are imposed on the governors are important issues for the study of law and politics. Nevertheless, claims that liberal constitutionalism provides a compelling critique of judicial approaches that disregard interpretivism have had little resonance for those to whom they are directed. That disagreement persists about reliance on liberal constitutionalism to evaluate judicial power is hardly surprising; debate about liberal constitutionalism boils down to a debate about liberalism itself.[60] The close association between liberal constitutionalism and limited government helps explain why critics of an active judiciary find appeals to this concept more persuasive than do proponents. The argument for a restrictive judicial role does not persuade those who believe that the normative purposes of a bill of rights should not principally enforce a limited state.

Dario Castiglione attributes the limited appeal of liberal constitutionalism to the failure of its proponents to recognize the relevance of new theoretical concerns for the contemporary state. Castiglione argues that the institutional relationships and procedures deemed appropriate to regulate and limit political power in the past are anachronistic as political theories of the constitution because they remain "anchored to eighteenth- and nineteenth-century models." By appealing to limited government, and expecting that courts interpret rights in a manner that preserves this notion, liberal-constitutional scholars neglect the following important questions for contemporary constitutionalism: How should new "generations" of rights be integrated within a constitution? And what are the implications of autonomous powers within and beyond the state for sovereignty and accountability? These, he suggests, are questions for which "new political thinking is urgently required."[61]

Weinrib similarly views liberal constitutionalism, when predicated on the limited state, as anachronistic. To reach back to a tradition of judicial conservatism as the appropriate methodology for this new task is to misunderstand the significance of the new version of Canadian constitutionalism. She argues that the Charter has purposively transformed the values and institutional responsibilities embodied in the Canadian constitution. The role of the courts is to give effect to these new constitutional norms. But in the process, these norms should not be equated with traditional notions of limited government. Instead, they embrace more contemporary concerns with respecting human dignity: "The final version of the Charter firmly mandated elaboration of the content of the rights, and perhaps more importantly the justification of limits upon those rights, in the mode of international human rights instruments and post-war domestic constitutions. The Charter, in other words, was to provide a living constitution for a liberal democratic state, a constitution that honoured the equal human dignity of all members of Canadian society."[62]

Weinrib argues that critics of judicial activism fail to recognize that the judicial deference or conservatism they demand is inconsistent with the philosophy of the Charter. In her view, their defence of judicial deference, while laying "claim to the high ground of democratic process," rests on a commitment to an "unchanging and unchangeable political order, in which the state is minimal, human nature is fixed, and persistent identity-based inequality is untroubling."[63] In short, it is an impoverished understanding of democracy, based on a "thin and outdated idea of majority rule."[64]

Weinrib turns the critics' objection to judicial activism on its head. She argues that judicial activism arises not when courts overturn legislation but when they fail to prevent governments from making discretionary choices that restrict dignity (by upholding traditional conceptions of morality or family) or when they refuse to invalidate other outmoded (and in her view unprincipled) choices:

Contrary to the critics' complaint, it is the deferential, conservative justices who have been impermissibly activist. They have consistently ignored the values of the Charter text, its political history and its stated institutional roles. These justices evoke the ideologies of morality and family that the Charter text ultimately repudiated. They re-make the rules of Charter analysis at will in order to reach the results they desire. In the guise of interpretation, they not only impose their own personal values – those timeless ideas of human nature prized by the critics of judicial activism – they also take up an institutional role that the Charter does not vest in them. If the problem is illegitimate judicial creativity, they are the ones who consider the Charter a blank canvas on which to express their own fundamental values.[65]

Not surprisingly, equality-seeking theorists disdain the emphasis on limited government and its prescription of a restrictive judicial role. They do not view courts as external to the social-policy process but as legitimate state actors who can and should interpret rights in a manner that helps overcome or respond to social and other prejudices that prevent equitable treatment. Many equality-seeking groups shy away from arguments based on negative liberty or the limited state. They believe the Charter can and should be used to change hegemonic and traditional views of discrimination and equality. They portray discrimination and inequality as arising not necessarily from the failure to apply the law uniformly but, on the contrary, from the law's identical application to different groups. Justice Rosalie Abella aptly characterizes this in terms of the need for state actors "to treat us differently to redress the abuses our differences have attracted."[66]

Linked to this concern is that liberal constitutionalism portrays rights in universal and abstract terms divorced from culture, society, or power. Feminists argue that, depending on the issue, the supposedly "neutral" universal paradigm of liberal constitutionalism both excludes and assimilates women's concerns. Issues of power – women's treatment in the workplace, home, and family – are said to be private and thus excluded from constitutional review. But other issues, where gender affects women differently than men – for example, rape, harassment, pregnancy, and discrimination – are viewed by liberal constitutionalism from a universal (and, many suggest, male) norm. By failing to take into account the significance of gender, feminist scholars argue that a universal approach distorts and misunderstands women's experiences. Liberal constitutionalism dismisses calls to consider the cultural, sexual, and racial dimensions of how legal rules are interpreted. As Judith Squires suggests about the fit between liberal constitutionalism and the politics of difference: "It is not the fact that structural provisions delimit the political that is of concern, but the current criteria upon which the delimitation is made. A key concern (as addressed within feminist and difference literature) is that representative mechanisms in particular function to exclude differences which ought to be politically recognized. It is the form (not the existence) of the boundaries that are subject to challenge, and it is the constitutional procedures governing representation that are the most obvious focus of concern to difference theorists."[67]

AN ALTERNATIVE PERSPECTIVE: SHARED RESPONSIBILITY

Instead of seeking to define the judiciary's role to correspond with rival claims of its purported guardianship of democratic principles or, alternatively, its democratic deficit, I prefer to offer a different perspective. I am no more persuaded that judicial hegemony is appropriate than I am that judicial review should be constrained to reflect a narrow or strict interpretation of constitutional provisions or to enforce the limited state. A better way to assess how a bill of rights affects judicial and political power is to think of constitutional judgments as a shared responsibility. As I will argue in the next chapter, this shared responsibility should be conceived in relational terms.

The idea of shared responsibility is at least as old as is the experiment with judicial review of a constitution. Some of the founding fathers of the United States conceived of constitutional interpretations as requiring "coordinate review" where each branch of government may interpret the constitution for itself in questions that are properly before it.[68] In 1787 James Madison recognized that the "exposition of the laws and Constitution devolves upon the Judiciary" but nevertheless queried "upon what principle it can be contended, that any one department draws from the Constitution greater powers than another, in marking out the limits of the powers of the several departments?" He believed that the constitution did not provide for "a particular authority to determine the limits of the Constitutional division of power between the branches of the Government." Adjustments must be left to "the departments themselves," and if this is not possible, the remedy must come from "the will of the community, to be collected in some mode to be provided by the Constitution, or one dictated by the necessity of the case."[69]

Contemporary versions of a coordinate approach similarly emphasize that constitutional interpretation should be a shared endeavour and not the final prerogative of the judiciary. John Agresto portrays the role of the court as "a coequal and contributing branch of government" that should be "checked as well as checking, independent but not absolute."[70] Agresto characterizes the notion of judicial supremacy as constitutionally intolerable yet suggests that "strict judicial quiescence is a constitutional mistake." He proposes a better way of resolving the concerns with judicial imperialism:

In many ways the perfect constitutional solution to the problem of interpretive finality and judicial imperialism would have been for the judiciary to possess the same legislative relationship to Congress as that which governs the executive.

Just as Congress, by special majority, can override a presidential veto, a similar process could from the outset have been established to review judicial objections. To have subjected judicial "vetoes" to the same process of review as to that to which the Constitution subjects presidential vetoes would have been the most unobjectionable method of combining the benefit of active judicial reasoning and scrutiny with final democratic oversight. It would have been the perfect balancing of the principle of constitutionalism with active popular sovereignty.[71]

It is not obvious that the legislative override in the Charter would satisfy Agresto's idea of a "perfect constitutional solution" because a simple rather than special majority can invoke it. Manfredi, however, is supportive of the override. He interprets the override as a way to ensure that "the legislative and executive branches of government possess *equal* responsibility and authority to inject meaning into the indeterminate words and phrases of the Charter."[72] The relational view of shared responsibility I propose in the next chapter envisages the legislative override in section 33 as an opportunity for political judgment about the Charter, but only in exceptional circumstances of profound disagreement with judicial rulings. The more important emphasis for political judgments about the Charter, I will argue, occurs at the time of legislative debate and before passage of contentious legislation.

Brian Slattery applies the idea of a coordinate approach to Canada and in so doing rejects the view that courts should be presumed to be the exclusive caretaker of the constitution. He argues that the Charter should be viewed as distributing constitutional duties and review powers among the government, legislatures, and the courts – each being equally mandated to pursue the Charter's goals:[73]

[Courts, government, and Parliament] differ somewhat in their particular aptitudes, experience, and expertise, and sometimes also in their assessment of what ails members of the community and the proper course of treatment. Citizens dissatisfied with treatment received from one body may seek a second opinion, and the body rendering that opinion may take into account the credentials of the first. Although the various bodies may at times be at odds with one another, they more usually work in a coordinated way, for only thus are they able to achieve the broader goals they all share. Each body recognizes that it would be unable to minister alone to the needs of the entire community and that the pool of wisdom present in the group as a whole is far greater than that held by any single member. This model of the *Charter* then, lays stress on the equal responsibilities of the various branches of government to carry out the *Charter*'s mandate and the reciprocal nature of their roles. I will call it the Coordinate Model.[74]

Viewing Parliamentary/Judicial Relationship in Dialogic Terms

The notion of shared responsibility for constitutional judgments underlies the assumptions of some scholars who extol the virtues of constitutional dialogue, which has become a popular way of conceiving the judicial/legislative relationship. Like the coordinate model, a dialogic perspective rejects an essential claim made by fundamental-rights scholars – that the project of protecting rights requires judicial hegemony for the articulation of rights and resolution of conflicting claims.

The idea of dialogue between Parliament and courts, and between Parliament and the people, is implicit in the work of Peter Russell. Russell warns of the need to strike a balance between respect for judicial decision making and automatic reverence for legal resolutions of complex social problems:

Unquestionably Canada can benefit from the rationality which a thoroughly researched, well reasoned judicial decision can bring to the resolution of a difficult question of social or political justice ... But, while acknowledging these possible benefits, we should not lose sight of the possibility that excessive reliance on litigation and the judicial process for settling contentious policy issues can weaken the sinews of our democracy. The danger here is not so much that non-elected judges will impose their will on a democratic majority, but that questions of social and political justice will be transformed into technical legal questions and the great bulk of the citizenry who are not judges and lawyers will abdicate their responsibility for working out reasonable and mutually acceptable resolutions of the issues which divide them.[75]

Although Russell accepts that well-reasoned judicial decisions can enrich political and popular deliberation, he does not believe that courts should necessarily have the last word on issues of social and political justice. Thus, the override in section 33 is central to Russell's conception of checks and balances because it preserves citizen involvement in resolving contested issues of social justice, which he sees as an essential activity of a political community. The override allows for "reasoned discussion in a publicly accountable forum to the great issues of justice." Court decisions can be overridden by Parliament but this political decision will be influenced by broader public reflection and debate (at first indirectly and later directly because temporal limits on using the override will have ensured that an election has occurred before it can be renewed).[76] As Russell suggests:

Both courts and legislatures are capable of being unreasonable and, in their different ways, self-interested. By providing a legislative counterweight to judicial power the Canadian *Charter* establishes a prudent system of checks and balances which recognizes the fallibility of both courts and legislatures and gives closure to the decisions of neither. A legislature's decision to use the override, it must be remembered, is not ultimate. It is good for only five years. After five years it can be reviewed but not without re-opening the issue for public debate and discussion.[77]

Slattery invokes the idea of "continuing dialogue" between courts and legislatures in his discussion of the coordinate model. But, unlike those who have in mind a more judicial-centric approach to interpretation, Slattery argues that the vitality of the Charter rests less upon the "policing" aspect of the actions of other branches of government[78] than on how it affects those bounded in a first-order way: to assess the reasonableness of their own actions in light of fundamental rights and to act accordingly.[79]

The role of dialogue in the parliamentary/judicial relationship garnered considerable attention after an influential paper by Peter Hogg and Allison Bushell.[80] Although Hogg and Bushell do not develop in depth how they envisage dialogue, their view is premised on the assumption that dialogue will be largely judicially driven. It will occur principally (although not exclusively) around court decisions on whether legislation is reasonable and the changes required to bring legislation into accordance with judicial rulings. Unlike Russell and Slattery, who see Parliament and courts as sharing jointly in the responsibility for interpreting the Charter, Hogg and Bushell portray Parliament's role as clearly secondary under the constitutional division of labour. Parliament can choose to accept the absence of the contentious (and now invalid) legislation; it can comply with court decisions by revising legislation to satisfy judicial dictates; or it can override the court's judgment (viewed by many, although not necessarily Hogg or Bushell, as being tantamount to throwing a constitutional temper tantrum). In all of these options, Parliament's role is entirely reactive. The judiciary speaks – Parliament listens.

Conceiving of the legislative/judicial relationship as a dialogue is not, by any stretch of the imagination, a Canadian innovation. American commentators have long characterized the interaction between courts and other branches of government in dialogic terms.[81] A good example is the work of Alexander Bickel. Bickel refers to the "endlessly renewed education conversation" that occurs between the Supreme Court and the public as a "conversation, not a monologue."[82] As one commentator has described Bickel's vision of dialogue: "The Court's many constituents, including the public and the Congress, respond by words and actions to the Court's decisions – and the Court must listen to the response. The Justices do not necessarily reverse themselves when their decisions are unpopular – no functioning guardian of fundamental rights could justifiably do so. But they are certainly aware of opposition when it exists."[83]

Michael Perry goes even farther in describing constitutional interpretations of rights as a form of dialogue. Whereas Hogg and Bushell see dialogue in terms of how "best to reconcile the individualistic values of the *Charter* with the accomplishment of social and economic policies for the benefit of the community as a whole,"[84] Perry credits judicial review as facilitating the evolution of political morality: "In the constitutional dialogue between the Court and other agencies of government – a subtle, dialectical interplay between Court and polity – what emerges is a far more self-critical political morality than would otherwise appear, and therefore is likely a more mature political morality as well – a morality that is moving (inching?) toward, even though it has never always and everywhere arrived at, right answers, rather than a stagnant or even regressive morality."[85]

An alternative perspective comes from Barry Friedman, who considers dialogue a useful way to conceive of the judiciary's role. He prefers this to legitimacy-based claims that focus on whether and how the non-elected status of courts can be reconciled with the democratic and majority precepts of representative politics. But, unlike some other proponents of constitutional dialogue who imbue the concept with normative attributes, Friedman conceives of dialogue in descriptive terms.[86] He describes how courts actually operate in society. Friedman sees dialogue as inevitable, flowing from the fact that the "constitution is spacious and admits of diverse interpretations."[87] In his descriptive account of dialogue, courts play two roles: that of speaker and that of shaper or facilitator of constitutional debate.[88] He suggests that dialogue is a fitting portrayal of judicial involvement which is more interdependent and interactive than generally portrayed.[89]

The Canadian version of dialogue differs somewhat from the American concept owing largely to the structural differences between the two nations' bills of rights. The Charter's general-limitation clause in section 1 has encouraged judges to place more emphasis on evaluating the reasonableness of the means chosen to pursue a legislative objective rather than on the merits of the objective itself.[90] Thus, the combination of the Charter's structure and the judiciary's approach to judicial review (in which the courts rarely prevent Parliament from pursuing a specific legislative objective) focuses a considerable part of the parliamentary/judicial exchange on how to pursue legislative objectives in a manner that is consistent with the courts' "reasonableness" concerns and interpretation of proportionality rules. Another significant structural difference stems from the Charter's opportunity for explicit disapproval of judicial decisions, in the form of the legislative override in section 33.

Claims that constitutional interpretations of rights should be viewed in dialogic terms have generated criticism on both sides of the border. Charter sceptics believe that only representative forums are appropriate venues for deciding what priority should be attached to conflicting social values. This is as much an argument against a bill of rights as it is against a dialogic interpretation. Some argue that the "undue" emphasis on rights distorts the way issues are debated and restricts the voices that are given regard. As a result, it makes little sense to view judicial decisions or legal arguments as making a valuable contribution to meaningful dialogue. As Allan Hutchinson argues:

The truncated dialogue of adjudication ... is a caricature of democratic dialogue in which the dumb spend too much time knocking on the door of the deaf. Ordinary people do not take part in constitutional litigation and, therefore, never have the democratic opportunity to speak for themselves. It is almost perverse to liken judicial review to a dialogue or debate between citizens and the state about the reasonableness of government action. If there is any debate, it is between different branches of government: citizens' complaints only provide an occasion for a discussion in which those citizens can only listen hopefully and can only speak episodically in the high-priced words of an arcane legal vocabulary.[91]

Other critics of the concept of dialogue, particularly as it is portrayed by Hogg and Bushell, consider this exchange more in terms of a monologue (judicial rather parliamentary). As Morton suggests, "obeying [judicial] orders is not exactly what most of us consider a dialogue."[92] Morton argues that this model of dialogue is not persuasive. In Canada, the legislative override is simultaneously portrayed as an essential element of dialogue and as a constitutional power that will likely, and many think should, be dormant. This leads Morton to question whether those who champion Charter dialogue would still be as enthusiastic if the override were used more often. From his perspective, Parliament should engage in dialogue by actively using the override whenever it disagrees with a judicial ruling.[93]

Manfredi and James Kelly also wade into the debate. They criticize the decision of Hogg and Bushell to characterize legislative amendments, made after earlier legislation was set aside by the judiciary, as examples of dialogue. Manfredi and Kelly argue that the characterization is misleading because courts play an important role in framing the options available for legislative responses.[94] Manfredi dislikes the dialogue metaphor, at least as used by Hogg and Bushell, because it uncritically equates judicial interpretation of the Charter with the Charter itself. In doing so, the dialogue metaphor denies Parliament credit for having a role in giving meaning to Charter values that are independent of judicial views.[95]

Scepticism also exists regarding the dialogue metaphor's characterization of judicial review in the United States. Mary Ann Glendon rejects the premise that a meaningful dialogue occurs around rights principles. Instead, she depicts the discourse as impoverished because of the absolute and often trivial claims that are made in the name of rights entitlement.[96] A different criticism of a dialogic explanation of judicial review indicts proponents of an active judiciary. The dialogic metaphor enhances and justifies claims for judicial power to articulate norms that constrain legislative decision making, even when these do not arise from the obvious or logical requirements of the constitution. The charge of promoting judicial activism via constitutional dialogue arises from the claim of some dialogue proponents that constitutional interpretation should not be bound to the literal meaning of the text but may require intellectual embellishment to apply these abstract values to pressing social concerns. The judiciary's job is to give meaning to public values.[97] Critics of the characterization of judicial dialogue argue that reliance on this metaphor is little more than a trendy concept used to conceal the sanctioning of judicial activism. As Earl Malz suggests:

The effect of constitutionally-based judicial activism ... give[s] judges an enormous advantage over other participants in the debate. It is this added advantage that dialogue theorists must justify.

The establishment of such a judicial advantage can only be justified if two conditions are satisfied. First, the judges must bring a *unique* perspective to the debate over fundamental issues of public policy. Second, there must be some reason to believe that that perspective is somehow superior to that of other governmental decisionmakers, and thus leads to an improvement in the overall decisionmaking process. An examination of representative case law demonstrates that neither of those conditions exists in the real world.[98]

Others suggest that the appeal to dialogue does not constitute a method or approach for theorizing about the law. Consequently, it does not capture the hard question, which is not whether people should talk but rather "what they should say and what (among the various ideas communicated) they should believe."[99]

In earlier work, I suggested that it may be useful to view the Charter as promoting ongoing conversations between Parliament and courts.[100] I preferred to think in terms of conversations rather than dialogue because the former suggests more fluidity and implies less structure and formality. My emphasis on conversation presumed that Parliament was not restricted to simply reacting to judicial outcomes but rather contributed to constitutional interpretations. Thus, I envisaged conversations as occurring in both directions. Parliament could express its perspective on how to interpret the Charter when evaluating legislative initiatives and their implications for protected rights. This could be communicated through records of parliamentary deliberations and also through the selective use of legislative preambles that set out Parliament's assumptions. These, and other relevant considerations, would be conveyed to courts if legislation was subsequently challenged under the Charter. When the judiciary reviewed the legislation, the reasons in judgments would provide Parliament a context for helping it determine how to respond to negative rulings.

Continued reflection about the intersection of judicial and political Charter judgments, however, has dampened my enthusiasm for conceiving of Charter interpretations in dialogic terms. A serious reservation I have with use of dialogue or a dialogic-like metaphor is its association, by others, with a more judicial-centric approach to constitutional interpretations than I am prepared to concede as necessary or desirable. Furthermore, dialogue connotes discussion, as if the partners were speaking directly to each other. But the message from courts is filtered through the interpretations of legal analysts and these judgments may influence the message that is received. Similarly, the message of Parliament is conveyed, in part, through the legal arguments of government lawyers. Judges, however, may dismiss or discount this message if they are not persuaded by the way that government lawyers have argued the case.[101] Indirect exchanges will occur. These may take the form of a legislative preamble to communicate legislative intent, the arguments of government lawyers to explain why the legislation should be interpreted as consistent with constitutional rights, or the reasons in a legal judgment that nullifies legislation. But the emphasis on expressing the reasons for a particular constitutional interpretation should not be mistaken with how each set of actors reaches judgments, even when these judgments are influenced, to some degree, by anticipation of the reaction and judgment of others involved in the interpretive exercise.

Another difficulty with the dialogue metaphor, especially in its portrayal of the parliamentary/judicial relationship in Canada, stems from its largely procedural focus – the opportunity for legislative response to judicial outcomes – which does not distinguish between different stages of judicial review. In particular, it does not differentiate between the rights-oriented dimension of defining normative values in the Charter and the more policy-laden task of assessing the reasonableness of complex policy objectives. In the former dimension, the authoritative force of a court's decision exists by virtue of the fact that the issue of whether a fundamental right has been restricted relates to the *raison d'être* for judicial involvement. Arguably, this contrasts with the less authoritative force of the policy-inquiry dimension of review when the court assesses the merits of how complex legislative objectives are translated into legislation. This latter inquiry into the reasonableness of legislation entails tasks and skills that bear more resemblance to policy analysis than they do to the skills or methodology for which judges can reasonably claim to have expertise (this will be discussed more fully in the next chapter). Furthermore, it is important to recognize that legal review and political evaluation of legislative goals do not necessarily share the same focal point or sense of priority as to the relevant issues that should guide policy choices. Legal consideration for rationality and proportionality are distinctly different queries from legislative interest in accommodation and mediation and concern for effectiveness, comprehensiveness, and practicality. As a result, the different focal points of making accepted and effective policy, on the one hand, and external assessments of its fit with proportionality criteria, on the other, may themselves enhance the appearance and extent of the conflict.

Rather than view this shared constitutional responsibility in terms of dialogue, I suggest that it instead be considered in relational terms. Parliament and the judiciary each have a distinct relationship to a Charter conflict. Not only are they situated differently relative to such a conflict but they reach their judgments about how rights should structure policy conflicts based on the distinct institutional characteristics they possess and the responsibilities that characterize their roles. Another aspect of the relational approach emphasizes the relationship under the Charter between Parliament and the judiciary, arising from the need to reflect upon and react to the other's judgment. Judgments are influenced by the foreseeable knowledge that they may not be the final word on the reconciliation of rights and values. A relational approach conveys the separate yet interconnected approaches taken to render judgment. Unlike many explanations of constitutional dialogue, it contemplates the Charter's significance more in terms of requiring careful scrutiny by each institution of governance than in terms of the judiciary policing or correcting the "wrong" decisions of the legislature. In this sense, the approach has much in common with Slattery's theory of coordinate responsibility. I will develop this approach in the following chapter and discuss its implications for institutional assumptions and practices.

3 A Relational Approach to Charter Judgments

A relational approach assumes that both Parliament and courts have valid insights into how legislative objectives should reflect and respect the Charter's normative values. Yet their judgments may be different. The benefits of conceiving Charter judgment in relational terms arise from the responsibility each body incurs to respect Charter values, from the exposure to judgments made by those differently situated, and from the opportunity to reflect upon the merits of contrary opinion. The normative goal is not that Parliament aspire to ensure that legislation addresses all judicial concerns or, alternatively, that the judiciary defer to Parliament's judgment. Rather, it is that each body satisfy itself that its judgment respects Charter values, particularly when faced with the other's contrary judgment. Thus, a relational approach is informed by the assumption that parliamentary and judicial judgments be guided by a degree of modesty about the superiority of their conclusions and by respect for the other's contrary interpretation. Respect is measured by a sincere effort to understand the reasons and motivations that led to a contrary assessment, even if each ultimately disagrees with the other.

In this chapter, I begin by discussing the different responsibilities of courts and Parliament and how these bodies influence Charter judgments. I then turn to the question of political responsibility in the face of contrary judicial judgment, and I conclude the chapter with suggested changes to institutional practices and assumptions that flow from viewing Charter interpretations in relational terms.

DIFFERENT VANTAGE POINTS
— DIFFERENT RESPONSIBILITIES

Although Parliament and the judiciary share responsibility for making judgments about the Charter, political and judicial officials approach Charter issues differently. The governing party defines a policy agenda to implement legislation aimed at promoting a public interest. In this process, the consideration of rights may be part of, but not necessarily the singular or discrete focus of, legislative judgment. How Charter values may be affected is incorporated into a larger policy inquiry that defines and evaluates the merits of proposals to address social concerns, anticipates factors that might undermine the attainment of objectives, and identifies alternative ways to pursue objectives to minimize Charter conflicts.

The judiciary has a different relationship to the Charter. It enters the policy dispute later and its role comes singularly at the behest of citizens or others with standing[1] who claim a violation of Charter rights. The judiciary passes judgment about whether legislation adequately complies with Charter values only after the legislation has been passed and subject to constitutional challenge.[2] The court's task is not to decide how best to reconcile conflicting values but instead to assess the constitutional validity of the specific legislation or state action that is subject to Charter challenge. Interpreting or defining rights lies at the core of judges' review function and is a conscious and deliberate part of judgment. One need not accept the claim that the judiciary is uniquely equipped to interpret rights to recognize the significance of the judiciary's relative insulation from public and political pressures. Distanced from the immediate pressures arising from political protests, internal party conflicts, and the desire to retain or attain power in elections, judges have more independence when determining how Charter principles should direct particular conflicts. The more dispassionate focus that is afforded by the judiciary's distance from the immediate conflict may provide judges with more liberty to identify legislative decisions that impose unwarranted or undue restrictions on fundamental rights.

This judicial emphasis on the rights dimension of a social-policy conflict has influenced claims for a judicial-centric approach in resolving Charter conflicts. For example, Lorraine Weinrib, in a startling claim, argues that Canada's transformation into a constitutional state has replaced a "defective form of governance." It has done so by depriving legislatures of their "general supremacy over the essential features of liberal democracy."[3] But the implication of this characterization, that political judgment is defective when contrasted with the judiciary's responsibility and capacity to "develop and apply constitutional norms,"[4] is both too cynical and too narrow. It is too cynical because it denies any moral value to Parliament's role in reconciling Charter conflicts, and is too narrow because it confines the meaning of constitutional values exclusively to what evolves from legal rulings.

The proposition that only judges are capable of making conscious and principled decisions where rights are affected underestimates the extent to which Charter evaluation has become an intrinsic part of the policy process. As discussed in Chapter 1, the federal government has institutionalized a process where government lawyers in the Department of Justice evaluate government bills for their consistency with Charter values. Most provincial governments have also adopted procedures by which government lawyers identify the possible Charter implications for bills and work with departments and ministers to reduce the likelihood that legislation may be ruled inconsistent with the Charter.

Parliament may not place the same emphasis on rights, particularly as articulated by judges or legal scholars. But this does not mean that legislative decisions that may give rise to a rights-based challenge are inherently unjustified. Not all legislation pursues majoritarian or utilitarian objectives at the cost of rights. For example, consider the parliamentary response to Supreme Court judgments dealing with the rules that govern sexual assault trials, which is discussed in Chapter 5. In contrast to the judiciary's exclusive focus on the right of the accused to a fair trial, Parliament's approach asserted that a fair trial must co-exist with respect for the equality and privacy of victims, who disproportionately are women. Parliament's disagreement arose not from a lack of respect for rights but from its different judgment about the priority that should be accorded to the conflicting rights and values at issue. Although Parliament's interpretation was controversial, in part because many contest the assumption that it has a legitimate role in reconciling rights conflicts, a judicial-centric approach to Charter judgment is not the only way to view constitutional responsibility.

While the Charter has required that greater attention be paid to rights in the development of policy, it is a serious mistake to expect that this increased focus does or should imitate judicial assessments. Parliament assumes an important responsibility to interpret rights principles and to resolve rights conflicts, arising from an essential task of democratic governance – making political judgment about how to mediate among disparate opinions, assumptions, and expectations. With the introduction of the Charter, legislative decisions also should take into account whether they are consistent with its normative values.

Unfortunately, too often commentators equate this aspect of political responsibility – to respect Charter values – in terms of "Charter

proofing" legislation. By this they mean that all potential judicial Charter concerns with legislation should be anticipated and redressed. But
if this is the case, Parliament is not really contributing to judgment
about the reasonable reconciliation of Charter conflicts. Rather, the
decision is being made by the government's legal advisers, based on
their discretionary assessment of judicial concerns. In contrast, the argument in a relational understanding of the Charter is that Parliament's constitutional judgment may have a different focus than legal
opinion, reflecting its distinct responsibilities and different vantage
point, relative to Charter issues. Parliamentary judgment requires careful consideration of how to pursue legislative objectives in ways that are
consistent with the Charter's normative values. Reflection on judicial
concerns, and the reasons for contrary judgment, are important considerations. Yet these should not be the entire focus of, or a substitute
for, Parliament's reasoned judgment. The idea of Charter-proofing
legislation against a judicially defined standard does not give sufficient
consideration to the different perspective that Parliament might bring
to constitutional judgment. Parliament's judgment about how to reconcile conflicting values may be different from expectations of what
the courts might say. Yet it may also be reasonable.

The Charter's introduction is recent enough that often the interpretation of rights, and their relevance for legislative policies, have
not been addressed. If Parliament fails to make a careful judgment,
and instead chooses to rely entirely on expectations of what the courts
might say, it may forego important legislative objectives or adopt legislative measures that are less ambitious or comprehensive than required, because of inaccurate assumptions that courts would find
these faulty.[5] Despite the best attempts of legal advisers, it is difficult
to anticipate how the judiciary will rule on a particular legislative challenge. Much depends on the quality of the argument a government
makes and the strength of the record it is able to compile to demonstrate the reasonableness of Parliament's judgment. Thus, confining
legislative objectives to those for which legal advisers can confidently
predict legal "success" may lead to risk-aversion that distorts policy
objectives and undermines Parliament's ability to pursue legislative
objectives effectively.

REFLECTING ON DIFFERENT JUDGMENTS

Shared responsibility for interpreting the Charter does not presume
consensus. Where Parliament is particularly committed to legislation
that has been ruled unconstitutional, these decisions will often be appealed to the Supreme Court. Parliament and the Supreme Court may

have fundamental differences about how conflicting rights and values should be resolved. The higher status associated with the language of rights (as opposed to interests or wants that are assumed to be the daily stuff of political compromises) and the tendency to associate rights disputes with legal rather than political resolutions may undermine political willingness to disagree with a judicial Charter decision. Yet not all rights claims are equally damning indictments of state actions.

The prestige and status of the language of rights obscure the fact that not all activities that are claimed to be a right necessarily warrant strict political or judicial vigilance. Freedom of expression is a good example of how a fundamental right can generate a broad range of claims, not all of which represent the kind of activity that deserves careful protection from state interference. Few would agree that expressions of opinion on matters of public policy should be constrained simply because those on the receiving end are sensitive to criticism. But it is not so obvious that the same degree of vigilance is appropriate for protecting other expressive activities, such as solicitation for prostitution purposes in residential neighbourhoods, hate speech that incites violence, or advertisement of tobacco products. We would all like to have our choices and desires respected in the social-policy decisions of government. But to say that our preferences constitute rights is not a persuasive way of conceiving of rights. A claim to a right flows not from our preferences for particular social outcomes but from our legitimate expectations that we will not incur artificial or discretionary barriers preventing us from participating in debates about public values and social policies or receiving equal effects of the law.

Opposition to a judicial-centre approach in resolving Charter conflicts does not mean that Parliament should not heed judicial concerns simply because it wishes to pursue legislation that has been struck down as a violation of the Charter. Where disagreements arise, Parliament should reflect upon the concerns that led the judiciary to invalidate legislation. The more serious the rights infringement, the more cautious Parliament should be before pursuing a course of action that is inconsistent with the spirit of the judicial ruling. The legal rulings that should raise the loudest alarm bells for Parliament and citizens are those in which the Supreme Court has concluded that legislative activity is inconsistent with core Charter rights.

My use of the term "core rights" refers to the most fundamental reasons why a polity believes that it is necessary to protect certain forms of human conduct from undue interference or from arbitrary coercion by the state. This is a philosophical exercise about the broad purposes of a right, rather than an inquiry into the actual intents of the framers.

The importance of linking claims of rights to the broad purposes of a bill of rights is to help sort core from less fundamental-rights claims, for the purpose of evaluating whether legislative restrictions on these are justified.

I think of core rights as constituting a broad range of requirements necessary for the people to govern themselves in a representative system of government, so that the exercise of power is based on consent rather than on coercion. For this reason, core rights should be extremely difficult for Parliament to restrict. Free political expression is a core right because it allows for the scrutiny of the ideas and the actions of those wielding or seeking to exercise power. Free association is similarly classified in this way because it enables similarly minded individuals to organize and coordinate their social and political actions when responding to political decisions. Religious freedom, the ability to challenge societal views on morality, and the ability to create and express opinions on art and literature are all examples of core rights because they allow members of society to contribute to public debate about values and political objectives that influence social policies. These rights, along with the requirement of regular elections, the ability to be a candidate for political office, and the ability to vote, enable political challenges to and replacement of political leaders through regularly held elections.

Core rights also include the conditions necessary to ensure the just treatment of individuals in their encounters with the coercive powers of the state, such as due process and freedom from arbitrary arrest and detention. Equality is certainly a core right. The full measure of equality is a philosophically charged subject, for which no singularly accepted definition will emerge. Without entering into a debate about the full requirements of equality, whether, for example, it should be measured in terms of substantive sharing of resources or more narrowly confined to equal treatment before the law, even a fairly narrow view of equality prohibits the use of legal rules that operate in an arbitrary and non-generalist manner. The importance of equal treatment under the law arises from the requirement in a democracy that power not be fixed in any one body or group or sustained by threats, coercion, arbitrary rules, or discrimination. All individuals in a polity have a legitimate expectation of the opportunity to contribute to and participate in decisions that affect their political and personal lives. No individual can be considered to have this, or to enjoy liberalism's promise of being able to pursue his or her own substantive goals, if discriminated against on the basis of personal characteristics or denied the dignity all are owed as human beings in their interactions with those who exercise power on behalf of the state. Equality in the Charter envisages more than equal treatment before and under the law. It also encompasses the right to the equal protection and equal benefit of the law without discrimination based on social and political judgments that accord lesser value to some identities or personal characteristics.

Disagreements will arise about what constitutes a core right and how to evaluate the merits of state actions that conflict with these. Does the state have a valid role to address power or disparities in resources that may distort or restrict the meaningful opportunity for some members of the polity to exercise their rights? Free political expression is a core right. Yet during elections the costs of advertising means that wealthier individuals and groups have greater opportunity to influence public debate. Their purchase of advertising can help shape the electoral agenda by giving more prominence to some issues or particular perspectives in a public debate. Can restrictions on political advertising be justified if their purpose is to promote greater equity in opportunities to exercise democratic rights of participation?

The attempt to distinguish between more and less important rights claims when evaluating state actions is certainly contentious. Since serious disagreements arise when assessing the relative importance of different claims to a right, some may question the merits of making these distinctions. My purpose in distinguishing between core and peripheral rights claims is not to provide a finite list that discourages discussion about whether a particular claim to a right deserves robust protection. Rather, it is to encourage those making rights claims, and, more important, those who must assess them and determine the validity of impugned state actions, to give serious thought to the importance of the rights claim and the implications of state-imposed restrictions for the functioning of the democratic polity and the obligation to treat all members of the polity with dignity and respect.

I anticipate the following questions, especially from those who accept a judicial-centric approach in resolving Charter conflicts: "Don't all judicial decisions that rights have been violated equally represent statements that fundamental constitutional norms have been violated?" And, "Shouldn't the fact that the judiciary has declared that legislation violates the Charter be taken as the final resolution of the Charter conflict?"

Two responses are appropriate. Even when a court rules a Charter right has been infringed, reasonable differences may exist about how the Charter conflict should be resolved. One can have a commitment to respecting fundamental rights, reject relativist thinking, and still be sceptical that rights claims must inevitably prevent Parliament from pursuing a legislative objective that has some implications for protected rights. The broad manner in which the judiciary has interpreted some rights in the Charter precludes the automatic conclusion that the mere recognition of a Charter conflict necessarily determines the constitutional legitimacy of legislation. Charter protection may be extended to claims that are marginal or peripheral to the philosophical purposes of a bill of rights. As a result, these rights claims may not reflect the kind of moral or normative claim against the state that warrants strict scrutiny.

Moreover, reasonable disagreements may arise when the judiciary reinterprets a common law rule in light of Charter values. The absence of legislation, hence reliance on the common law rule, means that Parliament has not made clear its assessment of the relative balance struck between Charter principles and law enforcement or other public concerns. Consequently, when the judiciary revises a common law rule, it is not aware of Parliament's perspective. Subsequent legislative judgment might differ from the judiciary's newly formulated rule. The mere fact of this difference does not automatically render Parliament's judgment invalid.[6]

The second response is that the authoritative force of a judicial ruling may vary depending on the nature of its disagreement with legislation. For example, does the problem stem from the fact that the court considers the legislative objective inconsistent with fundamental rights? Or is the problem instead that the legislative means chosen to pursue the legislative objective are deemed unreasonable? Arguably, the authoritative force of the court's ruling may be less in the latter context, with its focus on the reasonableness of the legislative means.

Although assessments of reasonableness are part of the judiciary's responsibility in developing the common law and are an important part of administrative-law considerations, the courts' emphasis on proportionality in review of the Charter is worrisome. No matter what objective veneer is placed on criteria such as rationality and minimal impairment, these judicially determined proportionality criteria engage judges in a close analysis of the minute details of legislation that may involve discretionary judgment about the utility or prudence of other legislative possibilities. These assessments present particular challenges for the judiciary because they presume an evaluation of the merits of impugned legislation in terms of how the policy was conceptualized and drafted and of the utility and effects of alternative and often hypothetical scenarios.[7] Yet policy development is necessarily subject to discretionary judgments based on relevant expertise, comparative experience, and informed best estimates. It is often difficult to predict how ambitious legislative objectives might be achieved or to demonstrate empirically whether and how the harm that legislation is directed towards will be redressed. The discretionary nature of policy development reveals the artificial quality of evaluating whether the means chosen were rational or significantly more restrictive than some other hypothetical possibility. Even to claim that precise policy means exist to pursue identified objectives suggests false confidence that society possesses the requisite and appropriate methodology to predict how to remedy problems or to anticipate all mitigating circumstances that may compromise the realization of a legislative objective. Furthermore, the government but not the judiciary can rely on extensive resources when developing policy.

The evaluation of policy choices is not an exercise for which judges can claim to have particular expertise or unique insights. Judges' knowledge of social problems will be of a generalist form, which may make it difficult for them to undertake independent assessments of social science and behavioural research that have been relevant to the legislative decision being reviewed. This suggests the possibility that Robert Presthus raises, of judges filling in the gaps with their own "generalized normative axioms."[8] Alternatively, judges may be dependent upon the assessment of this data by others who have an ideological commitment to a particular interpretation: "It has always proved difficult to integrate specialists into the adjudicative process. Specialized information is usually provided to judges through the medium of expert witnesses and consultants or through popularized written versions of the information ... The expert witnesses are paid by the respective parties, and they are almost invariably partisan. The popularizations share the usual defects of the genre. They simplify, and sometimes they mislead."[9]

An example of the difficulty judges incur when evaluating specialized knowledge arose when the Supreme Court reformulated a common law rule to allow extreme intoxication to be used as a defence to crimes of sexual assault, discussed in Chapter 5. In the legislative response that followed, scientists who appeared before Parliament indicated that the legal assumption that underpinned the court's reason for making a significant change to a common law rule was erroneous: the court misunderstood the relationship between intoxication and automatism.

This idea that not all rights claims are equal, and that these differences are relevant to judging the merits of state actions, finds support in the work of others. In the early days following the adoption of the Charter, Peter Russell and others warned about the problems a polity will incur if citizens and politicians fail to accept that difficult decisions will have to be made about the appropriate scope of rights. Russell argues that the simplistic language used in the debate about whether or not to adopt the Charter, which implied that the idea of protecting rights was no more complex than writing them down in a constitutional bill of rights, had the effect of reifying rights. Rights were portrayed as if they were possessions that people held in their entirety or not at all. But as Russell says, this zero-sum approach to rights disguises the important questions that arise when trying to evaluate the merits of state actions that may conflict with claims to a right. He refers to universal rights and freedoms as the core values or ideals common to all contemporary liberal democracies, such as political freedom, religious toleration, due process of law, and social equality. These, he argues, will not likely encounter serious risk from government because in Canada there is no serious disagreement about their importance. But controversies will inevitably arise when determining the appropriate limits on other less fundamental values.[10]

The distinction between core and more peripheral rights is also implied in the work of Charles Taylor. Taylor, who does not specifically use the term "core right," nevertheless discusses the importance of distinguishing between fundamental rights and those rights claims of lesser importance, which he refers to as privileges and immunities. The context for this distinction is a discussion of the variants of liberalism in Canada: a procedural-oriented model outside Quebec as contrasted with a more collectivist-orientated model in Quebec.[11] What most distinguishes these variants of liberalism is how they conceive of the role of the state. The procedural model is premised on the assumption that, if the state promotes substantive goals, it may impair the ability of those who disagree with these outcomes to pursue their own notion of the good or to be treated with equal respect. Quebec, with more collective goals defining the state's policy agenda, violates this procedural model. Yet for Taylor, the more collectivist model need not conflict with liberalism. A society can be organized around a definition of a substantive goal or the good life without adversely effecting those who do not share this definition. But if this is so, it must be extremely diligent in protecting its minorities and, in particular, those who do not share the public definition of the good. This requires respect for fundamental rights. These rights, which are the same ones "that have been recognized [as fundamental] from the very beginning of the liberal tradition," must, at the same time, be distinguished from less fundamental claims (or privileges and immunities).

There is something exaggerated, a dangerous overlooking of an essential boundary, in speaking of fundamental rights to such things as commercial signage in the language of one's choice. One has to distinguish between, on the one hand, the fundamental liberties – those which should never at any time be infringed and which therefore ought to be unassailably entrenched – and, on the other hand, the privileges and immunities which are important but can be revoked or restricted for reasons of public policy (although one needs a strong reason to do so).

A society with strong collective goals can be liberal, on this view, provided it is also capable of respecting diversity, especially when this concerns those who do not share its goals, and provided it can offer adequate safeguards for fundamental rights.[12]

Use of the Legislative Override

Although legislation can often be revised to address judicial concerns without compromising the legislative objective, on rare occasions this may not be the case. Judges may flatly disagree with Parliament's contention that its objective is important enough to restrict rights or they may fault the legislation for how it was conceptualized and designed. Parliament may decide that satisfying the judiciary's assessment of reasonableness would seriously compromise an important legislative objective, and that this legislation is justified, despite the judiciary's concerns.

The Charter provides a mechanism for resolving such serious disagreements – the legislative override of section 33. This political power, however, is extremely contested and remains controversial for the very reasons that divide many critics and supporters of the Charter. The override should not be thought of in mutually exclusive terms: either it is intrinsically antithetical to the purposes of the Charter or, alternatively, it represents a non-problematic way to give effect to majority will. Neither approach gives sufficient attention to the possibility that the override could be used for both appropriate and inappropriate reasons. Critics of the override are correct in fearing that it could undermine a central purpose of a bill of rights: to protect minority rights from contrary political judgments. The majoritarian qualities of the override exist both in terms of the initial decision itself (because a simple majority in Parliament is all that is required to support its use) and in terms of any subsequent decision to renew it (because temporal restrictions will ensure that an election has occurred, affording voters an opportunity to express their views on the issue).

Yet the very reasons for doubting whether a single, correct answer exists to rights conflicts, or whether Charter conflicts should be resolved only by judges, are also reasons for rejecting the view that the override is inherently in tension with right-based decisions. This is not to suggest, in any way, that legislative choices to use the override will necessarily advance rights-based principles. But they may. For example, if Parliament failed to convince the Supreme Court to give more appreciation to equality and privacy when interpreting the rules for sexual assault trials, use of the override to sustain Parliament's judgment could be viewed as consistent with, rather than contrary to, Charter values.[13]

At some point in the political evolution of the Charter, it will be worthwhile to encourage a more reasoned public and political understanding of the override. What needs to be addressed with respect to the override is the appropriate normative assessment that should guide its use and the procedures that are most likely to facilitate this assessment. A relational approach to the Charter, which conveys the importance of reflecting upon the reasons and concerns for contrary judgments, provides a framework for thinking about these criteria.

Parliament may not always agree with how the Supreme Court has reconciled conflicting rights and values. However, the override should not be viewed as a mechanism of raw power for reinstating Parliament's judgment. Before considering use of the override, Parliament should give serious consideration to whether it can revise legislation in a manner that satisfies judicial concerns, without seriously compromising the integrity or effectiveness of the legislative objective. If it has failed to convince the court that its judgment is justified, Parliament should revisit the merits of its judgment: specifically, is the right in question too fundamental to be overridden, and is the objective important enough that it justifies being given primacy in the Charter conflict?

The judiciary's judgment is not influenced by a desire to maintain popularity or secure a political future by satisfying public opinion. For this reason, serious reflection upon the Supreme Court's reasons for ruling legislation inconsistent with fundamental rights should precede any contemplation of the override. The argument against a judicial-centric approach should not be construed as arguing for moral relativism – as if any political decision can be justified on the basis of popularity or that fundamental human rights can be forsaken for reasons of expediency, custom, or popularity. Wrong or unjust answers to political conflicts certainly exist. For example, I consider discrimination against lesbians and gay men in social benefits and legal status as fundamentally wrong. I have difficulty accepting that the override is normatively justified to restrict a core right, such as the fair treatment and dignity of all human beings. As a general rule, a polity should be extremely critical of political decisions that are motivated or inspired by intolerance and prejudice.

What follows from this discussion is that the override should not be used pre-emptively, or before a ruling from the highest court, because this would deny the polity the benefit of a relational approach to judgment. It would omit the Supreme Court's contribution to constitutional deliberation.

If government decides that use of the override should be considered, its proposed use should compel higher and different criteria than those associated with majority approval in Parliament or a provincial legislature. The ensuing discussion should confront the implications of denying the right, rather than the popularity of the measure. Consideration of the override should be the occasion for political or parliamentary hearings with opportunities for public involvement, which will add different perspectives to the debate. The process should allow for a free vote, independent of partisan constraints, sustained by a larger than normal parliamentary majority. The purpose of this higher threshold is to focus deliberation on the consequences of using the override. It is not simply to find consensus for the decision or respond to public opinion.

Political uncertainty about the merits or validity of the override has resulted in little political deliberation about its uses. The exception is when the Alberta government, in 1999, proposed legislation (which later died on the order paper) that would have established a procedure for using the override. Bill 38, the Constitutional Referendum Amendment Act, would have required the government to submit its intent to use the override to a referendum. Had a majority of the voters approved this, the government would then have been required to introduce legislation containing the override. If a majority rejected the proposal, the government would not introduce the legislation.

This idea of basing a decision on whether to use the override on prior approval in a referendum raises a number of concerns.[14] Minorities are particularly vulnerable to this kind of process because the passions and level of debate that arise from the yes/no option may not provide the kind of environment conducive for thoughtful and principled engagement about rights and governmental responsibilities. Another concern with subjecting the use of the override to a referendum is that it removes an important source of pressure that government should incur when proposing the override. Those who wish to restrict rights should bear the onus for demonstrating why the action is justified. But the focus of the attention is removed, or at least redirected, when the decision is based largely on the will of the people. Although the Alberta referendum process would not have required the legislature to pass the legislation containing an intent to use the override, even if a majority of voters had earlier approved its use, it would have been extremely unlikely that a government would vote against this option in the legislature particularly since it initiated the process in the first place.

CHANGES THAT ARISE FROM VIEWING THE CHARTER IN RELATIONAL TERMS

A number of suggested changes to institutional assumptions flow from viewing the Charter in relational terms. The basic premises of a relational view are that responsibility for constitutional judgment is shared, Parliament and courts should satisfy themselves that their decisions respect Charter values, and each should respect the role and different perspectives that the other brings to its judgment.

Considerations for Political Judgment

My argument against a judicial-centric approach does not lessen citizens' valid expectation that legislative decisions reflect principled judgments about whether they are justified in light of the constitution's normative values. The federal government's internal process of scrutinizing proposed governmental bills for Charter consistency is an important element in responsible political judgment. But those who defend legislation in Charter litigation are not the same officials who evaluate bills or develop policy. Thus, it is essential that government lawyers who defend legislation not only have a solid understanding of the policy purposes and objectives of legislation but be familiar with the concerns that animated the choice of legislative means. This is particularly important in light of the emphasis in judicial review on the proportionality element of section 1. In the development of a record of the considerations that influenced policy concerns, relevant studies, comparative experiences, and previous legislative initiatives will help provide a foundation to support a government's argument that its legislation is important and justified.

But this may not be enough. No matter how impressive the record a government compiles, an important element that may be missing is whether Parliament itself made a sincere effort to ensure that legislative choices respect Charter values. It may be more difficult for a government to make a persuasive claim that the judiciary should be influenced by Parliament's judgment about the reconciliation of a Charter conflict if there is little indication that Charter concerns were given significant consideration by Parliament.

The government should encourage and support more robust parliamentary scrutiny of bills where these have Charter implications. It can facilitate this by specifically alerting Parliament about the reasons a government wishes to proceed with a bill that incurs a *substantial* Charter risk, *even if the minister of justice believes that the bill has a credible chance of surviving litigation.* This is different from the current political interpretation of the statutory obligation, which is to advise Parliament only where no credible Charter argument can be made. As discussed earlier, not only has this not occurred, but the political and bureaucratic culture affecting the process of Charter-vetting almost guarantees there will not be a report. The purpose of this different interpretation is to focus parliamentary deliberation on the justification of a legislative action which the government anticipates will likely culminate in litigation under the Charter.

This report should be introduced during second-reading debate and form a central focus for each of the two parliamentary committees that regularly examine bills that may have constitutional implications. The report should be viewed as an opportunity for the government to explain publicly why the course of action is justified, despite obvious or perceived tensions it raises with Charter values. The report should emphasize the nature of the rights conflict but do so in a way that avoids overly technical or "lawyerly" debates about conflicting interpretations of judicial precedents. It should also provide information relevant to the debate about the merits and justification of the legislative objective. This might include information on the harm or social concern that the legislation seeks to address, the significance of the rights infringement, why obviously less restrictive measures are not being utilized, and the degree of anticipated Charter risk.

Moreover, the government should recognize the need of committees for appropriate time to study the bill and to hear from non-governmental witnesses with opinions about the constitutional status and merits of the proposed legislation. Although Justice officials will provide important insights with respect to the reasons for rejecting alternative legislative means, or for narrowing the scope of the legislative objective, these committees should have access to their own legal expert(s). Legal advisers representing Parliament, rather than the executive, may bring different perspectives on Charter considerations.

It is important to distinguish parliamentary scrutiny from the kind of Charter analysis that takes place within the executive. Clearly, a system of executive-based rights scrutiny is welcome. For public officials in departments and agencies and ministers who bear ultimate accountability, it provides necessary advice about specific legal difficulties that can be anticipated and enables ministers to revisit policy objectives, assess alternative means, and ultimately make more responsible political decisions about whether to recommend that legislation be introduced. The purpose of parliamentary Charter scrutiny is neither to establish a rival or parallel procedure for undertaking risk-assessments nor to use rights language in a partisan manner to delay or block government initiatives. The objective is for Parliament to be aware of the consequences of legislation for protected values, so that when assessing the constitutional merits of a bill, making recommendations, and, ultimately, voting, Parliament has sufficient knowledge to reach careful judgment about whether legislation is reasonable and justified.

Deliberation by Parliament provides opportunity for broader public and judicial reflection on the assumptions and concerns that animate legislative decisions. A fulsome record of debate, most likely to occur at committee stage, which discusses reasons and concerns that motivated a particular course of action, could be helpful in defending legislation from Charter challenges. Judges have never before had reason to consider, systematically, Parliament's intent where rights are implicated. While snippets of parliamentary records have on occasion been introduced by government lawyers when litigating Charter conflicts, the lack of regular parliamentary assessment of Charter issues, or public explanation by the government at the time of policy development, have made these records easy to downplay as mere anecdotal evidence.

As experience with the Charter evolves, and familiarity increases, the importance of constitutional rights in setting the normative standards for legislation should give Parliament a greater claim to a central role – and perhaps a more conscious purpose – in evaluating the justification of legislation in light of Charter values. Some may characterize any semblance of parliamentary scrutiny as being simply the result of a well-orchestrated effort by the government to give credibility to a governmental decision – a democratic form of window dressing for decisions that have already been made. This scepticism, however, does not duly consider the significance of parliamentary disagreement or the independent judgment of interest groups and individuals who appear before parliamentary committees. The public record of these opinions can make it difficult for the government to orchestrate Charter assessments. Moreover, failure of the government to address serious Charter concerns, whether raised by parliamentarians or by independent groups and commentators, is a risky enterprise if courts begin to take a closer look at the reasons for and background of legislative judgments.

Not everyone may accept that Parliament should aspire to make its legislative intent more clear with respect to Charter issues.[15] Robert Nagel would likely disagree that Parliament should be more conscious and expressive of how it views the relationship between legislative objectives and their effects on constitutional norms as articulated by courts. He argues that insistence that legislative processes be assessed from a jurisprudential perspective, in which one seeks a rational link between the objective and means or the empirical validation of harms needing redress, "belittles political dialogue and participation" whose processes "depend on trusting and honoring the reactions of the public to the experience of being governed."[16] Nagel is likely correct in fearing that preoccupation with judicial concerns may distort the ebb and flow of legislative debate. But this is not what is being suggested here. Rather, I am proposing that Parliament assess the implications of legislative choices for Charter norms and satisfy itself that these choices are consistent and justified. It is difficult to believe that the legislative process will be harmed by encouraging Parliament to address issues that are relevant to its determination of the justification of proposed bills, such as how serious the rights infringement is, whether the initiative represents a compelling objective, and whether it can be accomplished, practically and effectively, by using significantly less restrictive means. While these questions bear a resemblance to the Supreme Court's criteria first developed in *R. v. Oakes*[17] for evaluating the justification of legislative restrictions on rights, they are questions befitting any careful evaluation of social policy.

Others may wonder whether a focus on rights in political decision making might denigrate legislative decision making. Rainer Knopff worries about the tendency in Canadian political culture to see the Charter as the soul of the Canadian constitution – as if this statement of rights is the constitution's exclusive focus, rather than representative government, federalism, and, more generally, inherited principles of British constitutionalism.[18] His concern is enhanced by what he identifies as the inflationary nature of rights claiming. He worries that the Charter may erode the already sagging legitimacy of Parliament by undermining its ability to engage in deliberation and to seek moderation.[19]

Whether the Charter will undermine Parliament's legitimacy and credibility to make good legislative decisions is an empirical question, for which it is premature to offer conclusive answers. I question the assumption, however, that the inflated tenor of rights is such a problem that it renders Parliament incapable of working towards reasoned and careful judgment. Unless political rhetoric so paralyses Parliament that it cannot function properly (in which event the Charter is only a very small part of a much larger problem), rights rhetoric is not categorically different from other exaggerated political claims. For Knopff, the crux of the issue is not so much whether one institutional arrangement is more likely than another to produce exaggerated claims; rather, it is which set of institutional arrangements is best suited to counteract this tendency. Yet, even if a bill of rights encourages an inflationary use of rights, and the language of rights makes compromise more difficult, many will welcome the power of courts as an effective check on the executive, in light of the weakness of the House of Commons and provincial legislatures and the absence of a powerful or effective second house.

As for the concern about whether the emphasis on rights will undermine the power of debate to produce laws for the common good, I am not convinced. Parliament may have a different interpretation from courts on how to reconcile Charter conflicts. Rights claims can vary both in their importance and in their relevance to Charter values. Consequently, not all rights claims necessarily warrant strict vigilance in their protection, whether from Parliament or courts. Yet it is difficult to anticipate how the public interest or common good, however defined, can be pursued when core fundamental rights are suppressed.

Considerations for Judicial Judgment

The difficulty of assessing the reasonableness of complex legislative decisions is probably one of the most serious challenges of judicial review. Judicial deference to legislative decisions that restrict rights is not an obvious answer to the difficulty the judiciary incurs. The Supreme Court's analytical distinction between whether a right has been infringed and the reasonableness of the legislation responsible for the infringement has the possibility of minimizing its focus on the former while placing an undue emphasis on policy-laden assessments of the latter. If a court is not duly sensitive to whether legislation is justified, ruling that a right has been infringed becomes a hollow gesture if legislation is easily sustained under the reasonableness evaluation. Section 1 analysis does not, and was not intended to, replace a court's critical judgment of whether fundamental rights have been violated. Critics of earlier forms of a limitation clause were likely correct in their concern that undue judicial deference toward legislatures would undermine the significance of the Charter.[20] Furthermore, if legislation is easily or routinely upheld, public and political officials may not be duly attentive to the implications of policy choices for fundamental rights if they incur little risk that legislation will be invalidated.

Two considerations may help judges decide when, and under what circumstances, more or less consideration should be extended to Parliament's judgment about how to pursue complex social-policy objectives. One of these arises from an approach the Supreme Court has occasionally taken, although not in a consistent manner. I refer to the court's practice of distinguishing between more and less serious rights claims for the purpose of evaluating restrictions on these. In other words, the court should consider distinguishing core from more marginal rights claims when evaluating the justification of impugned legislation. The court has already rejected the idea that a hierarchy should exist among conflicting rights.[21] Yet, at the same time, it has been willing to distinguish between the core meaning of a right and more marginal aspects of the rights claim when evaluating the burden that the government should satisfy for justifying legislation that restricts the right in question.

When the Supreme Court reviewed free-speech claims involving obscenity and hate speech, a majority concluded that the claimed expressive activity was quite peripheral to the value of speech in a liberal polity that recognizes the equal dignity of all. Hence, where legislation promotes a compelling purpose and the nature of the particular rights claim is quite marginal, restrictions are easier to justify than in other circumstances. This indication seems to be judicial acknowledgment that not all rights claims that the court recognizes have, or should be viewed as having, the same normative persuasion or should compel the same degree of protection. It is as if the court is mindful of how its chosen approach to judicial review, particularly in the context of free-speech jurisprudence, restricts the persuasive force of concluding that a right has been infringed. The infringement itself is almost of a secondary order of importance to the broader question of whether the legislation is justified.

What is being suggested here is that the Supreme Court should more regularly evaluate the significance of rights claims when evaluating legislative restrictions. This contextual approach will be valuable in terms of conveying a stronger indication of the normative message that is associated with rulings or rights violations. For example, a judicial ruling that free speech in the context of tobacco advertising has been restricted simply does not carry the same moral or normative message as a ruling that legislation has restricted political speech. A risk that accompanies the court's failure to differentiate between more serious and less serious rights violations is that it may, over time, weaken the moral authority of judgments and their acceptance by political officials and the public.

A second consideration for judicial judgment is that, where the Supreme Court is unsure about whether or not to accept the inevitable governmental claim that the legislation is reasonable and impairs rights and freedoms no more than is necessary, the court may find it useful to examine the quality of the process that led to the political judgment. Just as the government should respect judicial concerns when the court rules that legislation violates a right, and reflect seriously upon the normative message that may be conveyed in a judicial ruling, judges should similarly have respect for political judgments about how best to pursue complex social-policy objectives.

This argument for respect is not that courts should accept whatever judgment Parliament reaches. The judiciary, however, should be sensitive to whether the government and Parliament have consciously reflected upon Charter values and undertaken sincere measures to reconcile conflicts in a principled and sensitive manner. Once the Supreme Court concludes that the legislative objective is important enough to justify restricting rights, where a careful attempt to reconcile conflicting values appears to have been made, judges may want to exercise caution before invalidating legislation where they do not believe that the legislation is fundamentally unjust or that the legislative means chosen are obviously excessive. This reason for caution arises from how the judiciary is situated, relative to this dimension of the Charter conflict. As argued above, assessments of reasonableness pose particular difficulties for the judiciary.

It is important to emphasize that the possible influence the legislative decision-making process may have on judicial judgment cuts both ways. If the parliamentary record is spotty on the justification for the legislative objective, this may help those who have impugned the validity of legislation. The absence of public deliberation on the relevant merits or consequences of legislation may reinforce arguments that Parliament gave insufficient consideration to the consequences of legislative decisions for Charter values. Perhaps if the Supreme Court were less prepared to accept that legislation is a reasonable limit on a protected right, in the absence of little more than the rhetorical assurances of government lawyers, this would provide necessary incentive for a government to encourage more parliamentary deliberation about the justification of legislation from a Charter perspective.[22]

CONCLUSIONS

Judgment on the justification of rights from a Charter perspective should be considered dynamic rather than static. It entails presenting reasons for judgment and reflecting upon and responding to the reasons for contrary judgment. More careful parliamentary deliberation may help the courts better understand the reasons and assumptions that influenced legislation. Judicial decisions, in turn, shed light on important perspectives that were overlooked by Parliament – such as unwarranted distinctions for who receives benefits or unintended consequences of legislation.

The contested nature of rights claims and legitimate differences about uses of state power to remedy social problems suggest why it is not helpful to think of a bill of rights in terms of a rigid "rights template," which assumes that legislative judgment that lies beyond its judicially defined parameters is inherently illegitimate. I like to think of the Charter as embodying the Canadian polity's code of conduct, or its philosophical ethos, which expresses the normative values that should influence decisions about the exercise of state power, the benefits and burdens to which citizens are subject, and the recognition of status and allocation of entitlements. But these ideals and values may give rise to different, but nevertheless reasonable, interpretations.

The idea that Parliament and the judiciary share responsibility for Charter judgment is clearly at odds with the view that courts alone have legitimacy for reconciling Charter conflicts. A relational view of Charter interpretation does not claim to produce the correct answer for resolving rights conflicts. The very idea that a correct answer or, failing that, an obviously superior one will emerge from judicial review is naive. A relational approach emphasizes the importance of exposure to the judgment of those who are differently situated, relative to the Charter conflict, as well as the importance of reflecting upon the merits of contrary opinions.

No matter how principled or eminent judges may be, it simply does not follow from the increased judicial role contemplated by the Charter that Parliament ceases to have a legitimate role to interpret how rights principles affect issues of social policy. This is not a role that will be insulated from judicial review. It is a role that, depending on how it is performed, may validly influence judicial judgments. A question that often comes up in the legitimacy debate is: "Are judges or elected representatives more likely to have better answers to rights conflicts?" My answer is: Why must a polity choose one set of institutional actors and excuse or exclude others? Better answers are likely to emerge when they are the products of carefully reasoned judgments about whether state actions are justified in light of a polity's fundamental normative values. A bill of rights offers the opportunity to justify restrictions on protected rights. But justification is not the same thing as having one set of institutional actors policing another, whether this takes the form of a judicial-centric approach or, alternatively, an uncritical use of the override.

4 Tobacco Advertising

Those who are sceptical about the benefits of a bill of rights can hardly find a better example of how judicial review can hinder and distort legislative objectives than the Supreme Court's 1995 ruling in *RJR-MacDonald Inc.*[1] The Supreme Court decision in this case overturned federal legislation that sought to discourage young Canadians from becoming smokers. What makes this particular case so useful for Charter critics is the combination of the court's decision to elevate tobacco advertising to the status of constitutionally protected expression, judges' willingness to suggest that their judgment is superior to Parliament's on how to pursue this complex legislative objective (even though marketing strategies and knowledge of addictive behaviour are far more relevant than legal expertise), and Parliament's meek and submissive response to the court's ruling. In short, this case demonstrates how judicial review of rights claims can undermine political will to exercise independent judgment about how best to pursue a course of action deemed to be in the public interest, even when the rights claim is far removed from the philosophical purposes of protecting rights from state actions.

The impugned legislation, the Tobacco Products Control Act, had been in effect since 1989 and had the ambitious objective of discouraging tobacco consumption, particularly among impressionable young people. Specifically, its purposes were:

- to protect the health of Canadians in light of evidence implicating tobacco use in the incidence of numerous debilitating and fatal diseases;

- to protect young persons and others from inducements to use tobacco products and consequent dependence on them; and
- to enhance public awareness of the hazards of tobacco use by ensuring the effective communication of pertinent information to consumers of tobacco products.

The legislation pursued these objectives by prohibiting the advertising and promotion of tobacco products offered for sale in Canada and by requiring that manufacturers of these products display a non-attributed message on their packages describing the health effects of tobacco and listing its toxic ingredients. The health warning on tobacco-product packages was to indicate that: cigarettes are addictive; tobacco smoke can harm children; cigarettes can cause fatal lung disease, strokes, and heart disease; smoking during pregnancy can harm a woman's fetus; smoking can kill smokers; and tobacco smoke causes fatal lung disease in non-smokers. The tobacco industry vigorously opposed the legislation when it was being debated, and, soon after the Tobacco Products Control Act came into effect, the industry sought to have the act declared unconstitutional on the grounds that it violated the Charter right to freedom of expression.[2]

THE MAJORITY JUDGMENT IN *RJR-MACDONALD INC.*

The Tobacco Products Control Act was written in a way that was intended to convey the message that Parliament had given consideration to the Charter and had been convinced that the legislation was constitutionally justified. The legislative purpose was defined as responding to a national public-health problem of substantial and pressing concern. This phrasing was chosen to suggest the reasonableness of the legislation, by restating the Supreme Court's own normative criterion for demonstrating that legislation is important enough to restrict the protected rights enumerated in the Charter.[3] The statement of purpose also indicated Parliament's desire to protect young persons from the dangers of tobacco products, to the extent that is reasonable in a free and democratic society. Again, the wording was deliberate, restating the standard in section 1 of the Charter for justifying restrictions on rights. But, despite the act's appeal to these normative standards for restricting rights, a 5–4 majority ruled that the legislation imposed an unreasonable restriction on freedom of expression and struck down the provisions that had banned advertising and promotion and required the non-attributed health warning. The majority's ruling indicated that parliamentary concerns of harm were insufficient to convince enough judges of the constitutional validity of the legislation, absent evidence of how the legislation would redress these harms.

Reactions to this ruling among those who have not closely followed the trajectory of the Supreme Court's approach to expression may well be puzzlement (how could the court possibly think of tobacco advertising as the kind of expressive activity befitting constitutional protection?) followed by surprise at the conspicuous absence of a judicial explanation for how tobacco advertising facilitates any of the purposes traditionally associated with a bill of rights. A descriptive explanation for the Supreme Court's conclusion that tobacco advertising is entitled to constitutional protection is that this is the logical conclusion of the court's approach to interpreting expression in the Charter. But this explanation does not address the merits or wisdom of the court's approach.

In its earliest Charter jurisprudence, the Supreme Court discussed the nature of the principles and values that underlie expression. These were said to include the pursuit of truth, participation in the community, and individual self-fulfillment.[4] But the court no longer seems interested in ascertaining whether the expressive activity in question advances these values. This became apparent in a 1990 reference case when the court extended free-speech protection to include solicitation for prostitution purposes. In this case the court confirmed that the Charter protects "all content of expression, irrespective of the meaning or message sought to be conveyed."[5] What has been particularly striking about the court's rulings on free expression since the reference on prostitution is the lack of theoretical explanation for why constitutional protection should extend to all forms of expressive activity.[6] By the time the court ruled in *RJR-MacDonald*, it had abandoned any commitment to engage in a philosophical inquiry about the reasons for protecting the expressive activity in question. Instead, the court fell back on what has become a formal and normatively empty standard: Does the activity convey or attempt to convey meaning?

In *RJR-MacDonald*, the attorney general conceded that the legislation conflicted with free expression in the Charter and therefore did not mount an argument to suggest otherwise. Any other argument – that tobacco advertising did *not* constitute free speech – would likely have fallen on deaf ears in light of the accumulating Supreme Court jurisprudence which has made it abundantly clear that the court is not prepared to entertain the idea that commercial advertising is exempted from constitutional protection.[7] The government, however, did not concede the free-speech claim in one aspect of this case – the issue of whether the requirement of a non-attributed health warning violated speech.

The closest the Supreme Court came to assessing the importance of the speech claim itself was in that part of Justice La Forest's dissenting ruling that the non-attributed health warning did not violate protected expression.[8] At worst, the required warning constituted a technical infringement of speech. But the Charter does not require eliminating miniscule constitutional burdens. Legislative decisions that increase the costs of exercising a right need not be prohibited where the burden is "trivial" or "insubstantial." As La Forest stated: "The only cost associated with the unattributed warning requirement is a potential reduction in profits. In my view, this is a cost that manufacturers of dangerous products can reasonably be expected to bear, given the health benefits of effective health warnings."[9]

In light of the court's willingness to recognize almost any form of expression as a constitutionally protected activity, it had no trouble concluding that tobacco advertising was a protected right. Since the legislation obviously restricted tobacco advertising and promotion, the only substantive Charter determination for the court was whether the legislation was a justifiable restriction on expression under section 1.

Tobacco legislation fails section 1 test

Justice McLachlin wrote the majority decision in *RJR-MacDonald*, with then Chief Justice Lamer and justices Iacobucci, Sopinka, and Major concurring. Justice McLachlin emphasized that Parliament must demonstrate that its law is justified and stated that the section 1 inquiry was, by its very nature, a fact-specific inquiry that required proof of the justification of law and not just speculative warnings:[10]

The bottom line is this. While remaining sensitive to the social and political context of the impugned law and allowing for difficulties of proof inherent in that context, the courts must nevertheless insist that before the state can override constitutional rights, there be a reasoned demonstration of the good which the law may achieve in relation to the seriousness of the infringement. It is the task of the courts to maintain this bottom line if the rights conferred by our constitution are to have force and meaning. The task is not easily discharged, and may require the courts to confront the tide of popular opinion. But that has always been the price of maintaining constitutional rights.[11]

True to her warning, Justice McLachlin concluded that the government had failed to satisfy her that the legislation was justified and set aside the impugned provisions.[12] McLachlin specifically rejected the proposition that this was an appropriate occasion for judicial deference to Parliament's decision. She suggested that deference would undercut "the obligation of Parliament" to justify limits on protected rights and would in fact "substitute *ad hoc* judicial discretion for the reasoned demonstration contemplated by the *Charter*."[13] McLachlin asserted that no matter how important Parliament's objective may seem, if the government cannot demonstrate that the means by which its legislative goals will be achieved are reasonable and proportionate to the infringement of rights, the law should fail.[14]

In her view, the Tobacco Products Control Act failed all elements necessary to justify the legislation as a reasonable limit on protected expression. McLachlin was critical of the use of a ban on all advertising and promotion, particularly in light of the government's failure to introduce evidence about the utility of less intrusive measures. She was particularly upset that government lawyers had not included in evidence a study, commissioned by the government before the legislation was passed, that had examined alternatives to a comprehensive ban. This exclusion from evidence led to McLachlin's conjecture "that the results of ... studies must undercut the government's claim that a less invasive ban would not have produced an equally salutary result."[15]

She also concluded that the legislation was not rational because neither direct evidence nor reason suggest a causal connection between the legislative objective of decreasing tobacco consumption and the legislative decision to prohibit tobacco trademarks on advertisements for other products. In her view, it was "hard to imagine how the presence of a tobacco logo on a cigarette lighter ... would increase consumption; yet, such use is banned."[16] She concluded that the court should not accept the "mere intuition" of Parliament that this strategy would work because the Charter's requirement that legislation be demonstrably justified and reasonable should be based on "rational inference from evidence or established truths."[17]

Many (including the dissenting judges) could challenge this dismissal of Parliament's approach as being based only on intuition. However, what was equally troubling was Justice McLachlin's willingness to suggest an alternative legislative strategy, which the majority endorsed as constitutionally superior to Parliament's approach.

Justice McLachlin clearly was not prepared to accept the validity of a complete advertising ban and advanced her own version of a Charter-acceptable legislative strategy. This arose out of her comment that, "as a matter of common sense," lifestyle advertising may have a tendency to discourage those who might otherwise cease tobacco use from doing so.[18] She subsequently repeated the idea that one can conclude "as a matter of reason and logic that lifestyle advertising is designed to increase consumption." The context for these statements was her suggestion that Parliament should have utilized restrictions on lifestyle advertising instead of a more comprehensive ban on all tobacco advertising[19] and that, had it done so, the court would have viewed the legislation as a reasonable impairment of freedom of expression.[20]

This "common sense" observation was rendered without arguments or evidence presented to the court to demonstrate that such a partial approach would be effective. McLachlin apparently had little regard for the obvious contradiction inherent in her putting forth her own intuitive observation as a constitutionally valid option, while having just dismissed, as inadequate, Parliament's approach because she thought it was based on intuition rather than on evidence.[21] What makes this contradiction so glaring was that Parliament's legislative strategy, unlike McLachlin's, was not a spur-of-the-moment one but embodied more than twenty years of reflection on health studies, tobacco-related death rates, and other jurisdictions' sucesses and failures in the compaign against tobacco consumption.[22] In reviewing the bill, the parliamentary committee involved heard from more than one hundred organizations representing a variety of perspectives, including medicine, transport, advertising, smokers' and non-smokers' interests, and tobacco production.[23]

More to the point, she had little regard for the judiciary's lack of expertise on choosing policy means and the court's repeated acknowledgment that it is precisely this task, of determining the strategies and details of complex social policy, that properly distinguishes parliamentary from judicial responsibility and competence.[24] Her approach was also inconsistent with the court's earlier indication that it must appreciate that it is not always possible for Parliament to identify the precise means for achieving an objective. As Justice Sopinka had stated three years earlier:

It is often difficult, if not impossible, to prove in the ordinary way whether a particular measure will in fact achieve its objective. Accordingly, if Parliament, a legislature or other governmental body had a reasonable basis for concluding that the measure would achieve its objective, that is ordinarily a basis for concluding that there is a rational connection between the measure and the governmental objective. Accordingly, although the government could not prove that advertising toys on television had a manipulative effect on children, nor that hate propaganda actually promoted hatred against an identifiable group, nor that pornography caused harm to women, the fact that there was sufficient evidence to provide a reasonable basis for the legislature to adopt the impugned legislation in aid of its objective was sufficient to save it.[25]

It is difficult to appreciate why recognition of the difficulty of identifying precise and effective legislative strategies to combat difficult social problems did not have more influence on the judicial evaluation of Parliament's attempt to discourage smoking. As one commentator suggests, the objective of preventing serious harm caused by tobacco use "outweighs any other objective yet considered by courts under section 1,"[26] particularly since data suggests that tobacco use is the leading preventable cause of addiction, disease, disability, and death in Canada (the 38,000 annual premature deaths attributable to tobacco in Canada are alarmingly close to the 42,000 Canadian fatalities suffered in the Second World War).[27] The fact remains, however, that the majority did not share this assessment of the importance of the legislation, as indicated by Justice McLachlin's suggestion that "care must be taken not to overstate the objective" because "if the objective is stated too broadly, its importance may be exaggerated" and the task of evaluating the justification of restricting a right may be compromised.[28]

DISSENTING JUDGMENT

Both the majority's inferences about why the government had not introduced evidence to support the ban on advertising and the suggestion of an alternative legislative strategy provoked criticism from Justice La Forest, who wrote the dissenting opinion, with justices L'Heureux-Dubé, Gonthier, and Cory concurring. The minority thought it unwise for judicial conjecture about the contents of documents unavailable to judges to "displace the overwhelming evidence that the prohibition was a reasonable one." Parliament had a reasonable basis, after twenty years of research and legislative experimentation, to believe that all tobacco advertising stimulates tobacco consumption.[29] The emphasis by tobacco companies in their own marketing documents on the colour and "look" of tobacco packages demonstrated "that the companies themselves recognize that even purely "informational" advertising has an important effect on consumption."[30]

The minority characterized tobacco legislation as the archetypal case in which the Supreme Court should be prepared to give Parliament substantial latitude in choosing the legislative means it considers the most appropriate for addressing the social problem concerned. Justice La Forest reminded the majority that courts are not specialists in the realm of policy making and that this is a role properly assigned to Parliament because it has the necessary institutional resources to enable it to compile and assess social-science evidence, to mediate between competing social interests, and to protect vulnerable groups.[31] As he argued:

Tobacco consumption is a multifaceted problem which requires intervention from a variety of public authorities on a number of different fronts. Parliament has adopted an incremental solution by prohibiting advertising without, at the same time, prohibiting the consumption, manufacture or sale of tobacco. In so doing, it has chosen a policy approach that strives to balance the rights of tobacco smokers and manufactures against the legitimate public health concerns arising from tobacco addiction including, most importantly, the special vulnerabilities of young Canadians. In my view, it is not the role of this Court to substitute its opinion for that of Parliament concerning the ideal legislative solution to this complex and wide-ranging social problem.[32]

Justice La Forest also disagreed with McLachlin's speculation about the effectiveness of a partial ban, in this case on lifestyle advertising, suggesting that the court's making of this policy recommendation was not only inconsistent with judicial expertise but also contrary to the court's recognition of the proper institutional division of labour. Noting the "ingenious" tactics developed by tobacco companies to circumvent restrictions in other countries that had adopted partial advertising prohibitions, La Forest concluded that Parliament had "compelling reasons for rejecting a partial prohibition on advertising" and indicated that it was inappropriate for the court to substitute its opinion: "It would be highly artificial for this Court to decide, on a purely abstract basis, that a partial prohibition on advertising would be as effective as a full prohibition. In my view, this is precisely the type of 'line drawing' that this Court has identified as being within the institutional competence of legislatures and not courts."[33]

ASSESSING THE JUDICIAL DECISION

Arguably, the conflict over tobacco advertising is not about rights at all. At issue is a policy disagreement between tobacco companies' economic interests to maximize profits and maintain or increase market share and the government's objective to dissuade impressionable young people from becoming smokers.

Because I associate the philosophical purposes of a bill of rights with protecting the conditions essential for self-government (discussed in the previous chapter), it is difficult to accept that corporations should be able to avail themselves of a system of rights to challenge government actions. Corporations use their financial resources to influence policy and put pressures on government to change legislation. But the goal of safeguarding the conditions for democracy, and the associated liberties of citizens, suggests that the focus of a bill of rights should be on protecting the human component of the polity. Corporations' economic interests should not be mistaken for fundamental rights simply because the activity in question – advertising – is a form of expression.

For the same reasons that corporations are denied a right to vote, they should not be able to invoke protected rights intended for human beings as tools to veto policies they dislike. Thus, the court's elevation of a corporate economic interest to the status of a constitutional right seems ill-conceived.

The court's decision to interpret expression so broadly as to include tobacco advertising was a discretionary decision, emanating from the court's decision to interpret the Charter's protection for expression without reference to the significance, importance, or nature of the expressive activity. An alternative approach would have been to define the scope of this abstract principle incrementally, on a case-by-case basis. This would exclude speech claims that are far removed from the philosophical reasons associated with liberalism's legitimate concern to protect from state interference those expressive activities related to the healthy functioning of a democratic polity, however broadly interpreted.

It is disappointing that the Supreme Court has not adhered to its original inclination to inquire whether the expressive activity at issue relates to the kinds of goals the court elsewhere has said underlie the liberal concern for freedom of expression: seeking and attaining the truth; encouraging participation in social and political decision making; and cultivating diversity in forms of individual self-fulfillment in a tolerant and welcoming environment for speakers and listeners.[34] Had the court engaged in a more purposive or thoughtful discussion of why free expression is important, it seems unlikely that tobacco advertising would have been found to warrant constitutional protection.

It is clear that the Supreme Court does not like the idea of relying on definitional limits to constrain the scope of protected expression. Nevertheless, it is important to realize that the court has imposed definitional limits on some rights, including expression. For example, the court has indicated that violent activities may be excluded from the scope of the Charter's protection of speech.[35] This is logical because it would greatly trivialize the significance of constitutional rights were murder or physical violence to be treated as protected speech, subject only to reasonable limits. Similarly, before the court ever addressed whether the Charter protects commercial expression, it applied definitional limits to exclude the right to strike from the scope of the Charter's protection. Two reasons were given. One is that the Charter is not principally concerned with economic interests, which is how striking was characterized. Second, the court indicated that, if it upheld a right to strike, it would subsequently be required to intervene in economic disputes between governments and their public-sector unions. This, in the court's opinion, was a task for which it was not qualified.[36] It is difficult to understand why one form of economic activity (striking by labour unions) should be beyond the Charter's protection, while another form (corporate advertising) is protected.

But even accepting the decision to classify commercial advertising as protected expression, it can still be argued that the Supreme Court should have minimized the vigilance with which it protected this particular right claim. In other rulings the court has warned against taking "a restrictive approach to social science evidence" that requires "legislatures to choose the least ambitious means to protect vulnerable groups."[37] It has also indicated that, where a rights claim is only "tenuously connected to the values" underlying a protected right, restrictions on that right are easier to justify, as in the case of restrictions on hate literature.[38] Specifically, when the "kind of expression [claimed as a right] does not stand on an equal footing with other kinds of expression which directly engage the 'core' of the freedom of expression values," the court should apply a lower governmental burden for demonstrating the reasonableness of the legislative objective.[39] In this vein, restrictions on commercial speech have been easier to justify than other infringements on expression.[40]

Those who are not convinced by this argument, or worry that judicial deference may undermine the vitality of the Charter, likely find comfort in Justice McLachlin's explanation for why judicial deference was not appropriate: "To carry judicial deference to the point of accepting Parliament's view simply on the basis that the problem is serious and the solution difficult, would be to diminish the role of the courts in the constitutional process and to weaken the structure of rights upon which our constitution and our nation is founded."[41] However, this statement would be more appropriate in another context; where, for example, the legislative infringement on speech undermines the robust and healthy functioning of a liberal-democratic polity or restricts artistic and cultural expressions that reflect diverse and contrary views. McLachlin's position ignores the difference between the need for the court to be vigilant when protecting fundamental rights and its role in reviewing an economic-policy disagreement where the language of rights has been invoked strategically, to dress up a corporate-policy interest that does not reflect any reasonable moral or normative claim on society.

Citizens may have different views on the logic or effectiveness of controlling tobacco advertising. However, democratic principles of representative government generally assume that policy disagreements should be resolved in the representative branch of government. Apart from the necessity that courts arbitrate jurisdictional disagreements between different levels of government in federal states, political conflicts should be subject to judicial review only when state action has implications for fundamental rights. Yet by elevating tobacco advertising to the level of constitutionally protected expression, the court transformed a purely political issue, involving conflicting economic and political interests, into a constitutional debate over fundamental rights. It is important to emphasize the consequences of this judicial approach. To state the matter simply, the more broadly that courts interpret rights, the more often will judges be required to don the hat of the policy analyst and assess the reasonableness of the means chosen to pursue social policy. In *RJR-MacDonald*, once the court concluded that speech was violated, it was drawn into the middle of a complex and multifaceted policy debate.

When the judiciary assesses the reasonableness of legislative initiatives, it is engaging in a discretionary form of policy analysis, pure and simple. There is no other way to describe accurately what is involved when the courts assess whether legislative means are reasonable: Is there a rational connection between the legislative objective and means chosen? Did the legislation impair rights as little as practically possible? And are the salutary effects of the legislation sufficient to justify its deleterious effects? All three questions inevitably lead judges to query whether a better way existed to pursue the legislative objective. Yet judges lack the policy background and access to resources necessary for an educated evaluation of complex policy options. In *RJR-MacDonald*, an informed assessment of Parliament's chosen means to discourage tobacco consumption would properly require review of issues related to marketing strategies, behavioural research, and health studies. These are subjects for which legal training provides virtually no guidance but which are peculiarly suited to Parliament, with its access to the necessary resources and comparative knowledge to develop policy.

A related concern arises from the Supreme Court's willingness to dismiss Parliament's objective, influenced to a considerable extent by the perception that government lawyers had not done a good job at defending the legislation, and also by Justice McLachlin's willingness to advance her own speculative option as a more reasonable strategy. The entire majority discussion of whether the legislation comports with judicially created proportionality criteria demonstrates the ill fit of this form of judicial evaluation to complex social problems. Rarely is a preferred or superior policy strategy for implementing Parliament's will readily identifiable. The notion that an optimum policy option is just waiting to be found – the one with the least restrictive implications for protected rights – is particularly misguided in the context of discouraging tobacco consumption. At the best of times, policy making is not a scientific endeavour that allows those responsible, or those scrutinizing their decisions, to determine the best solution to complex social problems, whether from a rights perspective or from a practical one. But it is particularly difficult to measure the effects of tobacco advertising on consumption. Even to suggest that this measurement is attainable, let alone achievable by means of Justice McLachlin's recommended strategy, misunderstands the nature of the policy challenge. It suggests false confidence that those responsible for making difficult policy choices have the requisite knowledge to determine how to change human behaviour with regard to an addictive habit. Moreover, policy developers must anticipate the many ways in which tobacco companies will attempt to undermine this objective because of their fundamental and vested interest in encouraging tobacco consumption.

Thus, it is worrisome to see Parliament's strategy for pursuing this complex social policy evaluated against judicial interpretations of whether the means chosen were significantly more restrictive than some other hypothetical possibility. By structuring the conflict in this way, those who opposed the legislative initiative were at a distinct advantage. Inconclusive social-science data and behavioural/health studies make it difficult to challenge, empirically, tobacco companies' twin claims: that less restrictive measures are required to satisfy reasonableness criteria, and that, because no clear causal linkage can be established between advertising and tobacco consumption, restrictions on advertising are not rational.

Another problem with such judicial vigilance in enforcing the court's minimal impairment and rational-connection criteria is that these criteria are not necessarily the ones that should preoccupy Parliament. Since tobacco advertising does not embody the kind of civic activity or human right that justifiably warrants close judicial monitoring for evidence of rights infringement, there is no reason for assuming that Parliament should share the court's preoccupation with these issues. Legislative efficiency may not be an appropriate criterion for choosing a particular legislative strategy if the result is a serious infringement of a fundamental right. But this is simply not the case here. Tobacco advertising was labelled a right not because it advances any of the values normally associated as warranting protection in a bill of rights but because of the court's particular approach to expression.

INFLUENCE OF COURT'S DECISION ON SUBSEQUENT LEGISLATION

In light of the marginal nature of the speech claim in this case, and the difficulties inherent in judicial review of Parliament's choice of policy means, a forceful response from Parliament might have been anticipated. Yet this did not happen. Less than a year after the court's decision, the federal Liberal government introduced new legislation (Bill C-71) that represented a weaker version than the legislation that had been struck down by the Supreme Court.

The new tobacco legislation has purposes similar to those of the previous and now nullified legislation.[42] Yet it is not as comprehensive in scope. Health lobbyists, who testified in parliamentary hearings, expressed concern that the legislation would not be as effective as required because of its failure to ban all forms of tobacco advertising.[43] They argued that any form of advertising and promotion of tobacco products risks undermining the objective of discouraging young people from smoking.

This legislative response provides a clear example of how judicial review can influence the parameters of policy debates and political priorities even when Parliament is attempting to pursue a compelling public interest in which fundamental human rights are not seriously implicated. Then health minister David Dingwall made it clear that policy developers had moved "painstakingly" to examine the Supreme Court's decision "line by line" to ensure that the new legislation would be constitutionally valid and that they had sought two independent consultations on the constitutional validity of the bill.[44] The lines of the court's ruling that were particularly influential stemmed from the speculative comment by Justice McLachlin that restrictions on lifestyle advertising would have been constitutionally preferable to a more comprehensive ban on all advertising and promotion of tobacco products. The departments of Health and Justice worked closely together to develop a new legislative scheme that would have a good chance of withstanding future judicial scrutiny. A senior health official confirmed the influence of the lifestyle dimension of the court's ruling on the legislation's design: "We have taken those parameters and that is how we've crafted the bill, so that any promotion that appeals to youth or is associated with youth or has a lifestyle connotation is an area that is restricted. We feel we have taken a lot of care to reflect the guidance provided by the Supreme Court."[45]

Mark Tushnet argues that judicial review can seriously distort the policy process by encouraging inappropriate attention to judicial concerns and insufficient attention to political examination of contentious issues. Echoing the concerns of earlier commentators such as James Bradley Thayer and Alexander Bickel, Tushnet warns that judicial review might inject too many constitutional norms into the lawmaking process, which could interfere with or replace legislative consideration of more important issues. But, at the same time, judicial review can debilitate decision making by encouraging legislatures to enact laws without sufficient regard for constitutional considerations because of the knowledge that elected representatives can rely on courts to strike down constitutionally errant legislation:

> The problem of policy distortion arises when legislators take what the courts say about the Constitution's meaning too seriously, and the problem of democratic debilitation arises when legislators and their constituents do not take the Constitution's meaning – or more precisely, their own views about that meaning – serious enough ... A legislator may fail to give enough weight to constitutional concerns about welfare reform but may give too much weight to the Supreme Court's constitutional pronouncements when considering whether to enact a statute about the distribution of sexually explicit materials over the information superhighways. But, precisely because legislative views about the Constitution's meaning *may* differ from the courts', the problems of distortion and debilitation may sometimes occur simultaneously.[46]

The judicial/parliamentary saga on tobacco advertising reinforces Tushnet's point about policy distortion. Parliament gave too little consideration to judicial views on the constitutional concerns with restricting tobacco advertising, while the "line by line" approach, designed to emulate the court's suggestion of a preferable legislative strategy gave far more attention to this suggestion than it warranted. Both from a democratic and from a public-policy perspective, it seems extraordinary that a judge's speculative comment would have such influence on the design of legislation that addresses a complex social problem which baffles the policy experts and can hardly be said to fall within the court's competence. Yet, if Parliament paid too much attention to this aspect of the Court's judgment, it can also be faulted for having paid too little attention to the court's equation of protected expression with tobacco advertising. At no time in the debate did the government or Parliament question the persuasiveness of the court's judgment, despite the marginal nature of the free-speech claim. Both accepted, at face value, the court's ruling that a fundamental right had been restricted by the regulations on tobacco advertising.

Another example of how the Charter helped distort the way this policy issue was conceived and debated was the prominence of rights talk in the evaluation of the bill before the two parliamentary committees that studied it. Interest groups and individuals exhibited a marked tendency to appeal to rights and the specific reasons and conclusions of the court when assessing the bill. Supporters of the legislation emphasized the dissenting judges' acceptance of the legislation and the need to convert only "one more" judge to the cause. Critics highlighted the majority's reasons and argued that Bill C-71 had not duly addressed its concerns.

This emphasis on rights was not without consequences. The government was not prepared to reintroduce comprehensive legislative measures (which would have required more careful attention paid to how these might be defended in subsequent litigation) or to invoke the legislative override to restore Parliament's original judgment about the importance of a comprehensive ban on the promotion and advertising of tobacco products. The latter option was discussed within, but dismissed by, cabinet.[47]

From a pragmatic perspective, it is understandable why the government would have been tempted to heed the majority's policy suggestion, particularly with its attendant message that this would likely be considered a constitutionally valid way of discouraging tobacco consumption. The government was obviously anxious to avoid suffering another judicial setback. Nevertheless, the prudence of framing this policy around the majority's "common sense" observation is highly questionable. Disagreements expressed during parliamentary committee hearings about whether lifestyle advertising affects consumption suggest uncertainty about how effective this legislative strategy will be. They also raise doubts about whether the legislation will be immune from successful Charter challenge on the same grounds that were used to defeat the previous legislation.

Tobacco companies oppose even these less encompassing legislative restrictions and have focused much of their considerable criticism of the new legislation on its targeting of lifestyle advertising. They argue that the legislation will have no demonstrable effect on the decisions of young people or others about whether or not to smoke, and, consequently, that it amounts to little more than a token effort to give the appearance that the government is doing something effective.[48] As one tobacco executive testified before the parliamentary health committee:

There is not one scintilla of direct evidence that the bill will be successful in achieving its stated effect, which is reducing the consumption of tobacco. To put it bluntly, the rhetoric says one thing and the bill says another. No factual evidence has been given to you or to anyone to explain how this bill will accomplish its announced objectives, but the facts of the past decade in regard to smoking prevalence among Canadians tell us first that oppressive legislation does not work and has not worked, and secondly, that every single forecast to the contrary has always been wrong.[49]

Other critics, who feel threatened by the legislation, have argued that since there is no evidence of any causal connection between decreasing tobacco consumption and prohibiting advertising tobacco logos on products or at events, the legislative means are not rationally connected to the objective.[50]

As anticipated, tobacco companies have invoked the Charter in an effort to have the legislation declared unconstitutional. The majority's emphasis in *RJR-MacDonald* on the need to demonstrate that the legislation will actually achieve its objective provides a potentially potent advantage for the tobacco industry in its argument that the legislation is not rational. This will place the court in an awkward position. The composition of the court has changed substantially since the earlier legislation was struck down. Nevertheless, the court's ownership of the policy strategy adopted, to restrict lifestyle advertising, will likely make it politically difficult to rule that this revised legislative approach is not reasonable. Yet, since the new legislation raises Charter issues that are very similar to those in the previous case – specifically, whether legislative goals should be upheld if evidence does not exist to demonstrate that the legislation will actually address the intended harms – the court may find it difficult to provide a compelling response to a question that will likely be raised in Charter litigation by the tobacco industry: "In the absence of empirical evidence that restrictions on lifestyle advertising are effective in discouraging tobacco consumption, how does the new legislation come any closer to satisfying the majority's requirement in *RJR-MacDonald*, that the legislation means be based on 'rational, reasoned defensibility'[51] as opposed to the 'mere intuition' which the court ruled to be inadequate?"

TWISTS AND TURNS IN THE LEGISLATIVE SAGA

As the 1997 federal election neared, and speculation increased that sporting events like the Grand Prix might not be staged because of restrictions on tobacco sponsorship, the federal government announced that it would amend the legislation to exempt the racing industry from the scope of the new advertising restrictions. The announcement came shortly after Canada's three major tobacco manufacturers warned in newspaper advertisements that if the legislation was passed it would "inevitably lead to the cancellation of many events" and would cost thousands of jobs and millions of lost tourism dollars.[52]

The proposed amendment to exempt the racing industry from sponsorship restrictions drew criticism from the Reform Party and the New Democratic Party, both of which wanted much tougher and comprehensive legislation to restrict tobacco advertising. It also threatened to expose the legislation to even greater vulnerability in the courts. The tobacco industry tried to use this new exemption to strengthen its claim that the legislation was not constitutional. Three of Canada's major tobacco companies, Imperial Tobacco, RJR-MacDonald, and Rothmans, Benson and Hedges, filed a court challenge arguing that the government could hardly claim that the legislation was reasonable under the Charter since it "has shown willingness to modify restrictions on rights guaranteed by the Charter supposedly enacted by the House of Commons and by the Senate for health reasons to further its own political purposes."[53] The Reform Party also commented on the vulnerability of the legislation if exemptions were made for political purposes: "If the government exempts auto racing in the Tobacco Act, other groups will be sprinting to the courts. [Minister Allan Rock] knows that. What possible defence will this government offer at that time in court for exempting one event but not others?"[54]

New legislation (Bill C-42)amended the legislation passed one year earlier (Bill C-71) and created a five-year exemption for all events and activities that had received tobacco sponsorship before 25 April 1997, when Bill C-71 became law. The scope of the exemptions was broadened from those originally announced. This was almost certainly done to reduce the Charter vulnerability of exempting only the racing industry. The government tried to put the best face on these changes, claiming that the amendments strengthened the legislation because, after five years, all sponsorship would be banned, which would give groups "more time to adjust and to find alternate sponsors."[55] However, a more probable explanation is that, during the course of evaluating the proposed amendments, the Department of Justice warned of the high Charter risks that would be incurred if exemptions were based solely on discretionary political decisions. Exemptions for only some events would make it much more difficult to convince the judiciary that the legislative means are rational or comply with the minimal-impairment criterion.

CONCLUSIONS

Some might be tempted to characterize the resolution of this legislative conflict as a good example of Charter-dialogue, one that demonstrates how judicial review can lead to legislation that is more sensitive to fundamental rights without necessarily compromising the pursuit of valid legislative objectives: the Supreme Court expressed its concerns and Parliament, with careful reverence for judicial opinion, responded.

However, this particular legislative conflict raises the question of whether it should have even been dealt with under the Charter and subjected to its constraints. What is troubling in this case is that at no stage of the debate did it seem to matter that the "fundamental" Charter right at stake – tobacco advertising – was not a right in any philosophical sense but a right created by judicial decree. The government neither contested the claim that tobacco advertising deserved constitutional protection nor discussed publicly whether its objective warranted more comprehensive legislation (which, given the court's prior ruling, would inevitably have led to discussion of whether the enactment of the legislative override was justified).

This judicial decision and the political reluctance to challenge the use of rights discourse had important consequences. Most obviously, it allowed the conflict to be reviewed in the judicial arena rather than in the realm of representative politics and, in the process, changed the manner in which the relevant issues were identified and assessed – that is, by whom, and according to what criteria. Instead of Parliament assessing the legislation in terms of workability and practicality, judges reviewed it from an entirely different perspective: whether the objective was rationally connected to the means and whether its effects impaired rights as little as some other, hypothetical strategy might.

It is understandable why a government may not welcome the possibility of another judicial setback. But when a renewed legislative initiative is designed to correspond to a judicial suggestion about complex policy options, it is entirely possible that more appropriate guidance, which draws upon previous trials and errors, comparative experiences, and informed best estimates, will be forsaken. A consequence may be impractical or less effective legislation. The policy distortion flowing from judicial review is particularly worrisome when it prevents Parliament from pursuing legislative objectives deemed important and results in legislative choices that may not be considered desirable. The need to respect fundamental rights may represent justifiable constraints on policy discretion. But when distortion occurs to have legislation comply with an extremely marginal rights claim, this serves to confirm the sceptics' concern that a bill of rights may unnecessarily, or unjustifiably, undermine the pursuit of legislative objectives in the public interest.

5 Sexual Assault Trials

Parliamentary and judicial judgments have in the past reflected sharply different assumptions about how to reconcile the conflicting values that arise in sexual assault trials. Although the Charter has had a profound influence on how both the courts and Parliament approach the legal treatment of sexual assault trials, these institutions have accorded different priorities to the relevant principles at stake. For courts, the primary consideration has been the right of the accused to a fair trial. For Parliament, the prism has been more complex and involves consideration of how legal rights can be reconciled with equality considerations. The latter concern has arisen from the effects of sexual assault on women and from the gendered interpretation of legal rules.

Parliamentary/judicial disagreements have arisen not only with respect to the constitutional merits of statutory rules about consent and evidence but also over the desirability of judicial changes to the common law. This chapter analyses the juxtaposition of political and judicial judgments about how to interpret Charter principles in the context of sexual assault trials. It begins by examining the disagreement that arose over the court's interpretation of sections of the Criminal Code known as rape-shield provisions. It then discusses a different dimension of this disagreement, which emerged after the Supreme Court changed a common law rule to allow incidents of extreme intoxication to be used as a defence in sexual assault trials. It concludes with an analysis of parliamentary/judicial differences over when and how those accused of sexual assault can gain access to the private therapeutic records of those who press charges.

SEXUAL HISTORY AND CONSENT

R. v. Seaboyer

The *R. v. Seaboyer* decision of 1991 initiated the parliamentary/judicial conflict over the rules of sexual assault trials. A majority of the Supreme Court deemed unconstitutional sections of the Criminal Code, known as rape-shield provisions, which prevented women's sexual histories from generally being introduced as evidence by defence lawyers. Parliament had considered this legislation necessary because of the concern that judge-made rules were prejudicial towards women. Judges had routinely allowed evidence of women's sexual histories, with inferences frequently made that consent in earlier circumstances in all likelihood meant that consent had been given in the incident at trial or that the woman was not a credible or truthful witness.

The court, in a 7–2 decision, struck down the legislation for violating the principles of fundamental justice (section 7) and presumption of innocence (section 11(d)). The court did not question the importance of the legislation but thought that its effects were too restrictive because of the potential to exclude evidence "of critical relevance to the defence."[1] The majority judgment, written by Justice McLachlin with Chief Justice Lamer and justices La Forest, Stevenson, Iacobucci, Sopinka, and Cory concurring, concluded that a woman's sexual history could be relevant and necessary for a fair trial.[2] The majority ruled that the impugned legislation should be set aside and judges should use their discretion to distinguish between necessary and irrelevant evidence.[3]

The dissenting judgment of Justice L'Heureux-Dubé, in which Gonthier concurred, contained a sharp rebuke of those judges, particularly at the trial level, who have succumbed to biases in the law that reflect unfair, stereotypical myths about women and rape. This scepticism about judicial impartiality led to the suggestion that Parliament was justified when trying to legislate a different paradigm for sexual assault trials:

Parliament exhibited a marked, and justifiedly so, distrust of the ability of the courts to promote and achieve a non-discriminatory application of the law in this area. In view of the history of government attempts, the harm done when discretion is posited in trial judges and the demonstrated inability of the judiciary to change its discriminatory ways, Parliament was justified in so choosing. My attempt to illustrate the tenacity of these discriminatory beliefs and their acceptance at all levels of society clearly demonstrates that discretion in judges is antithetical to the goals of Parliament.[4]

The majority's decision generated widespread concern from women's groups, who believed that it would discourage sexual assault victims from proceeding with criminal charges. The decision reinvigorated criticism that assumptions in the law with respect to sexual assault trials treat the female victims of such crimes unfairly.[5]

Legislative Response: Bill C-49

The federal government was not prepared to accept this judicial decision as the final word on the rules governing sexual assault proceedings. After substantial lobbying by women's groups, followed by extensive consultation with them, the justice minister was persuaded to undertake substantial changes to the Criminal Code through Bill C-49, which addressed the issue of consent in particular. The legislation, which received all-party support, amended the Criminal Code to define consent and to make it clear that relevant inferences cannot be drawn from a woman's conduct or from her previous sexual history.[6] The legislation also made it more difficult for the accused to use mistaken belief as a legal defence. Under previous legislation, an accused, if able to persuade the judge or jury of an honest belief that the victim had consented, could be acquitted. However, the new legislation required that the accused take reasonable steps to ascertain that the complainant was consenting and it explicitly stipulated that mistaken belief about consent is not to be accepted when it arises from intoxication, recklessness, or wilful blindness.

In response to the court's rejection of the blanket exemption on evidence of a woman's sexual past, the legislation provided judicial guidelines for determining admissibility; for example, it stipulated that evidence that a complainant has engaged in previous sexual activity is not admissible to support an inference that she is more likely to have consented to the sexual activity in question or is less worthy of belief. The legislation further stipulated that evidence of a woman's sexual history can be included only when it is clearly relevant to the issue at trial and when its probative value is not substantially outweighed by its prejudicial effects.

The legislation was controversial and reactions to it revealed profoundly different views about how to ensure a fair trial without debasing sexual assault victims. Critics of the legislation, in particular defence counsel, argued that a man can honestly but mistakenly believe that a woman has agreed to the sexual act in question and therefore the preclusion of this defence would undermine the right to a fair trial. Critics also disagreed with Parliament's definition of consent, which they characterized as a "grotesquely distorted view of relations between men and women" – one more suited to contract law than to "the way such things happen in the real world." These assumptions were rejected, vigorously, by a number of women's groups who argued that, if men are in any way uncertain about whether consent was granted, they should take reasonable steps to ensure that their partner has consented and, if still uncertain, abstain. They also rejected the view that the legislation should be guided by "realistic vision[s] of sexual relations" which, in their opinion, perpetuate the view that women's words, when it comes to sexual relations, cannot be taken at face value.[7]

The bill was studied extensively by a parliamentary committee established for that purpose. Parliament then addressed and responded to the Charter concerns raised in a manner that was neither dismissive of rights-based criticisms nor intimidated by suggestions that the judiciary was the more appropriate venue for resolving conflicts over the rules of sexual assault trials.

What was most significant about political handling of this issue was the government's attempt to approach conflicting rights in a way different from the one followed in the court's decision. Parliament agreed with the government's position – that the Charter issues involved more than respecting the right of the accused to a fair trial and presumption of innocence. Also relevant were the equality rights of women in section 15 and their rights to security of person in section 7. This more complex interpretation of how the Charter should apply clearly distinguishes political from judicial judgment. For the majority of the court in *Seaboyer,* only one rights-holder has a Charter interest in this issue: the accused.

Parliament's alternative assessment was made explicit in a legislative preamble for all – in particular, judges – to read. The intent of the preamble was twofold: to serve as an education device for courts on how to approach sexual assault trials, and to provide a statement of parliamentary intent in anticipation of a subsequent constitutional challenge to the legislation. The preamble indicated Parliament's grave concern about sexual violence and abuse in Canadian society and its sense that judicial decisions should be made within the context of reconciling conflicting rights: those of the accused to a fair trial and those of women to equality and security. It suggested that, notwithstanding the Supreme Court's concerns about the exclusionary rule, Parliament believed that "evidence of the complainant's sexual history is rarely relevant and that its admission should be subject to particular scrutiny, bearing in mind the inherently prejudicial character of such evidence." One does not have to strain too hard to interpret this statement as Parliament's belief that the Supreme Court did not interpret these conflicting rights in *Seaboyer* in an appropriate manner because insufficient regard was given to the equality rights of women.

One can think of a preamble as representing a stage in a conversation between elected and judicial officials on how the Charter should be interpreted and applied to the particular case at hand. What is attractive about the use of the legislative preamble is that it makes explicit the concerns and intents animating legislative decisions and leaves less room for courts to ascribe objectives to Parliament. This is a more honest and forthright way of attempting to justify a legislative objective than relying on government lawyers to speculate, after the fact, about the reasons behind a legislative decision.

Parliament's Intent to Define Consent Upheld

Parliament's tough rules, which make it difficult for an accused to suggest mistaken belief about whether consent was granted, were at issue in *R. v. Ewanchuk*.[8] This case did not involve a constitutional challenge of Bill C-49. Nevertheless, the defence tried unsuccessfully to claim a defence that is no longer allowed by Parliament's post-*Seaboyer* legislation. In this case, the accused initiated several sexual advances towards a woman, despite her repeated statements of "no." He was acquitted at trial of sexual assault in which his defence was that consent had been implied. A unanimous Supreme Court in February 1999 upheld the appeal of his acquittal and used its discretion to enter a conviction against him.

The court ruled that, where an accused argues mistaken understanding in a sexual assault case, the judge must be convinced that the accused "honestly believed *that the complainant had communicated consent.*" Any other belief, however honestly held, is not a defence. Furthermore, for this claim to be accepted, the accused's mistaken belief "cannot be reckless, willfully blind or tainted by an awareness of any of the factors" enumerated in Bill C-49. At any point, if the complainant has expressed a lack of agreement to engage in sexual activity, "it is incumbent upon the accused to point to some evidence from which he could honestly believe consent to have been re-established *before* he resumed his advances."[9]

Justice L'Heureux-Dubé, who accepted the principal judgment of Justice Major, felt compelled to speak out against what she considered to be prejudicial and discriminatory statements from the earlier Alberta Court of Appeal ruling. In supplementary comments, she indicated her concern about the statement of Justice McClung that the complainant did not present herself to the accused "in a bonnet and crinolines." This statement, in her view, should not be condoned:

"[These comments] help reinforce the myth that under such circumstances, either the complainant is less worthy of belief, she invited the sexual assault, or her sexual experience signals probable consent to further sexual activity. Based on those attributed assumptions, the implication is that if the complainant articulates her lack of consent by saying 'no,' she really does not mean it and even if she does, her refusal cannot be taken as seriously as if she were a girl of 'good' moral character."[10]

In her view, the Court of Appeal's treatment of this case reinforces her conviction, expressed earlier in *Seaboyer*, that Parliament was justified in attempting to halt judicial reliance on myths and stereotypes in sexual assault complaints:

Complainants should be able to rely on a system free from myths and stereotypes, and on a judiciary whose impartiality is not compromised by these biased assumptions. The *Code* was amended in 1983 and in 1992 to eradicate reliance on those assumptions; they should not be permitted to resurface through the stereotypes reflected in the reasons of the majority of the Court of Appeal. It is part of the role of this Court to denounce this kind of language, unfortunately still used today, which not only perpetuates archaic myths and stereotypes about the nature of sexual assaults but also ignores the law.[11]

Bill C-49 was subject to specific Charter challenge later in *R. v. Darrach*, in which a unanimous court upheld the provision that restricted the use of previous sexual activity as evidence. In evaluating Bill C-49, the court ruled that the provisions relating to consent do not undermine the right to a fair trial. The legislation prohibits the use of evidence of past sexual activity only when offered to support two specific, invalid inferences; these are that a complainant is more likely to have consented to the sexual incident and that she is less credible as a witness by virtue of her prior sexual experience.[12]

EXTREME INTOXICATION AND LEGAL BLAME: *R. V. DAVIAULT*

An important instalment in this parliamentary/judicial disagreement about how Charter principles affect sexual assault proceedings arose as a result of the controversial 1994 judicial ruling *R. v. Daviault*.[13] In this case a 6–3 majority ruled that the Charter required that a common law rule be changed to allow extreme intoxication as a defence to sexual assault. The issue of whether and how intoxication should mitigate criminal responsibility has been before the courts for many years. Before the Charter, the Supreme Court's interpretation of the common law had established the rule that self-induced intoxication is never a defence to offences of general intent, which include crimes such as sexual assault. However, in *R. v. Daviault,* the majority ruled that extreme intoxication can be used as a defence in sexual assault trials if an accused can prove, on a balance of probabilities, to have been so intoxicated as to be in a state akin to automatism or insanity. In the court's view, to exclude the possibility of this defence of extreme intoxication violates the Charter.

Justice Cory, for the majority,[14] ruled that it is not valid under the Charter to prohibit an acquittal where an accused is so intoxicated that reasonable doubt exists as to whether he or she had the capacity to form the minimal mental element required for a general-intent offence.[15] To uphold the common law position would violate the principles of fundamental justice in section 7 and the presumption of innocence in section 11(d).

The case arose after a sixty-five-year-old woman, confined to a wheelchair, was sexually assaulted by a male acquaintance. The acquaintance, a chronic alcoholic, visited her home and arrived with a forty-ounce bottle of brandy. The victim drank part of a glass of brandy and then fell asleep in her wheelchair. When she awoke during the night, the acquaintance appeared, grabbed her chair, wheeled her into the bedroom, threw her on the bed, and sexually assaulted her. She later discovered that the bottle of brandy was empty. The acquaintance, who had spent the day drinking at a bar, testified that he had no recollection of what had occurred between drinking brandy at the woman's home and awakening later, nude in her bed. Nevertheless, he denied sexually assaulting her. He was charged with one count of sexual assault. The trial judge found that, although the accused committed the offence, he should be acquitted because reasonable doubt arose as to whether, by virtue of extreme intoxication, he had possessed the minimal intent necessary to be convicted of sexual assault.

The majority was troubled by the prospect that, if unmodified, its common law rule would have the effect of substituting blame for becoming intoxicated with blame for committing a sexual assault. In its view, this substitution was not legally appropriate. The majority rejected the government's contention that the "blameworthy" nature of voluntary intoxication justified a continuation of the common law approach. It stressed that voluntary intoxication is not a crime and that studies do not demonstrate that the consumption of alcohol necessarily leads to crime. Though voluntary intoxication may be reprehensible, it does not mean that the consequences of this behaviour are predictable.[16] Thus, for the majority, if the common law rule led to an

accused being convicted, despite reasonable doubt about the existence of one of the essential elements of the offence, this would offend
the Charter's presumption of innocence.

An accused in an extreme state of intoxication akin to automatism or mental
illness would have to be found guilty although there was reasonable doubt as
to the voluntary nature of the act committed by the accused. This would clearly
infringe both ss. 7 and 11(d) of the *Charter* ... It simply cannot be automatically inferred that there would be an objective foresight that the consequences
of voluntary intoxication would lead to the commission of the offence. It follows that it cannot be said that a reasonable person, let alone an accused who
might be a young person inexperienced with alcohol, would expect that such
intoxication would lead to either a state akin to automatism, or to the commission of a sexual assault. Nor is it likely that someone can really intend to get so
intoxicated that they would reach a state of insanity or automatism.[17]

The majority concluded that no urgent policy objective justified
continuing with an approach that does not satisfy Charter concerns.[18]
Furthermore, it ruled that the existing rule was so "drastic" a violation
of the Charter "and so contrary to the principles of fundamental justice" that it was not necessary to consider whether it should be considered a reasonable limit under section 1. In abandoning the analysis of
reasonableness under section 1, the majority relied on its earlier discussion in *R. v. Swain*[19] that the court need not ascertain whether a
common law rule is reasonable under section 1 but instead can create
a new common law rule.[20]

In formulating a new approach, the majority ruled that drunkenness
will be a defence to crimes of general intent but only in those situations where the degree of intoxication is so severe as to be akin to automatism.[21] The majority speculated that the automatism defence
would be available "only in the rarest of cases."[22]

Dissenting Opinion

In dissent, Justice Sopinka, with justices Gonthier and Major concurring, rejected the implication of the majority's ruling that sexual assault offenders who are extremely intoxicated are not morally
blameworthy. The minority characterized sexual assault as a heinous
crime of violence and that moral "opprobrium is not misplaced in the
case of the intoxicated offender." Individuals who commit a sexual assault while in a state of extreme intoxication deserve to be stigmatized
and their moral responsibility "is similar to that of anyone else who
commits the offence of sexual assault."[23] Where the accused through

his or her own fault brings about this condition of automatism, that there may not be volition to commit an offence does not negate blame for their subsequent conduct.[24]

The minority also disagreed with the majority's concern that convicting extremely intoxicated sexual assault offenders violates the principles of fundamental justice. The dissenting judges, offering a different conceptual view of the principles of fundamental justice, argued that these principles and the values upon which they are based justify convicting sexual assault offenders who are extremely intoxicated. The principles of fundamental justice are predicated upon the "moral responsibility of every person of sound mind for his or her acts." A drunkenness defence in sexual assault would negate that principle of moral responsibility:

Central to [the Charter's] values are the integrity and dignity of the human person. These serve to define the principles of fundamental justice. They encompass as an essential attribute and are predicated upon the moral responsibility of every person of sound mind for his or her acts. The requirement of *mens rea* is an application of this principle. To allow generally an accused who is not afflicted by a disease of the mind to plead absence of *mens rea* where he has voluntarily caused himself to be incapable of *mens rea* would be to undermine, indeed negate, that very principle of moral responsibility which the requirement of *mens rea* is intended to give effect to.[25]

Daviault was not subject to a new trial. The victim died before a second trial could be held. A Quebec court judge ruled that, if Daviault's lawyers were required to rely on transcripts of previous testimony, this would violate the principles of natural justice.[26] This ruling left the prosecution without the foundation for a case, resulting in acquittal.

Public Reaction to the Daviault ruling

The *Daviault* decision demonstrates how the Charter can have important implications for social policy even in the context of judicial interpretation of the common law. The court's development of the common law rule with regard to extreme intoxication raised the following important policy questions: Should society accept that an individual, who commits a sexual assault while intoxicated, be judged less blameworthy than one who commits the same crime while sober? Should the intoxicated sexual assault offender be viewed as morally blameless, from a legal perspective? What should be the degree of culpability when an intoxicated individual inflicts harm upon another?

Public reaction to the majority ruling in *Daviault* was overwhelmingly critical. This negative reaction indicated that a substantial segment of the Canadian public placed more emphasis on responsibility and legal culpability than on legal considerations of whether an offender possesses the requisite guilty intent, because of self-induced intoxication. Academics also waded into the debate with varying assumptions about legal concepts of blame and social-legal norms of responsibility. Women's groups and feminist scholars were particularly upset with the decision. They feared that it would send what they considered to be an inappropriate message to courts and to sexual assault offenders: that offenders, if intoxicated, are not to be blamed for the sexual assaults they inflict. Elizabeth Sheehy wrote: "By acquitting men of assault charges using the extreme intoxication defence, judges have belittled the severity of the crimes in their rulings. In effect, the judges have perpetuated the notion that such 'aberrations' in male behaviour should not be considered criminal. The accused who have been acquitted of assaulting women, due to extreme intoxication, in effect have received the message that they did nothing wrong, that they were not responsible for their actions, and that they were victimized by the prosecution."[27]

Many were also troubled by the fact that the court did not conceive of sexual assault as an equality issue. Instead, judges were preoccupied with the legal consideration of the "moral blameworthiness" of an extremely intoxicated accused person who had committed a sexual assault. As Isabel Grant argued, to excuse men who are violent against women because they are intoxicated denies women equal protection of the law. In her view, for equality in the Charter to be effective, "relatively advantaged members of society [must] be required to take responsibility for not becoming intoxicated and harming more vulnerable members." However, the majority ruling "utterly fails even to address this issue" and portrays violence and sexual assault as gender-neutral.[28] As Grant stated:

In *Daviault* there is no reference to, nor was argument heard on, the need to guarantee women equal protection of the law and equal benefit of the law in a society where women have historically been targets for male violence because they are women. There was no reference in the case to the gendered nature of sexual assault nor to the fact that ninety-nine per cent of sexual assaults are committed by men and that ninety per cent of the victims are female ... The only rights mentioned in *Daviault* were those of the accused. His disabled, elderly female victim was virtually invisible.[29]

Criticism of the majority ruling was not confined to Canada. The U.S. State Department expressed concern about the ruling in its annual report on human rights, suggesting that the establishment of an extreme-drunkenness defence might diminish the significance of Canadian laws that seek to protect women against violence.[30]

The predominantly negative public reaction to the decision was itself controversial. Some legal commentators were troubled both by the public reaction and by the media coverage, which, they said, highly exaggerated the likely application of this new defence of extreme intoxication,[31] to the point that rapists who had consumed a few drinks were said to be legally protected.[32] Some suggested that the public criticism revealed a failure to comprehend why "the prospects of acquittal should rise with progressively severe intoxication."[33]

Not all commentators believed that the court had gone too far in recognizing a defence of extreme intoxication. Some were critical of the majority's decision not to extend drunkenness as a defence for general-intent crimes where the level of intoxication is less extreme than circumstances akin to automatism. Their criticism is that, by failing to change the rule to these lesser forms of drunkenness, the court continues to substitute drunkenness for the mental element of a crime.[34] Another criticism is that the court imposed a burden of persuasion on an accused to demonstrate extreme intoxication[35] and that, as a result, an accused might be convicted even after having raised a reasonable doubt as to the degree of intention or voluntariness of his or her conduct.[36]

Compounding the controversy about the decision, and the reaction to it, was the quick reliance by other courts on what the Supreme Court had indicated would be a defence applicable only in rare circumstances. In a period of little more than six months, beginning with the release of the court's ruling in *Daviault* on 30 September 1994, at least five individuals accused of assault or sexual assault were able to secure acquittals using the Supreme Court's *Daviault* ruling.[37] Apparently, either lower courts ignored the court's sense of strictness in satisfying the extreme intoxication test in *Daviault* or the expert testimony used in trials proved the Supreme Court wrong in its expectation that few cases of alcohol-induced automatism would arise. Widespread reporting of these decisions helped to heighten public concern that the *Daviault* ruling would exempt sexual offenders from legal responsibility. The possibility that wrongly decided lower court rulings would be corrected upon appeal did little to allay this concern. As one commentator suggested, even if jurisprudence eventually reduces the incidents of over-reliance on this defence, a deeper problem must be addressed – that is, the law's treatment of violence against women.

Both sexual assault and wife abuse have shown themselves to be areas in which the faith our legal system places in triers of fact is to some degree misplaced.

Myths and stereotypes continue to abound in these areas, despite concerted feminist attempts to debunk them. Triers of fact may too readily accept a claim that the accused would not have engaged in assaultive behaviour had it not been for the affects of alcohol consumption, and may also too quickly accept that the accused had reached the *Daviault* level of drunkenness. As a result, *Daviault* may actually generate a greater number of acquittals than it ought, many of which may not be appealed.[38]

The *Daviault* ruling, and the application of this new intoxication defence by lower courts, generated divergent opinions about whether and how Parliament should respond. Some women's groups were so troubled by *Daviault* that they argued for a swift legislative response to reverse this change in the common law rule. A coalition of women's groups staged a national day of action with the hope that this would put sufficient pressure on the government to reform the law.[39] In response to mounting pressure from women's groups, the Department of Justice organized a meeting of women activists and lawyers to elicit their input for changes to the defence of intoxication. However, some legal commentators were disturbed by what they considered to be misguided public apprehension and believed that Parliament should not consider legislative means to reverse the *Daviault* rule. Instead, Parliament should consider broader reforms to the Criminal Code[40] as well as legislation to address recklessness or negligence associated with crimes committed in a state of intoxication.[41]

Bill C-72: Parliament's Response to Daviault

The government responded to *Daviault* with Bill C-72, which reflected an approach markedly different from that of the majority judgment on several key issues. While the Supreme Court had looked at the issue through the prism of the rights of the accused, the legislation focused on how the intoxication defence would affect the equality rights of women, since they are disproportionately the victims of sexual assaults. As then Justice Minister Allan Rock told Parliament: "The time has come for us ... to recognize that women are not equal in this society, for a number of reasons. One of the symptoms of that inequality is the extent to which they are victims of violence by men, and alcohol is very much tied up in that, statistically ... and factually and demonstrably. Let's say so expressly. Let's also acknowledge that inequality is depriving them of the very Charter rights contemplated in the sections that are mentioned [in the preamble to Bill C-72]."[42]

Concern for equality was reflected in Parliament's refusal to allow an intoxication defence, in its approach for assigning blame and responsibility for sexual assault, and, perhaps most strikingly, in the language it used to convey its judgment about the resolution of conflicting Charter values. The new legislation, it was said, revived the principle of accountability, which is "urgently needed" on this issue[43] (an obvious implication being that the court's judgment had eroded accountability).

Bill C-72 restored the pre-Daviault common law position that self-induced intoxication cannot be used as a defence against charges for general-intent offences that involve violence, such as assault and sexual assault. It accomplished this goal by excluding the intoxication defence for the purposes of both the physical and mental elements of an offence. The innovative feature of the legislation was that it set out a standard of care in the field of self-induced intoxication that reflects the principle of accountability for actions arising from that state. The legislation borrowed from penal-negligence jurisprudence and defined a standard of fault that makes individuals criminally responsible for actions that depart markedly from this standard. It means that individuals who voluntarily become so intoxicated that they lose conscious control of their behaviour, or lose awareness for what they are doing, causing harm to others while in that state, will be considered to have breached the standard of care required in the Criminal Code. Breach of this standard of care is sufficient to result in criminal liability. It would prevent an accused from using the intoxication defence because intoxication itself would be the basis of criminal fault for the offence. By becoming voluntarily intoxicated and then threatening or harming the bodily integrity of another person, an individual has failed to comply with the standard of reasonable behaviour. With this standard of care in place, judges are relieved of the burden of evaluating the significance of intoxication in terms of criminal intent, not to mention the task of deciphering exactly how drunk a person has to be before being incapable of forming intent.

Rock characterized this standard of care as reflecting the "widely shared values of Canadians" about the responsibility of intoxicated persons to avoid harming others. It is a standard of duty that individuals owe others in society to ensure that they do not violate the integrity of each other's bodies. If individuals become so intoxicated that they lose control and then commit a crime of violence, they fail to meet the standard of care that society has imposed on its members.[44] Rock described the bill as a reflection of Parliament's "strong, moral principle that those who commit violent acts towards others while voluntarily intoxicated should be held criminally responsible."[45]

Another important difference between the court's judgment and Parliament's approach was with respect to the issue of moral responsibility.

Clearly, Parliament had a different view on the moral relevance of intoxication and criminal liability in sexual assault offences. The legislation rejected the majority judgment that individuals should be viewed as morally innocent when they commit an assault while in a state of extreme intoxication. Unlike the court, which worried that an accused unable to rely on this state of extreme intoxication as a defence could be denied fundamental justice, the legislation was premised on the assumption that individuals have personal responsibility for their actions and that failure to live up to this societal obligation has criminal consequences.

Rock advised Parliament that, in developing the legislation, the Department of Justice had carefully considered the constitutional implications of its approach and that he believed that Parliament should be able to convince the Supreme Court that its approach is a reasonable response to a pressing social concern.[46] In deciding to build the legislation around the notion of a standard of care, the government abandoned an earlier plan to enact a new offence of criminal intoxication[47] because it concluded that this approach had "grave" policy and constitutional problems.[48]

The bill received all-party support when it was presented to Parliament. Opposition parties indicated that the purpose of legislation was to "neutralize" the "negative effect" of the *Daviault* judgement and to reflect Parliament's "zero-tolerance" position on violence and the violation of women's rights to security of the person and the equal protection and benefit of the law.[49] Some members believed that Parliament should pass the bill right away, without going to committee.[50] However, Rock thought that the House of Commons Standing Committee on Justice and Legal Affairs should examine the bill to hear evidence on some constitutional aspects of the bill. He suggested that, in the event that the legislation was later challenged under the Charter, it would be "terribly important" to establish a foundation of "the evidence on which the Parliament of Canada opted for this approach to the issue."[51]

The Standing Committee on Justice and Legal Affairs faced the dilemma of either hearing from a large number of witnesses and not having the bill passed before the summer, or limiting the number to allow the legislation to pass before the summer recess. In order to allow the bill to pass more quickly, the committee decided to limit the number of groups appearing. For the government's purposes, the most important witnesses were scientists who would address the Supreme Court's assumption about the link between intoxication and automatism.

The committee heard from three prominent scientists who stated categorically that the court had misunderstood the concept of automatism.

They testified that alcohol, in and of itself, cannot induce a state akin to automatism. Automatism occurs "as a consequence of various physical and psychiatric disorders affecting brain function." An alcohol-induced blackout itself does not constitute evidence "that the person so affected was unconscious or in a state of automatism" at the time of the events. Usually, memory of these blacked-out events can be recovered, indicating that there must have been consciousness present at the time. While there may be cases of unconscious behaviour akin to automatism that can be caused by alcohol, these are likely to occur only where there is a pre-existing disease or physiological imbalance – organic brain disorder, hypoxia, or low blood sugar. These conditions should be detectable and evidence of them should be obtainable for trials. Thus, they testified that the court's treatment of automatism, which equated this condition with a blackout, represented a serious error in understanding the concept, and that the court's new Daviault alcohol-induced automatism defence was indefensible in scientific terms. In this, and in other cases where a sexual assault defence has relied on a high level of intoxication akin to a state of automatism, there have been reasons "to doubt the scientific validity of the testimony" upon which judicial decisions were based.[52] The committee was also advised that, in the view of the Canadian Psychiatric Association, existing defences in the Criminal Code are more than adequate to deal with any of the special conditions that supposedly occur out of drunkenness.[53]

Rock confirmed that the government was influenced by this "uncontradicted testimony that there is no scientific evidence that alcohol acting alone can medically produce automatism or a state akin to automatism."[54] Parliament was also influenced by the scientific testimony and expressed doubt, conveyed in a legislative preamble, about the very assumption upon which the court's intoxication defence was based: that intoxication leads to automatism.

Upon the bill's return to the House of Commons two months later, Reform members criticized the government for what they perceived to be an unwarranted delay in the process of responding to a social issue of grave importance. In their view, the bill should have been put on a "fast track" to show Canadians that their elected representatives shared their concerns about public safety and justice.[55] Rock indicated that the committee experience was valuable because it provided not only indication of widespread support for the bill but also "an important record" of the reasons for the legislation. The bill was passed with minor amendments,[56] including a statement in the preamble expressing Parliament's doubt about the linkages between intoxication and automatism in response to the scientific evidence heard by the committee.

Preamble

As was the case with Bill C-49, Bill C-72 contained a lengthy preamble stating the philosophical premises of Parliament's approach. The preamble was a conscious element of the government's attempt to provide the Supreme Court with justification for Parliament's judgment. Rock himself expressed the hope that the preamble would positively influence judicial scrutiny of the legislation: "We must not underestimate the value and scope of the preamble to the bill. It is an expression of the reasons and considerations that have led Parliament to legislate in this way. These reasons and considerations have been written down and may usefully guide the courts in applying these amendments to cases that come before them."[57]

The preamble began with reference to Parliament's grave concern about the incidence of violence in Canadian society and its recognition that violence has a "particularly disadvantaging impact on the equal participation of women and children" and on their Charter rights to security of the person and equal protection of the law. This in itself was a significant departure from the court's approach, which did not examine the relationship between an intoxication defence and equality but instead focused exclusively on the rights of criminal suspects. The preamble also stated Parliament's "moral view" that individuals in a state of self-induced intoxication who violate the physical integrity of others are "blameworthy in relation to their harmful conduct and should be held criminally accountable for it." This clearly contradicted the majority's concern that blame for voluntarily becoming intoxicated should not be substituted for fault to commit the offence.[58]

The preamble expressed Parliament's scepticism about the foundation for the Court's judgment, namely, the presumed link between intoxication and automatism. It did so by stating that, while Parliament recognizes a "close association between violence and intoxication" and the "potential effects of alcohol and certain drugs on human behaviour," it is also "aware of scientific evidence that most intoxicants, including alcohol, by themselves, will not cause a person to act involuntarily."

The Judicial Strategy

Despite the substantial differences between the legislation and the majority's concerns, the government tried to minimize the extent to which the legislation overturned the court's opinion in *Daviault*. Rock stated, repeatedly, that Parliament's intent was not to "reverse the court's decision in *Daviault*" but to address problems or limitations with the common law approach to the issue.[59] Despite this statement, some have described the legislation as representing an "in your face" response to the Supreme Court[60] because it contradicts the very premises of the court's ruling and reflects Parliament's negative view of the merits of the court's judgement on this issue.

The disagreement between Parliament and the Supreme Court on the relevance and moral implications of the extreme-intoxication defence led to the suggestion, considered but later rejected by the government, that the legislation be subject to a reference case to test its constitutionality. During deliberations on the bill in the Senate, after the House of Commons had passed the legislation, Rock indicated that the government was considering referring the bill to the court to "save the time and expense of private litigants" if genuine questions persisted about the legislation's validity and to "avoid uneven results" in trial courts' dealing with the issue, before the law was clarified.[61] Later, Rock suggested that the public interest would be better served by having the legislation take effect without delay. But he indicated that the government might reconsider a reference case if a lower court were to strike down the new Criminal Code provision.[62]

ACCESS TO VICTIMS' PRIVATE RECORDS

Within a few years of Bill C-49's passage, women's groups and those who worked with rape-crisis centres became aware of a trend in sexual assault cases: defence counsel seeking and receiving access to a wide range of women's private medical and therapeutic records. Some women's groups attributed this to defence lawyers' determination to find alternative ways to undermine the complainant's credibility in an attempt to encourage them to withdraw their charges.[63]

In the 1995 case of *R. v. O'Connor*,[64] the Supreme Court ruled on whether defence lawyers in sexual assault cases could get a judicial order to compel those who have access to a complainant's confidential records (produced by counsellors and doctors who have treated alleged victims of sexual assault) to provide those records for defence purposes. At the time, no legislation addressed this issue and so the judiciary relied on the common law. The court ruled that these records are relevant, but it split 5–4 on what the law governing their release should be.

Supreme Court's Ruling

The court was profoundly divided, not just in terms of the vote, but on whether judicial interpretation of legal rules discriminates against women and on the relevance of equality considerations in the context of sexual assault. The case involved a Roman Catholic bishop who was charged with rape and indecent assault relating to incidents alleged to have taken place between 1964 and 1967 when he was the principal of a native residential school. In the initial trial, the presiding judge had ordered disclosure of the complainant's entire medical, counselling, and school records in response to the defence counsel's argument that these records were necessary to test the complainant's credibility. This court order was made without any inquiry into the relevance of the records or consideration of how to balance a complainant's privacy right with the right of an accused to a fair trial. The Supreme Court, by a 5–4 majority, ruled that, when therapeutic records are in the hands of third parties, access should not be difficult to obtain because these records may be relevant and necessary for full answer and defence in a fair trial.

The majority opinion on this issue was written jointly by Chief Justice Lamer and justice Sopinka, with justices Major, Iacobucci, and Cory concurring. The majority established a two-stage process for determining whether or not to grant access to therapeutic records held by third parties. The first stage is to determine whether there should be an order to produce these records for the judge and the second stage is for the judge to determine whether or not these records should be released to the accused. At the first stage, the onus is on the accused to establish that the information in question is "likely to be relevant."[65] However, the majority established a low threshold for demonstrating relevance because the accused should not be placed in a "Catch-22" situation of having to make submissions to the judge without precisely knowing what is contained in the records.[66] The threshold for satisfying onus is simply a requirement to prevent the defence from engaging in "speculative, fanciful, disruptive, unmeritorious, obstructive and time-consuming" requests for access to records.[67] In the majority's view, information contained in third-party records might be relevant in sexual assault cases for the following reasons:[68]

- they may contain information concerning the unfolding of events underlying the criminal complaint;
- they may reveal the use of a therapy which influenced the complainant's memory of alleged events; and
- they may contain information that bears on the complainant's credibility, including testimonial factors such as the quality of their perception of events at the time of the offence, and their memory after the alleged event.

Once likely relevance has been established, the trial judge must determine in stage two whether these records should be available to the accused. This requires that the judge weigh "the salutary and deleterious effects of a production order" and determine whether a decision not to provide the accused with access "would constitute a reasonable limit on the ability of the accused to make full answer and defence." In the majority's view, decisions about access to complainants' private records involve a "balancing process" that must recognize the competing claims of a constitutional right to privacy and the right to full answer and defence. However, the right to privacy should not result in the "possibility of occasioning a miscarriage of justice" by unduly restricting an accused's ability to access relevant information.[69]

The dissenting opinion differed in a number of significant respects. The minority established a substantially higher threshold for demonstrating likely relevance, attached far greater importance to privacy, claimed that equality issues should be considered when determining whether defence counsel should gain access to complainants' records, and suggested that judges should keep in mind "the extent to which production of records of this nature would frustrate society's interest in encouraging the reporting of sexual offences."[70] Written by Justice L'Heureux-Dubé, with justices McLachlin, La Forest, and Gonthier concurring, the minority opinion characterized the assumption that private therapeutic or counselling records are necessary to a full answer and defence as "highly questionable." In the minority's view, access to these records is more likely "to derail than to advance the truth-seeking process."[71] Both privacy and equality rights justify "a presumption against ordering" production of complainants' records.[72] Moreover, equality is a relevant Charter consideration in this issue because sexual assault overwhelmingly affects women, children, and the disabled.[73] The minority noted that judges should be aware of the "pernicious role" that past evidential rules in the Criminal Code and the common law have played in the legal system. Its judgment cautioned judges to be careful "not to permit such practices to reappear under the guise of extensive and unwarranted inquiries into the past histories and private lives of complainants of sexual assault."[74] A legal system should not devalue the evidence of complainants of sexual assault by "*presuming* their uncreditworthiness"[75] and judges should be sensitive to the difference that vulnerability and gender may make in the application of criminal-justice rules.[76]

Another significant departure from the majority's reasoning was the minority's reconciliation of the conflicting rights claims in this conflict. It argued that, while the right to full answer and defence is of central importance, it must co-exist with other constitutional rights rather than trample them. In the minority's view, the notion of balancing conflicting rights is the wrong imagery for sexual assault trials because access to a complainant's record is rarely necessary for a fair trial and restrictions on this might actually enhance privacy and equality.[77]

The majority's decision alarmed women's groups who believed that it established too low a threshold for obtaining access to complainants' private records. Critics argued that the ruling reinforced "destructive myths" associated with sexual assault, for example, that women who report rape, as opposed to other crimes, are likely to be "liars, discreditable, or easily duped."[78] Some predicted that women would be forced to choose between reporting sexual assault and seeking therapy to deal with its traumatic effects,[79] while others suggested that sexual assault centres would do whatever was necessary to ensure a women's confidentiality, including shredding documents and no longer taking detailed notes at counselling sessions.[80] Some also worried that the court's decision would hurt sexual assault centres that were unable to afford the expenditures of time and money involved in challenging subpoenas for records and attending court, thereby reducing the support available for victims.[81]

Bill C-46: Choosing the Minority Judicial View

Following the decision, the federal government indicated that it thought the majority judgment had set too low a threshold for gaining access to complainants' private medical records, and, to address the problem, it introduced Bill C-46. The government stated that the "public's confidence in the criminal justice system is weakened when complainants' records are disclosed without regard to their Charter rights to privacy and equality."[82] Once again, a significant difference in the parliamentary and judicial judgments is the relevance of equality rights in sexual assault trial proceedings. One commentator characterized Bill C-46 as "a direct, almost point by point repudiation" of the majority judgment.[83]

Bill C-46 established a two-stage process for obtaining access to records but the criteria imposed for gaining access were considerably more difficult to satisfy than those set out in the majority judgment in *O'Connor*. Underlying the legislation was a rejection of the majority's view that sexual assault complainants' private records are of such great relevance to a fair trial that access to them should be granted frequently. The legislation did not contradict the majority's conclusion that the Charter requires that records be produced where the accused establishes their likely relevance to an issue at trial. However, the bill sought to influence how judges decide whether relevance has been established. It did so by stipulating, in the first stage, that certain grounds used in the past by defence counsel to obtain access to complainants' records are not, on their own, sufficient to establish relevance. It also differed from the majority decision by imposing additional criteria the judge must use in stage two before ordering that records be produced. In addition to weighing the salutary and deleterious effects of this decision on the accused's right to make full answer and defence and on the right to privacy and equality, judges must consider the following:

- the extent to which the record is necessary for the accused to make a full answer and defence;
- the probative value of the record;
- the nature and extent of the reasonable expectation of privacy with respect to the record;
- the extent to which production of the record is based on a discriminatory belief or bias;
- the potential prejudice to the personal dignity and right to privacy of any person to whom the record relates;
- the interest of society in encouraging the reporting of sexual offences;
- the interest of society in encouraging the provision of treatment for complainants of sexual offences; and
- the effect of the determination on the integrity of the trial process.

What was significant about the legislation is how closely it resembled the minority view that, in addition to the accused's right to make a full answer and defence, equality and privacy rights were necessary considerations in an order to produce private records for defence purposes. The factors that judges were expected to take into account were almost identical to those cited in the dissenting judgment, of which the majority accepted the first five but not the last three. The majority rejected explicitly the idea that privacy should be considered during the inquiry for production stage, suggesting that this would unduly restrict an accused's access to information which may be required for a full answer and defence,[84] and it did not indicate that equality issues were relevant either at the inquiry for production stage or for the release of records to defence counsel. The legislation also differed from the majority decision in two other ways. In the second stage of the process (giving access to the defence), it stipulated that equality again should be considered. Furthermore, it imposed different disclosure requirements on the crown. The majority had ruled that, whenever a complainant's records are in the hands of the crown, the complainant ceases to have a privacy interest in them and the crown is required to disclose these to the defence.[85] The legislation forbids the production of a record relating to a complainant or witness unless that individual has expressly waived his or her privacy rights.

Interest-Group Submissions

Bill C-46 was subject to considerable commentary by interest groups who appeared before the House of Commons Standing Committee on Justice and Legal Affairs. Debate about the bill was reminiscent of the debate five years earlier on Bill C-49, with opinion sharply divided on whether the legislation was constitutionally valid. As before, reconciliation of competing views was hindered by profound differences in philosophical and conceptual understandings of how legal rules affect women and what priority, if any, should be attached to equality considerations.

Rights claims were a prominent feature of commentaries both critical and supportive of the legislation. Criminal defence lawyers viewed the accused as being the only rights holder at issue and argued that the right to a fair trial was unduly restricted by other legislative considerations that establish "artificial hurdles" for determining whether records were likely relevant to a full defence. In their view, the legislation changed the standard for the production of records from one of presumptive production, emphasized by the majority in *O'Connor*, to presumptive exclusion. Consequently, the legislation "[would] have the effect of depriving accused persons of relevant information"[86] and would create a "significant potential for miscarriage of justice" that would be "a disgrace to the administration of justice."[87]

Women's groups and service providers, particularly those representing rape-crisis centres, also invoked Charter rights in their arguments in support of the legislation. But the rights central to this issue, from their perspective, were the equality, privacy, and security of women, who are most likely to be the victims of sexual assault. They rejected the claim that the legislation would compromise the right of an accused to receive a fair trial because private records would rarely, if ever, be relevant.[88] At the same time, they supported the legislation for addressing what they considered to be inappropriate judicial rules and approved of Parliament's intent to try to introduce equality and privacy rights into judicial considerations.

Preamble

The legislation received support from all parties and was prefaced with a preamble stating Parliament's intent.[89] The preamble reveals

Parliament's view that court orders for access to private records should consider a number of Charter rights: equality, dignity, and privacy as well as a fair trial. While the production of private medical records may be necessary "for an accused to make a full answer and defence," it may also breach rights to privacy and equality; hence, these judicial determinations "should be subject to careful scrutiny." The preamble does not explicitly rank these conflicting rights (no doubt because of the court's explicit aversion to promote a hierarchy of conflicting Charter rights).[90] Nevertheless, it contains an implicit message to the judiciary: courts, in the past, have not given due regard to other relevant Charter rights and the purpose of this legislation is to establish a more balanced set of rules to govern requests for access to private records.

The preamble prompted varied reactions from interest groups. Those supportive of the legislation approved of the preamble and its message that access to private records should be assessed in terms of the adverse effects for equality and privacy rights. Any reservations about the clause from women's groups concerned its placement in the legislation. Rather than stating Parliament's intent and theoretical assumptions about how the law should operate in a preamble, some would have preferred to see these important statements in the actual text of the Criminal Code. A concern was that, if not contained in the actual terms of the legislation, the judiciary would too easily forget the educative and theoretical messages when interpreting and applying the legislation.[91]

Those critical of the legislation were, not surprisingly, also critical of the preamble. They disputed the legitimacy of Parliament's desire to interpret the Charter differently from the court and were particularly offended by this bold pronouncement of intent, which they considered inappropriate.[92] Defence lawyers considered the message of the legislation as an affront to the judiciary because of its implicit suggestion that "the judiciary cannot be trusted to examine third-party records" or to "reach a proper determination." In their view, it is "a sad day" when legislation is passed that contains such a message.[93]

Additional Incentive to Pass Legislation: The Court's Ruling in R. v. Carosella

Two days after the introduction of Bill C-46, the Supreme Court in *R. v. Carosella* handed down a decision that reinforced the government's belief that legislation was necessary to establish the conditions for garning access to therapeutic records.[94] After the *O'Connor* ruling, many sexual assault centres began to shred notes and records of cases for fear of being compelled at a later date to produce these for a trial, and so violate their clients' privacy. The issue in *Carosella* was how to proceed in sexual assault trials when a claim has been made for access to private records that have already been destroyed; under these circumstances, is the right of an accused to make a full answer and defence breached and should the proceedings be stayed?

Once again, the Supreme Court split 5–4 on how to assess the relevance and necessity of access to private records for a fair sexual assault trial. The decision revealed even stronger philosophical disagreements than in *O'Connor*, with the same judges represented on the majority and minority sides. The majority stated that disclosure is a component of the right to make full answer and defence. Consequently, if the destroyed materials satisfy the *O'Connor* threshold test for disclosure or production, the section 7 right of the accused is breached.[95] The majority established new guidelines to determine what remedy is appropriate in sexual assault cases where the standard for relevance is met but the records have been destroyed. Either one of the following two factors justifies a stay of the criminal charges:[96] no alternative remedy exists to overcome the prejudice to the accused's ability to make full answer and defence; and irreparable prejudice to the integrity of the judicial system were to arise with the continuation of the prosecution. In this case, the majority concluded that both conditions were satisfied and suggested that confidence in the system would be undermined if the court condoned conduct designed to defeat the processes of the court, particularly by a sexual assault centre or similar organization "that not only receives public money but whose activities are scrutinized by the provincial government."[97]

The dissenting judges disagreed that there is a right to disclosure as part of section 7, suggesting that while the production of every relevant piece of evidence might be an ideal goal from the perspective of the accused, this goal should not be elevated to a right, the non-observance of which leads instantaneously to an unfair trial. Where evidence is unavailable, it is not enough to speculate that there is the potential for harm. For missing evidence to violate the Charter, "there must be a real likelihood of prejudice to the right to full answer and defence, in that the evidence if available would have been more likely than not to assist the accused."[98] The dissenting judges also thought that, had the trial judge conducted a proper inquiry into the need for these documents, the "likely relevant" test of *O'Connor* would not have been satisfied. Defence counsel's request for production of these notes "amounted to no more than a fishing expedition in the hopes of uncovering a prior inconsistent statement."[99]

Supreme Court and Parliament: A Meeting of Minds

Bill C-46 came into force in April 1997 and, as expected, was quickly challenged under the Charter. The constitutional survival of the legislation was anything but certain because it challenged core assumptions in the majority ruling. Nevertheless, in November 1999, the Supreme Court upheld the legislation in *R. v. Mills*,[100] accepting the validity of Parliament's attempt to articulate a different legal paradigm affecting how Charter concerns should be factored into sexual assault trial proceedings.

Before its ruling, the legislative rules for granting access to private records had presented lower courts with an interesting dilemma: which interpretation of the Charter should they follow, that of Parliament or that of the Supreme Court? The case before the Supreme Court was appealed after a lower court had ruled that Bill C-46 was unconstitutional. At trial the presiding judge concluded that the legislation undermined the balance between privacy rights and the rights of an accused to a fair trial, as enunciated by the majority *O'Connor* ruling. The judge faulted the legislation for having improperly created a presumption against disclosure and for ranking privacy rights above the rights of an accused to a fair trial. In the judge's view, it is impossible to countenance that a breach of the fundamental right to a fair trial could ever be considered a reasonable and justifiable limit. Consequently, the legislation should be struck down.[101]

The Supreme Court disagreed with these conclusions. As suggested above, Parliament's response to the *O'Connor* judgement was clearly persuaded more by the dissenting judicial view than by the majority opinion on the issue of access to medical and counselling records that are in the hands of third parties. Subsequently, at the time of the Supreme Court's ruling on *Mills*, this was a substantially different court than that during the *O'Connor* ruling. Two new justices were on the bench (Bastarche and Binnie), replacing judges on either side of the *O'Connor* decision (Sopinka and La Forest). In reviewing the legislation, the court had to confront whether it was willing to accept the obvious will of Parliament when that will was contrary to its own majority judgment. Three judges who had formed the majority judgment in *O'Connor* (Major, Iacobucci, and Cory) now in *Mills* accepted Parliament's alternative interpretation of the relevant rules for determining access to therapeutic records.

The majority decision, written jointly by justices McLachlin and Iacobucci, with justices L'Heureux-Dubé, Binnie, Bastarache, Major, and Gonthier concurring,[102] described the question of when accused persons should have access to private records of complainants and witnesses in sexual assault trials as a "vexed one."[103] The court suggested that, despite Parliament's determination to advance an approach that differs from one in the majority ruling, Parliament had struck upon a balance of rights and interests that was "scrupulously respectful of the requirements of the Charter." [104] The court ruled that Parliament need not duplicate the court's approach because a range of reasonable standards may exist.[105] When it ruled in *O'Connor*, the court was operating "in a legislative vacuum" and created what it considered to be the "preferred common law rule." However, this rule should not be considered "rigid constitutional template."[106]

What is significant about this characterization and the court's interpretation of Bill C-46 is the recognition and acknowledgment that Parliament does have a valid role to play in interpreting how the Charter applies to social conflicts and that its judgment need not replicate the court's judgment. The court expressed more modesty than it sometimes does when reflecting on its role in upholding Charter values. It acknowledged that the judiciary does "not hold a monopoly" on protecting rights and freedoms; Parliament also plays a role in this regard and is often able to act as a significant ally for vulnerable groups. Further, the court recognized that Parliament's role in protecting and promoting rights has been particularly important in the context of sexual violence:

The history of the treatment of sexual assault complainants by our society and our legal system is an unfortunate one. Important change has occurred through legislation aimed at both recognizing the rights and interests of complainants in criminal proceedings, and debunking the stereotypes that have been so damaging to women and children ... If constitutional democracy is meant to ensure that due regard is given to the voices of those vulnerable to being overlooked by the majority, then this court has an obligation to consider respectfully Parliament's attempt to respond to such voices.[107]

The court indicated the need for inter-institutional respect while invoking the dialogue metaphor to discuss the relationship between courts and Parliament. The court suggested that a "great value" in this dialogic relationship is the fact that each of the branches "is made somewhat accountable to the other."[108] It explained: "Just as Parliament must respect the Court's rulings, so the Court must respect Parliament's determination that the judicial scheme can be improved. To insist on slavish conformity would belie the mutual respect that underpins the relationship between the courts and legislature that is so essential to our constitutional democracy."[109]

CONCLUSIONS

The most significant feature of Parliament's role in the context of sexual assault trials has been its determination to assert an interpretation of the Charter different from the majority Supreme Court view. Parliament has challenged the judiciary to consider a more complex and substantive interpretation of how Charter principles apply to sexual assault proceedings. It has argued, forcefully and consistently, that the procedural rights of the accused must and can be reconciled with equality and privacy rights of women. In short, it has tried to introduce a different legal paradigm from that of the Supreme Court majority with respect to the rules that govern sexual assault trials.

In so doing, it has challenged dominant legal assumptions that the judiciary has exclusive prerogative for interpreting the Charter. Parliament has made it abundantly clear that elected representatives are not prepared to defer to judges on all interpretations of the Charter. This has been controversial among those who do not believe that Parliament has any business deviating from Supreme Court rulings and that its Charter responsibilities are, and should be confined to, correcting non-conformist legislation to satisfy judicial dictates. Yet Parliament's actions have not been inspired by contempt for the Charter or ignorance of its normative principles. On the contrary, Parliament has relied on the Charter to challenge the judiciary to consider the effects of legal rules for sexual assault trials on other Charter rights, namely, the equality, security, and privacy rights of women, who are disproportionately victimized by this crime. Moreover, the federal government has become aware of the possible influence of parliamentary deliberations on judicial review and has sought to use legislative procedures (parliamentary hearings) and drafting techniques (preambles) to communicate to courts the purposes and philosophy of the legislation. On this issue, the government is clearly broaching Parliament's legislative role as a legitimate expression of judgment on how the Charter should apply.

6 Regulating the Collection and Uses of DNA

Changing technology has helped to establish DNA analysis as an effective tool for law enforcement.[1] DNA evidence is one form of evidence which, in combination with other evidence collected, is used to support or rebut the crown's theory that a suspect or an accused person was at the scene of a crime. DNA typing is considered an effective and highly discriminating forensic tool because no two people have the same DNA pattern, except for identical twins. Skin cells, hair, blood, and semen will contain the same DNA and a person's DNA will not change over the course of his or her life. But alongside the potential benefits of DNA for law enforcement are "Orwellian possibilities"[2] that raise serious ethical and normative concerns relating to privacy and security.

Uncertainty about how courts would evaluate forensic evidence derived from DNA analysis, and reconcile law-enforcement interests with privacy concerns, provided the motivation for the federal government to introduce a legislative regime to regulate the conditions and rules with respect to the collection and storage of DNA samples. The challenges are enormous when crafting a careful and principled legislative regime that responds to a new and highly technical scientific development, the uses and implications of which may not be fully understood by public and political officials. Parliament has an obvious public policy interest in this effective and powerful tool for identifying criminals. Yet, at the same time, the Charter requires that those making policy decisions in this area respect individuals' right to be free from unreasonable search and seizure and protect their privacy and security. Concerns for privacy are difficult to anticipate, as are the full consequences of placing so much personal information about citizens in the hands of the state. Among the normative issues that arise when regulating the coercive powers of the state to obtain and use DNA evidence are:

- What are the relevant privacy interests with respect to the state's coercive powers to obtain, store, and use DNA analysis for criminal law enforcement?
- Should criminal suspects be compelled, against their will, to submit to testing for DNA analysis purposes and, if so, in what contexts and under what conditions? And
- Should this requirement to submit to the coercive powers of the state to obtain bodily samples for DNA analysis be considered legally analogous to other requirements of producing self-emanating evidence, such as fingerprints?

In the parliamentary deliberations on these issues, the tone of the political debate for evaluating policy options was not conducive for making Charter-sensitive decisions. A first regulatory regime was created with little parliamentary scrutiny. A second, subject to more deliberation, failed to take into account the normative merits of the respective positions of supporters and opponents and their relevance to Charter concerns. On one side of the debate, attention was focused almost entirely on how DNA would contribute to effective law enforcement – a position influenced by its potential to demonstrate factual guilt. The non-ambiguous qualities ascribed to uses of DNA to demonstrate or repudiate factual guilt encouraged the advocacy of generous and broad police powers to obtain and use DNA evidence. The assumption was that these powers are justified because no innocent person will have anything to fear.[3] But one of the problems with this way of framing the debate was that it marginalized or neglected other relevant concerns. For example, the emphasis on law enforcement resulted in little attention being given to issues of privacy, particularly by those who were keen to provide police with broad powers to obtain samples of DNA for crime solving. Yet privacy concerns arise in connection with the collection and uses of DNA and, as such, are of fundamental interest to all members of the polity, as are the uses of technology or coercive state powers in ways that may be intrusive, unfair, or discriminatory. The assumption that innocent people have nothing to fear from DNA also resulted in insufficient attention given in the political debate to the right to be free from unreasonable search and seizure.

On the other side of debate, government members responded by emphasizing the importance of Charter values in constraining the legislative options for using this new law-enforcement resource. But these arguments were presented in a defensive manner to justify proposed legislation that was based on risk-aversion. Blanket claims that judicial review of the Charter compels a specific response or precludes others had little resonance for those with a different policy perspective, at least in the absence of specific arguments about the normative concerns they represented.

The first section of this chapter discusses the creation of two legislative regimes which provide statutory authorization for police to obtain samples for DNA analysis. I then turn to how the Supreme Court has interpreted legal rights in the Charter and the remedies necessary for their breach, arguing that these decisions reflect evolving and highly discretionary judgments about the nature of justice and the meaning of a fair trial. The Supreme Court is struggling with how to interpret the degree of intrusiveness associated with the collection of DNA samples. This struggle is relevant for Parliament's choice of a DNA regulatory regime. In the absence of a settled and coherent jurisprudence, the DNA debates provided important opportunities for Parliament to contribute to constitutional judgment about how to reconcile Charter conflicts over the rules to govern the collection and uses of DNA evidence.

ESTABLISHING STATUTORY AUTHORIZATION TO COLLECT DNA EVIDENCE

The use of DNA evidence in Canadian trials dates back to the late 1980s. In the absence of statutory authorization for the collection of DNA samples by police officials, the judiciary has relied on the common law to evaluate its uses for law enforcement. A 1994 Supreme Court decision, *R. v. Borden*,[4] indicated a need for Parliament to address the conditions under which bodily substances can be lawfully obtained by the police for forensic DNA analysis. In this case, DNA evidence played an important part of a police investigation of two sexual assaults that occurred within a few months of each other. In one, an unidentified assailant left a semen stain on a comforter, and in the other a suspect was identified as the assailant from a police line-up. Police suspected that the same individual was guilty of both crimes. The accused was arrested for the second sexual assault. He declined to contact a lawyer when advised of this right and complied with a police request to provide samples of blood, scalp, and pubic hair. The police hoped that DNA testing would show that the accused was also the assailant in the first assault, by a comparison of his DNA against the semen sample. In drafting a consent form to authorize the obtaining of these samples, the police deliberately used the plural with reference to their inquiries, stating that the sample was for the purposes relating to their investigation*s*. This plural reference was the only indication the suspect was given that his blood would be used in the investigation of the first assault. Based on the analysis of the suspect's DNA samples, he was subsequently charged with sexual assault in the first crime.

The Supreme Court ruled that, since the police did not have statutory authority to take a sample of the suspect's blood, consent was required for this action to be considered lawful. The fact that the suspect had signed a consent form did not satisfy the court. The majority ruled that the proper test for determining whether consent had been given was not whether the decision was made voluntarily but whether a person has sufficient information to relinquish the right to be secure from unreasonable seizure. At a minimum, it was incumbent on the police to make it clear to the suspect that they were interpreting his consent as a blanket authorization for the use of the sample in relation to other offences for which he was a suspect.[5]

The court's reliance on the common law, and its conclusion that consent was required for the lawful taking of blood for DNA analysis, put pressure on the government to address this vacuum in the Criminal Code by introducing legislation to establish the conditions under which the police can lawfully compel suspects to provide bodily samples for law-enforcement purposes. Since the *Borden* decision, Parliament has passed two significant legislative measures. The first, Bill C-104, provides a statutory basis for obtaining DNA evidence, and the second, Bill C-3, establishes the conditions under which DNA evidence can be stored in a national data bank for later uses in unresolved crimes.

Legislation to Authorize Warrants for DNA Evidence (Bill C-104)

Bill C-104 provides statutory authorization to obtain samples for DNA forensic analysis. The legislation was introduced and passed in the House of Commons in a single day, 22 June 1995, with all-party support. As suggested, the need to provide police with a statutory authorization to collect samples for DNA purposes was apparent after the *Borden* decision. But an added impetus for the quick passage of the legislation was the political response to the tragic rape and murder of a Quebec teenager in her own home. Her family members wanted the police investigation to undertake DNA analysis to clear themselves from suspicion[6] and to obtain a DNA profile for the suspected killer.[7] Fears that courts might rule DNA evidence inadmissible led to the political characterization of this issue as urgent, a portrayal supported by opposition parties. For example, then Bloc Québécois leader Lucien Bouchard acknowledged that the circumstances were important enough to justify "exceptional speed" and "unanimity" in Parliament's treatment of the bill.[8]

Warrant Scheme to obtain samples for DNA Analysis

Bill C-104 amends the Criminal Code to provide a statutory authorization to compel suspects to submit to procedures that will allow bodily samples to be obtained for forensic DNA analysis. The legislation establishes in the Criminal Code a procedure under which the police can apply to a provincial court judge for a DNA warrant that would allow them to obtain samples from a person who is reasonably believed to have committed certain designated Criminal Code offences. These designated offences are principally offences of violence, such as sexual assault or murder, where it is likely that bodily substances associated with the offence will be found deposited at or in something associated with the scene of the crime. The legislation authorizes a peace officer to use "as much force as is necessary" for the purpose of executing the warrant where there are reasonable and probable grounds to believe that an individual is implicated in the designated offence. Samples are to be obtained by trained personnel and the procedures for taking samples are to be governed by principles of respect for human dignity and privacy.

The legislation authorizes three investigative procedures for collecting bodily substances: the plucking of individual hairs, the use of a buccal swab, and the taking of blood by pricking the skin surface with a sterile lancet.[9] Young persons are treated similarly to adults, with the exceptions that they have the right to have the samples taken in the presence of counsel or another adult and are subject to the rules of the Young Offenders Act with regard to prohibitions on publication and access to records.

The quick passage of the legislation effectively denied a role for the House of Commons to scrutinize the legislation in committee and to ask questions of government lawyers about its implications for the Charter, or to hear from non-governmental actors who might have had concerns about the legislation. The government emphasized to Parliament that the legislation was "carefully designed to respect constitutional requirements."[10] Then Justice Minister Allan Rock also indicated that, in drafting the legislation, the government was careful to abide by principles of human dignity and privacy and that the legislation reflected the Charter's requirement that adequate safeguards be in place.[11] The bill was referred to the Senate

Standing Committee on Legal and Constitutional Affairs, which reported the bill without amendment, despite having the following substantial concerns: [12]

- the list of offences for which a DNA warrant could be sought was too broad;
- the hearing for the warrant was to be conducted without the accused being present;
- the legislation did not require that the least intrusive method for obtaining a DNA sample be used; and
- the adults subjected to the DNA test, unlike the young offenders, were not permitted to have counsel present when the sample was taken.

After passing the legislation the government indicated that it would ask a different parliamentary committee, the House of Commons Standing Committee on Justice and Legal Affairs, to study the legislation a year after it had been in effect.[13] In 1998 the committee reviewed the DNA warrant provisions, along with the government's proposal to establish a national DNA data bank (Bill C-3, which at the time had been introduced but had not yet been subject to second reading). The committee reported that it was having difficulty understanding the full effects of the new warrant scheme on law enforcement and, under the terms of a standing order, asked the government to provide a comprehensive response to a number of queries.[14]

The government responded seven months later with a limited review of the DNA warrant scheme. The review was based on a questionnaire sent by the Department of Justice, in cooperation with the Department of the Solicitor General and the RCMP, to all provincial deputy attorneys general and to police associations.[15] The government received 186 responses indicating that DNA warrants were obtained in 500 investigations. The largest number were with respect to investigations dealing with sexual assault, followed by murder-related offences. Blood was the bodily substance reported most often to have been collected under a DNA warrant. A majority of respondents reported that the use of DNA evidence was a factor in guilty pleas and convictions.[16]

Divergent Views on the Legitimacy of Bill C-104

Despite the government's assurances at the time Bill C-104 was passed that it was consistent with the Charter, legal scholars have subsequently suggested that the legislation might be vulnerable to successful Charter challenge. Some question whether the authorization to take blood

samples for DNA analysis conflicts with the Charter's protection of individuals from unjustified, physical interference by the state.[17] This
issue is further complicated by judicial interpretations that have emphasized that a violation of the sanctity of a person's body not only requires higher burdens of justification by the state but may be
considered unlawful if it is carried out with unnecessary violence.[18]
Some are critical that police are authorized to use "as much force as is
necessary for the purpose of executing a DNA warrant" and suggest
that the law may be considered inhumane for a person who is a hae-
mophiliac or who has a phobia of needles.[19] A different concern is
whether the taking of blood for DNA purposes should be considered a
medical procedure that ought to be undertaken only by someone with
special training and overseen by a medical practitioner.[20] Only Quebec
requires that medical personnel take DNA samples[21] and the legislation does not specify the nature of training or experience required for
obtaining bodily substances for forensic DNA analysis. The government's own survey of how Bill C-104 has affected police practices reveals that, while a majority of the respondents reported that they had
received training in the investigative procedures, a small number of respondents, particularly from smaller detachments or departments
where DNA warrants had not yet been used, reported that they had not
received any training.[22]

At the time of writing, the Supreme Court has not yet reviewed this
warrant scheme for obtaining DNA evidence but it nevertheless has
commented favourably upon the legislation. In *R. v. Stillman*[23] Justice
Cory made the following comment in *obiter dicta*: "It would seem that
the recent provisions of the *Code* permitting DNA testing might well
meet all constitutional requirements. The procedure is judicially su-
pervised, it must be based upon reasonable and probable grounds and
the authorizing judge must be satisfied that it is minimally intrusive …
It seems to me that the requirement of justification is a reasonable
safeguard which is necessary to control police powers to intrude upon
the body. This is the approach I would favour."[24]

Bill C-3 – National DNA Data Bank

Bill C-3, representing the second phase of Parliament's DNA regime,
establishes a national DNA data bank for the purposes of solving previously unsolved crimes. The legislation was introduced into the House
of Commons in September 1997 and received royal assent in December 1998. It establishes two databases. One contains DNA profiles from
bodily substances found at the scene of a crime, and the other contains
the DNA profiles of persons previously convicted of certain crimes.

Police will be able to cross-reference information in the databases to help solve earlier unsolved crimes. The legislation allows for samples to be taken for the data bank from individuals once they are convicted of serious offences including murder, sexual assault, or break and enter. The bill also grants limited authority to take samples retroactively from convicted criminals who are considered dangerous offenders or who have been convicted of more than one sexual offence or murder.

Shortly before the legislation was introduced, the Supreme Court handed down judgment in *R. v. Stillman*, in which a majority concluded that the common law does not authorize the taking of DNA samples without consent or a warrant. This ruling had a substantial influence on how Bill C-3 was designed and defended. As will be argued below, the Department of Justice's interpretation of *R. v. Stillman*, and the advice that Justice lawyers provided the government about the scope of the bill, led to criticism from the Reform Party and from police organizations that the government was being unduly risk-averse at the expense of effective law enforcement.

R. v. Stillman

In this controversial 1997 decision, the Supreme Court indicated that it would interpret the taking of samples for DNA analysis very differently from the taking of fingerprints, with respect to Charter consideration. The case arose following the rape and murder of a teenage girl in 1991. The 6–3 majority decision, written by Justice Cory with Chief Justice Lamer and justices La Forest, Sopinka, Iacobucci, and Major[25] concurring, ordered a new trial for the murder suspect and excluded vital evidence derived from hair samples, dental impressions, and buccal swabs. The excluded evidence had been obtained without the suspect's consent and before legislation existed to authorize police to obtain bodily samples for DNA purposes. The majority concluded that to admit this evidence would result in an unfair trial. In so doing, it extended the privilege against self-incrimination, which is normally associated with testimonial evidence, to other forms of evidence including DNA analysis of body samples. As will be discussed below, this decision to exclude factual evidence obtained in violation of the Charter generated considerable debate on and off the bench.

The autopsy of the victim revealed a blunt trauma to her head, semen in her vagina, and a human bite mark on her abdomen that had apparently been placed at or after the time of death. At trial, Stillman's conviction was based primarily on four pieces of evidence obtained at the time of his arrest: teeth impressions, DNA analysis of mucous found in a discarded tissue, hair samples, and buccal swabs.

The DNA extracted from Stillman was found to match the DNA of the semen found in the victim's vagina. Dental impressions and the bite mark found on the teenager's body were found to be somewhat consistent.

Since no legislation was in place to authorize a warrant for this kind of search, the police relied on the common law search power. The majority concluded that not only was the police action inconsistent with the common law but the common law rule itself could not be sustained under the Charter. It ruled that the suspect's right to be free from unreasonable search and seizure was seriously violated[26] and that the police had also contravened his section 7 Charter right to security of the person. The majority characterized the taking of the bodily samples as "highly intrusive" because the police had violated "the sanctity of the body," which is "essential to the maintenance of human dignity." Thus, the police action represented an "ultimate invasion of the appellant's privacy."[27]

The majority also ruled unconstitutional the use of dental impressions obtained without the suspect's consent, which was the most intrusive aspect of the search. In so doing, it rejected the government's claims that the taking of dental impressions should be considered analogous to the routine practice of fingerprinting. Government lawyers had argued that the common law should be interpreted to allow this identification procedure upon arrest. To support this proposition, reference was made to Justice La Forest's judgment in *R. v. Beare*, which stated that a suspect has a reduced privacy expectation upon arrest and that this justifies fingerprinting.[28] However, in *Stillman* the majority ruled that the common law power of search incidental to arrest cannot be so broad as to encompass the seizure of bodily samples in the face of a refusal of consent. Otherwise, the common law rule would itself be unreasonable, since the rule would fail to balance properly the competing rights involved.[29] The majority also suggested that Parliament's decision to amend the Criminal Code in order to provide a statutory basis for obtaining bodily substances for DNA forensic testing (Bill C-104) indicated that it had acknowledged the intrusive nature of seizing bodily samples.[30]

Dissenting judgments were written by justices McLachlin, L'Heureux-Dubé, and Gonthier, who disagreed that the right of an accused against self-incrimination should be extended to encompass evidence obtained from DNA samples. Justice McLachlin suggested that the privilege against self-incrimination should be confined to testimonial evidence and should not extend to "the search of persons or premises or to the seizure of physical evidence, except in the case of physical evidence

derived from testimonial evidence."[31] Justice L'Heureux-Dubé acknowledged that serious concerns arise where a search involves a person's
bodily integrity. But these concerns vary along a spectrum.[32] In this case,
she considered the search as imposing "minimal affronts to the appellant's bodily integrity."[33] When it comes to the taking of bodily substances, such as hair, saliva, or mucous for DNA typing comparison,
L'Heureux-Dubé thought that an analogy should be drawn with fingerprinting; the methods by which hair and saliva samples may be obtained
are quite straightforward and, in her view involve little, if any, inconve-
nience.[34] While these may be more intrusive than subjecting a person to
a "frisk" search, more offensive investigative procedures have been
permitted at common law.[35]

Political Debate on Bill C-3

The bill was considerably more controversial than Bill C-104. Opinion
was sharply divided on what priorities should be attached to perceived
Charter concerns, the nature of Charter constraints, and the balance
that should be struck between these and law-enforcement objectives.
Specific questions focused on when DNA samples should be obtained
in the criminal-investigation process and whether DNA analysis should
be considered conceptually similar to fingerprinting with respect to its
Charter implications.

   In parliamentary debate, the government faced criticism for unnecessary reverence for the Charter. Reform MPs, and law-enforcement officials who appeared before one or both committees studying the bill,
argued that the government had given undue consideration to the privacy and legal rights of criminal suspects at the expense of effective law
enforcement. The government referred frequently to the *Stillman*
judgment as the reason to resist pressure to broaden the scope of the
bill to make it easier to obtain DNA samples from criminal suspects or
to take them from a broader range of previously convicted criminals.
Adding to the controversial nature and confrontational tone of debate
were the following factors: unsettled jurisprudence resulting in disagreement about the implications of the majority's judgment in *Stillman;* questions regarding the weight to be attached to the Department
of Justice's interpretation of relevant rulings; disagreement about the
degree of intrusiveness of various methods to obtain DNA evidence;
and public and political pressures to ensure the most effective uses of
DNA evidence for law-enforcement purposes.

   Although the majority ruling in *Stillman* made clear that police cannot
compel a suspect to provide bodily samples for DNA evidence without a

warrant, it did not resolve a number of issues relevant to the Bill C-3 debate. Among the most contested issues not addressed were: Does DNA testing require a different standard of authorization than required for collecting other forms of physical evidence that emanate from a suspect? Is the retroactive dimension of the data-bank regime constitutional? And can suspects be compelled to provide bodily samples for the DNA data bank at the point of arrest or is it necessary to wait until after conviction?

Unlike the first part of the DNA regime (Bill C-104), which was not subject to extensive parliamentary scrutiny, Bill C-3 was examined by committees in both chambers, although the most in-depth study occurred before the House of Commons Standing Committee on Justice and Human Rights. Charter considerations were prominent in individuals' and groups' evaluations of the bill. Some argued that a principal threshold for assessing the legitimacy of allowing police to obtain samples for DNA testing should be the degree of intrusiveness. However, commentators were deeply divided on what constitutes intrusive procedure. A particularly contentious issue was whether the process for obtaining samples for DNA purposes is, and should be interpreted under the Charter as, conceptually distinct from other investigative tools such as identifications in line-ups, fingerprinting, or breath samples.

Many of the philosophical concerns identified with the bill were similar to those raised earlier by academic commentators after the passage of Bill C-104. Several witnesses disagreed profoundly with the suggestion made by some – that taking a bodily sample for DNA purposes constitutes only minimal intrusion. Yet others – who thought that the scope of the bill was too limited – were equally adamant in their view that the collection of DNA samples is not unduly intrusive. Police officials argued that the taking of samples of bodily substances for DNA analysis is simply a modern and more effective method for achieving the purposes served by fingerprinting persons who are charged with criminal offences.[36] They argued that, since fingerprinting does not require a warrant and can be done lawfully at the time of arrest or charge rather than at conviction, there was no reason why the bill could not validly authorize police to obtain samples for DNA purposes upon arrest or charge, as opposed to the bill's stipulation that this occur only after conviction.

Police representatives claimed that the government's interpretation of Charter concerns had rendered the bill "impotent"[37] and raised three objections, which attracted the sympathy of Reform MPs but did not change the eventual the scope of the legislation. The first objection was that the DNA samples for the data bank could only be collected after an individual had been convicted of a crime and not when a suspect was first arrested or charged. The police representatives argued that samples should be taken at the point of arrest to discourage suspects, out on bail, from fleeing the jurisdiction because of concerns that their DNA might also be used to convict them of another crime they had committed.[38] Second, police were critical of a provision allowing a judge to exempt an individual from providing a sample if the judge was satisfied that the impact on the privacy and security of the person would be grossly disproportionate to the public interest. The objection of police officials was that this provision could open the floodgates for appeals.[39] Third, they argued that the retroactive dimension of the bill was too narrow.[40] The bill allowed for the collection of DNA samples from already convicted prisoners for limited and specific crimes. It stipulated that a court might grant authorization to take a DNA sample from a person who, before the legislation was passed, had been declared a dangerous offender, convicted of more than one murder committed at different times, or convicted of more than one sexual offence in which a sentence of imprisonment of at least two years had been imposed.

The government relied heavily on its legal advisers in the Department of Justice to explain the nature of Charter concerns to parliamentarians and to refute publicly the constitutional validity of proposed amendments. The high visibility of these officials resulted in the Justice Department becoming a target of critics, who suggested that not only had the government been unduly influenced by its legal advisers but that these officials had exaggerated the degree of Charter risk.

The department made clear its position on the constitutional implications of proposed amendments both in public statements about the legislation[41] and in individual officials' testimony before both parliamentary committees that examined the bill. For example, in response to one query, about why more previously convicted criminals would not be compelled to provide DNA for the data bank, a senior Justice official noted that the department has a natural reluctance to include any retroactive dimension into legislation and that if Parliament attempted "too much" it likely would endanger the "whole project."[42] Justice officials also argued that to alter the scope of the bill, by allowing the taking of DNA samples at the time of arrest, as an automatic procedure and without specific judicial authorization, would carry a high risk of being found to offend sections 7 and 8 of the Charter.[43]

Police officials and their spokespersons were not satisfied by the explanations from the Department of Justice.[44] Their testimony before the parliamentary committees was peppered with criticisms of Department of Justice officials for being "so inexplicably concerned" about protecting criminal suspects from DNA procedures.[45] The Canadian Police Association, intent on contradicting the claim that Charter considerations would not allow for DNA samples to be obtained at the point of arrest, produced an independent and contrary legal opinion. The author of this opinion, lawyer Tim Danson, concluded that no credible argument supported the proposition that if Bill C-3 were amended to permit the DNA testing at the time of arrest, the legislation would be found unconstitutional.[46] A representative of the association indicated that his organization would pay for a constitutional reference to the Supreme Court to determine whether their proposed amendment was consistent with the Charter.[47] Danson also supported a reference case,[48] suggesting that if Parliament chose to utilize in its DNA legislation standards similar to those for obtaining fingerprints, the judiciary would likely defer to Parliament's intent.[49]

The government ignored suggestions for a reference case to the Supreme Court. But its subsequent actions amounted to a de facto reference. In an attempt to resolve the contradictory claims about the constitutionality of allowing DNA evidence to be obtained at the point of arrest, the assistant deputy minister of justice[50] sought legal opinions from three eminent former justices, Justice Martin Taylor of the British Columbia Court of Appeal, Charles Dubin, former chief justice of the Ontario Court of Appeal, and Claude Bisson, former chief justice of the Quebec Court of Appeal.[51] Each jurist agreed with the Department of Justice's assessment of the police proposal – that to have DNA taken at the time of arrest would not withstand judicial Charter scrutiny. The question asked of each of the three legal experts was the same: "Would the automatic (i.e., authorized in statute but without prior judicial authorization) taking of a bodily sample (i.e., blood, hair or buccal swab) for analysis and retention of the resulting DNA profile in the national DNA data bank from a person on his being arrested or charged with a designated offence violate the guarantees of the *Canadian Charter of Rights and Freedoms* and, if so, would it constitute a reasonable limit within the meaning of section 1 of the Charter?"

Dubin's opinion suggested that society's interests in using DNA to solve crimes "are not sufficient to outweigh the intrusive nature of bodily sample seizures." In the absence of reasonable and probable grounds to link an individual to a particular unsolved crime, "it is unreasonable to seize that individual's bodily samples merely on the chance that they may be linked to such a crime."[52] Bisson expressed scepticism about whether a statutory authorization to take bodily samples as soon as a person is arrested or charged, without judicial authorization, would meet the justice minister's own criteria to ensure "fairness for those who would be involved in such a regime."[53] Bisson concluded that it is difficult to see how this provision could be justified as a minimal impairment to the Charter and therefore satisfy section 1.[54] Taylor suggested that courts would likely regard the compulsory taking of bodily substances for DNA analysis, without prior judicial approval, in a significantly different light than the compulsory taking of fingerprints of arrested persons. Such an act would infringe both sections 7 and 8 and was unlikely to satisfy section 1 criteria.[55] Taylor suggested that the different implications of DNA for privacy necessitate judicial authorization for DNA:

Having in mind that DNA analysis of the sample taken can be used for many purposes other than criminal identification, the compulsory taking of such samples without judicial authorization would *not* in my opinion be regarded by the courts, for *Charter* purposes, in the same way as the taking of fingerprints. The difference would be found in the much greater extent of invasion of personal security and reasonable expectation of privacy.

...

Not everyone can be expected to share the high level of confidence expressed within the scientific community concerning the reliability of DNA analysis as a means of connecting the guilty, rather than the innocent, with criminal activity. Certainly some skepticism is to be expected in Canada today regarding the handling of bodily substances by public authorities. When DNA samples pass out of the control of the arrested person into that of the State, the uses to which they may be put depend not only on the law as it is and may become, but also on the competence of those who take control of them and their willingness to obey the law. The uses to which DNA may be put in providing personal information regarding the individual, while known to go well beyond the field of criminal identification, are at present only partly and imperfectly understood. Such factors as these will, in my opinion, be found by the courts to render the taking of DNA samples against the will of the individual particularly significant in terms of both denial of reasonable expectation of privacy and invasion of security of the person.[56]

In its attempt to win the battle of rival legal opinions, the government released copies of all three legal opinions and indicated confidence that Bill C-3, as drafted, would survive Charter scrutiny.[57] Yet these opinions did not satisfy the Canadian Police Association or soften criticisms of the Department of Justice. Danson charged that the department's decision not to ask whether the retroactive dimension of the legislation had to be confined to the three categories of convicted criminals referred to in the bill was both convenient and appalling. He claimed that Justice officials "knew they would not get an opinion that supported the department's position."[58]

Some parliamentarians criticized the timing of the independent judgments, which were obtained after the committee had concluded its hearings. Earlier, the committee had divided on the issue of whether DNA samples should be obtained at the time of arrest or at conviction.[59] MP Peter MacKay suggested that the government's purpose in securing the legal opinions "was to influence the deliberations of the vote that will take place on Bill C-3" yet it was not prepared to give parliamentarians sufficient time to consider fully these important legal opinions.[60] The chair of the committee responded to criticism by suggesting that the government had no obligation to share legal opinions that it pays for and obtains in the normal course of its business.[61]

House of Commons Debate

Debate in the House of Commons revealed that many opposition members were not persuaded by the government's claim that Charter considerations prevent the taking of bodily samples from criminal suspects at the time of arrest. Discussion was highly partisan and became even more divisive when the government announced that it would invoke closure to shorten debate. Those most critical of the legislation were members of the Reform Party, who emphasized law and order as the most important consideration in the policy debate. Reform members either disagreed with the government's interpretation of Charter concerns or expressed the opinion that these should not be allowed to frame the parameters of legislative choices if they were to result in weaker legislation. They did not accept the argument that obtaining samples for DNA analysis could not be treated in a manner similar to the taking of fingerprints,[62] indicating that the opinions of the three jurists had little influence on their assessments. One MP suggested that the government should not be so timid as to base legislation on fear of what the Supreme Court might say, given the evolving nature of Supreme Court jurisprudence and the absence of what he considered a sustainable or logical reason to deny the taking of DNA samples at the time of charge.[63] Another Reform MP argued that, before Parliament passed legislation that might be overly cautious, the government should first check with the Supreme Court about whether allowing samples to be obtained at the point of arrest would infringe the Charter.[64]

But not all Reform MPs thought that the government should be so worried about ensuring that the legislation was consistent with the

Charter. One MP suggested that, if the bill passed without the amendments recommended by police officials, the legislation would give Canadians a false sense of security. Rather than ensure the bill was consistent with the Charter, it was "more important to give tools to ensure that victims have more rights than criminals."[65] Another MP suggested that, if required, the government should invoke the notwithstanding clause to allow for the taking of samples at the time of arrest.[66]

Government members disagreed with the claim that the bill was weak or ineffective. But, at the same time, arguments that the Charter constrained its options figured prominently in government members' justification for rejecting proposed changes to satisfy police officials or Reform members.[67] In response to criticisms that the government was more interested in protecting criminal suspects than the rights of law-abiding Canadian citizens, some Liberal MPs criticized Reform members for proposing amendments that would be unconstitutional.[68]

The bill was passed in the House of Commons without the amendments desired by the Reform Party or by police officials. The Senate Standing Committee on Legal and Constitutional Affairs examined the bill but its members were subject to considerable pressure by the government not to make any changes that would delay passage of the legislation.[69] The Senate committee agreed to report Bill C-3 without amendment on the basis of an undertaking by the solicitor general that the government would introduce legislation to address some of the committee's concerns, particularly in relation to privacy.[70] Also included in this undertaking was the creation of an independent advisory committee with representation from the Office of the Privacy Commissioner to oversee the administration of the DNA data bank, the requirement of an annual report by the RCMP commissioner to the solicitor general on the operation of the DNA data bank, the promise of legislation to bring within the ambit of the DNA data bank those offenders who are convicted in the military justice system, and a provision for parliamentary review every five years.[71]

The data bank went into operation on 30 June 2000. An estimated 28,000 samples were collected from convicted offenders during its first year of existence.[72]

UNSETTLED JURISPRUDENCE — AND
THE IMPLICATIONS FOR PARLIAMENT

The question of how Charter principles should constrain the coercive powers of the state to compel criminal suspects to provide bodily samples for DNA analysis requires substantive judicial policy decisions.

These decisions will be influenced by normative assumptions about the requirements of a fair trial and its relationship to the integrity of the justice system, the merits of an exclusionary as opposed to proportional approach in the evaluation of evidence that has been obtained in a manner that conflicts with Charter values, and the weight that should be attached to privacy and other relevant concerns. To date, the lack of a singular and objective resolution of these questions is indicated in the serious substantive differences among Supreme Court judges on how to conceptualize DNA evidence when assessing its implications for Charter values. The lack of agreement on the bench has given rise to a lively commentary alleging an intellectually inconsistent judicial approach to the granting of remedies.

This issue is important for the DNA debate because, next in importance to the question of what constitutes a Charter breach in terms of obtaining and using DNA evidence is the question of whether courts will include or exclude this evidence if it is obtained in breach of a legal right. The latter question is obviously of critical importance to the law-enforcement objectives of the state.

The following analysis of the court's approach to legal rights in the Charter and remedies for their breach is intended to demonstrate the extent of the discretionary nature of the policy choices inherent in the court's task. This is relevant to the role of Parliament for several reasons. First, it demonstrates that there is no settled Charter jurisprudence on issues affecting the collection and uses of DNA. Second, it makes clear the difficulty in anticipating what courts might say on relevant issues. Third, it raises the possibility that risk-aversion based on anticipation of future rulings might distort legislative choices, resulting in weaker legislation than the court may subsequently determine is constitutionally required. Fourth, the discretionary nature of judicial value judgments raises institutional and normative questions about whether Parliament also has a valid role to play when contributing to constitutional judgment about defining reasonable legal rules to govern the collection and uses of DNA.

Evolving Legal Rules

The Supreme Court's record with respect to the due-process values so celebrated by many legal commentators, and the remedies for their breach, is incurring serious strains. Before the Charter was adopted, the court defined legal rights in a narrow and minimalist fashion. Trial fairness was not interpreted as requiring the exclusion of illegal or tainted evidence but was evaluated "according to its ability to produce an accurate result, and by the fairness of the procedures employed during the conduct of the hearing."[73] The right to counsel did not include the right to talk to a lawyer in private, many accused did not have access to defence counsel, this absence of counsel was not deemed to prevent a fair trial, the prosecutor was not required to disclose evidence to the accused, and the promise of a fair trial did not guarantee the right of appeal.[74] As Kent Roach suggests, if an accused was looking for due process in Canada before the Charter, he or she was better to go to Parliament than to court because the practice of criminal justice bore a stronger resemblance to a crime-control model than to a due-process one.[75]

The Supreme Court, with a few stops and starts along the way, has interpreted the legal rights in the Charter in a far more expansive manner than it had under the Canadian Bill of Rights and has given broader effect to a due-process model of justice. The term due process is a shorthand reference to a broad range of assumptions about how the legal rules should operate and what the role of the state should be vis-à-vis individual suspects.[76] Although the concept of due process was not intended to apply to the Charter because its drafters preferred the more procedural connotations associated with the principles of fundamental justice,[77] it signals the primacy of demonstrating legal guilt rather than factual guilt and raises a number of obstacles to conviction in order to protect the rights of criminal suspects.

Under its due-process emphasis on the legal rights in the Charter, the court has expanded significantly the right of those arrested to consult legal counsel. The court requires that police inform suspects of their right to counsel whenever they are detained and that they must not elicit evidence until a suspect has had an opportunity to consult a lawyer. This right to counsel is not easily waived. Before the judiciary accepts that a suspect has waived this right, it is necessary to ensure that this did not arise either because of failure to inform a suspect of the possibility of accessing legal aid[78] or because of the suspect's failure to appreciate the gravity of making incriminating statements without consulting a lawyer, whether because of intoxication,[79] insufficient mental acumen,[80] loose lips, or police trickery resulting in incriminating statements to an undercover agent despite an initial intent to refuse to answer police questions.[81] So enamored is it with this due-process model of justice that the Supreme Court, after a lengthy history of giving more weight to criminal law-enforcement needs than to due-process concerns, has gone almost as far in the other direction as the system allows and now offers an even stronger protection for due-process values than that provided by American courts.[82]

But this emphasis on a due-process approach has not occurred in harmony with other values in the Charter. The Supreme Court has

struggled greatly, and in the opinion of many has failed, to develop a
consistent approach when defining legal rights in the Charter and, significantly, determining the appropriate remedy for their breach. The
relevant section for remedies is section 24(2), which provides:
"Where, in proceedings under subsection (1), a court concludes that
evidence was obtained in a manner that infringed or denied any rights
or freedoms guaranteed by this Charter, the evidence shall be excluded if it is established that, having regard to all the circumstances,
the admission of it in the proceedings would bring the administration
of justice into disrepute."

In 1987 the court offered its first comprehensive discussion of how
to determine whether to admit or exclude evidence that had been
obtained in breach of the Charter, in *R. v. Collins*.[83] The *Collins* decision was considered a compromise between the rigour of the American exclusionary rule and the common law position that all relevant
evidence is admissible regardless of how it was obtained. The court
indicated that relevant considerations included: what kind of evidence was obtained, which right was infringed, whether the infringement was serious or of a more technical nature, whether it occurred
as a result of wilful or flagrant police conduct as opposed to being
committed in good faith, whether it arose in circumstances of urgency or of necessity, whether other investigation techniques were
available, and whether the evidence would have been obtained in any
event.[84]

As jurisprudence on remedies evolved, the court began moving away
from the balancing approach contemplated by section 24(2) towards
what has become, in some contexts, an automatic exclusionary rule.[85]
The court has changed its emphasis from "all the circumstances" stipulated in section 24(2) and central to *Collins*, to focus predominantly on
the fairness of a trial.[86] Then Justice McLachlin, in an analysis of the evolution of the court's section 24(2) approach,[87] attributed the origins of
this new exclusionary rule to a concurring judgment of Justice Sopinka
in *R v. Hebert* in 1990, where he suggested, in *obiter dicta*, that if a judge
decides that the admission of the impugned evidence would render the
trial unfair, there is no need to explore other factors in *Collins*, such as
those having to do with the seriousness of the violation.[88] Subsequent
cases built upon this suggestion. A majority approved Sopinka's dictum
in *R. v. Elshaw*[89] and the court approved it unanimously in *R. v. Broyles*.[90]
By the time the court ruled in *R. v. Mellenthin* in 1992, Justice Cory held
that if a trial was unfair, this itself determined the section 24(2) analysis:
"it is clear that the admission of the evidence would render the trial unfair and there is no need to consider the other factors referred to in
Collins."[91]

Concerns with the Court's Approach to Trial Fairness

The court's new emphasis on trial fairness has generated considerable discussion as to whether this is the most appropriate way to approach the granting of remedies. In deciding what constitutes a fair trial, the court has relied heavily on a distinction between what it has labelled as "real" evidence and "conscriptive" evidence. Real evidence exists independent of a Charter breach whereas conscriptive evidence is obtained or produced as a result of violating a suspect's rights – for example, incriminating statements made by the suspect without his or her being advised of the right to a lawyer. The court has tended to rule that real evidence will not compromise a fair trial whereas conscriptive evidence will. The crucial threshold for the court's determination of whether a trial is fair is if the right of the accused to be free of self-incrimination has been respected. The court assumes that to admit conscriptive evidence is equivalent to calling an accused as a witness against himself or herself, contrary to the common law principle that the state has the burden for demonstrating guilt. As a result of this approach and these assumptions, the court has tended to exclude conscriptive evidence almost automatically.

What has complicated matters is the court's decision to expand the nature of conscriptive evidence to include non-testimonial evidence where this evidence emanates from a criminal suspect, examples being breath samples, participation in police identification line-ups, and now DNA tests. A particularly difficult issue for the court, given its emphasis on trial fairness, is how broadly the privilege against self-incrimination should be interpreted. Though it is clear that the court is extremely reluctant to allow evidence that would have the effect of compelling an accused to testify against himself or herself, it has had difficulty developing a coherent theoretical framework to determine how to apply this concept to other forms of non-verbal evidence that emanate from the accused. Specifically, how far should the idea of preserving a fair trial be extended to protect individuals against incriminating themselves in the sense of cooperating in investigations that produce evidence which can be used to help demonstrate their guilt? What about fingerprinting someone who has been arrested or obtaining samples for DNA evidence? This evidence emanates from an accused. Does its inclusion as evidence render a trial unfair? Why or why not?

As was discussed above, a majority of the court does not consider fingerprinting and obtaining non-consensual samples of bodily substances for DNA purposes upon lawful arrest as conceptually analogous. It has concluded that, when a person is arrested on reasonable and probable grounds and is compelled to submit to having fingerprints taken, this does not constitute a search and seizure for Charter purposes.[92] Therefore, if there is no violation of the Charter, no section 24(2) consideration arises about whether the ensuing evidence would render a trial unfair.

But this does not address the issue of why requiring an accused to cooperate in fingerprinting would not render the trial unfair, whereas the same is not the case for using DNA evidence. In distinguishing between fingerprinting and DNA samples, the court's focus was principally on the degree of intrusiveness and the threat to privacy. Moreover, historical timing likely has more to do with explaining the court's distinction in how it treats these forms of evidence than any conceptual distinction between the effects of fingerprinting and DNA analysis with respect to a fair trial. Fingerprinting was used and accepted by courts long before the Charter was adopted and before the court had adopted a more due-process approach to justice.[93] This comfort level contrasts with relative unfamiliarity with legal considerations of bodily substances for DNA analysis.[94]

David Paciocco suggests that what underlies the court's concern about DNA and other forms of incriminating non-testimonial evidence may not be trial fairness at all but the fact that the police have occasioned a serious Charter violation by conducting an unauthorized search and seizure or infringing upon privacy.[95] But if notions of privacy are really what prompt judicial concern, then the court should re-think its policy decision that fair trials are the important threshold for excluding evidence and give greater consideration to privacy or other policy considerations.[96] Paciocco argues that the court's reliance on a fair-trial approach to section 24(2) is a matter of discretionary choice, as opposed to a legal imperative. In his view, Canadian jurisprudence has outstripped the theory about rendering a trial unfair: "It is a stretch to treat evidence emanating from the accused but obtainable without his participation as the functional equivalent of forcing him to participate in his prosecution. All the accused need do to furnish blood, for example, is to bleed, something that can be done without any degree of real participation."[97]

If the reason for judicial reticence about DNA really rests on concerns for privacy or protecting against unreasonable search and seizure, this raises important issues for the court to address. For example, what remedies are appropriate if this evidence has been obtained in a manner that violates the Charter? If the relevant issue were how the evidence has been obtained, rather than the nature of the evidence itself, would a reasonable statutory authorization to empower police to obtain body samples for DNA analysis resolve Charter difficulties?[98]

Opportunity to Revise Judicial Approach

After initially hearing argument and reserving its decision in *Stillman*, the Supreme Court ordered a re-hearing of the case and expressed its willingness to reconsider the principles it had earlier developed with regard to whether evidence obtained in a manner that violates the Charter should be included or excluded at trial. Eleven parties were granted intervenor status, representing seven federal and provincial attorneys general and law and civil liberties associations.[99] Most of the parties hoped for a significantly modified approach or at least a return to the flexibility and emphasis on proportionality which were implied in the *Collins* decision.[100]

This case was seen as a good opportunity for the court to reassess its approach to section 24(2) because of the potential implications of extending its exclusionary rule to circumstances involving DNA analysis – in particular, the possible significant disjunction between legal and factual guilt.[101] But the court did not modify its approach to any significant extent.[102] The majority confirmed that it would continue to emphasize the fairness of a trial. In what has been characterized as the retention of a "technical, rigid approach,"[103] the majority ruled that the DNA samples in this case should be viewed as "conscriptive" evidence and therefore subject to the exclusionary rule, because they had been obtained without consent or statutory authorization and their use was tantamount to having an accused give self-incriminating evidence.[104] The majority emphasized the importance of determining whether real evidence exists in a "useable form" to ascertain whether admitting this evidence would undermine a fair trial. Physical or tangible evidence should be assessed differently if it can be obtained or analysed only as a result of an unauthorized search and seizure.[105] Moreover, since Canadians think of their bodies as the outward manifestation of themselves,[106] it is "repugnant to fair-minded men and women to think that police can without consent or statutory authority take or require an accused to provide parts of their body or bodily substances in order to incriminate themselves." Therefore, it follows that "the compelled use of the body or the compelled provision of bodily substances in breach of a *Charter* right for purposes of self-incrimination will generally result in an unfair trial just as surely as the compelled or conscripted self-incriminating statement."[107]

Alan Young characterizes the court's approach as being fraught with inconsistencies. The court failed to explain how conscriptive evidence affects the fairness of a trial. An important part of the court's explanation for why DNA samples should be considered conscriptive evidence rested on the absence, at the time it was produced, of a lawful mechanism to compel an accused to provide this evidence. But he queries whether this characterization makes sense.[108] If the unlawful nature of the evidence produced in *Stillman* was the reason its inclusion would render the trial unfair, Bill C-104 addressed this concern and was in existence at the time of the court's ruling.

The dissenting judges worried that the court had strayed too far from the idea in *Collins* and the intent of the Charter to avoid an almost automatic exclusionary rule. Justice L'Heureux-Dubé argued that to broaden the exclusionary rule to "unforeseen situations" may lead to judges digging themselves "into a hole."[109] She interpreted the inquiry into section 24(2) as having become so complicated that it is a wonder "how trial judges will ever be able to resolve the issues arising under s. 24(2) in order to ensure that justice is done."[110]

What is the Significance of Judicial Record for Parliament?

Incomplete jurisprudence on issues relating to Parliament's policy objectives, together with the court's struggle to establish the meaning of trial fairness and the importance of privacy and security provided a timely and important opportunity for Parliament to contribute to constitutional judgment about how Charter values should guide considerations for regulating the collection and use of DNA evidence. Charter considerations clearly influenced the government's decision about the scope of the data-bank legislation and how it defended its policy choices. Worried about the prospects of judicial nullification of its legislation, the government decided to undertake what some might interpret as a more sensitive approach to the collection and uses of DNA evidence than might otherwise have occurred. Thus, the government's policy response might be viewed as evidence of the Charter's positive influence on legislative choices that might infringe on protected Charter rights.

This clearly was the image the government attempted to convey.[111] In parliamentary debates, government members went out of their way to portray the legislation as being born out of respect for Charter principles by contrasting their approach with their opponents' lack of sensitivity for the Charter. Those who were not persuaded by government claims that its interpretation of the Charter was appropriate, and that the Charter constrained (and rightly so) the scope of the bill, were chided for being anti-Charter and even "unCanadian" for their alleged willingness to infringe upon individual rights.[112] Reform MPs were asked, sarcastically, whether they had "heard of the Constitution or the Charter of Rights and Freedoms."[113]

Yet, despite appearances that the Charter improved this policy debate, that judicial review, or the prospects of it, constrained legislative choices so as to ensure that these give effect to the polity's fundamental values and rights commitments, there was a troubling quality about the way political choices were made and political debate unfolded. The opposition focused on law enforcement without due attention to privacy or other normative values in the Charter. As argued in Chapter 3, citizens have legitimate expectations that legislative decisions are consistent with Charter values. Yet, in relying on the Charter to reject the opposition's demands, the government did not acknowledge the degree to which its position depended on the interpretation of a limited jurisprudence that had not yet examined many of the issues central to the policy debate. Case law reflects underdeveloped theoretical inquiries about how to conceptualize the rights in question or how to resolve tensions between policy objectives and Charter principles. The *Borden* and *Stillman* decisions provided some insights into how particular judges will approach some of the issues related to the collection and uses of DNA evidence. But the extent to which these rulings provide authoritative guidance to many of the concerns that were central to debate on Bill C-3 should not be exaggerated. Thus, it was misleading for the government to suggest, as it did during the DNA debate, that the Charter provided settled and conclusive answers to relevant issues such as: What is the conceptual distinction between DNA samples and fingerprinting in terms of evaluating the coercive powers of the state to compel suspects to provide evidence? What criteria are required for a reasonable statutory authority that would allow police to obtain samples for the DNA bank? Can samples be obtained retroactively from already convicted criminals? Are there circumstances or conditions under which samples can validly be taken at the point of arrest or must this wait until after conviction?

What is troubling about the government basing its policy on expectations about what might emerge from a nascent and unsettled jurisprudence is that this strategy gave insufficient attention to the fact that the Supreme Court's decisions in *Borden* and *Stillman* relied on the common law because no relevant legislation existed. The assumption implicit in the government's position was that its choices were determined by, and must be drawn exclusively from, the relevant jurisprudence. Yet the court's judgment on the legislative regime may be different from the judgment it reaches when determining how the common law should be adapted in light of this new technology and Charter considerations. The reason for this difference is that reliance on the common law occurs when Parliament has not provided its perspective in the form of legislative judgment. As such, Bill C-3 should have been viewed as an important occasion for Parliament to contribute to constitutional judgment about how to reconcile public-interest concerns with Charter values. Not only was it difficult to predict how jurisprudence would evolve on this issue, but utilizing a risk-averse approach based on what the court might say in the future ran the risk of adopting less ambitious or comprehensive measures than may have been constitutionally required.

A different concern relates to the government's lack of substantive explanation about the merits of its preferred approach. Rock did refer to fairness in his discussion of the proposed measures in the first bill. But the overall tone of the political debate in the second bill was legalistic and defensive: what the Charter would allow as viewed through the lens of Justice lawyers. Legal opinions on what the court might say were used to restrict the parameters of debate rather than to encourage consideration of how Charter principles should affect judgment about the merits of proposed amendments to the bill. Reference to possible judicial Charter rulings became the substitute for principled arguments about why the state should not compel criminal suspects to provide samples for DNA analysis at the point of arrest rather than at conviction, why privacy is important and how it should affect the collection of DNA evidence, or the priorities that should be attached to conflicts between law-enforcement needs and the right to be secure from this kind of search. In short, the government provided little in the way of an explanation for the normative assumptions and values underlying its legislative choices.

In the final analysis, some might conclude that government's position is more compelling than suggested by the opposition: that there should be warrants to authorize police before DNA samples can be obtained and that, for purposes of a DNA bank, this should occur at the point of conviction rather than at arrest. But arguments to convince opponents of the merits of this view would have been more persuasive than reliance on legal and technical explanations of what the Supreme Court might or might not say if and when it reviewed the legislation.

Such heavy reliance on Justice lawyers to defend the government's legislation resulted in their becoming the targets of criticism. Yet criticizing Justice officials for the legislative choices made was unfair. Their role is to provide the minister of justice with an assessment of the Charter risks and of whether or not a credible argument can be made to justify legislation that will likely be subject to Charter litigation. It is the government's responsibility to decide how to interpret this legal advice when determining the appropriate balance that should be struck between conflicting rights and policy objectives. The government was constrained by the advice of Justice lawyers only to the extent that it chose to be.

Had the government wanted to proceed with legislation that allowed for DNA testing earlier in the criminal process, or that included a broader retroactive dimension, it could have asked the Supreme Court to provide an opinion in a reference case, taken a chance and tried to persuade the court in future litigation about the reasonableness of its actions, or had the minister of justice report to Parliament that the government was proceeding with a course of action that had been identified by its legal advisers as high risk. All these choices were available, but they were forsaken and without explanation.

Conclusions

Law-enforcement objectives, which emphasize the need for easier rules to compel suspects to provide samples for DNA analysis as early as possible in the criminal-investigation process, stand in tension with protecting individuals' privacy and right to be secure from unreasonable search and seizure. As such, reconciling these conflicting perspectives represents exactly the kind of decisions that are often claimed to justify a bill of rights. Many believe that the principled assessments that are required to protect rights are best made in an environment that is not subject to emotions that arise from public and partisan deliberations, particularly when these are influenced by recent memories of a specific or series of horrific crimes. For example, Don Stuart suggests that, without judicial review of the Charter, politicians would "have been unable to resist the political expediency of pandering to the perceived need to toughen penal responses" to crime.[114] He argues that an entrenched bill of rights, while no panacea because courts can be unduly deferential to legislatures, is nevertheless the best way of ensuring more just principles in assessing the uses of "massive State power against an individual."[115]

The judiciary's liberty from partisan or public pressures is an important reason for valuing judicial review of coercive state powers. Yet an important distinction must be made between judicial evaluation of the merits of legislation and judicial evaluation of the legitimacy of the discretionary conduct of police or others exercising coercive powers. While judicial review in both contexts is valuable for shedding light on whether coercive state powers are justified, it should not be assumed that legislative judgment, where different from judicial opinion, is necessarily unreasonable. As was argued in Chapter 2, the philosophical nature of rights claims and the normative nature of societal values raises serious doubt about the principled/non-principled dichotomy used by some to distinguish judicial from political judgments. Legislative choices may reflect unjust and reprehensible answers. But to assume that contrary legislative judgment is inherently unreasonable is both too cynical a view of Parliament and too narrow a portrayal of constitutional judgment. The idea that judicial answers are necessarily correct implies judicial infallibility, which has no basis in human and historical experience. Moreover, it suggests that constitutional conflicts can be resolved by a search for a singular correct answer, when in fact they may be amenable to a range of reasonable answers. For this reason, a polity may be doing itself a disservice by giving so much responsibility to courts to determine reasonable answers to legislative conflicts. My argument rests not on distrust of the judiciary or discomfort with the idea that judges may come to a resolution of various interests and rights different from that of Parliament. Rather, it is based on the concern that excessive reliance on judicial wisdom could result in Parliament reneging on its responsibility to make principled political decisions.

Despite the centrality of Charter concerns to the development of a DNA legislative regime, this issue proved a poor example of the Charter's salutary potential to improve the quality of political deliberation about the justification of state actions in light of the Charter's normative values. The initial bill, C-104, which established a statutory authorization for police to compel suspects to provide samples for DNA purposes, was rushed so quickly through Parliament that no opportunity existed for parliamentarians or non-governmental actors to assess it properly or raise questions. The second bill, C-3, occasioned little by the way of vigorous debate about the merits or justification of proposed and alternative measures.

Regardless of whatever personal or normative judgment one brings to bear on questions such as how much force police should be able to exert when compelling suspects to provide body samples for DNA analysis, whether samples should be obtained at the time of conviction rather than arrest, or how broad the retroactive dimension of legislation should be, the most troubling aspect of the debate was the lack of inclination to make a careful political judgment about the reconciliation of conflicting values or to argue policy positions on the basis of their merits. Those who are more concerned about law-enforcement needs may not have been persuaded even had the government explained its assumptions about privacy or security. But careful consideration of complex and controversial legislative initiatives is more likely to occur when the government defends its position on the basis of explained assumptions, values, and objectives instead of simply waiving a Charter flag with the hope that reverence for legal opinions will silence alternative perspectives.

By failing to engage Parliament in a normative debate about the merits of different policy options, and how Charter values should constrain uses of the state's coercive powers, the government has largely ceded this terrain to the judiciary. Since the Supreme Court is struggling with policy questions related to how it views issues relevant to a DNA regime, as well as its approach to remedies which will influence how the DNA scheme will ultimately be assessed, this would have been an optimum time for Parliament to offer careful and reasoned judgment about how it envisages the relative importance of the issues and what priority it attaches to them.

7 The Rules and Exemptions for Search Warrants

A year after the *Stillman* ruling, the Supreme Court handed down another decision, *R. v. Feeney*,[1] that again had significant implications for law enforcement. In May 1997 a 5–4 majority reversed itself on the validity of a common law rule that had allowed police, under certain conditions, to enter a home without a warrant to arrest a suspect. The court's decision in *Feeney* was controversial because the majority's treatment of the privacy rights of a suspected murderer resulted in an order for a new trial and the exclusion of vital evidence in relation to the brutal slaying of an elderly British Columbia man. But controversy went well beyond the actual outcome and focused on the implications of the court's decision to change the meaning of the Criminal Code and create a new requirement that police obtain a warrant to enter private dwellings for the purpose of making an arrest. This decision was touted as the most troubling Charter ruling yet from a law-enforcement perspective.[2] It immediately created uncertainty about how the police should conduct themselves in circumstances that compel immediate action – for example, can they lawfully enter a dwelling without a warrant in urgent situations such as those involving domestic violence?

Worried about the implication of the ruling, several provincial attorneys general applied to the court to suspend the effects of the decision for six months to allow for a transition period before the new warrant requirement would take effect. The federal government shared the provinces' concerns that the ruling would adversely affect law enforcement and decided to enact new legislation. Although the court agreed to suspend the effects of its new rule, the temporary reprieve proved to be insufficient. Substantial consultations with provincial officials and police representatives delayed the introduction of legislation. Also complicating a quick legislative response was the timing of the ruling, which overlapped with a federal election. Once Parliament was convened, and with a new minister of justice in place, the legislation was so hastily rushed through Parliament that some parliamentarians resented their limited opportunity to assess the bill and held lingering doubts about its constitutional validity.

This chapter will analyse the interplay of the Supreme Court's judgment creating a new warrant requirement and the legislative response. Charter concerns figured prominently in the design and political defence of the legislation. But, unlike the government's approach in developing a DNA data bank, risk-aversion was not a central focus. This is not surprising since the intent of enacting legislation was to change the thrust of the court's new warrant rule to address concerns that this rule would unduly hinder law enforcement. The government's position demonstrated confidence that Parliament had a legitimate role to play to alter the balance of conflicting Charter values and public interests struck by the Court.

The partisan tone of the debate was not as confrontational as in the case of the DNA data bank. One reason for this may have been the different contexts in which the legislative initiatives were introduced. Charter concerns in the DNA debate were directed primarily at anticipating what the court might say in the future, with the hypothetical circumstances providing more opportunity for divergent opinions. In contrast, the context for debate about Parliament's new warrant regime was how to respond to concerns associated with a specific judicial ruling. Parliamentary criticism was directed more towards the court than to the government, as some members responded negatively to the majority's decision to place a higher priority on protecting criminal suspects' privacy rights than on law and order. Reinforcing Parliament's frustration was the fact that the bench was so divided on this issue, that had one judge voted differently, no legislative changes would have been required.

THE SUPREME COURT DECISION IN *R V. FEENEY*

The case arose as a result of the police investigation of the 1991 beating to death of an eighty-five-year-old man in rural British Columbia. The amount of blood at the crime scene indicated that the murder had been carried out in an extremely violent fashion. A police officer visited a suspect's dwelling, following tips from local residents. After the officer announced himself, and upon hearing no response, he entered the dwelling, without a warrant, and with his gun drawn he woke the sleeping suspect by touching him on the leg. Upon seeing blood on the suspect's shirt, the officer arrested the suspect.

Majority Judgment

The 5–4 majority decision was written by Justice Sopinka with justices La Forest, Cory, Iacobucci, and Major concurring. The majority ruled that the search was unlawful.[3] Before the *Feeney* case, the common law allowed the police under certain conditions to enter a dwelling to arrest a suspect without a warrant. These conditions required that: the police officer has reasonable grounds to believe that the person sought is within the premises; proper announcement is made; the officer believes that reasonable grounds for the arrest exist; and reasonable and probable grounds for the arrest would exist in the opinion of a judge. In addition, police were required, except in exigent circumstances, to identify and give notice of their purpose for entry. They were expected to request admission but could force entry where admission was denied.[4]

The majority concluded that the police did not comply with the common law rule because the third and fourth conditions were not satisfied. At trial the arresting officer testified that, at the time of entering the suspect's trailer, he had reason to believe that the suspect was involved in the murder but did not have sufficient reason to make an arrest. This changed after he observed blood on the suspect's clothing. The majority concluded that this testimony demonstrated that the officer did not have reasonable grounds for making the arrest at the time of entering the dwelling.[5]

Having ruled that the police failed to satisfy the common law rule as it existed, the court could have stopped at this point and sent the case back for a new trial. But the majority went far beyond what was required to resolve the issue. It ruled that the common law rule was itself inconsistent with the Charter. Justice Sopinka indicated that the earlier acceptance of warrantless arrests was based on a balance between privacy and effective police protection. But, in his view, this rule is no long valid under the Charter, because it gives insufficient consideration to privacy.[6] The Charter necessarily changes the analysis. Now, the privacy interest to be free from intrusions into one's dwelling outweighs the interests of law enforcement. For this reason, the old common law rule is invalid and warrantless arrests in dwelling houses are prohibited.[7]

Continuing with its activist course, the majority decided to interpret the Criminal Code as including a new requirement that a warrant must be obtained before searching for a person in a private dwelling. This is the practical equivalent of the court legislating. As such, it is rare because it represents an action that is contrary to conventional understanding of the separation of legislative and judicial responsibilities.

In introducing this new warrant requirement, Justice Sopinka suggested that the sanctity of the family dwelling is sufficiently important that there ought to be no forcible entry into a private dwelling unless the entry is authorized by judicial authority.[8] Just as prior judicial authorization is required for searches, prior judicial authorization should be required for entry into a home for purposes of arrest. But, since Parliament had not provided for this in the Criminal Code, the court would establish this requirement.[9]

Stephen Coughlan characterizes the court's decision to create a warrant requirement as an unprecedented example of "reading in" a different meaning for legislation. In the past, the court has relied on this rare power to "read in" a statutory requirement as part of the remedy that is granted. This generally means that the court is giving new meaning to legislation, often to broaden its scope to make it consistent with the court's interpretation of a right. But in this case, the court used the "read" in power to restrict the scope of a right. The right restricted was the very one the court had just created – privacy from having police forcibly enter one's dwelling – which can now be infringed with a warrant.[10]

Coughlan offers an explanation for this unprecedented judicial action. The court was not prepared to approve of police being able to enter homes lawfully without a warrant. Yet, at the same time, the court was not prepared to elevate the new right of privacy – to be free from intrusion by police – to such an absolute level that one's home becomes an inviolable sanctuary that would impede law enforcement. Thus, some qualification to the privacy right is required. That qualification is a warrant. But since a warrant requirement did not exist, the majority decided to create one.[11]

As will be argued below, the court's unusual decision to create a warrant requirement, by changing the meaning of the Criminal Code, raised serious concerns about how it would effect criminal law enforcement. Coughlan is critical of this action and suggests that, if the court had been so troubled by the prospect of warrantless searches for a person in a dwelling, it could have simply ruled that the common law does not allow these kinds of searches. This would have given Parliament the option of determining how to respond to this new common law requirement, without having to deal with the effects of a judicially imposed change to the Criminal Code.[12]

Under this new *Feeney* warrant rule, if the police need to enter a private dwelling to make an arrest, they must first obtain a warrant. This warrant would be authorized only if police have reasonable grounds to make an arrest and if they have reasonable grounds to believe that the person will be found at the address named. From the majority's perspective, this rule is important to ensure that "invasive arrests without a basis of reasonable and probable grounds" will be prevented, rather than remedied after the fact.[13]

The majority ruling left uncertain what circumstances might justify an entry into a private dwelling if police lack a warrant. The majority recognized that, in cases of "hot pursuit," society's interest in effective law enforcement takes precedence over the privacy interest of a suspect.[14] Although the majority did not elaborate on what constitutes a hot pursuit, or whether other circumstances might justify entering a dwelling without a warrant, it disagreed with the minority's view that, as a general rule, exigent circumstances justify a warrantless entry.[15] It also disagreed with the minority's suggestion that the preservation of evidence in the *Feeney* case justified a warrantless entry.[16]

Minority Judgment

The minority opinion diverged substantially from the majority's – so much so that it is difficult to understand how judges on the same court, interpreting identical constitutional rules in the same circumstances, could be so conceptually at odds about the application of Charter principles.[17] The dissenting judgment, written by Justice L'Heureux-Dubé with justices Gonthier and McLachlin concurring,[18] ruled that the police had complied with the common law rule[19] and that the rule itself could be sustained under the Charter. In the view of the minority, the Charter has not fundamentally changed the balance between privacy and the need to enforce the law, particularly in the investigation of violent crimes.[20] These justices suggested that it is unrealistic to assume that the police can never lawfully enter private premises without first obtaining a warrant, because this requirement "would severely impede the ability of police to capture persons suspected of criminal activity and to preserve evidence necessary to convict them."[21] Moreover, even if the minority thought that the search was inconsistent with the Charter, it believed that the police were authorized to enter the dwelling without a warrant because of the presence of exigent circumstances.[22] The minority rejected the idea that only circumstances of hot pursuit should permit the police to enter a dwelling without a warrant to arrest a suspect. The minority did not define, conclusively, the other circumstances what would be, but it indicated that the circumstances in this case qualified – the police had a "genuine fear that evidence of the crime will be lost."[23] In addition, a warrant was not required because of the extremely violent nature of the crime and the obligation to find out who the offender was as soon as possible.[24]

Following the majority's ruling, Feeney was granted a new trial, convicted of second-degree murder,[25] and in February 1999 was sentenced to life imprisonment.[26]

THE POLITICAL RESPONSE
TO COURT'S RULING

The decision took the federal government by surprise.[27] The Department of Justice had not expected the court to rule that the existing common law rule was unconstitutional or to read into the Criminal Code a new requirement to obtain a warrant before entering private dwellings for purposes of arrest. One reason for this surprise, apart from the unexpected degree of judicial activism, was that the court did not notify federal or provincial attorneys general of the pending constitutional change. The relevant rule for notification is Rule 32 of the *Rules of the Supreme Court of Canada*. This requires that, when a party raises a question of the constitutionality of a statute of Parliament or of a provincial legislature, notice must be provided to the attorney general of Canada and the attorneys general of the provinces. On receiving this notice, the attorneys general are permitted to intervene in the hearing. The court, however, does not have a similar obligation to notify the attorneys general when a party raises the constitutional validity of a common law rule – even if that party is the court itself. Thus, the court provided no notification that it would be changing a common law rule that would affect law-enforcement procedures.

A reason for alerting attorneys general when legislation is being challenged under the Charter is that Parliament or the provincial legislatures have an obvious interest when legislation may be nullified. This interest entitles them to make arguments and provide perspectives for the court to consider before rendering judgment. But the *Rules of the Supreme Court* implicitly assume that Parliament lacks sufficient interest in changes to common law rules to justify notifying the relevant attorneys general. This assumption is also reflected in judicial attitudes about the role of Parliament with respect to common law rules. Elsewhere, the court has suggested that the judiciary is the guardian of the justice system,[28] and since judges make the common law, deference is not owed to Parliament when changes to the common law are made in light of Charter values. This is because judges are simply changing the rules that they have made.[29] Implicit in this view is that, since Parliament did not make the law, changes to it should not be construed as having a significant effect on legislative priorities.

But this perspective gives insufficient consideration to Parliament's responsibility to legislate in the public interest. Parliament may not actively change a common law rule precisely because it supports the assumptions and values that underlie this rule. Parliamentary inaction does not mean lack of interest or concern about how legal rules affect particular social policies. The federal Parliament has jurisdiction over criminal law and has a legitimate interest in changes to common law rules, regardless of whether it has provided input into their original creation. In taking the unusual step in *R. v. Feeney* to read a new warrant requirement into the Criminal Code, the court's lack of notification meant that provincial and federal attorneys general were not given an opportunity to explain their views about the significance of this change, its constitutional propriety, or its implications for law enforcement. Furthermore, the majority's conclusion that the existing common law rule could not be sustained under the Charter did not involve any section 1 considerations. Once again, attorneys general may have had relevant arguments to make – in this context, on the reasonableness of the existing rule.

It is not clear that the majority fully comprehended the significance of its decision to change the Criminal Code to introduce a warrant requirement for searches in private dwellings. The court's new rule that police obtain a warrant for arrest, prior to entering a private dwelling, presented special difficulties for four provinces. New Brunswick, Quebec, Manitoba, and British Columbia each require that a crown prosecutor approve the charges the police propose to lay before an arrest warrant is sought. The process of prosecutorial vetting, when juxtaposed with the court's new warrant requirement, would result in delays in obtaining warrants and undermine the flexibility required by the police to make quick decisions to conduct searches where appropriate.

Moreover, uncertainty about what constitutes a hot pursuit, or whether other circumstances may justify an entry without a warrant, placed the police in a difficult situation. For example, are police lawfully permitted to enter a dwelling, without a warrant, when investigating violent crimes such as spousal abuse? Uncertainty about the implications of the court's ruling underscored a need for clear guidance on when, and under what conditions, police can enter private homes without a warrant, particularly in cases where danger is imminent and would be compounded by delay.

Immediately following the ruling, provincial and federal authorities responded with a varying range of temporary measures to permit police forces to continue performing their duties when searches of dwellings were involved. Different provinces and police officers also adopted "markedly varied positions" as to how the decision affected their powers to search.[30] Discussions between the federal and a number of provincial attorneys general revealed significant concerns about the precise implications of the new warrant rule.[31]

On 27 June 1997 the court, perhaps surprised by the scope of governmental concerns about the implications of its judgment, granted a rehearing to consider whether to allow a transition period before the requirement for a warrant was to take effect. British Columbia, which had standing in this case, asked the court to suspend the effects of the judgment for six months. The federal attorney general joined this action and was supported by Alberta, Quebec, and Ontario. In response, the Supreme Court granted a six-month transition period and delayed the requirement for a warrant to make an arrest in a dwelling from the date the judgment was issued. The judicial reprieve would expire on 27 November 1997. In the meantime, the previous common law rule continued to operate.

The federal government was not prepared to accept the implications of the *Feeney* rule. But the six-month judicial reprieve was not sufficient for Parliament to respond to the *Feeney* ruling. The introduction of legislation was delayed because of an accident of timing. At the time the decision was rendered, 22 May 1997, the federal Parliament had been dissolved. A federal election was held on 2 June and Anne McLellan was sworn in as justice minister on 11 June 1997. In mid-June the Department of Justice began consulting with provincial and territorial governments and police and legal organizations. The scope of these consultations delayed the introduction of legislation.

Although Parliament could have allowed the court's new warrant requirement to remain in effect, the government believed that legislation was necessary to clarify the rules for obtaining a warrant, in light of a lack of consensus in different jurisdictions on how to interpret the court's ruling.[32] The government was worried that, in the absence of clarification, police officials would be uncertain about the appropriate rules for conducting searches in private dwellings. This was an untenable situation. Police uncertainty might lead to decisions that resulted in evidence being excluded at trial. Alternatively, police might hesitate to enter dwellings even in circumstances where lives were at risk.[33] Legislation was also required to introduce flexibility in the warrant scheme, to accommodate different provincial approaches for issuing warrants.

Legislation (Bill C-16) was introduced on 30 October 1997. When it became obvious that Parliament would not be able to pass legislation before the lapse of the six-month suspension, a further extension was sought. On 19 November 1997 the Supreme Court granted an additional one-month reprieve (or, alternatively, until the date that the legislation received royal assent if this occurred before the one-month extension). The legislation was given third reading in the House of Commons and was passed, on 17 December 1997. It received royal assent the following day, with one day to spare before the second reprieve expired.

BILL C-16: ESTABLISHING A NEW ENTRY WARRANT REGIME

The majority ruling in *Feeney*, that the Charter changes the balance between privacy and law-enforcement concerns, along with relevant common law rules, presented Parliament with a number of principles to consider in its legislative response. These principles were: an individual's right to privacy in his or her dwelling outweighs society's interest in effective police protection; prior authorization is necessary before police can validly enter a dwelling to arrest a person; to obtain a warrant, police must have reasonable and probable grounds to arrest a suspect and believe that the suspect sought is within the premises in question; an exemption to this requirement for a warrant to arrest an individual in his or her dwelling are exigent circumstances such as a hot pursuit; and authorities are required to make a proper announcement before forcibly entering a dwelling.

Bill C-16 amends the Criminal Code to address the *Feeney* ruling. But Parliament's response was not a straightforward codification of the above judicial principles. A significant difference between the legislation and the majority *Feeney* ruling is the broad exemptions the legislation allows for entries without a warrant. The legislation alters the thrust of the majority's new rule by authorizing police to enter a private dwelling without a warrant in circumstances other than hot pursuit. It authorizes a warrantless entry if police "suspect that entry into the dwelling-house is necessary." Justice Minister McLellan acknowledged that suspicion involves a lower standard than that suggested by the court, but she indicated her belief that this standard was justified to prevent imminent bodily harm or death.[34]

The legislative response reflects Parliament's unequivocal view that circumstances, other than hot pursuit, may justify the police to enter a private dwelling even if a warrant has not been obtained. In this aspect, the legislation is much closer to the minority view in *Feeney*. It allows police to enter a private dwelling without a warrant where obtaining a warrant would not be practical for reason of "exigent circumstances." The legislation, intentionally, does not provide an exhaustive definition of these circumstances. Rather, it suggests two specific conditions that justify police entering a dwelling without a warrant, while also making it clear that these conditions do not exhaust the exemptions for requiring a warrant. The specific exemptions are where a police officer

- has reasonable grounds to suspect that entry into the dwelling-house is necessary to prevent imminent bodily harm or death to any person; or
- has reasonable grounds to believe that entry is necessary to prevent the imminent loss or destruction of evidence.

McLellan explained that the first exemption for a warrant is necessary to respond to situations of domestic violence, because police should not be unduly hampered in their ability to protect victims.[35] It is difficult to imagine that this exemption for a warrant would trouble the judiciary. But it is not clear how the Supreme Court will view the second exemption. The majority was not at all sympathetic to the minority position that the need to preserve evidence (at least in this context of the *Feeney* case) justified entering the suspect's dwelling without a warrant. Another difference between the legislation and the majority ruling is that the legislation dispenses with the judicial rule that police officers announce their presence before entering a dwelling, in circumstances where this announcement would expose them or others to harm or would result in the loss of evidence.

One of the most important differences between the legislation and the majority's new *Feeney* rule is the kind of warrant authorized. The majority ruled that, prior to an arrest in a private dwelling, the police must first obtain judicial authorization for the arrest and obtain a warrant to enter the dwelling house for the purpose of arrest.[36] The majority had indicated that the reason for requiring a warrant for arrest, rather than simply a warrant for entry, was to protect against unauthorized intrusions into a person's private dwelling.[37] Its intent was to prevent such unauthorized entries rather than to rely on judicial remedies to redress breaches of privacy, after the fact.

Practical concerns explain why the government chose not to replicate the court's rule. Under the legislation, there is no requirement that a person be charged before police obtain the warrant to enter a private dwelling. Instead, the legislation allows police to obtain a warrant to enter a dwelling house. Once inside, they can then rely on the power that is already provided in the Criminal Code (section 495) to arrest the person without a warrant.[38] This approach was taken because its flexibility accommodates different provincial procedures for issuing warrants. The court's rule – that police first obtain a warrant for the person's arrest, before obtaining authorization to enter the dwelling – would have caused difficulty for those provinces that require approval from a crown prosecutor to vet the allegations before an individual can be charged. It would have meant that, before police could enter, an arrest warrant would have to be obtained and a suspect would have to be charged with a crime. But the necessary scrutiny by the crown prosecutor before criminal charges could be laid would have delayed obtaining a warrant. Such delays would be especially worrisome in those circumstances that necessitate immediate action. McLellan suggested that the majority's approach would be "particularly problematic" for police work and indicated that divergence from the majority's rule was necessary to reconcile an expectation to privacy with the needs of law enforcement: "[If police want to arrest someone in a dwelling but must first obtain a warrant for their arrest] this would mean that the police would have to formally charge the person before obtaining an authorization to enter. It is my opinion that such a requirement would end up unduly hampering the work of the police and be particularly problematic in the provinces of New Brunswick, Quebec and British Columbia, where the crown must approve the charges the police propose to lay before an arrest warrant is sought."[39]

A Justice lawyer has suggested that, once the police have obtained an authorization to enter the premises, they need not make an arrest if they find out they were mistaken in their belief that the suspect had committed the alleged crime.[40] What is uncertain is whether the standard for obtaining a warrant to enter a dwelling is high enough to satisfy the court, particularly if the legislation has this effect of allowing police to decide if they have the right person to arrest once they are inside the dwelling. Defence lawyers have expressed doubts about whether the decision not to require a warrant for arrest prior to entry is consistent with the majority's ruling.[41]

As is increasingly becoming the case when Parliament enacts legislation that is likely to be challenged under the Charter, the legislation includes a preamble to explain Parliament's concerns and the assumptions that have influenced the legislation. In this particular legislation, McLellan indicated that the preamble was important so that Parliament could convey its belief that the legislation should not "restrict development of the common law with regard to exigent circumstances" or "limit police powers of entry for purposes other than arrest or apprehension."[42]

PUBLIC AND POLITICAL SCRUTINY

The tight time-frame for legislative development left Parliament little opportunity to study the bill. Nevertheless, the government was determined to pass the legislation before the suspension of the court's judgment expired, because of concern for how law enforcement would be affected if the law were to revert to the *Feeney* rule. As McLellan informed the Senate committee studying the bill:

[I]t is imperative that Parliament pass[es] Bill C-16 before December 19 of this year. To begin with, should Parliament fail to pass Bill C-16 by December 19, we return to the state of affairs as it existed immediately after the Feeney decision. It was clear in the aftermath of the Feeney decision that there is no consensus among the jurisdictions as to how the police should obtain the constitutionally required entry warrants. A return to such legal inconsistency and lack of clarity would bring the administration of justice into disrepute.

Without clear guidelines and without the backing of a law passed by Parliament, law enforcement agents, on the one hand, run the risk of creating solutions to the warrant requirement in Feeney which are themselves unconstitutional. This in turn could result in substantial acquittals on the basis that the police violated the Charter rights of the accused.

On the other hand, fear of misinterpreting Feeney may cause police to cease all entries into dwellings to arrest.[43]

Both the House of Commons and the Senate heeded the government's concern to pass the legislation within the allotted time to avoid reverting to the *Feeney* ruling. Nevertheless, in both chambers, parliamentarians expressed considerable resentment that they had insufficient time to scrutinize the legislation properly.

Scrutiny by Committee

The House of Commons Standing Committee on Justice and Legal Affairs Committee formally indicated its lack of satisfaction with the time allowed for its role in the legislative process in its report to Parliament. In that report, the committee stated:

The Department of Justice, caught by surprise by the result in *Feeney*, conducted, from a standing start, an accelerated consultation, policy development, legislative drafting process which seemed to satisfy those involved in it. This Committee, however, is not satisfied by the time allowed for its role in the legislative process. The Committee had only several days to receive, absorb and analyze the issues dealt with in Bill C-16. The process allowed only a short time for the Committee to invite and consider submissions from witnesses. Those who appeared before us did so under severe time constraints and, even so, were of great help to us in our role as lawmakers. The accelerated timeframe, however, did not allow the Committee to benefit fully from all the detailed submissions it would have liked to consider on the complex issues dealt with in *R. v. Feeney* and in Bill C-16 itself.[44]

Some parliamentarians expressed concern that, because of insufficient opportunity to hear from more witnesses or make substantial amendments, the legislation might pass with serious Charter concerns left unaddressed. One Reform member expressed doubt about whether the authorization for a warrantless search to prevent the destruction of evidence was consistent with the court's ruling and was frustrated by the lack of opportunity for the committee to hear from more witnesses,[45] particularly about Charter concerns.

[This bill] has consequences as far-reaching as those of any bill that I have ever voted for since I've been a member of the House ... [W]e have a mess on our hands and we're dumping it on the front-line police officers.

I don't think we have properly addressed the problem created by the Supreme Court of Canada's decision on the Feeney case ... I don't know whether the justice department had sufficient time or whether they were running up against a deadline that encompassed us as well, but I'm not satisfied with this bill. We'll be supporting the bill, but it's not going to answer the problem that the Supreme Court of Canada's decision on the Feeney case has created.[46]

Another member also worried about whether, because of haste, Parliament was unknowingly passing legislation that might have lingering constitutional problems: "I have grave concerns about putting through a bill basically at the gunpoint of the Supreme Court, and doing so in such a way that it may be flawed. Are we to hurry this bill through and have the same thing happen at some court level in this country, where again there is an interpretation put on a search, where evidence is excluded, and we wind up having to go through this process again? We should be very concerned about doing it right the first time."[47]

The committee recognized the irony of the situation – that, by agreeing to an unnecessarily expedited procedure, it was contributing to the "alarming emasculation of Parliament as an institution."[48] One government member suggested that the government should signal to the Supreme Court and to the Justice Department just how much time Parliament needs to deal with new legislation, particularly where Charter issues arise. He called for the establishment of a protocol to address circumstances where the court imposes a time-frame for Parliament to respond to a negative ruling. He was particularly upset that a ruling that might necessitate Parliament's response was handed down without consideration for the fact that Parliament was not sitting. To

prevent a reoccurrence, a process should be in place to exempt temporarily the application of a court's decision, perhaps by a short-term
application of the notwithstanding clause:

I'm sure the Supreme Court didn't plan it, but it's most unfair to say this is a
job for Parliament at a time when Parliament is dissolved and it didn't have any
real prospect of coming back for three, four or five months.

I think our government should develop a protocol for that purpose ... Hopefully, Parliament would adopt the protocol and say if this ever happens again,
this is the procedure we want to use. It's like a temporary mini notwithstanding
kind of protocol.[49]

The committee also recommended that the minister of justice consult with provincial and territorial counterparts and establish a requirement that formal notice be given to attorneys general where changes
are being contemplated for common law rules, so that they can decide
whether or not to seek intervenor status. It also recommended that, in
cases of "major public importance," the Supreme Court stay execution
of its judgments for determinate periods of time to allow for legislative
redress. The committee requested that the government provide a comprehensive response to its report in accordance with standing order
109.[50] In its reply to the committee, the government argued that judicial independence prevented it from changing Rule 32 of the *Rules of
the Supreme Court of Canada* so as to include a requirement that attorneys generals be notified when common law rules might be found
inconsistent with the Charter.[51]

CONCLUSIONS

As argued in chapter 3, a salutary benefit of a relational approach to
Charter judgment is that it can improve the quality of scrutiny that is
brought to bear on uses of state power that affect rights. Flowing from
this is the idea that judgment about the Charter is fluid – that no single
institution has the only valid perspective or insight into questions
about the justification of state actions. Implicit here is the need for
critical reflection upon the merits of contrary judgments. However,
this ideal was not met in the development of a warrant regime for
entering homes for criminal investigations.

No opportunity existed for the government to apprise the Supreme
Court of its perspective on the question of whether and how the com-
mon law rule must change or on the court's decision to read into the
Criminal Code a warrant requirement. The notification rule did not

encompass these situations, likely because it was premised on the faulty assumption that Parliament does not have a valid interest in changes to common law rules. The court's decision to introduce a warrant requirement in the Criminal Code cannot, under any circumstances, be claimed to be an issue on which Parliament is a disinterested and non-legitimate party.

The nature and degree of the court's activism also diminished the salutary benefits of inter-institutional scrutiny of whether legislation appropriately reflects Charter values. The majority went beyond what was required to indicate its concern that, under the Charter, the common law can no longer allow the police to enter private dwellings without prior authorization. The court could simply have ruled that the common law does not allow for warrantless searches, without having taken the additional step of judicially legislating. Parliament and courts have distinct responsibilities and different qualities that affect their contribution to the resolution of constitutional conflicts. The role of courts is not, and never has been, to legislate. Focusing only on abstract principles can have serious and unintended consequences when applied to specific circumstances. This problem was demonstrated by the confusion and uncertainty that arose from the Supreme Court's failure to anticipate how its new warrant requirement would affect law enforcement in exigent circumstances or what its effects on law enforcement would be in provinces that have different procedures for granting warrants.

The government's response to the Charter with respect to issuing warrants was not as risk-averse as in the case of the DNA data bank regime. This is not to suggest that Charter concerns were not central to the legislative approach. However, the government decided that the need for a more flexible approach for issuing warrants, because of the different procedures used in some provinces, justified legislation that was considerably different from the rule created by the court. Parliament supported this position. The legislative approach was influenced by the expectation that, if it was explained in a preamble (and in future legal arguments), the court would exercise some degree of deference towards Parliament's judgment. This willingness to develop a warrant regime that differs from the court's revised rule suggests that Parliament does not accept a judicial-centric view of constitutional judgment. Its awareness that it has a legitimate role to play when rendering Charter judgments, even where these may differ from the court's approach, was reinforced by Parliament's criticism of rules that do not require the court to notify attorneys general when the Charter might lead to a reinterpretation of a common law rule. The recommendation of the House of Commons committee that the federal government develop a protocol to overcome potential problems that arise from rulings that change common law rules reflected Parliament's assumption that it should have the opportunity to reflect upon how Charter values should be accommodated in legislation, and not simply placed in the position of having to accept, without change, new judicially imposed rules.

Yet serious time constraints under which the legislation was developed compromised Parliament's ability to reach reasoned judgment. Governments and courts need to develop mutually acceptable guidelines and assumptions about the transition period for legislative responses to judicial Charter rulings. Six months can be harrowing for a parliamentary response under optimal conditions. But when Parliament is not even sitting, it is almost impossible to expect that Parliament can reach a careful judgment on a complex and important social policy within such a short period.

8 Equality Claims of Lesbians and Gay Men

The visibility of sexual politics has increased substantially over the past twenty years "beyond the wildest imaginings of activists caught up in the surge of liberationist politics" of the late 1960s.[1] Nevertheless, for those who encounter harassment arising from their sexual orientation, and endure discrimination in forms that heterosexual Canadians have neither experienced nor probably can fully comprehend, the pace of legislative change may seem painfully slow. Lesbians and gay men encounter continual reminders of the significance of their sexual orientation in a culture that considers heterosexuality the norm, favours relationships that comply with this norm, and treats those who differ from it in various disparaging ways.

The federal government's decision in 1969 to implement Pierre Trudeau's famous declaration that the state has no business in the bedrooms of the nation resulted in the liberalization of laws on divorce, birth control, and abortion and in the decriminalization of homosexual activity. But it would take more than two decades before the legislative agendas of provincial and federal governments would acknowledge, let alone begin to redress, the various dimensions of legal discrimination endured by lesbians and gay men.

In 1971 lesbian and gay activists made a number of demands for legislative changes that are said to have launched a decade of gay militancy in Canada. Assessments by interested observers reveal a lengthy, bitter, and not entirely successful campaign to address demands and remedy grievances.[2] Lesbian and gay activists in Canada had little reason to look either to the judiciary or to representative institutions as allies in their causes. Courts routinely upheld legislative denials of social benefits by utilizing exclusively heterosexual definitions of family or marriage. Alternatively, courts ruled that, in the absence of a statutory basis to support lesbian and gay claims of entitlement, judges were not empowered to assess the merits or fairness of legislative distinctions that denied benefits and recognition to those in same-sex relationships.[3] At the same time, the pattern of political behaviour was steadfast refusal to acknowledge or redress claims that discrimination occurs not only from blatant prejudicial treatment of lesbians and gay men but also from the exclusive recognition of heterosexual relationships in social policies, because this norm influences the statutory recognition of spouses, families, benefits, and responsibilities. Legislation was not the only cause of unfair treatment of lesbians and gay men. Employers and landlords could discriminate against them with relative impunity. Judicial relief would not be forthcoming as long as courts or tribunals rejected claims that differential treatment was discriminatory on the grounds that human rights codes did not identify sexual orientation as a prohibited ground of discrimination and that legislation did not conceive of lesbians and gay men as constituting families or spouses.

The gay-liberation movement has invoked a variety of methods in its quest for social and legal reforms. But the use of rights claiming in legal challenges to legislation has become a significant element of reform strategies since the adoption of the Canadian Charter of Rights and Freedoms.[4] The Charter encourages this strategy of rights claiming and provides a new strategic site to redress inequality. The greater visibility of rights claiming, arising from the constitutional lens through which these claims are now viewed, fosters broad challenges to the justification of social-policy choices. Lesbians and gay men argue, with different theoretical and policy emphases, that reliance on heterosexuality, as the foundation for social and legal policies, is discriminatory. To base criteria of eligibility and recognition on heterosexual status affects the scope of entitlements for social benefits and excludes those who do not conform to this norm. Denying benefits and status for some relationships for no other reason than individuals' sexuality undermines the basic dignity and humanity of those adversely affected.

Yet arguments that substantive legislative changes are required to redress sexual discrimination in legislation and in legal assumptions are repudiated by many who are convinced that the moral and social norms for Canadian society are, and should remain, the heterosexual family unit. The dominance of this paradigm has been established through centuries of moral claims, supported and reinforced through overlapping cultural, religious, political, legal, and media messages. Many are not prepared to question or reject what they consider their foundational moral beliefs, or accept that this paradigm manifests itself in unfair and unjust treatment for lesbians and gay men.

This chapter focuses on the intersection of judicial rulings on lesbian and gay Charter claims and legislative reforms. Judicial Charter decisions have been extremely important in advancing the policy objectives of lesbian and gay groups. Although not all jurisdictions have complied with the anti-discrimination principles set out in the handful of landmark Supreme Court rulings on lesbian and gay equality claims, a majority of governments have now passed comprehensive legislative reforms that remove policy distinctions which denied benefits and recognition to those in same-sex relationships. The chapter begins with a discussion of debates within the relevant communities regarding the prudence of relying on a rights tradition historically intolerant and insensitive towards the claims of lesbians and gay men. Then, early political debates about the scope of equality and its application to questions of discrimination against lesbians and gay men are examined. Following this, the nexus between judicial Charter decisions and legislative reforms at the federal and provincial levels of government is analysed. The jurisdictions examined are those that have introduced substantive reforms and one other, Alberta, which has indicated strong resistance. The chapter concludes with an examination of the question of marriage, which is the most contentious issue yet to be resolved with respect to the scope of lesbian and gay equality.

LESBIAN AND GAY STRATEGIES TO REDRESS DISCRIMINATION

Lesbian and gay activists did not initially see the Charter as a likely tool for their liberation, and some still doubt the prudence of relying on a legal rights tradition that previously had not questioned the legitimacy of discriminatory treatment of lesbians and gay men. A range of views arise around questions such as whether rights litigation represents a useful strategy to attain social and legal changes or what the most appropriate and inclusive ways are for the law to conceptualize lesbian and gay identities, aspirations, and relationships.

Theoretical misgivings about how the law interprets and defines policy reforms relevant to lesbians and gay men, along with the tenuous promise of judicial decisions that are so dependent upon the philosophical assumptions of judges, explain why some lesbians and gay men view rights not as ends in themselves. Rather, rights are seen in strategic terms as tools used to promote social reform.[5] Yet many consider the strategic use of rights for social change fraught with perils.

Miriam Smith, who has examined the lesbian and gay reform move-ment in Canada, demonstrates how litigation under the Charter has influenced and changed political strategy. While equality seeking has remained constant, the nature of how equality is pursued has changed. Whereas once the strategy involved the deployment of rights claims as part of a broader political project of building the lib-eration movement and its organizations, it now has the pursuit of le-gal change as the overriding goal.[6] But this pursuit of legal change is occurring within the context of a liberal framework and some worry about the influence this will have on what kinds of reforms are pursued and their implications for lesbians and gay men.

Appeals to equality, with its liberal emphasis on treating everyone the same, may hold hope for some claims of recognition and provide remedies for blatant forms of legal discrimination. But a serious con-cern many have is with the alleged "neutral" norm against which differences are assessed. Questioned in particular is the desirability of appealing to the ideal of treating everyone the same when that "same" is actually premised on a heterosexual norm. Hegemonic as-sumptions in social policy and in law that families, spouses, and mar-riage are heterosexual underlie doubts about whether rights claiming can overcome discrimination against lesbians and gay men.

A particular concern with the liberal rights paradigm is associated with the tendency of courts and society to view lesbian and gay issues from the perspective of minority rights. Some believe that this per-spective will undermine more substantive reform efforts. Lesbians and gay men who neither desire nor are in relationships that are analo-gous to traditional heterosexual relationships worry that reliance on a liberal (and essentially heterosexual) paradigm of equality will dis-courage attempts to make claims for social and legal acceptance of al-ternative lesbian and gay identities.[7] Didi Herman believes that a minority-framework model, which portrays lesbians or gay men as a special category or class of people in need of protection against dis-crimination, occurs at the expense of examining the assumptions that underlie dominant social relations and that perpetuate and sustain discrimination.[8] As a result, the perceived normality and implied su-periority of heterosexuality remain unquestioned.[9] "Representing les-bians and gay men as an immutable minority may restrict rather than broaden social understandings of sexuality. Lesbians and gay men are granted legitimacy, not on the basis that there might be something problematic with gender roles and sexual hierarchies, but on the basis that they constitute a fixed group of 'others' who need and deserve protection. Arguably, then, human rights frameworks thus regulate new identities in ways that contain their challenge to dominant social relations."[10]

A different concern with the minority paradigm arises from treating lesbians and gay men as a homogenous group, identified in terms of their common characteristic of sexual orientation. Although sexual orientation is presented in terms of gender neutrality, some believe that a gay male standard is promoted. Lesbians and gay men may both experience oppression arising from the "social and political structures of sex and gender," but some argue that lesbians experience inequality in different ways than gay men.[11]

Concern about the implications of appealing to a liberal norm of sameness, which many believe is premised on heterosexuality, is compounded by criticism of the patriarchal nature of heterosexual relationships. Many feminist scholars portray the family as the institutionalization of patriarchal relations with male domination of women in sexual, reproductive, and labour spheres[12] and question the prudence of replicating a family paradigm for lesbian relationships.[13] Shelley Gavigan views the family as offering few advantages for lesbian relationships because she considers the family as an ideological construct that produces and sustains the subordination, poverty, and violence of women. She expresses doubts about whether the social and legal concept of spouse can be removed from its heterosexual familial context and applied in a non-problematic way to a lesbian context.[14] Similarly, Herman warns that, by appropriating familial ideology, lesbians and gay men may be supporting the very institutional structures that have created and now sustain women's oppression.[15]

Scepticism about the prudence of arguing that same-sex partners should be considered spouses, or that same-sex relationships should be considered analogous to heterosexual family relationships, is predicated on the assumption that, but for their adaptation to same-sex partners, these social concepts have otherwise fixed attributes (built upon a sexual hierarchy that subordinates women). Scepticism is also predicated on the expectation that, if those in same-sex relationships replicate these social concepts, same-sex partners will be the unfortunate recipients of relationships that generate and sustain inequality.

But not all are troubled about the implications of adapting formerly heterosexual notions of family or spouse to lesbian and gay relationships. Many are optimistic about the promise of a liberal-rights paradigm. They are hopeful that recourse to rights claiming under the Charter will expose the extent to which the family unit, as traditionally perceived in social policies, is based on a heterosexual norm. This exposure is part of the political project of arguing that, if social policies do not accommodate differences, they are discriminatory. The very act of questioning the definition of spouse or family represents a profound shake-up of institutional and societal assumptions about relationships. Rights claiming, in this context, raises new questions about what is family and what are the appropriate criteria for recognizing familial relationships and conferring benefits and recognition. These questions are more likely to challenge than to reinforce existing assumptions. It is this reform potential, in fact, that underlies so many opponents' criticism of Charter-inspired policy changes. These changes are criticized precisely because they threaten the traditional understanding of family.

The reform potential of the Charter explains the enthusiasm of many lesbians and gay men who measure the Charter's benefits in terms of its dynamic role of encouraging, compelling, and giving legitimacy to social-policy changes. The Charter is seen as a new venue to pursue social-policy reforms. The rights framework it provides does more than attach legitimacy to rights claiming. The Charter changes political and social discourse and offers new opportunities to challenge political and societal norms in the privileged and respected language of rights. Many are hopeful that courts will use their powers to grant remedies to Charter violations to force representative institutions to redress the discriminatory features of social policies that have excluded lesbians and gay men from their scope. Thus, many reject the idea that the reliance on rights hinders progress. For example, Kathleen Lahey is optimistic about the Charter's reform potential. She acknowledges that there will be serious bumps along the way, particularly from judicial decisions that honour the traditional family as a justification for continued discrimination against lesbians and gay men or that confer legitimacy on incremental legislative reforms.[16] Nevertheless, she concludes that Charter equality jurisprudence can lead to significant policy reforms. This is particularly important in a federal state like Canada because, without the Charter's unifying influence, lesbians and gay men would be forced to address discrimination in the various existing human-rights codes. Furthermore, unlike an appeal to human rights legislation, Charter litigation can more effectively produce broad policy rules that apply beyond the immediate party in litigation.[17]

EARLY POLITICAL RESPONSES TO EQUALITY DEBATE

At the time of debate about the Charter, there was little political support for the propositions that legislative policies, which are based on heterosexual concepts of family, spouse, or marriage, discriminate against lesbians and gay men and that equality imposes a moral obligation on governments to redress systemic discrimination. Quebec was the only province to prohibit discrimination on the basis of sexual orientation in its human rights legislation.[18] As will be discussed later, almost two decades would pass before the federal government and most other provincial governments introduced similar protection in their human rights legislation.

When the Charter was first drafted, it was extremely difficult to anticipate how it would affect judicial rulings on lesbian and gay rights claims or to predict whether judicial decisions would have an influence on the political will to introduce legislative reforms. The equality rights in the Charter do not specifically mention sexual orientation as a prohibited ground of discrimination. The political leaders responsible for the creation of the Charter were not prepared to include this specific protection for lesbians and gay men. Section 15 (1) of the Charter provides: "Every individual is equal before and under the law and has the right to the equal protection and equal benefit of the law without discrimination and, in particular, without discrimination based on race, national or ethnic origin, colour, religion, sex, age, or mental or physical disability."

Then Justice Minister Jean Chrétien gave two reasons for not including sexual orientation in the Charter. First, the grounds in the proposed clause were already recognized by society and therefore were capable of "more ready definition" than other proposals. Second, it was preferable to have an open-ended wording than to add some new categories while excluding others.[19] Chrétien indicated that it would be up to the courts to determine whether other prohibited grounds of discrimination, such as sexual orientation, were also included.[20] Both explanations suggest indifference and lack of political commitment to the idea of extending the scope of equality to protect lesbians and gay men from discrimination. But they do not suggest outright opposition. The federal Liberal government was willing to rely on judicial discretion to decide whether the Charter's equality provision would be interpreted in a manner that proscribes discrimination on the basis of sexual orientation.[21]

As will be shown later, the tendency of political actors to wait for judicial rulings before acknowledging that the Charter's principles do or should prohibit discrimination on the basis of sexual orientation has become a pattern of political behaviour. The Charter's section 15 equality rights were delayed from coming into force for a period of three years. The delay was intended to give both federal and provincial governments the opportunity to revise legislation so as to make it compliant with the Charter. Federal and provincial departments of justice and attorneys general conducted audits of legislation to identify serious Charter breaches. Most jurisdictions passed omnibus legislation to address obvious breaches of equality rights. Notably, however, these amendments did not address discrimination on the basis of sexual orientation. Political resistance to recognize lesbian and gay rights and to redress discrimination in legislation led to a "wait and see what the courts say" attitude. Some lawyers involved in the auditing process acknowledge that the exclusion of discrimination on the basis of sexual orientation from the scope of provincial audits was not inadvertent. Rather, it resulted from an unwritten policy that was influenced by uncertainty about how Charter jurisprudence around sexual orientation would evolve and by political and bureaucratic reluctance to delve "unnecessarily" into such a controversial issue.[22]

Governments in most jurisdictions have shown little inclination to introduce legislative reforms until judicial rulings make it clear that the status quo cannot be constitutionally sustained. An early example of this reluctance arose in the 1985 discussion paper, *Equality Issues in Federal Law*, in which the federal Progressive Conservative government suggested that the Charter does not require a fundamental reassessment of the normative values in legislative priorities. It failed to acknowledge that federal legislation discriminated against lesbians and gay men and did not indicate whether the Charter should be interpreted to prevent this form of discrimination. For instance, the government did not discuss the merits of how lesbians and gay men were treated by the Canadian Armed Forces or the Royal Canadian Mounted Police, which both had policies stipulating that lesbians and gay men would not knowingly be recruited and would be dismissed upon discovery of their homosexuality.[23]

This discussion paper was assessed by a parliamentary subcommittee on equality rights, which issued a unanimous report recommending substantial changes to federal legislation and policies to redress discrimination against lesbians and gay men.[24] Its work has been characterized as exhibiting "uncharacteristic independence," which is attributed, in part, to freedom from party discipline arising from the very nature of its task – a broad policy inquiry as opposed to a review of specific legislation.[25] Yet the subcommittee's report appears to have had little immediate effect on convincing the government to redress discrimination against lesbians and gay men.

The government published its response in 1986 in another report, *Toward Equality*, which was tentative and non-committal in addressing the subcommittee's recommendations. The tone of this report indicated that the government viewed the Charter not as imposing new normative standards to which Canadian governments must adhere but as reflecting general principles that should be influenced and constrained by existing beliefs on contentious issues. For example, it did not indicate that discrimination against lesbians and gay men should be considered unlawful. Instead, it suggested that issues related to sexual orientation give rise to "social dilemmas" that cannot readily be reconciled.[26] The government acknowledged that courts would likely rule that sexual orientation is encompassed by the guarantees of section 15 of the Charter[27] but did not indicate whether or how legislative priorities would change if this were to occur.

Comments to the media by then Justice Minister John Crosbie suggested that the government had not ruled out policy changes. But Crosbie did not appreciate the extent of internal party dissent. More than half of the sitting Conservative MPs opposed the subcommittee's recommendations to redress discrimination on the basis of sexual orientation.[28] Thus, while Crosbie may have believed that the government's commitment would "naturally" entail legislation to amend the Canadian Human Rights Act (CHRA),[29] internal division would undermine reform efforts. Internal opposition also inhibited the government's willingness to convince the RCMP and armed forces to eliminate their anti-homosexual policies.[30] Several years later, the military agreed to abandon these policies, but the impetus came not from the federal government but from the judiciary.[31]

In 1986 Ontario became only the second province to amend its human rights code to include sexual orientation as a prohibited ground of discrimination,[32] nine years after the Ontario Human Rights Commission made this recommendation.[33] David Rayside attributes the success in passing this controversial amendment, which originated as an "innocuous piece of housekeeping," to an "unusual constellation of political factors, almost all of them beyond the control of the pro-gay lobby."[34] But more substantial legislative reforms to redress discrimination against lesbians and gay men would not be passed anywhere in the country for more than a decade after equality rights had first come into force.

JUDICIAL RULINGS AND NEW PRESSURE FOR LEGISLATIVE CHANGE

Despite legislative inaction, judicial rulings emerged from various jurisdictions which suggested that courts were reassessing the justification of traditional policy choices that denied benefits for same-sex partners. A steady stream of lower court and tribunal decisions confirmed the expectations of some drafters of the Charter that courts might interpret section 15 in a manner that includes protection from discrimination on the basis of sexual orientation. These decisions occurred several years before the Supreme Court first ruled on this issue.

Among other things, the lower courts ruled: the denial of medical coverage to same-sex partners is discriminatory and infringes upon equality;[35] the absence of sexual orientation as a prohibited ground in the *CHRA* violates equality;[36] and (a dissenting judgment) the restriction of marriage to heterosexual couples violates equality.[37]

These Charter decisions involving lesbian and gay rights claims, together with the Supreme Court decision that followed, indicate that a significant evolution is under way in terms of how the judiciary conceives of discrimination. Courts have moved well beyond an earlier pre-Charter period when judges tolerated exclusions from social benefits based on moral claims that homosexuality was deviant behaviour or when judges condoned legislative judgements that lesbians and gay men were not entitled to family-based social benefits or legal recognition of their relationships. Courts have begun to look more critically at the purposes and effects of legislative distinctions. This approach is manifesting itself in a re-evaluation of legal approaches to discrimination, with a new focus on respect for human dignity and acceptance of difference as foundations for equality. Judicial review of equality under the Charter has encouraged judges to reach beyond the restraints of earlier legal analysis rooted in formal and definitional claims of family or spouse. A nascent judicial culture increasingly is questioning the validity of the choices upon which exclusionary policy distinctions have been based, and challenging government arguments that traditional values are appropriate reasons for perpetuating discrimination or denying wide-ranging remedies.

Canada (AG) v. Mossop

The first Supreme Court ruling indicating that governments would likely have to redress discrimination against lesbians and gay men occurred in 1993. In this case, *Canada (AG) v. Mossop,*[38] the Supreme Court did not deal directly with the question of whether section 15 of the Charter protects against discrimination based on sexual orientation. Nevertheless, the court expressed its sympathy with this interpretation of section 15. The case arose after a federal public servant was denied bereavement leave to attend the funeral of his same-sex partner's father. The question before the Supreme Court was statutory rather than constitutional. It was whether denying same-sex partners the benefits given to heterosexual couples is consistent with the Canadian Human Rights Act. The majority ruled that it was inappropriate to interpret the act's family-status provision so broadly as to include same-sex families, particularly in light of Parliament's specific choice not to include sexual orientation in the act as a protected ground.[39] The minority disagreed that the interpretation of the act's family-status provision should exclude same-sex families.[40]

A significant feature of the majority's ruling in this case was the suggestion that the court's decision might have been different had the argument of discrimination been based on a Charter claim. In the period between the original claim and the Supreme Court's involvement, the Ontario Court of Appeal had ruled in *Haig v. Canada* that the CHRA should be interpreted to include sexual orientation as a prohibited ground of discrimination,[41] a decision that Justice Minister Kim Campbell decided not to appeal. Then Chief Justice Lamer, writing for the majority, indicated that had Parliament decided to include sexual orientation in the list of prohibited grounds of discrimination, his interpretation of the scope of the family-status provision might have been entirely different.[42] But in light of the acceptance by the federal government of the *Haig* ruling, a parliamentary amendment may not have been necessary to encourage the court to interpret family status as including same-sex partners.

Federal Justice officials interpreted this ruling as confirmation that Parliament would have to revise legislation to address discrimination against lesbians and gay men. Many provincial officials similarly anticipated Charter-based challenges to existing legislation. Yet legislative reforms to redress discrimination against lesbians and gay men would not become a political priority for many years, since governments were generally unwilling to contemplate these without a ruling from the Supreme Court that changes were constitutionally required. Still unknown at the time was how broadly the Supreme Court would interpret this protection from discrimination, or how the court would respond to governmental arguments that legislative distinctions that treat same-sex families differently from heterosexual families should be considered a reasonable limit on equality.

The first governmental attempt after the *Mossop* ruling to undertake substantial legislative reforms to redress discrimination against lesbians and gay men resulted in highly publicized failure. In 1994 the NDP government in Ontario introduced Bill 167, which sought to remove discrimination based on sexual orientation in more than fifty pieces of legislation and would have recognized same-sex partners as spouses. The unprecedented changes it proposed[43] "brazenly confronted heterosexual norms" deeply embedded in social policies.[44]

The proposed legislation attracted broad opposition, particularly in the wake of a Progressive Conservative Party by-election victory that was attributed, by many, to the party's opposition to the legislative package. This served to undermine support for the legislation within both the governing NDP party and the opposition Liberal Party, since some members feared retribution in the next election from constituents opposed to the granting of benefits to same-sex families.[45] When it became clear that the bill would not likely survive, the government indicated a willingness to consider amendments. However, these were insufficient to increase support for the legislation, even among some NDP members. Despite the disappointments many experienced with the defeat of the Bill 167, some lesbian and gay activists were relieved, particularly in light of proposed changes the government was willing to make in order to pacify critics. Lahey suggests that some of the changes would have made existing differences in the treatment of same-sex partners, opposite-sex partners, and married couples even more pronounced.[46] Whatever the reasons for political resistance to these changes, however, partisan opponents of the legislation failed to anticipate that in the near future they would be compelled by the judiciary to address the same issues. Moreover, when that time came, they would be legislating under the added pressures and constraints arising from a constitutional judgment that discrimination is not justified. When Bill 167 was being developed, the Attorney General's office had legal opinions from its own advisers suggesting that providing benefits for common-law but not same-sex relationships would likely fail in Charter litigation.

The only other jurisdiction willing to undertake substantial legislative reforms in the absence of an unequivocal judicial imperative from the Supreme Court was British Columbia. In 1995 the province, under an NDP government, became the first jurisdiction to allow same-sex partners to adopt children. Although the Adoption Act (Bill 51) generated considerable debate,[47] the government did not waiver under the pressure of criticism. Joy MacPhail, then minister of social services, defended the legislation for replacing the policy of "another generation" which no longer reflected current values with respect to complex family relationships.[48]

Miron v. Trudel and Egan and Nesbit v. Canada

In 1995 the Supreme Court released two same-day judgments which indicated that the Charter was having a significant influence on how the judiciary was interpreting equality claims. In both decisions, a core of the court (justices McLachlin, Cory, Iacobucci, and L'Heureux-Dubé), which would later form a new majority,[49] focused on the significance of legislative distinctions that deny benefits to those in non-traditional relationships and began to develop an equality-rights paradigm under the Charter that links equality with respect for human dignity.

In *Miron v. Trudel*[50] a 5–4 majority ruled that marital status is an analogous ground of discrimination for the purposes of section 15 and interpreted the definition of "spouse" as including unmarried common law couples. This decision had broad implications for policy choices that make distinctions between married and non-married relationships. Although the reference to common law spouse has in the past been used in the context of heterosexual non-married relationships, the majority opinion used language that was sexually neutral. The opinion was significant from the perspective of lesbian and gay rights. Its neutral language could be interpreted as a requirement that, not only are legislatures prohibited from discriminating between married and heterosexual common law couples, but that they should also not discriminate between those in married and in same-sex relationships.[51]

The issue in *Miron v. Trudel* centred on whether the definition of spouse used in the province's automobile-insurance policy violated the Charter's equality rights because it excluded common law partners. The effect of the policy was to deny a man insurance against injury under the policy of his female common law partner. This benefit would have been forthcoming had the couple been married. The purpose of the policy was to protect families by insuring against the economic consequences that may follow from the injury of one member. Justice McLachlin, speaking for the majority, ruled that an insurance policy that provided benefits only to married couples discriminated against non-married partners who live together, and that it did so not only by denying benefits to these people but also by conveying the message to them that their relationships are not valued as highly as married ones.[52]

The majority's reasoning in this decision underscored the significance of how the Charter has affected the way some judges approach the principle of equality. McLachlin defined equality as being dependent upon the recognition of human dignity, which she characterized as including personal autonomy and respect for one's identity: "[The principle of equality] recognizes the dignity of each human being and each person's freedom to develop his body and spirit as he or she desires, subject to such limitations as may be justified by the interests of the community as a whole. It recognizes that society is based on individuals who are different from each other, and that a free and democratic society must accommodate and respect these differences."[53]

McLachlin suggested that a corollary of the recognition of an individual's dignity is the recognition that it is wrong to withhold or limit "access to opportunities, benefits, and advantages available to other members of society, solely on the ground that the individual is a member of a particular group deemed to be less able or meritorious than others." Thus, differentiation in social policies that deny these benefits constitutes discrimination because it revokes the individual's right to realize his or her potential and to enjoy the freedom accorded to others, solely on the grounds of membership in a particular identity group.[54] "Discrimination on the basis of marital status touches the essential dignity and worth of the individual in the same way as other recognized grounds of discrimination violative of fundamental human rights norms. Specifically, it touches the individual's freedom to live life with the mate of one's choice in the fashion of one's choice. This is a matter of defining importance to individuals. It is not a matter which should be excluded from Charter consideration on the ground that its recognition would trivialize the equality guarantee."[55]

In ruling that equality was breached by a definition of spouse that applied only to married couples, the majority rejected the argument that, because marriage is socially valuable, marriage-based distinctions that affect entitlement do not constitute discrimination.[56] Justice McLachlin, without challenging the worth of marriage, argued that the relevant issue is whether marriage can be used to deny equal treatment to people on grounds that have nothing to do with their true worth or entitlement. Relying on Justice L'Heureux-Dubé's observation in *Mossop* about the validity of supporting non-traditional families,[57] McLachlin stated that it is not "anti-marriage to accord equal benefit of the law to non-traditional couples."[58] Her ruling did not preclude marriage from being used to justify legislative distinctions between married and non-married relationships. However, she indicated that, where marriage is adopted as the criterion to justify benefits, the state must demonstrate that marriage is "truly relevant to the goal and values underlying the legislative provision in question."[59]

As suggested above, the decision was significant for lesbians and gay men because the sexually neutral language used to depict common law relationships did not exclude same-sex partners from this revised notion of the legally recognized family. It was also significant because it revealed the willingness of a majority of the court to equate equality with protection from legislative distinctions that deny benefits based on identity and personal characteristics. Furthermore, the court equated a violation of equality with the symbolic message that emanates from differential treatment. This message confirms that human dignity is compromised where the denial of benefits is based on one's identity or personal characteristics. The denial of benefits suggests that the state deems those who are excluded to be less worthy of recognition or respect.

The dissenting judgment written by Justice Gonthier and with Chief Justice Lamer and justices La Forest and Major concurring, argued

that the differential treatment of married and non-married relationships was not prejudicial when considered in the larger context of
rights and obligations that uniquely and appropriately attached to
marriage.[60] The minority ruled that the legislature had a legitimate
ability to define the scope of "marriage-like" relationships and had no
obligation to extend all of the attributes of marriage to non-married
couples.[61]

The second ruling that day, *Egan and Nesbit v. Canada*,[62] sent a different and less-supportive message to lesbians and gay men about the justification of policy distinctions that deny them social benefits. *Egan*
represented the Supreme Court's first explicit decision on whether
section 15 prohibits discrimination on the basis of sexual orientation.
Although the court was unanimous in its conclusion that sexual orientation is an analogous grounds of discrimination for the purposes of
section 15(1), and therefore protected by the Charter, the "urgency"
of the need to introduce legislative reforms was weakened by the
majority ruling that the denial of same-sex benefits was constitutional.

At issue in *Egan* was the legitimacy of the federal Old Age Security
Act, which provided an allowance for the spouse of a pensioner who
was already receiving a guaranteed income supplement. Both entitlements were based on need. Spouse was defined, and interpreted by ad-
ministrators, as meaning persons of the opposite sex. Consequently
when James Egan applied for the monthly spouse allowance on behalf
of his same-sex partner, his application was denied because his partner
did not satisfy the definition of spouse.

A narrow majority of the court ruled that the "opposite-sex" restriction in the definition of spouse in the Old Age Security Act constituted
discrimination and violated equality in section 15(1). The majority
emphasized the importance of protecting human dignity by according
equal concern, respect, and consideration to all human beings. Justice
L'Heureux-Dubé captured this sentiment in the following statement
about equality: "Equality ... means nothing if it does not represent a
commitment to recognizing each persons' equal worth as a human being, regardless of individual differences. Equality means that our society cannot tolerate legislative distinctions that treat certain people as
second-class citizens, that demean them, that treat them as less capable
for no good reason, or that otherwise offend fundamental human
dignity."[63]

The majority also ruled that discrimination occurs both by denying
economic benefits to same-sex couples, and thereby depriving them of
equal benefit of the law, and by denying them state recognition of
their relationships, which withholds the respect accorded to others in
long-term relationships.

The legislation denies homosexual couples equal benefit of the law. The Act does this not on the basis of merit or need, but solely on the basis of sexual orientation. The definition of "spouse" as someone of the opposite sex reinforces the stereotype that homosexuals cannot and do not form lasting, caring, mutually supportive relationships with economic interdependence in the same manner as heterosexual couples. The appellants' relationship vividly demonstrates the error of that approach. The discriminatory impact can hardly be deemed to be trivial when the legislation reinforces prejudicial attitudes based on such faulty stereotypes. The effect of the impugned provision is clearly contrary to s. 15's aim of protecting human dignity, and therefore the distinction amounts to discrimination on the basis of sexual orientation.[64]

Justice La Forest, writing the minority four-member opinion that the act's opposite-sex requirement did not amount to discrimination for Charter purposes (Chief Justice Lamer and justices Gonthier and Major concurring), ruled that according benefits only to heterosexual partners "is both obvious and deeply rooted in our fundamental values and traditions, values and traditions."[65] The policy distinction between heterosexual and same-sex partners is "firmly anchored in the biological and social realities that heterosexual couples have the unique ability to procreate." This led to his conclusion that "marriage is by nature heterosexual."[66] However, Justice La Forest did not address why assumptions that were "obvious and deeply rooted" were not also discriminatory. Similarly, he did not address why it was essential or inevitable that procreation be considered the reason to distinguish marriage from other intimate relationships, an assumption that was queried by other judges.[67] La Forest's judgment reflected a reluctance to question whether the traditional privilege given to the heterosexual vision of the family had discriminatory effects. As a result, it was a departure from the court's recognition elsewhere that the ideal of equality means that a "law expressed to bind all should not because of irrelevant personal differences have a more burdensome or less beneficial impact on one than another."[68]

One of the five judges to rule that equality had been violated, the late Justice Sopinka, concluded that the discrimination was justified under section 1. His ruling, in combination with that of the four judges who concluded that the denial of benefits to same-sex partners did not constitute discrimination, meant that a narrow majority of the court upheld the validity of denying benefits to same-sex partners. Justice Sopinka accepted the argument of government lawyers that flexibility should be afforded Parliament in the extension of social benefits within a context that recognized new social relationships. Parliament must contend with fiscal constraints and the implications of these for the scope of social programs. He characterized the recognition of same-sex spouses as "a novel concept" and so concluded that inaction on this front did not amount to an unreasonable restriction on equality.[69]

Justices Cory and Iacobucci, who wrote a joint opinion that the legislation was unconstitutional, explicitly disagreed with the deference Sopinka accorded the legislative denial of benefits for same-sex partners. They argued that, if Parliament were exempted from its obligations, this would undermine the vitality of the Charter and belittle its purposes.[70] It would enable Parliament to "uphold legislation that selectively and discriminatorily allocates resources."[71]

The fact that four of nine judges ruled that the denial of benefits to same-sex partners did not violate the Charter, while a fifth upheld the denial as a reasonable limit, gave Parliament a reprieve from the pressure of revising social policies to make them more inclusive of same-sex relationships. What remained uncertain was the length of time or extent to which governments would be accorded latitude before being compelled to redress the discriminatory effects of social policies that deny benefits to lesbians and gay men. Prior to *Egan*, federal Justice officials had advised departments – drawing upon lower court rulings and *Mossop* – that legislative reforms were necessary under the Charter to remedy discrimination against lesbians and gay men. The *Egan* decision, however, was interpreted by federal departments and ministers as removing the pressure for immediate legislative reforms, and it had a similar effect for provincial jurisdictions.[72]

Human Rights Legislation

Despite the waning momentum for the reforms to social policies to redress discrimination against lesbians and gay men, *Trudel* and *Egan* conveyed the message that legislatively imposed discrimination could not likely be sustained indefinitely. Moreover, the *Haig* ruling indicated that human rights legislation would be considered inconsistent with the Charter as long as it did not protect lesbians and gay men from discrimination based on sexual orientation. For those governments that had not yet amended their human rights legislation, the *Haig* decision gave them the necessary impetus to act.[73]

In 1993 the federal Conservative government tried to amend the Canadian Human Rights Act but the legislation died on the order paper, after having generated substantial public controversy both within caucus and amongst lesbians and gay activists who objected to the bill's intent to define marital status in exclusively heterosexual terms.[74]

In the 1993 federal election campaign, Jean Chrétien promised that a Liberal government would amend the CHRA to prohibit discrimination on the basis of sexual orientation. However, it soon became clear that on this issue the Liberal government was no less prone to internal division than the Conservative government it replaced. Once elected, the Liberals showed little inclination to follow up on their commitment to amend the *CHRA*. When they finally did act, the impetus came partly from criticism of their silence on the subject[75] and partly from their own desire to redirect attention away from another failed election promise that was becoming an even larger political liability – the elimination of the Goods and Service Tax.[76]

In a political overture to critics of the bill,[77] including those within its own party, the government engaged in a strong rhetorical campaign to emphasize that amending the *CHRA* did not change its commitment to family values. The government made frequent statements that the changes to the *CHRA* would not lead to same-sex benefits, gay marriages, or gay or lesbian adoption.[78] This appeasement strategy included a legislative preamble in the bill which referred to "the importance of family as the foundation of Canadian society" and affirmed that "nothing in this Act alters its fundamental role in society." Yet the government's reference to family was conveniently vague. The ambiguity of its position encouraged critics of the legislation to claim that the government was ignoring the real possibility that courts could transform the legal recognition of families to include same-sex partners. The legislation passed 153–76 in a free vote in the House of Commons in May 1996 (with 28 Liberal MPs voting against it).[79]

When Ottawa amended the *CHRA*, three provinces still had not changed their human rights legislation to protect lesbians and gays from discrimination on the basis of sexual orientation. But they have now done so, or have had their legislation changed by judicial decree. Newfoundland amended its human rights legislation in 1997, two years after the Newfoundland Supreme Court ruled that "sexual orientation" must be read into the Newfoundland Human Rights Act.[80] Prince Edward Island followed with amendments in 1998. That same year, the Supreme Court ruled that Alberta's failure to protect against this form of discrimination violated the Charter. The Supreme Court read into the province's human rights legislation a new protection against discrimination on the basis of sexual orientation (discussed below).

Judicial Frustration with Legislative Inaction

Apart from amending human rights legislation, governments generally remained uncommitted to more substantive legislative reforms to redress discrimination against lesbians and gay men. In Charter challenges, governments attempted to justify the validity of legislation that denied benefits to same-sex partners, readily referring to *Egan* to support their argument that courts should be deferential when reviewing legislation that denied benefits to same-sex partners.[81] However, some judges showed little inclination to countenance arguments that more time was required or that the protection of the traditional family justifies denial of benefits to same-sex partners. For example, the Board of Inquiry (Ontario Human Rights Code), which reviewed the inability of lesbian and gay municipal employees to designate their partners for pension benefits, ruled that deference to the legislature was not warranted because there was no evidence of any governmental intent to extend benefits to same-sex spouses. The board ruled that the discriminatory effect of the words "of the opposite sex" be reinterpreted so that benefits be provided to same-sex spouses on the same basis as provided to opposite-sex spouses. It also rejected arguments that fiscal costs and procreation justified the denial of benefits to same-sex partners.[82] Similarly, in *Vogel v. Government of Manitoba*[83] and *Rosenberg v. Canada (Attorney General)*,[84] the Manitoba and Ontario courts of appeal, respectively, expressed frustration with government claims that judges should exercise deference to legislative decisions that continued to deny benefits or withhold recognition for same-sex partners. In *Vogel*, which involved denial of spousal benefits for employees' same-sex partners, the court characterized the case as an example where judges were required to rule on issues that legislatures had deliberately avoided.[85] In *Rosenberg*, Justice Abella was even more outspoken about the linkage between legislative inaction and arguments for judicial deference, suggesting that courts were required to make principled decisions about the justification of constitutional violations and not base decisions on "whether there might be a more propitious time" to remedy discrimination.[86]

The turning point for legislative reforms came with two Supreme Court decisions, in 1998 (*Vriend v. Alberta*[87]) and 1999 (*M v. H*[88]), which made it clear that the court was no longer willing to defer to legislative inaction. An increasing number of Supreme Court judges now began to emphasize a link between equality rights and recognition of the equal worth and dignity of individuals. In so doing, they expressed frustration with the lack of legislative initiative in making social-policy entitlements more inclusive. Two judges who had ruled in *Egan* that the exclusion of same-sex spouses did not violate equality (Chief Justice Lamer and Justice Major) now accepted the previous majority view that discrimination against lesbians and gay men is not a reasonable restriction of equality. The changing composition of the court also increased the size of this majority. The replacement of justices La Forest and Sopinka, who had upheld legislative distinctions that denied benefits for lesbians and gays, by justices Bastarache[89] and Binnie,[90] enlarged the majority supportive of lesbian and gay rights claims. Only one judge from the original *Egan* majority was still on the court. Justice Gonthier joined the majority view in *Vriend* but was the lone dissenting voice in *M. v H.*

Vriend v. Alberta

Judicial fatigue with legislative action was particularly apparent in *Vriend v. Alberta*. In this April 1998 decision, the court categorically rejected arguments for judicial deference. It was unanimous in concluding that the failure of Alberta's human rights code, the Individuals Rights Protection Act (*IRPA*), to protect against discrimination on the basis of sexual orientation violated equality in the Charter.

The Alberta government had repeatedly refused to amend the legislation to include sexual orientation as a prohibited ground of discrimination.[91] In the court's opinion, the government's omission of sexual orientation from its human rights legislation was tantamount to "condoning or even encouraging discrimination against lesbians and gay men." The court ruled that the failure to include protection from discrimination for lesbians and gay men "demeans the individual" and sends a "strong and sinister message" that lesbians and gay men are less worthy of protection as individuals in Canadian society.[92] In short, it sends to Albertans the suggestion that "it is permissible, and perhaps even acceptable, to discriminate against individuals on the basis of their sexual orientation … . As a practical matter, it tells them that they have no protection from discrimination on the basis of their sexual orientation. Deprived of any legal redress they must accept and live in constant fear of discrimination. These are burdens which are not imposed on heterosexuals."[93]

Government lawyers made two different arguments in favour of judicial deference for the legislative decision not to include sexual orientation as a prohibited ground of discrimination. The first was that the court should not rely on the Charter to assess the validity of the legislature's decision to omit sexual orientation from the *IRPA* because the Charter should not apply to legislative inaction. The court rejected this claim, ruling that the legislature's "silence" by omitting sexual orientation cannot be assumed to be neutral, and that if the court were to accept this argument it would have the effect of immunizing certain kinds of legislative decisions from Charter scrutiny.[94] The second version of the deference argument, also rejected by the court, was that the omission of sexual orientation as a prohibited ground of discrimination was justified under section 1. Government lawyers argued that the court should apply the same logic used by Justice Sopinka in *Egan* – elected representatives should be given the opportunity to adopt an incremental approach to expand the scope of the legislation to those whom the legislature determines to be in need of statutory protection.

Justice Iacobucci, who wrote for the court on the section 1 issue, ruled that it is "nonsensical to say that the goal of protecting persons from discrimination is rationally connected to, or advanced by, denying such protection to a group which this Court has recognized as historically disadvantaged."[95] He argued that groups historically targeted for discrimination should not be "expected to wait patiently for the protection of their human dignity and equal rights while governments move toward reform one step at a time." The Charter's guarantees will be reduced to "empty words" if governments "fail to pursue equality diligently."[96] The remedy granted by the court was to interpret the *IRPA* as including sexual orientation in the list of prohibited grounds of discrimination.[97]

Controversy in Alberta

The *Vriend* ruling and the judicial remedy granted resulted in substantial public outcry. The premier's office was inundated with as many as 3,700 phone calls a day. Many expressed extreme anger with the court's ruling and called upon the government to invoke the notwithstanding clause.[98] MLAs were also inundated with thousands of telephone calls, faxes, and letters supporting the use of the override.[99] Many members of the Conservative caucus supported proposals to use the override. Premier Ralph Klein, however, resisted this pressure, announcing on 2 April 1998 that the government would "obey the law."[100]

In fact, the ruling had not surprised the government. In anticipation that it would lose, it had established a four-member cabinet committee to review its legal options. Premier Klein indicated that nothing would be ruled out and implied that use of the legislative override would be one of the options considered.[101] Yet, despite his earlier indication that the override would be considered, Klein subsequently developed political reservations about invoking this power, likely becaue of the heavy criticism the government had incurred for its stated intention to use the override in an unrelated context.[102] This involved legislation that would have set limits for the amount of compensation provided to those who, as a result of provincial policies from the late 1920s to the early 1970s had suffered forced sterilization and confinement in Alberta provincial institutions.[103] The opposition criticized the government for relying on the override and for attempting to save money at the expense of restricting rights by allowing individuals to settle their claims in courts.[104] Hundreds of telephone calls in protest influenced the government, which, the day after the bill had been introduced, indicated that its intention to invoke the override had been a mistake.[105]

M v. H

The next and most significant judicial ruling in putting pressure on governments to introduce broad legislative reforms was *M v. H*, handed down 20 May 1999. The importance of *M v. H* stemmed from the court's unambiguous statement that same-sex partners must be treated with the same degree of respect and recognition given to heterosexual spouses, and also from its acknowledgment that this principle has far reaching consequences for social policy. Although the decision applied specifically to Ontario, the court's interpretation of equality had implications for all governments. As a consequence, a majority of legislatures have now passed comprehensive reforms to respond to this ruling.

At issue was the failure of Ontario's Family Law Act to (*FLA*) recognize same-sex relationships in its processes for resolving property and other issues arising from the dissolution of family relationships. The act utilized a heterosexual definition of spouse.[106] The Supreme Court, by an 8–1 margin,[107] ruled that the exclusion of lesbians and gay men from the scope of the *FLA* violated equality in a manner that is not justified under section 1. The majority opinion, written jointly by justices Cory and Iacobucci (with Chief Justice Lamer and justices L'Heureux-Dubé, McLachlin, Binnie, Bastarche,[108] and Major concurring), emphasized that the purpose of equality rights in the Charter is to "prevent the violation of essential human dignity and freedom through the imposition of disadvantage, stereotyping, or political or social prejudice" and to "promote a society in which all persons enjoy equal recognition at law as human beings or as members of Canadian society, equally capable and equally deserving of concern, respect and consideration."[109]

The majority ruled that, because the spousal definition in the *FLA* prevented persons in a same-sex relationship from gaining access to the court-enforced and court-protected support system, this denial imposed a financial burden on some lesbians and gay men and contributed to the vulnerability experienced by individuals in same-sex relationships. The majority characterized the failure to recognize lesbian and gay relationships under the act as discrimination because it promotes the view that individuals in same-sex relationships are less worthy of state recognition and protection. The court held that the exclusion of same-sex couples perpetuated the disadvantages incurred because of social prejudices against lesbians and gay men.[110]

The majority concluded that the violation of equality was not justified under section 1. Governmental lawyers argued that options other than statutory ones – available in contract law, for example – could address the economic dependence that may arise following the break-up of lesbian and gay relationships. The majority rejected this argument because these alternatives may be less flexible, impose more onerous requirements on claimants, and be available under more limited circumstances. In the majority's view, neither common law remedies nor the law of contract provide an adequate alternative to the spousal support provisions of the *FLA*.[111] These alternative options do not address the moral and societal implications of excluding lesbians and gay men from the *FLA*'s framework.[112]

Governmental lawyers had argued that the court was bound to the deference approach it adopted in *Egan*. Justice Iacobucci, who wrote the majority's section 1 reasons, ruled that a deferential approach was not warranted to justify continued denial of rights particularly since there was "no evidence of any progress with respect to this group since the inception of the spousal support regime." Iacobucci added that, if the legislature "refuses to act so as to evolve towards Charter compliance," the argument for deference "loses its raison d'être."[113] The majority ruled that, given the complexity of the necessary changes, the appropriate remedy would be to suspend the ruling for six months to give the Ontario legislature an opportunity to amend the law.[114]

Ontario's Response to M v. H

Prior to the *M v. H* ruling, the Progressive Conservative government of Mike Harris had been extremely reluctant to expand the scope of benefits for lesbians and gay men or to recognize same-sex relationships. The government's position in *M v. H* was that equality is not unduly violated by an exclusively heterosexual definition of spouse. Earlier, when the case had been before the Ontario Court of Appeal, the NDP government was in power and its attorney general had conceded that the existing definition of spouse was unconstitutional. The factum conceding this was removed from the court file and the attorney general under the Conservative government filed a revised legal opinion, arguing that the legislation was a reasonable limitation of equality under section 1.[115] This supports the argument made in Chapter 1, that the scope of the "credibility" or similar provincial political tests for evaluating whether legislation is consistent with the Charter is broad enough to be influenced by the ideological, partisan, and moral assumptions of different attorneys general.

After the Supreme Court ruled in *M v. H*, Premier Harris reacted by stating that the court's assumption did not coincide with his "definition of family." Nevertheless, despite his personal and political disagreement with the ruling, he indicated that government lawyers would study how the province could comply with the court's decision.[116] He also stated that the government would not invoke the legislative override because he did not believe its use was a valid political response to judicial rulings.[117] The Ontario government passed legislation near the end of the sixth-month reprieve from the *M v. H* ruling, which extended benefits to same-sex partners and provided legal recognition of their relationships in many statutes. However, this political response was made grudgingly. Governmental comments about the bill, and its very title, Amendments Because of the Supreme Court of Canada Decision in M v. H Act, 1999, make it plain that the government passed this legislation not because of considerations of fairness but because of the judicial imperative.[118]

Ontario's new legislation, which amended sixty-seven legislative acts, received unanimous support in the legislature. However, some commentators have criticized the legislative reforms for adopting a differential approach to the recognition of same-sex couples. Lesbian and gay partners are not considered spouses but are referred to as same-sex partners. The objection here is that the distinction between same-sex partners and heterosexual spouses may imply an inferior status for those in same-sex relationships. Furthermore, some believe that the changes do not go far enough. The court's ruling in *Miron v. Trudel* established the principle that common law partners cannot be denied benefits that are accorded to married partners. Left unstated was whether same-sex partners could be denied benefits that are given to those who are married. This is significant because the legislative changes made in Ontario do not grant same-sex partners all of the benefits that are given to married partners.[119] Some have characterized this legislation as reflecting separate but equal treatment. Martha McCarthy, the lawyer for one of the parties in the *M v. H* case, said that the government's approach represented "sexual apartheid" and announced that her client would be seeking a rehearing by the Supreme Court for clarification of whether the legislation is acceptable.[120]

Implications of M v. H for Other Jurisdictions

In *M v. H*, Justice Iacobucci provided a warning, applicable to all governments, that this decision "may well affect numerous other statutes that rely upon a similar definition of the term 'spouse.' "[121] According to Lahey's account in 1999, more than 360 provisions of federal law and substantial numbers of provisions in provincial legislation contained special rules that related to [heterosexual] "spouses," most of which conferred benefits.[122]

A significant political obstacle to passing legislative reforms to address judicial Charter concerns has been the political reluctance of many jurisdictions to apply the term "spouse" to same-sex relationships. Rayside argues that the broad scope of some proposed changes, such as those attempted earlier by the NDP government in Ontario, increased public anxieties about sexual diversity. Although the Canadian population now demonstrates more tolerance towards lesbians and gay men than it did in earlier times, this tolerance is most pronounced when sexual activity is dealt with as a private matter, a view that dovetails with human rights measures which speak largely to the rights of individuals. However, the implications of Supreme Court rulings broaden the legislative focus to include family relationships. In the use of the term "spouse" to define lesbian and gay partners, public opinion has been confronted with a shift from toleration for private activities to acceptance of same sex-relationships as an alternative to traditional family relationships. Given the extent to which heterosexual norms penetrate legislative programs and legal assumptions, proposed changes to recognize same-sex relationships bring to the surface what, for many, are extremely controversial issues. Legal recognition of same-sex spouses does not simply imply toleration of individual differences but suggests that same-sex relationships be considered the practical and moral equivalent to traditional family relationships.[123] This discomfort likely explains why such an innocuous term as "spouse" might give rise to such vehement opposition when extended to same-sex relationships.

The focus on the legal definition of "spouse" is also problematic for some lesbians and gay men who question the fairness of emphasizing partners in the context of benefit issues. For example, the Coalition for Lesbian and Gay Rights in Ontario (CLGRC) has argued that benefits should be available to individuals and not to couples.[124] As suggested earlier, issues related to the recognition of relationships are subject to diverse opinions within lesbian and gay communities.

Governments responded with varying degrees of urgency to revise the definition of spouse or redress gaps in the way opposite and same-sex families are treated in legislative provisions. Where the government response was characterized by inaction, this is likely explained by a desire to avoid introducing reforms that may be politically contentious until it is absolutely essential – more specifically, until the court has reviewed and nullified specific legislation in a given province.

Quebec
Consistent with being the first jurisdiction in Canada to prohibit discrimination on the basis of sexual orientation in its human rights

code, Quebec also was the first province to pass comprehensive legislation to extend to lesbian and gay partners the benefits accorded to
non-married partners of the opposite sex. Almost immediately after
the *M v. H* ruling, the Quebec National Assembly unanimously passed
Bill 32, An Act to Amend Various Legislative Provisions Concerning
De Facto Spouses. The intent of the act is to allow "*de facto* unions to
be recognized without regard to the sex of the persons concerned."[125]
The legislation, which was passed on 10 June 1999, extends the benefits conferred on common law couples to lesbians and gay men. It
affects almost forty acts, regulations, and by-laws, removing requirements that partners be heterosexual and replacing them with more
neutral language, such as "persons who live together in a de facto
union"; similarly where provisions refer to a union of persons of the
opposite sex, the legislation states that the union can exist of persons
of the same sex as well. However, one concern that lesbian and gay
groups have with their status in Quebec is that common law opposite-
sex couples are not as strongly protected under Quebec law as they are
in some other provinces. For example, they lack a scheme to qualify
for support payments after the dissolution of a relationship.[126]

British Columbia
At the time of the *M v. H* ruling, the British Columbia government had
already passed legislation that addressed some of the issues that were
central to this decision. In 1997 it introduced the Family Relations
Amendment Act, which recognized same-sex couples in law and
granted them many of the rights and obligations that common law
couples have with respect to child custody and child and spousal support upon the breakdown of relationships. Then attorney general Ujjal
Dosanjh indicated that, although he had received strong criticism
from many sectors, some of which bordered on hate mail,[127] the government would proceed with the legislation, which passed despite objections from Liberal members.[128] Some opposition Liberal members
acknowledged that the Charter compelled legislative changes, but they
opposed the term spouse and preferred the concept of "domestic partner" for same-sex couples.[129] Dosanjh criticized the domestic-partner
alternative for the following two reasons: by treating same-sex partners
differently from heterosexual spouses, it would undermine equality;
and the concept, as proposed, would provide too onerous a standard
to meet.[130]

Dosanjh interpreted the *M v. H* ruling as requiring more to be done
to guarantee equality.[131] In July 1999 the government introduced Bill
100, the Definition of Spouse Amendment Act, which proposed to
change the definition of spouse to treat same-sex couples in the same

manner as heterosexual couples with respect to wills, estates, inheritance, and related laws. Once again, Liberal members criticized the bill because of its intent to recognize same-sex partners as spouses.[132] Although the British Columbia government at the time was at the forefront of Canadian governmental efforts to redress discrimination against lesbians and gay men, its approach was criticized for lacking consistency and coherence. The British Columbia Law Institute objected to the different ways in which spousal status was referred to in various statutes and proposed a consistent definition of spouse throughout provincial legislation with respect to unmarried relationships.[133] Influenced by this concern, the government decided not to proclaim Bill 100 and in June 2000 a new attorney general, Andrew Petter, introduced the Definition of Spouse Amendment Act 2000 (Bill 21). This legislation was passed a month later and introduced a standard definition of spouse in provincial legislation. Petter characterized the bill as a continuation of the government's "commitment to equality for common-law and same-sex couples" to ensure that lesbians and gay men "should enjoy the same measure of protection and recognition, and indeed the same measure of responsibility, as loving couples who are of the opposite sex."[134] Petter stated that it is important for governments to send a "positive signal to society that this is a form of discrimination that is no longer acceptable."[135] The Liberal opposition again proposed the idea of a domestic partnership as an alternative to redefining spouse to include same-sex partners. Petter indicated that the government did not support this approach, which it perceived as an attempt to avoid substantive equality.[136]

Nova Scotia

In the case of Nova Scotia, the *M v. H* decision did not result immediately in legislative reforms. A year after the ruling, the provincial government introduced legislation that would have defined spouse to include same-sex partners, but it did not go beyond the first-reading stage.[137] Shortly after, the Nova Scotia Court of Appeal ruled in *Walsh v. Bona*[138] that equality was infringed by the Matrimonial Property Act, which grants a division of assets to legally married spouses but not to common law couples. The court gave the province a year to remedy the problem. This decision was sufficient to compel the government to attempt again to pass legislation to extend benefits to same-sex partners. Attorney General Michael Baker explained to the legislature that substantive legislative changes were required because of Charter jurisprudence.[139] Bill 75, passed in late November 2000, was omnibus legislation that amended several provincial laws to allow same-sex couples to receive the same benefits and responsibilities as opposite-sex common law couples, once they had lived together for three years.[140] The decision to require a cohabitation period of three years, whereas the requirement in the earlier, failed bill had been one year, was criticized.[141]

Bill 75 did not remedy the constitutional difficulties raised in *Walsh v. Bona*. But these were addressed in subsequent legislation, Bill 25, which was passed in June 2001. With this legislation, Nova Scotia became the first Canadian jurisdiction to grant lesbian and gay partners the right to register legally their relationships as domestic partners. Bill 25 amends the Vital Statistics Act to allow both common law and same-sex couples to register a domestic partnership. Upon registering a domestic partnership, a same-sex couple will have many of the same benefits and obligations as a married couple, including pension benefits and the division of assets at separation or death.

Saskatchewan

In July 2001 Saskatchewan passed Bill 47, which extends the same legal rights to unmarried opposite and same-sex couples as those enjoyed by married couples. Twenty-four legislative acts were revised in this omnibus legislation, including adoption laws. In speaking to the changes, Justice Minister Chris Axworthy indicated that the measures were necessary to comply with the legislature's "obligation to act when a court makes a finding that our laws are unconstitutional." The purpose of the amendments is to ensure that, "when two people enter into a relationship that is like a spousal relationship, the obligations they have toward each other's economic well-being are the same, regardless of marital status or sexual orientation."[142] The opposition criticized the government for going beyond what was required in the *M v. H* decision. It objected to the reference to same-sex partners as spouses and worried that, by referring to same-sex partners as spouses, the legislation would encourage gay activists to challenge their inability to marry as a Charter violation.[143]

Manitoba

The same day that Saskatchewan announced it was introducing comprehensive legislative changes (30 May 2001), Manitoba introduced Bill 41, which amended ten provincial acts to comply with *M v. H*. The legislation, which followed upon a comprehensive review of legislation conducted in the aftermath of *M v. H*, was passed a month later. It extends pension and death benefits to same-sex partners. It also recognizes the obligations to dependent partners upon the dissolution of their relationships. Attorney General Gord Mackintosh indicated that it was important that the province "respect the law, as well as the dignity, rights and security of all its citizens."[144] But the legislation does not address adoption by same-sex partners. Mackintosh stated that this change was not required because the Supreme Court had not commented on the issue. Commentators speculate that the government's avoidance of the subject was due to political opposition.[145] Political protests against the decision not to reform adoption laws led to the appointment of a panel, consisting of a judge and a lawyer, to study the issue of same-sex adoption and produce a report.[146]

Alberta

Alberta has shown considerably less inclination than many other provinces to respond to the implications of the *M v. H* ruling. Still, although Premier Klein suggested that his government would consider using the override to keep same-sex couples from being recognized as common law partners,[147] Alberta has not been immune to pressure to reassess and revise legislative decisions that discriminate against lesbians and gay men.

Shortly before the *M v. H* ruling, Alberta was still engaged in legislative reforms to comply with the implications of the court's earlier ruling, *Miron v. Trudel.* The province was under judicial pressure to address the issue of spousal support for common law relationships and was criticized for adopting a definition of spouse that was defined exclusively in heterosexual terms.[148] The Liberal opposition objected to the government's willingness to "spend countless dollars ... resisting court decisions the government doesn't like" instead of providing "enlightened leadership" on necessary and comprehensive legislative reforms affecting families and relationships.[149] A similar debate on whether lesbian and gay partners should be recognized as spouses occurred with respect to legislation that would govern division of pension benefits following the break-up of a marriage. The amendments, which would govern private-sector registered pension plans in the province, utilized a heterosexual definition of spouse.[150]

Despite the government's reluctance to introduce broad legislative changes to extend benefits to same-sex partners or recognize their relationships, it has incurred pressure to alter policy criteria in light of ongoing constitutional challenges. Concerned by the possibility of the judiciary unilaterally redefining spouse, and the implications this would have for all social policy, Alberta amended its adoption policy and utilized the term "step-parent," allowing one person in a lesbian or gay partnership to adopt the other's child. Lyle Oberg, minister of family and social services, indicated that the decision represented a defensive measure aimed at preventing the judge hearing the case from "reading-in" or classifying partners in same-sex relationships as legal spouses: [151] "What we are attempting to do is not have a judge read the definition of spouse into our 60 other pieces of legislation that contain the word spouse."[152]

An indication that the government had become more receptive, or perhaps more resigned, to addressing discrimination against lesbians and gay men arose in early 2001. The Intestate Succession Act was challenged under the Charter because it denies same-sex partners the ability to be recognized as the surviving spouse of a partner who dies without leaving a will. The Department of Justice was instructed not to contest the challenge.[153] A Justice official indicated that the department did not believe it could successfully defend the law in light of Charter jurisprudence. The legislation was subsequently declared a violation of equality rights. Presiding Justice Del Perras of the Edmonton Court of Queen's Bench decided against "reading-in" a new definition of spouse that would include same-sex partners, and instead suspended the legislation for nine months to allow the government to make the necessary changes.[154] At the time of writing, Alberta has not yet introduced legislation to address distinctions in benefits and recognition between same-sex and opposite-sex partners, despite a review, initiated by the Department of Justice in 1999, of existing legislative acts that deal with the concept of spouse.[155]

Federal Legislative Changes

Prior to the *M v. H* ruling, federal government strategists had debated whether legislative reforms to extend benefits to lesbians and gay men should come in the form of incremental changes or in a more comprehensive fashion. A central concern focused on how to manage political dissent within caucus. An interesting aspect of the debate has been the choice of words to characterize same-sex relationships. Political reluctance to adopt a same-sex definition of spouse may have been a significant factor in the federal government's response in 1998 to the Ontario Court of Appeal's judgment in *Rosenberg v. Canada*.[156] This case arose when the Canadian Union of Public Employees (CUPE) sought approval from Revenue Canada to amend its registered pension plan so as to allow employees to designate same-sex partners as recipients of survivor benefits. Not only did Revenue Canada refuse to recognize same-sex survivor benefits, but it threatened to de-register the entire pension plan if CUPE made the change.[157] CUPE unsuccessfully appealed this administrative decision to the Federal Court of Appeal and subsequently launched a Charter challenge that Revenue Canada's position violated equality rights. In 1998 the Ontario Court of Appeal ruled that the exclusion of same-sex couples from the pension plan was a violation of equality that could not be justified.[158] The remedy granted by the court was to read into the act an alternative definition of spouse which included same-sex partners.

The federal government decided not to appeal this judgment. This decision may have stemmed from an acknowledgment that the denial of recognition for same-sex relationships conflicts with the Charter's normative values. But a more pragmatic explanation focuses on the wider political, policy, and fiscal implications that would have arisen had the government been unsuccessful in defending the impugned provision. If the government lost at the Supreme Court level, it risked having the court interpret the word spouse to include same-sex partners.[159] If this occurred, it would cast constitutional doubt on all other legislation that confers benefits or responsibilities on the basis of a heterosexual definition of spouse.

Regardless of whether principled or pragmatic considerations governed the response to *Rosenberg*, the decision not to appeal conveyed a degree of resignation that the federal government would eventually have to undertake comprehensive legislative reforms to recognize same-sex relationships. Yet, shortly before the *M v. H* ruling, the federal government was still uncertain how it would proceed – specifically, whether it would it continue with incremental changes in reaction to specific judicial rulings or introduce comprehensive measures. Moreover, how would the government tackle the controversial issue of recognition of same-sex partners?

Political reaction to initiatives undertaken in the aftermath of the *M v. H* decision was pivotal in clarifying the federal government's choice of strategy.[160] Several months after the ruling, a significant internal conflict influenced the government's decision about how to recognize lesbian and gay equality rights. The government introduced Bill C-78 to overhaul the pension plans of 340,000 federal government employees.[161] One small part of the lengthy bill addressed survivor benefits for same-sex partners. The reference to the word "conjugal" in the context of lesbian and gay partners provoked strong criticism from some Liberal MPs who indicated that they intended to vote against the legislation.[162] A vote against the bill by the eight dissident MPs not only jeopardized the passage of the bill but threatened the government's survival if the vote became a confidence motion.[163] As it turned out, the pension bill passed by a 137–118 vote, with six Liberal MPs voting against it.[164]

The depth of opposition within caucus during the pension debate caused party strategists to rethink the government's incremental approach. Since it was thought that opposition would rise to the surface whenever specific legislative reforms were considered, some concluded that it might be better for the party to confine or focus the inevitable opposition to a single act.[165] The consideration of a comprehensive approach also coincided with an omnibus challenge to federal legislation by the Foundation for Equal Families, an advocacy group for the rights of same-sex couples under the law, which sought changes to fifty-eight federal statutes.[166]

Once the decision was taken to introduce comprehensive changes, the government attempted to tread a careful political path. It acknowledged agreement with the normative obligations imposed by the Charter while, at the same time, it attempted to placate critics' concerns by claiming that this agreement did not represent, and would not initiate, a new moral paradigm with respect to marriage. The political message conveyed by the government indicated that the Charter's protection for equality may preclude the continuation of legislative choices that deny lesbians and gay men benefits and recognition accorded to those in heterosexual relationships. The government, however, also believed that it could continue to define marriage as the privileged and exclusive domain of heterosexual spouses.

In February 2000, the government introduced the Modernization of Benefits and Obligations Act (Bill C-23), which amended sixty-eight statutes falling within the mandate of twenty federal departments and agencies. As the name of the act suggests, the government presented the bill as an attempt to "modernize" federal legislation by extending benefits and obligations to same-sex couples. It acknowledged that the reforms were required to satisfy the Supreme Court's jurisprudence on gay and lesbian rights and, in particular, the judgment in *M v. H*. At the time the bill was being debated in the House of Commons, more than thirty cases challenging federal legislation for discrimination against lesbians and gay men were outstanding.[167] The bill received royal assent on 29 June 2000.

Those developing the legislation attempted to avoid previous controversies that were associated with using the term spouse when recognizing lesbian or gay partners. The legislation introduced a new term, "common law partner," and expanded the common law definition of non-married relationships, which previously referred only to heterosexual partners, to include lesbian and gay partners. The bill was extremely controversial. Those supporting it argued that the contemplated reforms were not optional: the issue was whether Parliament should introduce reforms in an accountable, comprehensive, and rational manner or let the courts do so in a piecemeal, time-consuming, and expensive litigation process.[168] Although most groups who were sympathetic to the idea of expanding same-sex benefits supported the bill, some were disappointed by the government's failure to recognize lesbian and gay marriages.[169]

Not all participants in the debate agreed that compliance with the Charter necessitated legislative changes. For example, political scientist Ted Morton told the parliamentary committee studying the bill that Parliament could simply choose to ignore the relevant jurisprudence. He testified that the Charter did not require the reforms contemplated by Bill C-23. Characterizing the Supreme Court's gay-equality rulings as abuses of the court's power, he argued that Parliament should either ignore these judgments or reverse them by using the notwithstanding clause.[170]

The government encountered substantial opposition from within its caucus[171] and from the Canadian Alliance. By far the most contentious issue focused on whether and how the proposed changes would affect the traditional understanding of marriage. Canadian Alliance and some Liberal MPs worried that, by changing the common law definition of relationships to include same-sex partners, the bill would change how marriage is interpreted in law. Many of the claims made both inside and outside Parliament by elected representatives, interest groups, and the media characterized the legislation as an attack on marriage. Critics argued that the bill was a "pit stop along the way to having further amendments made to the entire institution of marriage or to the definition of marriage."[172] Charges that the legislation would undermine traditional marriage persisted despite denials by Justice Minister Anne McLellan that it would have this effect: "The approach chosen in this bill deliberately maintains the clear legal distinction between marriage and unmarried common-law relationships. The Government of Canada recognizes that marriage is of fundamental value and importance to many Canadians, but that value and importance are in no way undermined by recognizing, in law, other forms of committed relationships."[173]

McLellan was asked repeatedly to amend the legislation so as to make absolutely clear that the bill would not affect marriage. She emphatically rejected the need for clarification, suggesting that the legislation was clear and non-ambiguous and that its effects on benefits and obligations for same-sex partners would have nothing to do with marriage.[174] Nevertheless, the Standing Committee on Justice and Human Rights recommended amending the bill to make explicit that lesbians and gay men could not marry. The proposal was made despite the argument of NDP MP Svend Robinson that, by defining marriage exclusively in heterosexual terms, the proposed preamble "demeans and trivializes the recognition of the relationships of gay and lesbian people."[175]

The federal government eventually bowed to parliamentary and political pressure and accepted the Justice Committee's recommendation to amend the bill to make clear that the legislative changes would not alter the existing heterosexual definition of marriage.[176] This was not the first time the government had given in to pressure to identify marriage exclusively in heterosexual terms. Less than a year earlier, the government supported a Reform motion that stated that marriage would remain the lawful union of one man and one woman.[177] In the Bill C-23 debate, McLellan did not recant her previous conclusions that the bill would not affect the legal definition of marriage, but she stated that the clarification was warranted to assure Canadians that "the definition of marriage will not change."[178] The legislative preamble expressed Parliament's belief that marriage should remain an exclusively heterosexual relationship: "For greater certainty, the amendments made by this Act do not affect the meaning of the word 'marriage', that is, the lawful union of one man and one woman to the exclusion of all others."

Despite agreeing to the amendment, many critics were not satisfied. Canadian Alliance MP Eric Lowther argued that this preamble would not prevent courts from redefining marriage to include same-sex partners. An Alliance amendment, which was defeated, would have defined marriage and spouse in every statute affected by Bill C-23. Lowther suggested that this more comprehensive approach was necessary to "send a clear signal to the courts on behalf of the Canadian people that marriage should remain the union of a man and a woman to the exclusion of all other definitions."[179] Some Liberals shared this concern. Nineteen Liberal MPs voted against the bill at the reporting stage and seventeen voted against it in the final vote.[180] One Liberal MP explained his concern in terms of his lack of confidence that governmental lawyers would defend Parliament's will, suggesting that some officials in the Department of Justice have their own Charter agenda: "We have this very uneasy situation that worries a lot of us around here, that we are not entirely certain that the people who produce the legislation for the government, who advise the government on its legislation, are indeed as impartial as they should be."[181]

Many MPs who ultimately voted against the bill suggested that a large part of their opposition stemmed from the fact that eligibility for benefits would reflect a sexual relationship. They suggested, as an alternative, that legislative benefits should be based on dependent relationships between family members and possibly long-time friends. Lowther argued that it was odd for "private sexual intimacies between two people" to make up the "sole criteria" for benefits.[182]

McLellan stated that the passage of Bill C-23 would not preclude the possibility of recognizing other dependency relationships. However, this issue would require further review, particularly with respect to legal obligations.[183]

Recognition of same-sex benefits in no way prevents the recognition of different forms of dependency relationships that have not been traditionally included in Canadian social policy. But the argument of some critics of Bill C-23, that dependency relationships should replace sexual relationships as the basis for benefits, had a disingenuous quality. Many who proposed this idea argued that benefits should not be based on sexual relationships. Yet the sexual element of relationship recognition was not treated in a consistent manner. Many proponents of benefits for dependency relationships, as an alternative to same-sex benefits, did not seem to have any objections to maintaining benefits for married partners. Yet this form of relationship, which by law is confined to heterosexuals, clearly presumes a sexual element. Indeed, many critics of same-sex benefits continue to emphasize procreation as the reason for distinguishing between marriage and same-sex relationships.

THE QUESTION OF MARRIAGE

The questions of adoption and marriage are the most contentious issues yet to be resolved with respect to the scope of equality rights. Several jurisdictions have revised adoption laws either to allow one same-sex partner to adopt the other's children or to allow them to adopt jointly as parents. But only one jurisdiction, British Columbia, has indicated support for recognizing same-sex marriages.

Many politicians opposed to redefining spouse to include same-sex partners suggest that they share the deeply held convictions of their electoral constituents that this recognition is inappropriate – that marriage is, and should remain, a uniquely heterosexual institution. But it is not clear whether politicians are correct in their impression that their constituents overwhelmingly oppose same-sex marriage. While the idea of gay marriage is controversial, and politicians certainly hear from critics of the idea, they may exaggerate the number who are opposed to same-sex marriage. An Angus Reid poll conducted shortly after the *M v. H* ruling in 1999 suggests that, nationally, 53 per cent of respondents approved of gay marriage, with the largest support coming from Quebec (61 per cent) and from younger Canadians (66 per cent of those aged 18 to 34).[184]

The federal Parliament has jurisdiction over marriage but has not enacted legislation that defines the gender criteria for the institution.

Its statements on this issue have taken the form of preambles to other legislative enactments. Thus, the legal position that marriage takes place only between a man and a woman has arisen from the common law rather than from legislation. This heterosexual definition of marriage has been applied by Canadian courts dating back to 1866 and was reaffirmed in 1970.[185]

Common law rules are not immune to Charter-inspired changes. Several cases have appeared in the lower courts claiming that the inability of same-sex partners to marry infringes the Charter.[186] Several commentators in the Bill C-23 debate testified before the parliamentary hearings that the denial of marriage to gays and lesbians, particularly in the absence of a parallel system, might not survive a Charter challenge.[187] At the time Bill C-23 was being discussed in parliamentary committee, the Liberal Party was challenged at a national convention by its youth wing to recognize legal marriage for same-sex partners. This proposal by the Young Liberals of Canada, to "urge the federal government to extend the right for same-sex couples to be legally married,"[188] was defeated.

Since state recognition of marriage is a secular activity, as distinct from the optional religious element, the courts may be suspicious about the legitimacy of having the state sanction and recognize only heterosexual unions, particularly if no comparable opportunity exists for same-sex partners to gain legal recognition for their relationships. It goes without saying that many lesbians and gay men may never want to marry, just as many heterosexual couples choose not to seek state recognition of their relationships. But for those who do wish to marry, and the sole factor precluding them is interpretation of the common law, courts may decide to reassess this rule in light of the Charter.

In 2000 British Columbia's attorney general, Andrew Petter, announced that the government believed that same-sex couples should have the equal right to marry legally.[189] He subsequently indicated that the government would ask the British Columbia Supreme Court to provide guidance on whether the denial of the ability of same-sex couples to marry violates the Charter, indicating that his government would "argue strongly in favour of legalized, same-sex marriages." The British Columbia Supreme Court has since ruled that equality is infringed by this denial but that it is nevertheless reasonable under section 1, because marriage is a "deep rooted" institution set up to provide a structure for children.[190]

Alberta is the other jurisdiction to wade into the marriage debate, but with a very different position. The government supported private-member legislation adding a preamble to the Marriage Act which declared marriage to be a union of a man and woman. This was largely a symbolic gesture because provinces lack jurisdiction to define marriage.[191] In March 2000 the Marriage Amendment Act (Bill 202) was passed in a free vote within the government caucus. The amendment stated that it would operate notwithstanding the Charter. Liberal MPs criticized the use of the override, suggesting that it was dangerous to employ this tool in a pre-emptive or "prophylactic way."[192] Although the Liberal opposition supported the principle that marriage should be confined to those of the opposite sex, it argued that the government should recognize domestic partnerships that would include people of the same sex and extend benefits to those in these partnerships.[193]

CONCLUSIONS

The successful use of the Charter by lesbians and gay men to pursue social changes has had, and will continue to have, significant implications for social policies that make distinctions in benefits, recognition, and obligations based implicitly or explicitly on heterosexuality. It is only a matter of time before the whole range of social distinctions based on heterosexuality as the sexual norm, including adoption laws and the definition of marriage, are challenged in all Canadian jurisdictions.

Not surprisingly, Charter-inspired changes to legislation and legal assumptions are controversial. Depending on one's assumptions about the justification of historic legislative distinctions that recognize only heterosexual relationships, legislative changes to date are likely considered either inappropriate or insufficient. Those who do not accept the validity of Charter-inspired changes, because of religious, moral, or cultural beliefs, likely consider the pendulum as having swung too far towards recognizing lesbian and gay rights claims.

Alternatively, those who believe that social policies that recognize heterosexual relationships, while ignoring and denying benefits to same-sex relationships, likely view legislative changes as incomplete because not all jurisdictions have redressed gaps in the benefits accorded heterosexual and same-sex relationships and because lesbian and gay couples remain unable to marry legally.

Jurisprudence on lesbian and gay rights is still evolving. Yet governments have little reason to doubt the significance of what can only be characterized as a new legal equality-rights paradigm. This paradigm emphasizes that equality under the Charter requires not only equal benefits for lesbians and gay men but also that the state treat their relationships with dignity and respect. The message from the Supreme Court, reinforced by tribunals and lower and appeal courts, is that policies based on norms of the traditional and heterosexual family are constitutionally suspect in the absence of recognition and inclusion for same-sex relationships and families. Governments are gradually responding to these new judicial imperatives. At the time of writing, six provinces and the federal government have passed comprehensive legislative reforms. Others seem to be delaying legislative reforms as long as possible – until a litigant has successfully challenged their particular legislation.

But for these reluctant provinces, delay may have serious consequences. The Supreme Court is indicating that its patience with legislative reform is wearing thin. In the absence of satisfactory legislative changes, as construed by the court, more judicially imposed changes may arise through "reading" into statutes and reformulating definitions of spouse or through strongly worded judicial suggestions that will be difficult for legislatures to ignore. If governments renege on the responsibility to evaluate and make prudential and principled decisions about how to reassess the complex policy networks of social benefits and obligations, courts are likely to play a larger role in expanding the scope of benefits as well as assessing the merits and redefining the purposes of social policies. This is significant for the following reason. Lesbian and gay communities are not unanimous in how to conceive of family, relationships, and social and political entitlements. These divisions indicate that those who are closest to the relevant issues and, therefore, who are in the best position to judge their own interests, objectives, and policy hopes, may disagree on how the relevant issues and objectives should be conceived. Thus, the need to consult, engage in dialogue, and conduct research on issues central to social policy reforms is essential. Legislatures are better situated than courts to undertake this difficult and ambitious task. Yet, if legislatures are too slow in changing social policy, courts will likely become impatient with legislative indecision and more active in proffering remedies. The court's lack of resources to undertake social-policy reform suggests that judicially imposed solutions may provide only fragmented remedies for complex social-policy challenges.

9 Assessing the Charter's Influence

Two of the claimed virtues of a bill of rights are that it provides a set of rights that guard liberty[1] and ensures that these principles cannot be easily set aside. By implication, a bill of rights should benefit minorities who might otherwise be vulnerable to having their rights compromised when circumstances and sentiment for doing so are convenient or popular. Yet this idea has its sceptics. A more guarded vision of a bill of rights holds that, if a polity needs to codify fundamental values and rely on judicial review for their meaning to be persuasive, then a bill of rights may have little effect.

Scepticism about the protective capacity of a bill of rights dates back to founding American constitutional debates. James Madison, even while promoting the amendments that became known as the Bill of Rights, expressed doubts about the significance of their codification. The central normative concern for Madison was how to protect private rights from an oppressive majority, since the majority ultimately has power.[2] Madison believed that liberty depends largely upon a well-ordered constitution, consisting of a separation of powers and a system of checks and balances which, when combined with federalism, divides interests and factions.[3] Alexander Hamilton similarly argued that rights were protected through the well-crafted institutions of governance, suggesting that the "Constitution is itself, in every rational sense, and to every useful purpose, A BILL OF RIGHTS."[4]

A corollary of this argument is that, in the absence of a well-ordered constitution, rights may not be protected, even if enumerated in a constitutional bill of rights. As Robert Goldwin characterizes Madison's scepticism about the utility of a bill of rights: "Madison was cool to a bill of rights not because he was indifferent to private rights, but rather because he was devoted to them and thought declarations of rights had proven to be ineffective in protecting them. He sought something else, therefore: something with greater power, something commensurate with the threat of the security of the rights of the people, something sturdier than a 'parchment barrier.' "[5]

Rainer Knopff has shown similar scepticism in his consideration of the Charter's role in protecting rights. Knopff argues that, if the judiciary recognizes rights claims that lack broader consensus (which is not a foregone conclusion because judges usually share in this societal consensus), judges may issue rulings that support a rights claim but will be able to do little to compel societal or political compliance. Unless a fundamental societal consensus exists for the right being claimed, a bill of rights will be unable to prevent infringements arising from contrary political conduct. Yet, if this fundamental consensus exists, a bill of rights will not be necessary. A society will simply not tolerate unjustified restrictions on fundamental rights.[6]

This chapter examines the sceptical vision of a bill of rights with respect to the Charter's role in redressing discrimination against lesbians and gay men. I argue that the judicial and political reception of lesbian and gay equality claims contradict the expectations associated with the sceptical vision. The explanation for this rests, in large part, on the dynamic role the Charter performs in changing the assumptions and expectations of the polity. Opinion about how to conceive fundamental values is not static. The Charter, as the core element of a new constitutional paradigm, has contributed to more critical thinking about the meaning of rights and the implications of state actions for these. It is influencing assumptions about the judiciary's role in protecting rights and assessing discrimination, affecting interest-group behaviour, and shaping political responses to rights claiming, particularly where these claims are upheld by the judiciary.

REASSESSING THE SCEPTICAL HYPOTHESIS

The hypothesis associated with a sceptical view of a bill of rights can be stated as follows: *The Charter's potential to redress rights violations that lack fundamental consensus is doubtful because judges likely share this consensus and, therefore, will not provide relief for rights violations. Alternatively, judges may render rulings that uphold rights that are outside this consensus but, lacking power to enforce their rulings or compel public and political acceptance, these decisions will be, at best, hollow victories. In short, a bill of rights will be either ineffective or unnecessary.*

Judicial and political reception of the equality claims of lesbians and gay men should provide a good test of this sceptical hypothesis. The hypothesis provides several reasons for cautioning against expectations that the Charter will facilitate legislative reforms to redress historical discrimination that lesbian and gay men have incurred. First, since the judiciary in all probability shares the societal consensus about fundamental values, judges may not be predisposed to interpret equality in a manner that embraces protection from discrimination on the basis of sexual orientation. Not only has the Canadian judiciary historically been reluctant to question the validity of discriminatory treatment of lesbians and gay men, but the Charter lacks explicit recognition that discrimination on the basis of sexual orientation is constitutionally prohibited.

Second, even if the judiciary interprets equality in a manner that protects against this form of discrimination, legislative changes may not follow. Before the Charter was adopted, elected representatives steadfastly ignored political pressure from lesbian and gay activists to reform social policy. Thus, they may not be prepared under the Charter to cede judgment to courts on this particular social-policy terrain. If political opposition to the reform agenda of lesbian and gay rights activists remains firm, judicial rulings that support lesbian and gay rights claims may have little effect on policy decisions because courts do not have the means to compel adherence to their judgments or to draw upon the coercive powers of the state to enforce controversial rulings.

The possibility of a government deliberately ignoring a judicial decision that directly impugns its legislation is unlikely, because this would undermine the integrity of the rule of law. Still, it cannot be assumed that governments will accept the implications of a judicial decision that reflect legal or moral claims with which political leaders strenuously disagree. The Charter's inclusion of a legislative override allows the federal Parliament and provincial legislatures to set aside, temporarily, the effects of a judicial ruling on equality while still respecting the rule of law. The use of the legislative override is contentious. Nevertheless, if there is widespread opposition to a judicial ruling providing benefits for those in same-sex relationships, this may reduce the perceived political costs of using the override power.

Therefore, many conditions associated with a sceptical view of a bill of rights exist for lesbian and gay rights claiming. If this hypothesis is correct, the existence of the Charter should make little difference with respect to judicial and political reception of these rights claims.

Knopff adds another dimension to his sceptical view of a bill of rights. While he believes that the Charter is not necessary in Canada, he is not suggesting that it is irrelevant. Rather, Knopff argues that the Charter is harmful to the polity. Since consensus exists for fundamental rights, true violations will not occur. The only rights claims that will generally go to court will involve "second-level issues about which reasonable people may reasonably disagree."[7] But here Knopff worries that a bill of rights will erode the already declining legitimacy and credibility of representative institutions by undermining their capacity for deliberation and moderation. He views moderation as an important condition for a healthy polity. The language of rights, however, makes this difficult because it is "inescapably about claiming the uncompromisable trumps known as rights." It encourages participants "to speak the language of extremism both in and out of the courtroom."[8] "The courtroom politics of rights ... rhetorically gives these second-level disagreements the colour of truly fundamental ones. Courtroom partisans present themselves as the true defenders of fundamental rights, of the original consensus, and demonize their opponents as despoilers of all that is true and good ... What is merely a part is rhetorically disguised as the whole."[9]

Consideration of whether the harm thesis applies to rights claiming by lesbians and gay men raises two interrelated questions. Are lesbian and gay claims for inclusion in social-policy benefits a logical derivation of equality, in which denial of benefits contradicts a fundamental constitutional right? Or do these claims represent "second-level issues" around which tolerant people can expected to have reasonable disagreements?[10] In his harm thesis, Knopff does not specifically address the normative status of lesbian and gay equality claims to end discrimination in social benefits. Yet, elsewhere, he defends the case for recognizing domestic partnerships, which may include same-sex partners.[11]

CONTRADICTING SCEPTICAL EXPECTATIONS

Both judicial and political reaction to the equality claims of lesbians and gay men under the Charter challenges the expectations of the sceptical thesis. As argued in the previous chapter, the Supreme Court has ruled that legislative decisions that reflect the norm of the traditional and heterosexual family are constitutionally suspect in the absence of recognition and inclusion for same-sex relationships and families. In so doing, the court has cast doubt on the constitutional validity of a broad range of social policies across the country. This message has been reinforced by tribunals and by lower and appeal courts. Under the Charter, the judiciary initially has been less accepting than representative institutions of policy distinctions that deny entitlements and legal recognition for those in same-sex relationships. Of all the so-cial policies examined in this book, issues relating to the rights of lesbi-ans and gay men represent the greatest lag between how the Supreme Court interprets the Charter's statement of normative values and how elected representatives relate these to legislative decisions.

Yet, despite the gap between judicial and political opinion, political responses to Supreme Court rulings on lesbian and gay rights claims show far greater compliance with court rulings than what would be ex-pected from the sceptical view of a bill of rights. Political behaviour has generally been reactive. With few exceptions, governments have waited to be compelled by judicial rulings that specifically require them to in-troduce legislative changes to make social-policy benefits more inclu-sive of lesbian and gay relationships. But substantive reforms have been forthcoming. At the time of writing, six provinces and the federal Parliament have enacted comprehensive legislative reforms to address concerns raised by the Supreme Court in *M v. H*. Important questions remain unanswered, and the political responses to these are still un-certain, such as whether the court will interpret the Charter as prevent-ing legislatures from denying same-sex partners the ability to adopt children jointly and, more controversially, whether they have a right to marry legally.

Yet the extent of the response to date suggests that it is a serious mis-take to dismiss the Charter as ineffective for failing to generate swift and complete political compliance with controversial lesbian and gay rights rulings and the implications they raise for legislative distinctions based on sexual orientation. After so many years of denying the validity of lesbian and gay equality claims, it would be naive to expect that judi-cial decisions would immediately transform political attitudes and leg-islative agendas. The judicial imperative for more inclusive social policies, and the judicial insistence that social policies treat same-sex relationships with dignity and respect, could have been categorically spurned. But this has not been the case.

Moreover, those jurisdictions that have not yet complied with Su-preme Court rulings have not generally repudiated the legitimacy of these rulings. Their form of disagreement, if it can be construed in this manner, is inaction rather than rejection. But this suggests only tempo-rary avoidance until the Supreme Court hands down an imperative for reform in their particular jurisdiction.

Some might argue that judicial and political reception to rights claiming by lesbians and gay men supports, rather than challenges, the sceptical hypothesis. According to this alternative interpretation, the Charter has not contributed in any significant manner to social re-forms to implement gay rights claims. The breadth of policy reforms indicates that a new consensus has emerged which supports efforts to redress discrimination against lesbians and gay men as part of a more inclusive commitment to equality. The Charter is irrelevant to this consensus. Reforms would have occurred in any event, even had the Charter never been adopted, because where consensus for fundamental values exists the polity will not tolerate restrictions. One need only look at Australia, which does not have a bill of rights, to recognize a substantial increase over the last twenty years both in political mobilization by the gay liberation movement and in broader public and political acceptance of attempts to redress discrimination against lesbian and gay men.[12]

Yet it is difficult to imagine that extensive reforms would have been made in some Canadian jurisdictions for many years, perhaps a generation, without the Charter's influence. As will be argued below, the Charter has evolved in a dynamic way that has contributed in significant ways to this reform environment.

WHERE DOES THE INFLUENCE LIE?

An inherent difficulty in assessing the effects of a bill of rights arises in discerning the direction of influence. Do judicial decisions influence political and public opinion? Or do they reflect changes in values that are already under way? Robert Dahl's observation, made almost half a century ago, that courts will not be long out of step with legislative decisions (either ahead or behind) is important when thinking about the relationship between judicial and political judgments.[13]

Analysis by Gerry Rosenberg of the reform effects of landmark American judicial decisions provides a cautionary warning for expectations that judicial review of a bill of rights will have a causal effect on legislative reforms. Rosenberg argues that constraints within the American political system ensure that seldom will conditions be present that enable courts to produce significant social reform. These constraints include the limited nature of constitutional rights: not all social-reform goals can plausibly be presented as constitutional rights and the judiciary may be reluctant to change the meaning of existing rights or to recognize new ones. Courts lack sufficient independence from other branches of government to ensure that their decisions will be given effect: the appointment process may limit diversity on the bench or Congress may undermine a judicial ruling by writing a provision that does not give effect to a judicial objection. Finally, courts lack the tools to develop appropriate policies and implement decisions necessary for significant social reform.[14] Rosenberg concludes that U.S. courts will rarely be able to compel significant social reforms; at best, they can support the social-reform acts of the other branches of government. Even in rare circumstances when these constraints can be overcome, the judiciary's contribution to social reform is weak; it is more akin to the "cutting of the ribbon on a new project than its construction."[15] He argues that judicial involvement in school desegregation provides an example of the limited influence of judicial decisions. Even though school desegregation ostensibly represents the paradigm of a successful litigation strategy leading to social change, Rosenberg maintains that before Congress and the executive branch acted to achieve reform, courts had virtually "*no direct effect*" on ending discrimination in education. The same is true of halting discrimination in voting, transportation, and housing.[16] These institutional constraints apply equally to Canada.

Miriam Smith similarly raises caution about causal-based explanations of Charter-induced changes to social policies. Smith warns against simplistic assumptions that the Charter is responsible for social-reform activity and, by implication, the outcomes that emerge from the actions of social movements. The Charter may have encouraged gay and lesbian activists to emphasize the legal dimension of equality seeking. Nevertheless, its influence must be understood in the larger social and political context of an active gay-liberation movement.[17]

There has been a significant increase in the number of rights claims on the ground of sexual orientation from the mid-eighties. Not only has the number of cases increased, but such rights claims have occurred across the range of institutions of society. This is clearly an effect of the Charter. The increase in the number of cases appears relatively suddenly; hence, the increase in rights claims could not result from social change alone. On the other hand, the sociological and political changes of the seventies and eighties – the rise of the women's movement and the gay liberation movement, the struggle to create lesbian and gay community institutions at the grass roots of Canada's largest urban centres, the emergence of sizeable and visible lesbian and gay communities – created the pre-conditions for the rise of rights talk. After all, even with the most favourable legal structure, lesbian and gay rights claimants would be unable to pursue their claims if they were unwilling to be visible or if they felt they would be at risk of harassment for coming forward with a claim … The legal opening of the Charter would not in itself have been sufficient to generate equality seeking.[18]

Smith also emphasizes, however, an important dimension in the relationship between judicial review and social change which Rosenberg discounts. This is the dynamic effect that appeals to the normative principles in a bill of rights can have when motivating and enhancing the political and legal strategies of social movements, a theme that is discussed below. Arguably, Rosenberg understates the effect that judicial rulings may have on a reform-oriented environment, providing necessary and cumulative pressures for legislatures to revisit contested issues and reassess the justification of previous choices.

Charles Epp's comparative study of the uses and reception of rights claims adds additional layers to this question of the rights-protecting capacity of a bill of rights, and by implication its potential to produce legislative reforms to give effect to these rights. Epp emphasizes the relationship between a support structure for legal mobilization of rights claims and sustained judicial attention and support for these claims. He argues that a rights revolution will occur only where there is a support structure with a broad base in civil society: in short, where there is support for rights litigation such as rights-advocacy organizations, supportive lawyers, and sources of financing.[19] For different reasons than Rosenberg, he, too, warns against a view that exaggerates the role of a bill of rights in achieving social change:

Although it is common to argue that bills of rights empower judiciaries, that may be only a secondary effect of a much stronger relationship between popular movements and bills of rights. Judiciaries seem capable of deriving legitimacy from sources other than a bill of rights; and constituencies of support for judiciaries have not always been oriented toward a bill of right. But in systems in which there exist broad constitutional rights guarantees, popular movements seem especially capable of using contradictions between political practice and constitutional promise as a means for organizing support for their causes. And when such movements have had access to resources for legal mobilization, they have turned to the courts, creating the conditions for a new range of judicial activity. Thus a bill of rights provides popular movements with a potential tool for tying judicial power to their purposes.[20]

Epp argues that commentary on the Charter is generally guilty of exaggerating its influence. He characterizes the political and legal culture of Canada as having been influenced by a rights revolution. But he argues that this revolution pre-dates the Charter and was manifest in support structures that provided the foundation for the Charter and for creative judicial enforcement of its provisions.[21]

The development of the rights revolution rested heavily on the growth of a support structure for legal mobilization. All of the main elements of the support structure – rights-advocacy organizations, sources of financing (particularly government-provided aid), lawyers, and supportive government agencies – either

newly emerged or grew substantially in the seventies. Those developments provided the foundation for the rights revolution: they supported a steadily growing number of rights cases, they greatly contributed to the development of
rights provisions in the Charter, they developed the scholarship that supported
a vigorous judicial role in interpreting the Charter, and they brought new cases
under the Charter that provided the judges with the opportunities to enforce,
expand, and create the new rights.[22]

Admittedly, it is difficult to disentangle political opinion from influences that are independent of judicial rulings under the Charter. The
Charter does not exist separate from, or in isolation of, societal values
and institutional assumptions of governance. Yet, at the same time, the
Charter is not dormant or static. Rather, it is a dynamic rights instrument that is evolving in a manner that exerts significant influence on
judicial approaches, reform strategies, and political responses.

THE SIGNIFICANCE OF A NEW CONSTITUTIONAL PARADIGM

My purpose is not to construct a general theory of the circumstances or
conditions under which a bill of rights will produce social change commensurate with rights claims. Rather, it is to consider the more narrow
question of why the Charter has been effective in advancing the legislative reforms sought by lesbians and gay men to redress discrimination.
Nevertheless, in accounting for the role of the Charter in facilitating
these reforms, the explanation may have broader application.

A persuasive explanation for the influence of the Charter in recognizing rights claims that previously lacked support almost certainly has
many dimensions, including the societal and structural supports that
both Smith and Epp emphasize. Rights historically did not provide a
rallying call for political action in Canada similar to the American example. American popular movements seeking social reforms have long
been inspired by constitutional promises.[23] Nothing in the original
Canadian constitution can compare to the political and rhetorical
flourish of the American Declaration of Independence, constitution,
and Bill of Rights. Yet, in the last quarter of the past century, rights
language in Canada has become more frequent and vocal.

Epp is surely correct that the Charter, by itself, cannot explain the
increase in rights awareness and rights claiming. The globalization of
rights discourse meant that Canada would not be immune to rights
sensitivity, even had the Charter not been adopted. Nevertheless, far
more prominence is now being given to rights considerations in judicial, public, and political assessments of state actions than existed in

the years immediately before the adoption of the Charter. Moreover, Epp understates the significance of constitutional innovation in terms of influencing societal assumptions about fundamental values and changing judicial and political behaviour.

Thomas Berger, among others, has written not only about the incidents of intolerant treatment of minorities or those with dissenting opinions before the adoption of the Charter but also about the absence of remedies and lack of political and judicial will to redress rights violations.[24] The adoption of the Charter, and the declaration in 1982 that the constitution will be the supreme law of the land – forever changing the principle of "parliamentary supremacy" – have had a significant influence on governmental behaviour. The relationship between the Charter and lesbian and gay reform objectives raises the following question: *How is the new constitutional paradigm adopted in 1982 influencing the behaviour and assumptions of reform-motivated individuals and groups, courts, and representative institutions?*

The profound change to governing principles initiated by this constitutional innovation has provided new occasions and incentives for individuals and groups, judges, and political actors to reassess their assumptions about the meaning and scope of rights, how they conceive their own roles in relation to making, evaluating, or responding to rights claims, and whether and how rights claims should influence legislative priorities.

As judicial and political responses to the Charter evolve, more systematic and rigorous scrutiny is being undertaken concerning the effects of state actions on protected rights. The increased prominence of rights, as critical standards for evaluating the justification of state actions, encourages and focuses more attention on using rights claims to promote social reforms necessary to give effect to these claims. This strategy for change has been influenced by the broad interpretation generally given by the Supreme Court to Charter claims, as well as by the reform potential of judicially defined remedies, which the court is empowered and committed to grant. It has also been influenced by the broad popularity of the Charter, which affects political behaviour and constrains the way governments respond to judicial rulings that run counter to legislative decisions.

THE CHARTER'S INFLUENCE ON THE JUDICIARY

The Charter has had a significant influence on how the judiciary conceives of its role and responsibilities. This is not to suggest that Canadian judges would not be able to protect rights using the common law, administrative rules, or statutory interpretations, if so inclined. But the adoption of the Charter represented a turning point for the judiciary in terms of how it perceives and responds to its task. In its very earliest Charter decisions, the Supreme Court characterized itself as the guardian of the constitution and indicated that it must reassess the conservative and reluctant character of its earlier rulings under the Bill of Rights.[25] Under the Charter's influence, judges have re-evaluated their methodological approach and have consciously chosen to interpret rights broadly and to assess whether both the purposes and the effects of legislative decisions are consistent with the Charter's normative values. This has provided far broader opportunities to assess and question the merits of legislative choices.

It was not inevitable that the Charter would have this particular dynamic effect on judicial review. The pervasive conservative judicial culture that characterized judicial attitudes and behaviour led some commentators to speculate that the Charter would likely have little effect on judicial attitudes. This expectation followed from the principle of parliamentary supremacy, which had encouraged judicial restraint, and was thought to be "too deeply imbedded in the thought processes of Canadian lawyers and judges to be abruptly displaced through the adoption of the Charter."[26]

The judiciary could have interpreted the Charter's values narrowly and its recognition of limits on rights broadly. Had the Supreme Court done both, the approach to judicial review would have greatly reduced the incidents in which rulings find legislation to contravene the Charter. Nevertheless, Supreme Court judgments in early Charter cases present a stark contrast with the judicial approach and reasons in cases decided under the statutory federal Bill of Rights only a few years earlier, even when similar rights claims were at issue.[27] Charter sceptics F.L. Morton and Knopff argue that the fate of many Bill of Rights precedents "provides a particularly dramatic example of legal transformation without textual warrant."[28] The existence of this contrast indicates that the Charter has introduced a new era in terms of judicial attitudes and approaches to protecting rights. The Charter was critical to, and not merely coincidental with, changing judicial attitudes about the nature and scope of rights and the judiciary's responsibility in protecting these rights.

That the Charter would prompt judges to enlarge the discretionary nature of their adjudication of policy disputes is indeed the focus of some complaints about the court's approach to judicial review. Morton and Knopff view the Charter's significance in terms not so much of guaranteeing rights as of providing judges with "the power to make policy by choosing among competing interpretations of broadly worded provisions."[29] In so doing, they charge, the Supreme Court has "transformed itself" in a "dazzling exercise of self-empowerment" from "an adjudicator of disputes to a constitutional oracle" that is willing to pronounce on the merits and validity of a broad range of social policies.[30] What troubles Morton and Knopff is that this heightened role of evaluating social policy is inconsistent with their preferred view of judicial review, which should protect existing rights from democratic excesses – not broaden the scope of Charter provisions to, in effect, create new rights.[31]

SIGNIFICANCE OF NEW EQUALITY PARADIGM

The occasion to interpret and define rights has encouraged the judiciary to give more critical reflection to the relationship between protected rights and state actions. A heightened, more conscious sense of the courts' responsibility for protecting rights has also manifested itself in a re-evaluation of legal approaches to discrimination, with a new focus on human dignity and respect as foundations for equality. Changing judicial attitudes about the meaning of equality, and the judiciary's role in giving effect to this, have been extremely relevant for the judiciary's reception of lesbian and gay equality claims. Legal recognition of lesbian and gay relationships is in a period of transition. Courts are moving well beyond an earlier pre-Charter period, when judges tolerated criminal sanctions and the exclusion of lesbians and gay men from policy benefits, or condoned moral claims that defined homosexuality as deviant behaviour.

Although judges are expected to share in the societal consensus around most values, judicial review of the Charter demonstrates a willingness to re-examine and question the normative validity of legislative assumptions and objectives. The court has focused both on the intent and on the effects of social policies that deny equal dignity and respect for some. The emphasis on dignity and respect for enduring relationships has set in motion a process of examining whether constitutional norms should recognize same-sex family units as the legal and moral equivalents of traditional families.

The breadth and scope of judicial acceptance of lesbian and gay relationships and sexual conduct have not yet been tested. We know more about how courts view the legal status of same-sex relationships, particularly where these relationships are viewed as analogous to long-term heterosexual relationships, than we do about judicial views on homosexual conduct. The judiciary may not be as supportive of lesbian and gay rights where the claimed reasons for discrimination are more complicated than the omission of legislative benefits to same-sex relationships. This is suggested by the Supreme Court's judgment in *Little Sisters Book and Art Emporium v. Canada (Minister of Justice)*,[32] involving a gay and lesbian bookstore with a long-running conflict with Canada Customs, which routinely held up or seized shipments of materials on the grounds that they were obscene. Here, a central issue in the Charter conflict was whether the Supreme Court itself had contributed to this discretionary treatment. In an earlier decision, *R. v. Butler*,[33] the court had redefined the meaning of obscenity. A claim in the *Little Sisters* case was that this new definition of obscenity is discriminatory because it utilizes a single community standard for harm that is not sensitive to the specific circumstances or context of homosexual erotica and its relationship to lesbian and gay communities.[34] The court rejected this argument.[35] Although it accepted that the owners of the store had been discriminated against, the majority placed the fault on Canada Customs' insufficient staff, resources, and training to ensure fair and expeditious treatment of gay and lesbian bookstores.[36] The court ruled that one aspect of the customs legislation was invalid, namely, the provision establishing an administrative review process that places the onus on the importer to establish that goods are not obscene.[37] But the majority said that it was not practical to declare the legislation unconstitutional because of this clause alone.[38]

Despite the court's reluctance in *Little Sisters* to provide a remedy for discrimination against lesbians and gay men,[39] judicial interpretation of equality, as it applies to lesbians and gay men, has generally demonstrated the Charter's potential to transform legal culture in a way that critically examines the fairness and legitimacy of the dominant legal, social, and moral assumptions of legislative decisions. The Charter does not simply appear to coincide with this evolution. It has provided both the occasion and the foundation from which to reassess previous judicial assumptions and approaches.

CHANGES TO GAY REFORM STRATEGIES

Accumulating jurisprudence that is receptive to lesbian and gay equality claims, the authority of the Supreme Court, and the popularity of the Charter establish favourable conditions to emphasize a court-oriented, rights-based strategy to pursue legislative reforms. But this represents a significant change in the choice of political strategy and the role played by rights claiming. Before the Charter, the purpose of rights claiming was directed as much towards mobilization – to build a social movement around gay liberation – as towards specific legal and legislative victories. As Smith argues, the goal was to challenge "the dominant codes of society." This was important to the movement because "if lesbians and gay men were not free to be out, if they did not decide to be publicly visible, then the movement could not exist."[40] Under the Charter, the strategy changed to the pursuit of legal victories as goals in themselves.[41] Although this choice of strategy is contentious, for the reasons discussed in the previous chapter,[42] lesbians and gay men have actively utilized rights claiming with the expectation that legal victories will translate into legislative reforms: "The gay liberation movement in Canada had moved decisively away from equality-seeking and litigation by 1980; the fact that the movement's state-directed activism turned toward litigation and toward the specific interpretative framework of rights talk in the late eighties and nineties cannot be explained without reference to the Charter's impact."[43]

Had the Supreme Court spurned the equality claims of lesbian and gay men, this would almost certainly have influenced lesbian and gay strategies about where and how to pursue their reform objectives. Substantial constitutional setbacks would likely have encouraged lesbian and gay organizations to develop approaches that were not as court-centred or rights-dependent. Whether this would have been a negative occurrence depends entirely upon one's view of how to conceive and pursue reform objectives. For those activists who worry about the implications of a minority paradigm or the adoption of familial ideology, Charter victories may not seem as valuable as they do to others.

Yet the attention and legitimacy that derive from judicial validation of rights claims have provided lesbian and gay activists with an important resource in responding to arguments that would resist legislative changes. The rallying call may not be an appeal to historic promises, as it is in the United States, but instead to adherence to the very normative principles to which society has recently expressed commitment.

CHANGES TO POLITICAL BEHAVIOUR

To understand the political reception of lesbian and gay equality claims, it is important to remember the trajectory of legislative reforms to redress discrimination against lesbian and gay men. A significant reason why gay men and lesbians did not have earlier success in the political arena was the failure of both judges and political representatives to accept the premise of their normative claims. Had the Supreme Court dismissed Charter claims that distinctions based on sexual orientation do not violate equality, or continued to rule that legislative choices are reasonable where they favour heterosexual unions and families while failing to extend benefits to those in same-sex relationships, governments would not have the same imperative to introduce what were, and remain, controversial reforms.

At the time of the Charter's adoption, Quebec was the only province to include protection in human rights legislation against this form of discrimination. Other provinces eventually reformed their human rights legislation, but many did so only after courts had ruled that the absence of this protection was contrary to the Charter. In early Charter litigation, governments initially tried to maintain existing legislative distinctions that were based on the heterosexual family unit and, when unsuccessful, appealed lower court rulings to the Supreme Court. Legislative inclination to redress these policy distinctions did not generally arise until the Supreme Court made it clear that equality in the Charter does not permit the denial of benefits to lesbians and gay men or recognition of their relationships, and that the court does not accept this discrimination as a reasonable limit on equality.

As experience with the Charter increases, so does the willingness of political representatives to acknowledge that the Charter's normative values confer obligations on Parliament. In 1985 there was little indication that the federal government thought that equality rights in the Charter should constrain or influence its policy choices. The government did not conceive of the Charter as imposing new normative standards but as providing a statement of principles whose meaning, when applied to social conflicts, should be influenced by public opinion about contentious issues. In the specific context of legislative treatment of lesbians and gay men, the government did not believe that discrimination should be considered unlawful because it gave rise to "social dilemmas" that could not readily be reconciled.[44] This contrasts with the far greater acknowledgment in 2000 of the necessity for change and the acceptance of the normative claim for fair and equitable treatment of lesbians and gay men. Both in parliamentary discussion and in published material explaining the reasons and nature of the pending changes associated with the Modernization of Benefits and Obligations Act, the federal government acknowledged its normative obligations to respect core values enshrined in the Charter – in particular, equality.[45] This change has likely less to do with a different government being in power than with the gradual change in political acceptance of this interpretation of equality.

For those jurisdictions that have complied with this new judicial imperative to redress legislative distinctions that exclude same-sex partners from social-policy benefits, legislative changes have been defended politically as essential measures to comply with the Charter's normative values or, in some cases, to fulfil a judicially compelled requirement. Regardless of the nuance, legislative reforms have recognized lesbians and gay men as deserving of equal benefits and worthy of equal dignity and respect. This is significant because it suggests growing acceptance for the idea that legislative discrimination against lesbians and gay men violates a fundamental right. Remedying discrimination, in other words, is not being treated as a second-level issue.

Moreover, by prefacing these legislative changes as a necessary response to Charter imperatives, governments have stronger leverage against dissidents within their party and opposition members who have difficulty with the idea of recognizing same-sex partners as spouses. Opposition parties do not generally challenge the legitimacy of the Supreme Court's authority in defining Charter values. Thus, the legitimacy of the Charter and the authority of the court constrain the extent to which they can object to legislative reforms.

The popularity of the Charter and the high public regard for the Supreme Court[46] also make it difficult for governments which disagree with the moral view of the court to repudiate the legitimacy of Supreme Court Charter rulings. However reluctant governments may be to amend legislation to make social benefits more inclusive of same-sex relationships, they have not invoked the legislative override to provide a temporal reprieve from the need to comply with judicial rulings. Alberta has been the only jurisdiction to use the override, and this decision did not materially affect benefits for lesbians and gay men. The override was attached, pre-emptively, to legislation that defined marriage – despite the province's lack of jurisdiction to define marriage. If anything, this political statement linking the use of the override to an exclusively heterosexual definition of marriage may provide lesbian and gay activists with a useful resource in support of their argument that lesbians and gays should be able to marry legally. They can now claim that the Alberta government itself recognizes that the denial of marriage for same-sex partners conflicts with protected Charter rights. Moreover, there are signs of greater acceptance in Alberta for this new equality paradigm: the province's decision to undertake a comprehensive review of social policies, and, more important, its indication that it is willing to concede, rather than to challenge, the claim that the denial of recognition for same-sex relationships is unconstitutional.

CONCLUSIONS

Rights claiming by lesbians and gay men and judicial validation of these claims have exposed considerable legislative discrimination in Canada. Judicial rulings that same-sex families must be considered the legal equivalent to heterosexual families run contrary to the normative assumptions upon which social policies have traditionally been based.

A sceptical view of the reform potential of a bill of rights would expect to see neither judicial support for these claims nor political compliance with such judicial rulings, where the normative emphasis diverges so sharply from previous assumptions and practices.

The role of the Charter in contributing to legislative reforms has been complex and multidimensional. An important part of the story is the influence that Canada's new constitutional paradigm is having on judicial approaches and assumptions, on groups' behaviour and strategies, and on political responses to rights claiming, particularly where these are validated by the Supreme Court. The Charter has had a dynamic effect on how the judiciary views its institutional responsibilities, how it defines the methodology of reviewing rights claims, and how it evaluates impugned legislative decisions. It has provided an opportunity and reason for the judiciary to reassess its approach to discrimination, resulting in a new equality-rights paradigm that questions the validity of legislative distinctions that deny benefits or recognition to individuals on the basis of their sexual orientation. Lesbians and gay men have altered their reform strategies and have increasingly utilized legally based rights claims to pursue specific legislative changes. Receptive judicial rulings and the political significance of the remedies they offer have encouraged reliance on this particular strategy. Even though representative institutions initially lagged behind the Supreme Court, in terms of their commitment to this new equality paradigm, they are now coming to accept that equality precludes discrimination on the basis of sexual orientation. This reception is influenced by the role of the Charter in strengthening a rights culture, which is becoming strongly enough ingrained in Canadian political discourse that governments are not generally prepared to challenge the legitimacy of judicial rulings. Representative institutions are keenly aware that, at a broad societal level, the Charter has become a popular national symbol of justice,[47] providing an accepted set of normative standards from which to evaluate the justification for state actions and, by implication, the public values these reflect.

The significance of the reform role of the Charter also lies in the authority, opportunity, and incentive it has provided for broader societal reflection upon whether the values it embodies are actually being respected in legislative choices. The Charter focuses attention on the need to justify legislative distinctions that affect or deny rights. In so doing, it casts scrutiny on whether the reasons for differential treatment are consistent with equality, fairness, and justice. The normative message in these judicial gay rights rulings, about living up to the ideal of equality, has had considerable resonance for the polity. It appeals to one of the most cherished and highly regarded human rights, around which a strong consensus clearly exists.

Despite the cautious expectations about the ability of a bill of rights to protect rights claims that lack societal consensus, judicial and legislative reception of the equality claims of lesbians and gay men suggest a necessary and important qualification to the sceptical thesis. This qualification arises from the use of the Charter to expose gaps between the polity's commitment to fundamental values, as represented in the Charter and around which there is consensus, and the practices and institutional assumptions that fall short of these values. The qualification is the following: *The Charter may be effective in protecting rights claims that initially lack broad support when it is used to encourage or compel the polity to re-examine existing practices and reform these to adhere to the normative values around which fundamental consensus exists.*

The extent to which the polity is willing to reassess the normative merits of legislation choices also has implications for the harm thesis. If greater judicial and political support for the equality claims of lesbians and gay men follows from more critical reflection on the disjunction between equality and legislative distinctions that deny same-sex partners the benefits accorded to heterosexual spouses and families, doubt is cast on applicability of the harm thesis. If lesbian and gay rights claims lead to legislative reforms that provide for equality, it becomes difficult to accept that this form of rights talk represents merely second-level interests or that these rights claims are inappropriate for the judicial arena.

Conclusion

The Charter of Rights has had a significant impact on legislative agendas. The reasons for its influence are complex and multivaried. They stem from political, bureaucratic, legal, and cultural changes associated with the introduction of this new constitutional instrument for protecting rights. The establishment of rights as critical standards to evaluate the justification for state action is both sufficiently recent and profound that the judiciary and representative institutions are still adapting to the Charter's implications for governing. Still in flux are issues relating to how the Charter alters legislative and judicial responsibilities and the appropriate relationship between Parliament and the judiciary in the definition of how Charter principles direct and constrain legislative choices.

Throughout this book I have argued for shared parliamentary and judicial responsibility for resolving Charter conflicts. In so doing, I am arguing contrary to the tendency in legal and political analysis to accept a judicial-centric approach for interpreting the Charter. My perspective, as I have said, is not derived from scepticism about the salutary merits of the Charter, distrust of the judiciary, or criticism that its approach is too activist. Rather, it is informed by concern that excessive reliance on judicial wisdom to resolve contentious social conflicts will lead representative institutions to renege on their responsibility to make responsible decisions about how to reconcile compelling legislative purposes with the values espoused in the Charter.

Appeals to these normative values provide important guidelines to the resolution of Charter conflicts. Certain doubt may be cast on the legitimacy of obviously intolerant or illiberal objectives. But for many

Charter conflicts, legislative decisions infringing Charter values are not so patently incongruent with fundamental values that reasonable and tolerant people will overwhelmingly reject the validity of political judgment. That a right has been claimed does not necessarily clarify how a Charter conflict should be resolved. The applicability of abstract rights provisions to specific social conflicts will require difficult decisions about the significance of the rights claim, the importance of the policy objective, and the reasonableness of the particular legislative means chosen to pursue the legislative goal.

The Supreme Court's approach to judicial review, which distinguishes whether a right exists from the justification for the state action that conflicts with it, focuses attention on the need for careful judgment about what kinds of state actions are justified when they create tension with protected rights. In the making of these judgements, important questions will regularly arise about the role of the state, such as how active government should be when trying to anticipate and redress societal harms, and what its responsibilities are to respond to power imbalances that accrue because of unequal distributions of resources or power. Responses to these questions will be mired in political, philosophical, and subjective differences that reflect ideological and normative assumptions about the role of the state, human behaviour, and societal obligations. Moreover, these conflicts give rise to questions about institutional relationships: What standards or criteria should impugned legislation be evaluated against? And how much discretion should be given to representative institutions to define legislative responses to societal concerns? Thus, evaluating the merits of public-policy objectives that purport to be in the interests of society, and deciding about the appropriate resolution of conflicts between these and protected rights, may give rise to plural rather than singular reasonable responses.

The inevitability of serious disagreements about how the Charter should influence social policy has serious implications for the development of legislative agendas. If courts settle contentious issues, without Parliament first making known its judgment about how the Charter's principles should influence legislative objectives, Parliament will have forfeited the opportunity to influence how the judiciary views and assesses these conflicts. Moreover, if Parliament is seemingly cavalier about Charter obligations, the judiciary will have little incentive to be sensitive to its perspective. Consequently, legislation may be more vulnerable to judicial invalidation.

Another concern with a judicial-centric approach is that it provides only partial protection for rights. To assume that rights will and can be protected only by courts gives insufficient attention to the possible occurrence of rights infringements that may never be litigated. Only a fraction of legislative decisions will ever be subject to judicial review. Thus, legislation often represents a final and authoritative decision about how to balance rights, values, interests, and other policy perspectives. For this reason, the overriding goal of the Charter, of ensuring that state actions are consistent with its normative values, may not be fully realized if legislative decision making is not sufficiently guided by respect for Charter values.

For these reasons I have suggested that the salutary benefits of the Charter are best realized if Parliament accepts that it shares responsibility with the judiciary to make principled judgments about the justification for state actions. By this I do not mean that Parliament should simply assert its preferred view, without regard for judicial concerns, or gauge its options entirely on the basis of anticipation of what the judiciary might say. Neither Parliament nor the judiciary should aspire to replicate each other's judgment. The approach I envisage emphasizes that Parliament and the judiciary each satisfy themselves that their judgment is justified and, when differences arise, reflect on the opinion of those situated differently, relative to the Charter conflict. The significance of alternative judgments is not that they are necessarily more enlightened or principled. It is that they are made from different focal points and reflect distinct institutional responsibilities. The alternative perspectives brought to the resolution of a Charter conflict may address concerns overlooked or given insufficient attention in the other's judgment. In Parliament's case, a court's contrary judgment should be considered and its different concerns addressed, even if ultimately disagreed with. Before disagreeing with a judicial judgment, the nature and severity of the rights infringement should be part of any process of reaching judgment about whether a legislative objective is justified in light of its implications for protected rights and values.

When parliamentary judgment differs from judicial opinion about how to reconcile Charter conflicts, these differences can be expressed in several ways, depending on the nature of the disagreement. Parliament can object to how the judiciary reassessed a common law rule in light of the Charter, and pass legislation that assigns a different priority to the conflicting values involved. A different expression of disagreement may arise after legislation has been nullified. Parliament may decide to pass new legislation that differs from the Supreme Court's approach, with the deliberate intent of trying to convince the court that Parliament's perspective is reasonable and justified. In this case, the government lawyers will likely focus on section 1 arguments in defending Parliament's decision about the appropriate resolution of conflicting values. The most radical expression of disagreement will be to invoke the override, to allow the impugned legislation to stand notwithstanding the court's judgment.

The override, as an expression of profound disagreement with a judicial Charter ruling, should not be impossible to use. But it should be difficult. The burden of persuasion should rest on those supporting its use. If Parliament is to endorse a course of action that is contrary to judicial assessments of the appropriate resolution of conflicting values, it should satisfy itself that its judgment is justified and consistent with the normative standards in the Charter. Its focal point should not be the popularity of the measure. Rather, when Parliament disagrees with judicial rulings, the ensuing political discussion should confront the implications of denying the right and whether the legislative purpose is consistent with the values that are integral to a free and democratic society. One can hope that the demand for reasons to support overriding a protected right will make the override more difficult to justify. With this approach, too, Parliament may well find it less easy to hide behind prejudices that are not valid policy considerations.

As argued earlier, the more fundamental the right that is being infringed, the more difficult it should be to restrict. Although many may be troubled by the suggestion that some rights are more important than others, it is important to emphasize that not all rights claims are of equal importance, even when they receive judicial validation. Tobacco advertising is a good example of what I consider a marginal rights claim. Such advertising is far removed from the philosophical reasons for protecting expression from state restrictions. Judicial recognition of this right has more to do with the particular approach chosen by the court to review Charter claims than to any normative value associated with advertising or promoting tobacco products.

In contrast to the marginal nature of tobacco advertising, equality, and the right to be free from discrimination, epitomizes a core right. Its protection lies at the heart of the reasons why a polity wishes to protect rights from state interference. The importance of equality in a democratic polity is to ensure that all members are allowed to contribute to the making of decisions that affect their public and private lives and that they have equal expectations to the benefits and burdens of policies that affect them. Its protection is essential to the functioning of a democratic polity. For this reason, it is extremely difficult to imagine that legislative restrictions resulting in discrimination severe enough to require use of the override could be normatively justified. What is sadly lacking in the Charter, and in political conventions around its use, are accepted normative criteria for evaluating the justification for invoking this power.

Not surprisingly, in light of the nascent state of judicial and political approaches to the Charter, no settled pattern has arisen from parliamentary responses to judicial rulings. The social policies examined here reveal a range of legislative responses to the Charter, varying from an unwavering acceptance of how the judiciary has framed the relevant rights conflict to an openly confrontational position that challenges the very assumptions that underlie a legal ruling.

In some instances where legislation has been nullified, or when the judiciary has changed a common law rule in light of the Charter, the political reaction has been characterized by a high degree of risk-aversion, inspired by a desire to minimize the likelihood of losses in future Charter litigation. For example, the government's legal advisers worked closely with Health officials after comprehensive restrictions on tobacco advertising were nullified. Together, they developed a legislative scheme to restrict tobacco advertising that was based on a "cut and paste" approach to the majority Supreme Court ruling in *RJR-MacDonald*. The legislative response was characterized by a desire to "Charter proof" new legislation so as to address and anticipate the judiciary's specific and likely concerns.

While some might applaud this effort, as a welcome sign that Parliament is taking its obligations to respect Charter values seriously, I am far from convinced that risk-aversion is the best measure of responsible parliamentary judgment. An important distinction should be made between respecting fundamental rights when evaluating policy choices and opting for non-ambitious and ineffective legislative goals and means because of the possibility that courts may disagree with their reasonableness. Governing under the Charter requires careful decisions about how to pursue objectives in the public interest while respecting fundamental values. The significance of the rights restriction and its severity are both important considerations. But not all rights claims, even when validated by the court, necessarily warrant the same degree of vigilance in their protection from legislative objectives that Parliament deems important. Moreover, it is Parliament, not the judiciary, that has access to the extensive resources necessary for prudent and responsible policy choices about how to pursue legislative goals. These are located in a large bureaucracy with departmental specialists who, in developing policy, have been able to authorize comprehensive studies, access broader social-science materials, consult with experts in the relevant policy community and with non-governmental actors, borrow from the experiences of other Canadian and foreign legislatures, and utilize an institutional memory of how the policy objective has evolved, including the successes and failures of previous strategies.

It is this form of judgment, of reconciling Charter concerns with legislative purposes, that characterizes political responsibility. But fulfilling this responsibility is not necessarily realized by an uncritical adoption of judicial perspectives, particularly on the issue of how best to pursue a complex legislative objective. Judges' expertise lies more in defining rights than in suggesting appropriate ways to pursue complex legislative initiatives.

Quite apart from the fact that Parliament is better situated than the judiciary to identify the appropriate means to pursue policy, it is difficult to anticipate how the judiciary will rule on a particular legislative challenge, despite the best attempts of legal advisers. Charter jurisprudence is still evolving and the judiciary may not yet have addressed the relevant issues in a conclusive or consistent manner. When judges retire, their replacements may have a different interpretation of the relevant Charter principles.

Risk-aversion, focusing heavily on what a court might say, could also divert attention from other relevant concerns that may be important for effective policy decisions. In the context of regulating tobacco advertising, the government was seemingly indifferent about the merits of basing its new, revised legislation on unsolicited judicial advice. Yet serious questions arise about the relevance of judicial expertise to the objective of changing adolescent behaviour or addressing the effects of marketing strategies intended to induce smoking. The benefit of this policy wisdom was even more questionable in the face of health workers' emphasis on comprehensive rather than partial measures to discourage young people from smoking.

Risk-aversion also characterized the approach taken to establishing a DNA data bank. Here the government was strongly influenced by its advisers' interpretation of changes to the common law. Arguably, the Charter concerns at issue were far more serious than in the tobacco case and, for this reason, judicial perspectives were understandably central to framing the parameters of the legislative regime. Though the jurisprudence on this subject was far from complete and had not addressed many of the relevant issues, the assumption implicit in the government's position was that its choices were determined and constrained by the relevant jurisprudence. Yet the court has indicated that its judgment about the reconciliation of Charter values with public-interest concerns may be different when it interprets legislation as distinct from the common law. The reason for this is that Parliament may have valid perspectives that are not apparent when the court is relying only on the common law. Thus, the development of legislation to regulate uses of DNA provided Parliament with an important opportunity, for which it did not take full advantage, to contribute to constitutional judgment about how to reconcile Charter concerns arising from uses of this new technology for law-enforcement purposes.

Risk-aversion epitomizes a judicial-centric approach. The idea of "Charter proofing" legislation against a judicially defined standard does not recognize the legitimate political element of constitutional judgment about the priority that should be attached to conflicting values or about the ways to pursue worthwhile legislative objectives that might infringe, in some manner, on protected rights. Confining legislative objectives to those for which government lawyers can confidently predict legal success may lead to Parliament reneging on its responsibility to undertake initiatives in the public interest, and to pursue these effectively.

Not all governmental responses to Charter rulings have been characterized by risk-aversion. The best examples of Parliament assuming and acting on its responsibility for reconciling Charter conflicts occurred in responses to Supreme Court rulings about how the Charter affects sexual assault trials. Legislation challenged many of the assumptions central to judicial rulings. Parliament addressed concerns that trial judges had been influenced by prejudicial assumptions that women were somehow culpable for being raped. Legislation responded to the Supreme Court's ruling that would have allowed criminal defence lawyers easy access therapeutic records in an effort to undermine the complainants' credibility. Parliament also disagreed with the court on the issue of whether extreme intoxication should be a defence to sexual assault charges. Although the legislative responses reflected Parliament's profound disagreement with many of the assumptions central to judicial rulings, these differences were not expressed in a manner that was dismissive of the Charter's legitimacy. Rather, the differences were presented and debated in Parliament as an alternative interpretation of the Charter. In recognition that Parliament shares responsibility to make constitutional judgments about the Charter, its legislative responses were carefully framed as a stage in a conversation with the judiciary. The federal government, aware of the need to justify its alternative judgment, consciously used legislative procedures (parliamentary hearings) and drafting techniques (preambles) to communicate to courts the purposes and philosophy of each legislative decision.

The Supreme Court has indicated that it accepts that Parliament has a valid role to play when interpreting how to reconcile conflicting Charter values. Moreover, it has suggested that judicial views on how the Charter changes a common law rule should not be considered a rigid constitutional template that must be strictly adhered to by Parliament.

In other words, the court accepts that it does not hold a monopoly on Charter judgment and that a range of reasonable responses may be acceptable for resolving some Charter conflicts.

One lesson that has emerged from the juxtaposition of parliamentary and judicial Charter judgment in Charter conflicts is that responsible legislative responses to judicial rulings require more time than may be accorded by the Supreme Court. The court's decision in *R. v. Feeney*, which created a new requirement that police obtain a warrant to enter private dwellings for the purpose of making an arrest, and prompted the government to respond with legislation, underscores this point. If political decisions about how to reconcile Charter values with legislative objectives are to reflect careful parliamentary judgment, sufficient time is required for effective consultation and careful scrutiny. Thus, the judiciary should be conscious of the necessity for a realistic time-frame in the enactment of new legislation, which, in normal circumstances when Parliament is sitting, is likely a minimum of twelve months.

Sufficient time for an informed legislative response to a judicial ruling is one consideration. But prolonged legislative inaction raises other concerns. The latter response, and its consequences for those whose rights are being infringed, is understandably a serious judicial concern. The most significant Charter disagreement examined here focuses on the legitimacy of social-policy distinctions that are based exclusively on a heterosexual norm. The Supreme Court has denied the legitimacy of these distinctions and cast doubt on the validity of a broad range of social policies across all jurisdictions. Legislative inaction has characterized some governments' responses to Charter rulings on lesbian and gay equality claims. But this form of parliamentary reaction cannot be characterized as an example of principled judgment. Legislative inaction is not motivated by an attempt to persuade judges of a better way to reconcile conflicting Charter values or to assert the primacy of Parliament's judgment. If governments were profoundly opposed to these judicial rulings, they would use the override (although, as suggested above, overriding equality will be difficult to justify). Fear of political controversy may have discouraged use of the override. But if this is so, elected officials do not have sufficient confidence in the justification for such an extreme form of disagreement. Legislative inaction, rather than being an expression of political judgment, represents a stalling tactic, an attempt to bide time until circumstances are deemed more favourable for generating internal party consensus, or until further delay is no longer possible because of a judicial imperative that legislative reforms be introduced immediately.

These judicial/parliamentary disagreements raise an interesting question for the normative claim made throughout the book – that a reasonable resolution of Charter conflicts is not necessarily amenable to a singular correct answer. Is legislative refusal to comply with judicial gay rights rulings a justifiable and reasonable expression of disagreement? Do differences in citizens' moral or religious attitudes, with respect to how they view homosexuality, validate legislative inaction in the face of judicial rulings that existing legislation is unconstitutional?

In a word, no. As argued earlier, Parliament should be extremely cautious before imposing restrictions on core rights, such as equality. Arguing against a judicial-centric approach to Charter judgment does not justify moral relativism. The call for shared responsibility aims to have Parliament exercise principled judgment about the merits of legislative decisions. Its conclusions may diverge from judicial opinions. Yet, if legislation has significant implications for protected rights, it should be subject to careful and deliberate political evaluation to determine whether the objective is justified, with respect to the merits of the concern it addresses and the seriousness of the rights infringement.

The judiciary's liberty from political pressures and its particular focus on the rights dimension of a constitutional conflict are both reasons why Parliament should be particularly attentive to the normative messages about rights in judicial rulings. Where the Supreme Court has ruled that core rights have been infringed – those rights that relate to the very philosophical reasons a polity wishes to protect rights from state actions – these rulings especially warrant scrupulous political attention. The more serious the rights infringement, the more cautious Parliament should be before it adopts any action (or inaction) that would infringe this right.

The Supreme Court's rulings on lesbian and gay equality fall into this category of rulings that warrant scrupulous attention. The struggle to escape arbitrary treatment and the search for personal freedom have been defining features of Westeen civilization since the sixteenth century. In this context, it is difficult to conceive how legislative distinctions that have been created and sustained to perpetuate a heterosexual norm, while excluding differences, can be viewed as anything but a violation of equality. Individuals, for no reason other than their sexuality, are denied the legitimate expectation of the equal effects of the law. That people may differ in their moral or religious attitudes with respect to how they view homosexuality, or that the Charter does not explicitly state its intention to ban discrimination on the basis of sexual orientation, does not support a conclusion that this equality claim should be thought of as anything but a fundamental, core right.

If there is room for reasonable differences on the question of how the Charter's values affect social-policy distinctions that affect lesbians and gay men, it is more likely to arise around the issue of how equality should be respected, not if it should be protected. Reasonable disagreements may arise over the specific details of how recognition of same-sex relationships should take place. For example, must the term spouse be used to describe same-sex partners, or can a different term, such as common law partner, be adopted? Is a domestic partnership an acceptable alternative to marriage?

The argument that Parliament shares responsibility for constitutional judgment about the reconciliation of legislative objectives and Charter values is still very much of an ideal rather than a general description of existing practices. But it is an ideal that government and Parliament should work more deliberately towards attaining. Ronald Dworkin's insistence, more than two decades ago, that liberal societies should *take rights seriously* is well known and often cited.[1] This demand has appeal, at an abstract level. But since the applicability of abstract rights provisions to specific social conflicts will necessarily give rise to philosophical differences about the significance of the rights claim involved, the role of the state to redress social problems, the importance of the policy objective, and the reasonableness of the particular legislative means chosen to pursue the legislative goal, Dworkin's emphasis seems misplaced. Perhaps the more appropriate imperative is *to take seriously the obligation to render responsible judgment, particularly when rights are affected.* It is this aspect of judgment, the reconciliation of conflicting values and legislative objectives, that is a prime focus of Charter decisions. There is no valid reason to assume that this responsibility is uniquely conferred upon the judiciary. Nevertheless, the extent to which Parliament will be able to convince the judiciary about the merits of how it believes Charter conflicts should be resolved may be a direct reflection of the extent of its commitment to careful and principled judgment. To a considerable degree, Parliament is likely to get the kinds of judicial rulings it deserves. Where serious questions arise about the merits of legislative choices in light of the Charter's normative values, and these uncertainties have not been persuasively addressed in any public or transparent fashion, courts are understandably reluctant to accept Parliament's judgment.

A government can facilitate a far richer parliamentary contribution to Charter judgment than the restrictive option of simply reacting to negative judicial rulings. The federal government's conscious use of parliamentary hearings in responding to the Supreme Court's creation of an intoxication defence for sexual assault suggests expectations of a linkage between parliamentary deliberation and success in litigation. But there is little reason why the government should be so selective in viewing Parliament as an important venue for expressing political judgment on Charter issues. Government has a vested interest in passing legislation that will survive Charter litigation. Yet this may also coincide with necessary respect for Parliament's role to scrutinize bills for consistency with Charter values and to establish a public record of the reasons that legislation diverges from judicial interpretation of the Charter, as part of the project of establishing the merits of parliamentary judgment. Otherwise, legislative responses that reflect political disagreements with judicial rulings may be more vulnerable to judicial nullification. Moreover, the lack of any publicly available record indicating that there has been careful political judgment about how Charter values should guide and be reflected in legislation will reinforce the assumption, already prevalent in society, that the judiciary is the only capable and credible body to respect rights principles.

Notes

INTRODUCTION

1 Michael Mandel, *The Charter of Rights and the Legalization of Politics in Canada* (Toronto: Wall and Thompson 1989).
2 Peter W. Hogg and Allison A. Bushell, "The *Charter* Dialogue between Courts and Legislatures (or Perhaps the *Charter of Rights* Isn't Such a Bad Thing after All)," *Osgoode Hall Law Journal* 35: 1 (1997), 105.
3 Section 33 (1) provides that "Parliament or the legislature of a province may expressly declare in an Act of Parliament or of the legislature, as the case may be, that the Act or a provision thereof shall operate notwithstanding a provision included in section 2 or sections 7 to 15 of this Charter."

CHAPTER ONE

1 See, for example, Ronald Dworkin, "Liberalism," in Stuart Hampshire, ed., *Public and Private Morality* (New York: Cambridge University Press 1978); *Law's Empire* (Cambridge, Mass.: Harvard University Press 1986); *A Matter of Principle* (Cambridge, Mass.: Harvard University Press 1985).
2 In 1990 New Zealand adopted the Bill of Rights Act and borrowed from Canada this concept of executive scrutiny and parliamentary evaluation. Courts are given authority to interpret legislative enactments where possible, in a manner that is consistent with the protected rights and freedoms. But the Bill of Rights stops short of allowing judges to nullify legislation that conflicts with protected rights. Instead, it contemplates political scrutiny as

the method for deciding whether legislation is justified. The Bill of Rights Act requires in section 7 that the attorney general report to the House of Representatives where bills appear to conflict with the protected rights and freedoms. This intent to utilize political scrutiny was clearly the product of political compromise, necessitated by weak support for judicial review of an entrenched bill of rights that gave courts the power to declare offending legislation unconstitutional.

3 Britain passed the Human Rights Act 1998, which incorporates the European Convention on Human Rights into United Kingdom law. However, the act preserves parliamentary sovereignty. Courts have the duty to interpret all legislation in accordance with the convention as far as this is possible. Where this is not possible, courts are empowered to make a declaration of incompatibility. After that, government can decide whether or not to amend the offending legislation to make it compatible with the convention. Thus, the degree to which legislation respects rights concerns may rely, to considerable extent, on the willingness of Parliament and government to ensure that legislation is compliant.

4 Australia has not adopted a bill of rights but several jurisdictions have established a parliamentary committee to evaluate proposed legislation for consistency with rights and other principles of justice. Two Commonwealth Australian Senate committees are considered models for the parliamentary evaluation procedure anticipated in Britain. These are the Standing Committee on Regulations and Ordinances and the Standing Committee for the Scrutiny of Bills, which evaluate compliance with human rights principles. Other jurisdictions that have established committees are Victoria, with its Scrutiny of Acts and Regulations Committee, and Queensland, with its Scrutiny of Legislation Committee.

5 For a discussion of different judicial assumptions see Walter Surma Tarnopolsky, *The Canadian Bill of Rights*, 2nd edition, (Toronto: Macmillan Company of Canada Limited 1978), 128–167.

6 The Bill of Rights does not apply to the provinces.

7 This obligation arose from section 3 of the bill which was subsequently amended by section 29 of the Statutory Instruments Act, 1971. Tarnopolsky, *The Canadian Bill of Rights,* 125.

8 This regulation also required that all authorities with responsibility for making regulations forward proposed regulations to the Clerk of the Privy Council, who, in consultation with the deputy minister of justice, would examine them to ensure that a regulation "does not trespass unduly on existing rights and freedoms and is not, in any case, inconsistent with the purposes and provisions of the *Canadian Bill of Rights.* "

9 Section 6 of the Statutory Orders and Regulations, SOR/61–16, *Canada Gazette*, Part II, 25 Jan. 1961, 75.

10 Committee on Human Rights and Fundamental Freedoms, *Proceedings*. Bill C-79: An Act for the Recognition and Protection of Human Rights and Fundamental Freedoms, 20 July 1960, 332–4.

11 Elmer A. Driedger, "The Meaning and Effect of the Canadian *Bill of Rights*: A Draftsman's Viewpoint," *Ottawa Law Review* 9 (1977), 310–11.

12 Ibid., 311. He also believed that in the rare event that the Department of Justice initially overlooked a possible conflict with the Bill of Rights, any inconsistency with rights would be caught at the drafting stage and would still result in sufficient pressure to amend the legislation.

13 Ibid.

14 Ibid.

15 Tarnopolsky, *The Canadian Bill of Rights*, 128.

16 This was in 1975 when the government introduced an amendment to the Feeds Act that was returned from the Senate with a provision that conflicted with the presumption of innocence. Upon its return to the House of Commons, the minister of justice reported that the Senate amendment was an infringement of the Bill of Rights and this section was deleted. Driedger, "The Meaning and Effect of the Canadian *Bill of Rights*", 306.

17 For discussion of these, see Tarnopolsky, *The Canadian Bill of Rights*, 127–8.

18 *Law Society of Upper Canada v Skapinker* [1984] 1 SCR 357.

19 *Singh v. Minister of Employment and Immigration* [1985] 1 SCR 177.

20 *R. v. Schachter* [1992] 2 SCR 679.

21 *R. v. Oakes* [1986] 1 SCR 103.

22 *Hunter et al. v. Southam Inc.* [1984] SCR 145.

23 For a discussion of this tension and conflict, see Larry T. Taman, "The Role of the Attorney General in Litigating Charter Claims." Presented at the conference on *Equality: Section 15 and Charter Procedures,* Department of Education, The Law Society of Upper Canada, Toronto, 2 March 1985, M – 6; Grant Huscroft, "The Attorney General and *Charter* Challenges to Legislation: Advocate or Adjudicator?" *National Journal of Constitutional Law* 5 (1995), 138; J. Ll. J. Edwards, "The Attorney General and the Charter of Rights," in R.J. Sharpe, ed., *Charter Litigation* (Toronto: Butterworths 1986); Ian Scott, "The Role of the Attorney General: Constancy and Change in the 1980s," *University of Toronto Law Journal* 39 (1989); Kent Roach, "The Attorney-General and the Charter Revisited," *University of Toronto Law Journal* 50 (2000).

24 Donald J. Savoie, *Governing from the Centre: The Concentration of Power in Canadian Politics* (Toronto: University of Toronto Press 1999), 7.

25 James Kelly, "Bureaucratic Activism and the Charter of Rights and Freedoms: The Department of Justice and Its Entry into the Centre of Government," *Canadian Public Administration* 42 (1999), 478–80.

26 Ibid., 495–8.

27 "Role of the Department of Justice in the Government of Canada," Department of Justice, June 1995.

28 Peter H. Russell, "A Democratic Approach to Civil Liberties," *University of Toronto Law Journal* 19 (1969), 125–6.

29 David Kinley, *The European Convention on Human Rights: Compliance without Incorporation* (Aldershot, U.K.: Dartmouth Publishing 1993), 105.

30 For a more developed argument, see Janet L. Hiebert, *Limiting Rights: The Dilemma of Judicial Review* (Montreal: McGill-Queen's University Press 1996).

31 *R. v. Keegstra* [1990] 3 SCR 697 at 743.

32 Brian Slattery, "A Theory of the Charter," *Osgoode Hall Law Journal* 25:4 (1987), 714.

33 Exceptions are the minister of finance and the president of the Treasury Board, who lead their own central agencies. Savoie, *Governing from the Centre*, 338.

34 For a recent appraisal of Parliament's weakness, see C.E.S. Franks, "Parliament, Intergovernmental Relations and National Unity," Working Papers, (Kingston, Ont.: Queen's University, Institute of Intergovernmental Relations 1999).

35 C.E.S. Franks, *The Parliament of Canada* (Toronto: University of Toronto Press 1987), 221–2.

36 A telling example occurred with respect to the legislative response to a Supreme Court decision to change to a common law rule affecting the ability of police to enter private dwellings. This is discussed in Chapter 7.

37 Individual members have requested copies of reports from the minister of justice to explain conclusions reached from its process of evaluating bills. In the early days of the Charter, requests by committee members to speak to the person "who has certified a bill" in terms of the Charter were met with various explanations for why this was not possible. Included in these were that the concept or word "certify" is a "misnomer" for the process undertaken; that the person certifying a bill is the chief legislative counsel but he or she acts on the advice that is provided by the department; and that "ultimately, the guardian of our Charter advice is the human rights law section." Senate Standing Committee on Legal and Constitutional Affairs, 21 June 1993, 50:44–8.

38 Ibid., Senator Stanbury, 50:47.

CHAPTER TWO

1 These techniques included: a redefinition of sedition, one that was narrower than earlier common law interpretations, in a case in which the Quebec government had prohibited the distribution of religious pamphlets which were "expressive of a seditious intention" (*Boucher v. R.*

[1951] SCR 265); an interpretation of the preamble of the Constitution Act, which requires freedom of discussion and debate, to set aside provincial legislation requiring that newspaper presentation of the provincial policy satisfy the government's criteria of accuracy (*Reference re Alberta Statutes* [1938] 2 SCR 100); federalism grounds, to set aside Quebec legislation which sought to prohibit the propagation of communist ideology in the province (*Switzman v. Elbling and Attorney-General of Quebec* [1957] SCR 285); and an interpretation of tort law which held Quebec Premier Maurice Duplessis personally liable for having caused the wrongful cancellation of a liquor permit in a personal vendetta against Jehovah Witnesses in the province (*Roncarelli v. Duplessis* [1959] SCR 122).

2 *Harrison v. Carswell* [1976] 2 SCR at 218.

3 *Hunter et al. v. Southam Inc.* [1984] 2 SCR 145 at 155.

4 Hon. Bertha Wilson, "We Didn't Volunteer," *Policy Options* 20: 3 (April 1999), 8–11.

5 Miriam Smith, "Ghosts of the JCPC: Lessons for the Study of Law and Politics in Canadian Political Science," Paper presented at the annual meeting of the Canadian Political Science Association, Quebec City, 29 July–1 Aug. 2000.

6 Samuel V. La Selva, *The Moral Foundations of Canadian Federalism: Paradoxes, Achievements, and Tragedies of Nationhood* (Montreal: McGill-Queen's University Press 1996).

7 For a discussion of the linkage between democratic assumptions and fundamental rights' claims, see Janet L. Hiebert, *Limiting Rights: The Dilemma of Judicial Review* (Montreal: McGill-Queen's University Press 1996), Chapter 5, 97–106.

8 See Ronald Dworkin, "Constitutionalism and Democracy," *European Journal of Philosophy* 3 (1995). For Canadian versions, see David Beatty, "A Conservative Court: The Politicization of Law," University *of Toronto Law Journal* 41 (1991), 147–67, and *Talking Heads and the Supremes: The Canadian Production of Constitutional Review* (Toronto: Carswell 1990). See also Lorraine Eisenstat Weinrib, "The Supreme Court of Canada and Section One of the Charter," *The Supreme Court Law Review* 10 (1988), 469–513, and "Canada's Constitutional Revolution: From Legislative to Constitutional State," *Israel Law Review* 33:1 (1999), 13–50.

9 Lorraine Weinrib cites with approval the judicial claim that: "true democracy recognizes the power of the constitution–fruit of the constituent authority – to entrench the fundamental human rights and the basic values of the system against the power of the majority. Such a limitation of majority rule does not impair democracy but constitutes its full realization." Taken from *United Mizrahi Bank Ltd., et al. v. Migdal Cooperative Village, et al* (1995) 49 P.D. 221 (para. 47) (English translation), ibid., "Canada's Constitutional Revolution," 13, 15.

10 Ibid., 24.

11 Weinrib, "The Supreme Court of Canada and Section One of the Charter," 491 [note omitted].

12 Ibid.

13 Beatty, *Talking Heads and the Supremes: The Canadian Production of Constitutional Review,* 36

14 Beatty, "A Conservative's Court," 162.

15 Lorraine Eisenstat Weinrib, "The Activist Constitution," *Policy Options.* 20:3 (1999), 30.

16 Dworkin, "Constitutionalism and Democracy," 2.

17 Ronald Dworkin, *Taking Rights Seriously* (Cambridge, Mass.: Harvard University Press 1978), 149.

18 Ronald Dworkin, *Law's Empire* (Cambridge Mass.: Harvard University Press 1986), 381.

19 Ronald Dworkin, "Liberalism," in Stuart Hampshire, ed., *Public and Private Morality* (New York: Cambridge University Press 1978), 136.

20 Ronald Dworkin, *Taking Rights Seriously,* 124–30, 144–5.

21 Dworkin, "Constitutionalism and Democracy," 11.

22 Laurence Tribe, *American Constitutional Law,* 2nd ed. (New York: Foundation Press 1988), 15.

23 Owen M. Fiss, "The Supreme Court 1978 Term. Forward: The Forms of Justice," *Harvard Law Review* 93 (1979), 10.

24 Ibid., 12–13.

25 Michael J. Perry, *The Constitution, the Courts and Human Rights* (New Haven, Conn.: Yale University Press 1982), 2.

26 Andrée Lajoie and Henry Quillinan, "Emerging Constitutional Norms: Continuous Judicial Amendment of the Constitution – The Proportionality Test as a Moving Target," *Law and Contemporary Problems* 55:1 (1992), 285.

27 It is for this reason that Peter Russell suggests that the idea of protecting rights is deceptively simple. See Peter H. Russell, "Political Purposes of the Canadian Charter of Rights and Freedoms," *Canadian Bar Review* 61 (1983), 43.

28 Jeremy Waldron, *The Dignity of Legislation* (Cambridge, U.K.: Cambridge University Press 1999), 24–5.

29 Ibid., 153.

30 Ibid, 61 (emphasis in Waldron).

31 Ibid., 159–60 (note omitted).

32 Mark Tushnet, *Taking the Constitution away from the Courts* (Princeton, N.J.: Princeton University Press 1999). For comments, and response, see *University of Richmond Law Review* 34:2 (2000), 359–566.

33 See, for example, Duncan Kennedy, *A Critique of Adjudication (fin de Siècle)* (Cambridge, Mass.: Harvard University Press 1998); Allan C. Hutchinson and Andrew Petter, "Private Rights/Public Wrongs: The Liberal Lie of the

Charter," *University of Toronto Law Journal* 34 (1988); Mark Tushnet, "An Essay on Rights," *Texas Law Review* 62 (1984); Hutchinson, *Waiting for Coraf: A Critique of Law and Rights* (Toronto: University of Toronto Press 1995).

34 See, for example, Kimberlé Crenshaw, Neil Gotanda, Gary Peller, and Kendall Thomas, eds., *Critical Race Theory: The Key Writings That Formed the Movement* (New York: New Press 1995).

35 See, for example, Carol Smart, *Feminism and the Power of Law* (London: Routledge 1989); Lynn Hecht Schafran, "Is the Law Male? Let Me Count the Ways," *Chicago-Kent Law Review* 69 (1993); Catherine A. MacKinnon, *Feminism Unmodified: Discourses on Life and Law* (Cambridge, Mass.: Harvard University Press 1987).

36 Mary Eaton, "Lesbians, Gays and the Struggle for Equality Rights: Reversing the Progressive Hypothesis," *Dalhousie Law Journal* 17 (1994), 150.

37 Hutchinson, *Waiting for Coraf.* Joel Bakan is also sceptical about the ability of the Charter to promote the political and social changes that are necessary for social justice. Bakan, *Just Words: Constitutional Rights and Social Wrongs* (Toronto: University of Toronto Press 1997).

38 For a good review of different variations of interpretivism or originalism, understood as constitutional adjudication that accords authority to the text of the constitution or to the intentions of its adopters, see Paul Brest, "The Misconceived Question for the Original Understanding," *Boston University Law Review* 60 (1980), 204–38.

39 Peter H. Russell, Rainer Knopff, and F.L. Morton, *Federalism and the Charter: Leading Constitutional Decisions* (Ottawa: Carleton University Press 1990), 19.

40 See Cass R. Sunstein, "Constitutions and Democracies: An Epilogue," in Jon Elster and Rune Slagstad, eds., *Constitutionalism and Democracy* (New York: Cambridge University Press 1988), 327–53.

41 Gordon J. Schochet, "Introduction: Constitutionalism, Liberalism and the Study of Politics," in J. Roland Pennock and John W. Chapman, eds., *Constitutionalism* (New York: New York University Press 1979), 1.

42 James Madison, Federalist 51, *The Federalist Papers* (New York: New American Library of World Literature 1961), 322.

43 Schochet, "Introduction: Constitutionalism, Liberalism and the Study of Politics," 1.

44 In the American context, John Hart Ely has argued that constitutional provisions exist on a spectrum "ranging from the relatively specific to the extremely open-textured." The due-process clause, which provides that no state shall "deprive any person of life, liberty, or property, without due process of law," is an example of the latter. Ely suggests that the inability of this clause to provide determinate principles has resulted in its use to justify a diverse range of judicial interpretations, from the economic due-process interpretations in the *Lochner v. New York* era in the early part of the last century to the declaration of a right to abortion in *Roe v. Wade* in

the 1970s. John Hart Ely, *Democracy and Distrust: A Theory of Judicial Review* (Cambridge, Mass.: Harvard University Press 1980), 14–15.

45 Schochet argues that the rapid expansion of government, in response to the social, economic, technological, military, and political exigencies of contemporary society, has meant that the concept of constitutionalism, "once part of the standard vocabulary of the student of politics, is now seldom encountered, having fallen into apparent intellectual disrepute." Also contributing to its decline, as the object of scholarly focus, are the widespread reliance on written constitutions, which, ironically, has trivialized the meaning of the concept in terms of the ideological principles it conveys; and the rise of behaviouralism, and its attendant shift in emphasis from laws and institutional structures to systems and social settings and from normative philosophy to more "scientific" and "value-free" generalizations. Shochet, "Introduction: Constitutionalism, Liberalism and the Study of Politics," 5–9.

46 Cass Sunstein points to the "little-remembered" close of The Federalist, no. 19: "A rage for paper money, for an abolition of debts, for an equal division of property, or for any other improper or wicked project, will be less apt to pervade the whole body of the Union than a particular member of it." Sunstein, "Constitutions and Democracies: An Epilogue," 342n.20.

47 For a discussion on the centrality of property concerns to the constitution and its project of limited government, see Jennifer Nedelsky, *Private Property and the Limits of American Constitutionalism: The Madisonian Framework and Its Legacy* (Chicago: University of Chicago Press 1990).

48 F.L. Morton and Rainer Knopff, "The Supreme Court As the Vanguard of the Intelligentsia: The Charter Movement as Postmaterialist Politics," in Janet Ajzenstat, ed., *Canadian Constitutionalism: 1791–1991* (Ottawa: Canadian Study of Parliament Group 1991), 61.

49 Benefits are said to include its protection from arbitrary power (in that the use of public power for private ends is prevented by general rules that are impartially administered); the promotion of individual freedom (this is encouraged by the ability to plan one's objectives within a comparatively secure and predictable environment); government efficiency (associated with the division of institutional labour); and better governance (resulting from the mutual accountability of the powers of each branch of government). See Richard Bellamy, "The Political Form of the Constitution: The Separation of Powers, Rights and Representative Democracy," in Richard Bellamy and Dario Castiglione, eds., *Constitutionalism in Transformation: European and Theoretical Perspectives* (Oxford, U.K.: Blackwell Publishers 1996). See also Maurice Vile, *Constitutionalism and the Separation of Powers* (Oxford, U.K.: Clarendon Press 1996).

50 Richard Bellamy, "The Political Form of the Constitution," 27–8; 35–44; George P. Fletcher, "The Separation of Powers: A Critique of Some Utili-

tarian Justifications," in J. Roland Pennock and John W. Chapman, eds., *Constitutionalism* (New York: New York University Press 1979), 300.

51 Rainer Knopff and F.L. Morton, *Charter Politics* (Scarborough: Nelson Canada 1992), 139.

52 This indispensable character is derived from two aspects of judicial review. The first is its counter-majoritarian character: courts, liberated from the direct control of political majorities, are the only institution capable of safeguarding minority rights. The second is the role of adjudication in resolving complex political and moral disputes. As Manfredi argues, the "atmosphere of impartiality surrounding adjudication lends considerable moral legitimacy and authoritativeness to the decisions of courts on such issues." Christopher P. Manfredi, *Judicial Power and the Charter: Canada and the Paradox of Liberal Constitutionalism* (Toronto: McClelland and Stewart), 36–7.

53 Ibid., 37 [note omitted].

54 Ibid., 46.

55 Christopher P. Manfredi, *Judicial Power and the Charter,* 2nd ed. (Don Mills, Ont.: Oxford University Press 2001), 30–1.

56 Knopff and Morton, *Charter Politics,* 195–6.

57 Rainer Knopff and F.L. Morton, "Does the Charter Hinder Canadians from Becoming a Sovereign People?" in Joseph F. Fletcher, ed., *Ideas in Action: Essays on Politics and Law in Honour of Peter Russell* (Toronto: University of Toronto Press 1999), 287–8.

58 Standing Committee on Justice and Human Rights, Ted Morton, 15 March 2000, *http://www.parl.gc.ca/InfoCom/CommitteeEvidence.asp?Language=*E&Parliament=2&Joint=0&CommitteeID=65 (Minutes and Proceedings and Evidence only available on parliamentary website).

59 For Critical Legal Perspectives that challenge the claimed neutrality of legal rules, including the rules associated with liberal constitutionalism, see Allan Hutchinson and Andrew Petter, "Private Rights/Public Wrongs: The Liberal Lie of the Charter," *University of Toronto Law Journal* 38 (1988); Duncan Kennedy, "Form and Substance in Private Law Adjudication," *Harvard Law Review* 89 (1976), "Tortious Interference with the Contractual Relations in the Nineteenth Century: The Transformation of Property, Contract, and Tort," *Harvard Law Review* 93 (1980); Grant Gilmore, *The Death of Contract* (Columbus: Ohio State University Press 1974); Duncan Kennedy, *A Critique of Adjudication (fin de Siècle),* (Cambridge: Harvard University Press 1997).

60 Schochet, "Introduction: Constitutionalism, Liberalism and The Study of Politics," 8

61 Dario Castiglione, "The Political Theory of the Constitution," *Political Studies* 54 (1996), 434–5.

62 Weinrib, "The Activist Constitution," 29.

63 Ibid., 27.

64 Ibid., 27–8.

65 Ibid., 28–9.
66 As cited in Morton and Knopff, *The Charter Revolution and the Court Party* (Peterborough, Ont.: Broadview Press 2000), 67–8.
67 Judith Squires, "Liberal Constitutionalism, Identity and Difference," in Richard Bellamy and Dario Castiglione, eds., *Constitutionalism in Transformation: European and Theoretical Perspectives,* (Oxford, U.K.: Blackwell Publishers 1996), 209.
68 See Christopher Wolfe, *The Rise of Modern Judicial Review: From Constitutional Interpretation to Judge-Made Law* (New York: Basic Books 1986), 94.
69 Galliard Hunt, ed., *The Writings of James Madison* (New York: G.P. Putnam's Sons 1910), 403–4, as cited by Wolfe, *The Rise of Modern Judicial Review,* 95.
70 John Agresto, *The Supreme Court and Constitutional Democracy* (Ithaca, N.Y.: Cornell University Press 1984), 119.
71 Ibid., 134.
72 Manfredi, *Judicial Power and the Charter* (2001), 188, emphasis in original.
73 Brian Slattery, "A Theory of the Charter," *Osgoode Hall Law Journal* 25:4 (1987), 706.
74 Ibid., 707.
75 Peter H. Russell, "Political Purposes of the Canadian Charter," 52.
76 Peter H. Russell, "Standing up for Notwithstanding," *Alberta Law Review* 29: 2 (1991), 298.
77 Ibid., 298–301.
78 The court is not the only policing body here. Slattery views legislatures and the executive as having this role when they enact corrective statutes or use the override in response to a judicial ruling. Slattery, "A Theory of the Charter," 710.
79 Ibid., 707–9
80 Peter W. Hogg and Allison A. Bushell, "The Charter Dialogue between Courts and Legislatures (or Perhaps the Charter of Rights Isn't Such a Bad Thing after All)," *Osgoode Hall Law Journal* 35:1 (1997), 75–124.
81 For different variations, see Frank Michelman, "Law's Republic," *Yale Law Journal* 97 (1988); and Bruce Ackerman, *Social Justice in the Liberal State* (New Haven, Conn.: Yale University Press 1980).
82 Alexander Bickel, *The Morality of Consent* (New Haven, Conn.: Yale University Press 1975), 111.
83 Stephen L. Carter, "The *Morgan* "Power" and the Forced Reconsideration of Constitutional Decisions," *University of Chicago Law Review* 53 (1986), 851.
84 Hogg and Bushell, "The Charter Dialogue between Courts and Legislatures," 105.
85 Perry, *The Constitution, the Courts and Human Rights,* 113.
86 Barry Friedman, "Dialogue and Judicial Review," *Michigan Law Review* 91 (1993), 584–5, 653.
87 Ibid., 680.

88 Ibid., 668.

89 Ibid., 653.

90 The court looks at the constitutional merits of legislation but rarely concludes that the legislative purpose is so contrary to Charter values that it cannot be pursued under any circumstances.

91 Hutchison, *Waiting for Coraf,* 170 [note omitted].

92 F.L. Morton, "Dialogue or Monologue?" *Policy Options,* April 1999, 23.

93 Ibid., 23–6

94 Christopher P. Manfredi and James B. Kelly, "Six Degrees of Dialogue: A Response to Hogg and Bushell," *Osgoode Hall Law Journal,* 37 (1999). 513–27.

95 Manfredi, *Judicial Power and the Charter* (2001), 178–9.

96 Mary Ann Glendon, *Rights Talk: The Impoverishment of Political Discourse* (New York: Free Press 1991).

97 See Owen Fiss, "The Supreme Court, 1978 Term – Forward: The Forms of Justice," *Harvard Law Review* 93 (1979), 16–17.

98 Earl M. Maltz, "The Supreme Court and the Quality of Political Dialogue," *Constitutional Commentary,* 5 (1988), 380–1. Emphasis in original.

99 Steven D. Smith, "The Pursuit of Pragmatism," *Yale Law Journal* 100 (1990), 434–5.

100 See, by the author, "Parliament, Courts and Rights: Sharing the Responsibility for Interpreting the Charter," in James Bickerton and Alain G. Gagnon, eds., *Canadian Politics,* 3rd ed. (Peterborough, Ont.: Broadview Press 1999), 185–205; and "Why Must a Bill of Rights Be a Contest of Political Wills? The Canadian Alternative," *Public Law Review* 10 (1999), 22–36.

101 This seems to have been a factor in the majority's discomfort with the quality of the argument put forward to justify restrictions on tobacco advertising. See author, "Wrestling with Rights: Judges, Parliament and the Making of Social Policy," *Choices* 5 (1999), 10.

CHAPTER THREE

1 For example, corporations have been able to utilize the Charter to challenge legislative decisions.

2 A rare exception to this characterization would be if the court were asked for its opinion on the constitutional implications of proposed legislation in a reference case.

3 Lorraine Eisenstat Weinrib, "Canada's Constitutional Revolution: From Legislative to Constitutional State," *Israel Law Review* 33:1 (1999), 38.

4 Ibid., 39.

5 See Mark Tushnet, "Policy Distortion and Democratic Debilitation: Comparative Illumination of the Countermajoritarian Difficulty," *Michigan Law Review* 94 (1995), 245–301.

6 The court has indicated that Parliament may validly reconcile conflicting rights and values in a way different from the court's common law principle. See *R. v. Mills* [1999] 3 SCR 668, 710–11, 749, where the court indicated there may be a range of reasonable resolutions to Charter conflicts and that it did not have a monopoly on valid judgments.

7 This argument is developed more fully by the author in *Limiting Rights: The Dilemma of Judicial Review* (Montreal: McGill-Queen's University Press 1996), Chapter 4.

8 Robert Presthus, "Decline of the Generalist Myth," *Public Administration Review* 24 (1964), 216.

9 Donald L. Horowitz, *The Courts and Social Policy* (Washington: Brookings Institution 1977), 25–6.

10 Peter H. Russell, "Political Purposes of the Canadian Charter of Rights and Freedoms," *Canadian Bar Review* 61 (1983), 43–5.

11 Charles Taylor, *Reconciling the Solitudes: Essays on Canadian Federalism and Nationalism,* in particular "Shared and Divergent Values" (Montreal: McGill-Queen's University Press 1993), 155–86.

12 Ibid., 176–7.

13 The Supreme Court has upheld Parliament's legislative rules with respect to consent and how to assess evidence in sexual assault trials. See *R. v. Darrach* [2000] 2 SCR 443 and *R. v. Mills.*

14 For a discussion on the relationship between the legislative override and referenda, see Scott Reid, "Penumbras for the People: Placing Judicial Supremacy under Popular Control," in Anthony A. Peacock, ed., *Rethinking the Constitution: Perspectives on Canadian Constitutional Reform, Interpretation, and Theory* (Don Mills, Ont.: Oxford University Press 1996), 186–213.

15 For example, Jeremy Waldron is critical of attempts to elicit from Parliament an overarching legislative intent on specific issues of policy. He argues that to do so misunderstands the nature of legislative activity and arguments in which decisions reflect the hopes and purposes of not one monarch but hundreds of people with different and conflicting concerns. Waldron, *The Dignity of Legislation* (Cambridge, U.K.: Cambridge University Press 1999), 25–35.

16 Robert F. Nagel, *Constitutional Cultures: The Mentality and Consequences of Judicial Review* (Berkeley: University of California Press 1989), 116.

17 *R. v. Oakes* [1986] 1 SCR 103.

18 Rainer Knopff, "Populism and the Politics of Rights: The Dual Attack on Representative Democracy," *Canadian Journal of Political Science* 31:4 (1998), 697–8.

19 Ibid., 702.

20 See author's discussion of the evolution of the limitation clause in *Limiting Rights*, Chapter 2.

21 *Dagenais v. Canadian Broadcasting Corporation* [1994] 3 SCR 835 at 877.

22 I recognize the irony of this claim in light of the discomfort I have expressed elsewhere with the Supreme Court's ruling in the tobacco case (see
Chapter 4). The majority was particularly troubled by the weakness of the
government's case and, in the absence of evidence to justify the restrictive
scope of the legislation, struck it down. However, my focus is not simply on
the calibre of the legal arguments made or the depth of the stack of studies
or other materials that were entered into evidence. An important measure
of the quality of the government's reasons for restricting rights should be
in terms of the quality of legislative debate that produced the legislation.

CHAPTER FOUR

1 *RJR-MacDonald Inc. v. Canada (Attorney General)* [1995] 3 SCR 199.

2 Rob Cunningham, "R.J.R.-MacDonald Inc. v. Canada (A.G.): Reflections
from the Perspective of Health," *McGill Law Journal* 40 (1995), 231.

3 *R. v. Oakes* [1986] 1 SCR 103 at 138–40.

4 *Irwin Toy Ltd. v. A.G. Quebec* [1989] 1 SCR 927 at 976.

5 *Reference re ss. 193 and 195.1(1)(c) of the Criminal Code (Man.)* [1990] 1 SCR
1123 at 1181.

6 For discussion of the Supreme Court's jurisprudence on freedom of ex-
pression, see Kent Greenawalt, *Fighting Words: Individuals, Communities, and
Liberties of Speech* (Princeton, N.J.: Princeton University Press 1995); Jamie
Cameron, "The Past, Present, and Future of Expressive Freedom under the
Charter," *Osgoode Hall Law Journal* 35:1 (1997).

7 *Ford v. Quebec (Attorney General)* [1988] 2 SCR 712 at 766–7; *Irwin Toy Ltd. v.
Quebec (Attorney General)* [1989] 1 SCR 927 at 971; *Rocket v. Royal College of
Dental Surgeons of Ontario* [1990] 2 SCR 232 at 241–5.

8 *RJR-MacDonald*, 321–4.

9 Ibid., 324.

10 Ibid., 331.

11 Ibid., 329.

12 Justice Iacobucci proposed an alternative remedy. Like McLachlin,
Iacobucci was not prepared to conclude that the legislation complied with
minimal impairment in light of the government's decision to withhold
from the factual record evidence related to alternative options. He also
speculated that partial bans on lifestyle advertising, or restrictions on advertising aimed at adolescents, might have been considered reasonable. However, he differed from McLachlin in his view that instead of nullifying the
legislative scheme, a suspended declaration of invalidity of one year was
more appropriate. This would give Parliament an opportunity to revise the
legislation, with the status quo remaining in force in the meantime. He

concluded that this remedy was warranted "in light of the deleterious effects of tobacco products on those who use them and on society generally." Ibid., 352–6.

13 Ibid., 331 (emphasis in original).

14 Ibid, 329.

15 Ibid., 344–5

16 Ibid., 342.

17 Ibid., 329

18 Ibid., 342.

19 Ibid,, 344.

20 Ibid., 345.

21 Ibid., 329.

22 Although the Tobacco Products Control Act was the first federal initiative to legislate tobacco products, Parliament has considered the issue since 1963. In 1969 the House of Commons Standing Committee on Health, Welfare and Social Affairs held lengthy hearings on tobacco and the committee issued a report that recommended a ban on tobacco advertising. For a discussion of these efforts, see Cunningham, "R.J.R.-MacDonald Inc. v. Canada (A.G.)."

23 *RJR-MacDonald*, 278.

24 See, for example, *Irwin Toy Ltd.* at 993–4.

25 *Dickason v. University of Alberta* [1992] 2 SCR 1103 at 1195–6.

26 Cunningham "R.J.R.-MacDonald Inc. v. Canada (A.G.)," 239.

27 Ibid.

28 *RJR-MacDonald*, 335.

29 Ibid., 310–11.

30 Ibid., 311.

31 Ibid., 277.

32 Ibid., 314–15.

33 Ibid., 312.

34 *Irwin Toy*, 976.

35 Ibid., 970.

36 *Reference re Public Service Employee Relations Act (Alta.)* [1987] 1 SCR 313; *RWDSU v. Saskatchewan* [1987] 1 SCR 460; *PSAC v.* Canada [1987] 1 SCR 424.

37 *R. v. Butler* [1992] 1 SCR 452 at 505.

38 *R v. Keegstra* [1990] 3 SCR 697 at 761–3.

39 *R. v. Butler* [1992] 1 SCR 452 at 500; *Reference re ss. 193 and 195.1(1)(c) of the Criminal Code (Man.)* at 1136.

40 *Rocket v. Royal College of Dental Surgeons of Ontario* [1990] 2 SCR 232 at 247.

41 *RJR-MacDonald Inc,* 332–3.

42 For example, the new legislation prohibits sales of tobacco products to persons under eighteen years of age; requires health messages on packages of

tobacco products that are attributable to health authorities and that include detailed information about tobacco products and their emissions; prohibits the advertising of tobacco products, except product information and brand-preference advertising in publications with primarily adult readership or in materials mailed to adults and in places where young persons are not permitted by law; prohibits the distribution and promotion of tobacco products if any of their brand elements appear on a non-tobacco product that is associated with youth or that targets lifestyle; restricts tobacco advertising, in promotional material for events sponsored by tobacco manufacturers, to the bottom part of the material, where it can occupy no more than 10 per cent of the display surface, and to publications with primarily adult readership or venues where young persons are not permitted by law.

43 Proceedings of the House of Commons, Standing Committee on Health, Les Hagen, Executive Director, Action on Smoking and Health; Dr Jim Walker (treasurer, Physicians for a Smoke-Free Canada), 10 Dec. 1996, *http://www.parl.gc.ca/cgi-bin/committees352/english_committee.pl?sant*

44 House of Commons *Debates*, David Dingwall, 5 Dec. 1996, 7115.

45 Judy Ferguson, director general, Health Policy and Information, Standing Committee on Health, 6 Dec. 1996.

46 Mark Tushnet, "Policy Distortion and Democratic Debilitation: Comparative Illumination of the Countermajoritarian Difficulty," *Michigan Law Review* 94 (1995), 253 [note omitted].

47 Former health minister David Dingwall says that the cabinet discussed, but dismissed, his suggestion that the override be used following the *RJR MacDonald* decision. He also suggests that, while he expects the new legislation to pass judicial scrutiny, if it is nullified he thinks Parliament should use the override. Interview with author, Ottawa, 17 April 1999. See also "Use override clause against tobacco ads, ex-minister says," *Ottawa Citizen* 19 April 1999, A7.

48 Standing Senate Committee on Legal and Constitutional Affairs, Robert Parker, chair and chief executive officer of the Canadian Tobacco Manufacturers' Council, 1 April 1997, http://www.parl.gc.ca/english/senate/com-e/lega-e.htm.

49 Standing Committee on Health, Robert Parker, 9 Dec. 1996.

50 Senate Committee on Legal and Constitutional Affairs, Rick Dearden, legal counsel, Molstar Sports Entertainment, 3 April 1997.

51 *RJR-MacDonald*, 328.

52 "Dingwall softening on tobacco bill," *Globe and Mail*, 4 Feb. 1997, A1, A2.

53 "Tobacco companies fighting back," *Globe and Mail*, 22 April 1997, A1, A2.

54 House of Commons, *Debates*, Maurice Vellacott, Reform, 5 Dec. 1997, 2805.

55 Information bulletin, Health Canada, June 1998.

CHAPTER FIVE

1 *R v. Seaboyer* [1991] 2 SCR 577 at 616.
2 Ibid., 612–16
3 She outlined judicial guidelines for determining when evidence of a woman's sexual past should be included at trial. Ibid., 634–6.
4 Ibid., 707.
5 See, for example, Julian V. Roberts and Renate M. Mohr, *Confronting Sexual Assault: A Decade of Legal and Social Change* (Toronto: University of Toronto Press 1994).
6 Consent is defined as voluntary agreement to engage in sexual activity and cannot be inferred as having been granted in a number of situations. For example, consent cannot be assumed to have been granted where someone other than the complainant expressed the agreement, where the complainant is incapable of consenting to the activity, or where the complainant had initially consented to engage in sexual activity but subsequently expressed a lack of agreement to continue to engage in sexual activity.
7 For discussion of groups' reaction to and comments on Bill C-49, see Janet Hiebert, "Debating Policy: The Effects of Rights Talk," in F. Leslie Seidle, ed., *equity & community: the charter, interest advocacy and representation* (Montreal: Institute for Research on Public Policy 1993), 41–56.
8 *R. v. Ewanchuk*, [1999] 1 SCR 330.
9 Ibid., 361 (emphasis in original).
10 Ibid., 372–3.
11 Ibid., 376.
12 *R.. v. Darrach* [2000] 2 SCR 443 at para. 32.
13 R. v. Daviault [1994] 3 SCR 63.
14 With Justice L'Heureux-Dubé and Iacobucci concurring. Lamer and La Forest offered separate concurring opinions.
15 Historically, the sole element of a crime was the physical act itself. Over time, the law recognized that in addition to the physical act, a guilty finding also required that the accused must have intended to commit the prohibited crime. By the nineteenth century, the English common law began to allow evidence of intoxication in defence of some offences that contained a *mens rea* element. A landmark British ruling in 1920, *Director of Public Prosecutions v. Beard* [1920] AC 479 (HL) had a significant effect on the common law treatment of intoxication, with its distinction between the capacity to form intent and the actual formation of intent. This decision has been credited with influencing a fundamental paradigm in Canadian criminal law: that evidence of intoxication is admissible only in offences of specific rather than general intent.General-intent offences are understood as those requiring the minimal intent to do the prohibited act. Proof of intent is generally inferred from the commission of the act, on the premise that a

person intends the natural consequences of his or her actions. In contrast, specific-intent crimes are those generally more serious offences where the *mens rea* must involve not only the intentional performance of the act but also the formation of an ulterior motive. Most criminal offences are not specific-intent crimes but general-intent offences. The conventional judicial thinking in Canada has been that intoxication is not a defence to general-intent crimes because the level of intent is minimal and this element is not negated by drunkenness. The courts have treated sexual assault as a crime of general intent. Despite the Supreme Court's determination to distinguish general- from specific-intent offences, the court has struggled with the question of how to reconcile concepts of voluntariness and *mens rea* with evidence that an accused was intoxicated. The court has continued to maintain this distinction between specific- and general-intent crimes, despite growing division among its members over whether the distinction is coherent. This distinction has been the subject of substantial commentary. See David McCord, "The English and American History of Voluntary Intoxication to Negate Mens Rea," *Journal of Legal History* 11 (1990), 372–95; Heather MacMillan-Brown, "No Longer 'Leary' about Intoxication: In the Aftermath of *R. v. Daviault*," *Saskatchewan Law Review* 59 (1995), 311–33; Alan D. Gold, "An Untrimmed 'Beard': The Law of Intoxication as a Defence to a Criminal Charge," *Criminal Law Quarterly* 19 (1977), 34–85; Tim Quigley, "Specific and General Nonsense?" *Dalhousie Law Journal* 11 (1987), 75–125; Don Stuart, *Canadian Criminal Law: A Treatise*, 3rd ed. (Toronto: Carswell 1995), 387–401; Matthew Goode, "Some Thoughts on the Present State of the 'Defence' of Intoxication," *Criminal Law Journal* 8 (1984), 104–21.

In 1977 serious judicial differences emerged in the sexual assault case *R. v. Leary*. In *Leary* the court had to resolve conflicting interpretations between British Columbia and Ontario courts about whether sexual assault is a general-intent or specific-intent offence. The majority judgment confirmed that rape was a crime of general intent and that an accused cannot rely on the defence that self-induced intoxication meant he lacked the intent to commit the offence. In dissent, Justice Dickson, with two other judges concurring, ruled that the distinction between specific- and general-intent crimes is neither intelligible nor defensible in Canadian law: in short, it lacks a "legally adequate criteria" for distinguishing the one group of crimes from the other. In the dissenting judges' opinion, rather than being forced to rely on this incoherent distinction, the jury should instead convict only if it is satisfied that the accused knew either that the victim did not consent or was reckless as to whether she had consented. Drunkenness should be considered an element that the jury properly takes into account in resolving this question. In other words, the issue of drunkenness should be left to the jury, along with all the other relevant evidence, in deciding whether the accused knew that the victim was not consenting. See Stuart, *Canadian Criminal Law*, 398–9.

16 *R. v. Daviault*, 92.

17 Ibid., 91.

18 The court was influenced by its interpretation of the experiences of Australia and New Zealand, which have abandoned a similar rule. Evidence available to the court suggested that these jurisdictions have not experienced high levels of acquittals of intoxicated sexual assault offenders. Ibid., 92–3, 103–4.

19 *R v. Swain* [1991] 1 SCR 933.

20 *R. v. Daviault*, 93–4

21 Ibid., 100–1.

22 Ibid., 100.

23 Ibid., 119–20.

24 Ibid., 121.

25 Ibid., 119.

26 "New trial ruled out for drunk-defence claimant," Vancouver Sun, 28 April 1995, A14.

27 Elizabeth Sheehy, "The Intoxication Defence in Canada: Why Women Should Care," Executive summary prepared for the Canadian Advisory Council on the Status of Women, 14 Feb. 1995, 2.

28 Isabel Grant, "Developments in the Criminal Law: The 1994–1995 Term," *Supreme Court Law Review* 7(2d) (1996), 255.

29 Isabel Grant, "Second Chances: Bill C-72 and the *Charter*," *Osgoode Hall Law Journal* 33:2 (1995), 394.

30 "U.S. rebukes Canada over drunk defence," Toronto Star, 2 Feb. 1995, A13; "U.S. rights report questions Canadian drunk defence ruling," Halifax Chronicle-Herald, 2 Feb. 1995, C10.

31 Charles B. Davison, "Reality and Perception: A Gap in Criminal Justice (*Daviault* case)," *Law Now* 20(5) (April/May 1996), 6–9.

32 Don Stuart, "Parliament Should Declare a New Responsibility for Drunkenness Based on Criminal Negligence," 33 CR (4th) (1995), 289.

33 Patrick Healy, "Another Round on Intoxication," 33 CR (4th) (1995), 271.

34 Martha Shaffer, "*R. v. Daviault:* A Principled Approach to Drunkenness or a Lapse of Common Sense?" *Review of Constitutional Studies* 3:2 (1996), 321.

35 Stuart, who is disappointed that the majority in *Daviault* would "so casually reverse the onus of proof of this extreme intoxication defence," admits to a suspicion that the "onus was pragmatically reversed to justify the order of a new trial in the hope that there would be a conviction." In his view, the majority seems to want it both ways: "to assert fundamental *Charter* standards and yet make it virtually impossible for anyone charged with sexual assault to have a drunkenness defence." Don Stuart, *Canadian Criminal Law*, 405.

36 See commentaries by Patrick Healy, Isabel Grant, Tim Quigley, and Don Stuart, in "Criminal Reports Forum on *Daviault:* Extreme Intoxication Akin to Automatism Defence to Sexual Assault," 33 CR (4th) (1995), 269–94.

37 Standing Committee on Justice and Legal Affairs, Elizabeth Sheehy, "A Brief on Bill C-72, An Act to Amend the *Criminal Code*" 20 June 1995, 112A:9n.1.

38 Shaffer, "*R. v. Daviault:* A Principled Approach to Drunkenness or a Lapse of Common Sense?" 325–6 [note omitted].

39 "Last call for drunk defence," Toronto Star, 24 Feb. 1995, A1, A24.

40 The decision in *Daviault* was rendered while the Department of Justice was undertaking a substantial review of the General Part of the Criminal Code, which sets out rules that apply to the Criminal Code and to other laws that describe criminal offences. These rules are intended to reflect fundamental societal values and set out principles of criminal liability and responsibility, including defences that an accused can raise. Over the years, the legal community and successive governments have recognized a need to update and revise the Criminal Code. *Recodifying Criminal Procedure* (Ottawa: Law Reform Commission of Canada 1991).

41 Tim Quigley, "A Time for Parliament to Enact an Offence of Dangerous Incapacitation," 33 CR (4th) (1995), 287–8.

42 Standing Committee on Justice and Legal Affairs, Allan Rock, 5 April 1995, 98:22.

43 Standing Senate Committee on Legal and Constitutional Affairs, Rock, 28 June 1995, 46:23.

44 Justice and Legal Affairs, Rock, 6 April 1995, 98:5

45 Legal and Constitutional Affairs, Rock, 28 June 1995, 46:22.

46 House of Commons *Debates*, Rock, 27 March 1995, 11039.

47 Ibid., 7 Oct. 1994, 6718.

48 One concern was that the government did not want to establish a rule that would lead to a "drunkenness discount" by providing a sentence that was less severe by virtue of intoxication. Second, the government was not prepared to see individuals who have committed a sexual assault be convicted of a crime that is labelled something other than "assault." Third, the government was concerned that the prosecuting crown attorney would be in the position of having to argue contradictory positions at trial: in the context of the main charge, the argument would be that the person was not so intoxicated as to escape responsibility. Yet, in the context of a charge of criminal intoxication, the crown would be arguing that the person was intoxicated and therefore should be convicted of this new offence. Rock, House of Commons *Debates*, 27 March 1995, 11037–8; Justice and Legal Affairs, 6 April 1995, 98:5.

49 House of Commons *Debates*, Christiane Gagnon, BQ, 27 March 1995, 11044.

50 Ibid., Myron Thompson, Reform, 27 March 1995, 11048.

51 House of Commons *Debates*, Rock, 27 March 1995, 11048

52 See testimony of Dr Harold Kalant and Dr Perry Kendall (Addiction Research Foundation) and Dr John Bradford (head, Forensic Psychiatry, Royal Ottawa Hospital), Justice and Legal Affairs, 13 June 1995. After April 1995, evidence of the committee's meetings was no longer available in paper form in many libraries and soon after was available only on the Internet. *http://www.parl.gc.ca/InfoCom/CommitteeEvidence.asp?Language=E&Parliament=2&Joint=0&CommitteeID=65*.

53 Ibid., testimony of Dr John Bradford.

54 Legal and Constitutional Affairs, Rock, 28 June 1995, 46:23.

55 House of Commons Debates, Philip Mayfield, Reform, 22 June 1995, 14483.

56 Justice and Legal Affairs, 6 June 1995. A second amendment was to change a reference to "basic intent" to "general intent," as recommended by the Canadian Bar Association. Rock agreed to the amendment because the latter expression is better known to the law and to lawyers.

57 House of Commons *Debates*, Rock, 27 March 1995, 11039.

58 *R. v. Daviault*, 92. The majority suggested that, if the intentional act to become intoxicated voluntarily is substituted for the intention of committing the sexual assault, this would be "so drastic and so contrary to the principles of fundamental justice" that it could not be justified under the Charter.

59 Legal and Constitutional Affairs, Rock, 28 June 1995, 46:22.

60 This characterization is used by Shaffer in "*R. v. Daviault:* A Principled Approach to Drunkenness or a Lapse of Common Sense?" 329.

61 Legal and Constitutional Affairs, Rock, 28 June 1995, 46:23.

62 As quoted in "New law will slap down too-drunk-to-know defence," *Montreal Gazette* 10 Aug. 1995, A11.

63 House of Commons *Debates*. One MP reported to Parliament that he had heard of a workshop for defence counsel which provided tips on seeking medical, psychiatric, hospital, and immigration records as part of a strategy "to whack the complainant hard at the preliminary inquiry," the objective being to encourage complainants to have the charges withdrawn to avoid a grueling and embarrassing treatment in court. Gordon Kirkby, Liberal, 4 Feb. 1997, 7650.

64 *R. v. O'Connor* [1995] 4 SCR 411.

65 Ibid., 435–6.

66 Ibid., 438–9.

67 Ibid., 437–8.

68 Ibid., 439–41.

69 Ibid., 433–4.

70 Ibid., 504.

71 Ibid., 481.

72 Ibid., 490.

73 Ibid., 488.

74 Ibid.

75 Ibid. (emphasis in original).

76 Ibid., 489.

77 Ibid., 491.

78 Justice and Legal Affairs, Margaret MacGee, chair, National Council of Women of Canada, 12 March 1997.

79 "Court rules against rape victims," *Globe and Mail*, 15 Dec. 1995, A1.

80 As cited in Andrea Neufeld, "A.(L.L.) v. B.(A.): A Case Comment on the Production of Sexual Assault Counselling Records," *Saskatchewan Law Review* 59: 2 (1995), 354.

81 Justice and Legal Affairs, Catherine Kane, counsel, Criminal Law Policy Section, Department of Justice, 4 March 1997.

82 Backgrounder, press release, "An Act to Amend the Criminal Code (Production of Records in Sexual Offence Proceedings)," Department of Justice, 12 June 1996.

83 Bruce Feldthusen, "Access to the Private Therapeutic Records of Sexual Assault Complainants," *Canadian Bar Review* 75 (1996), 562.

84 *R. v. O'Connor*, 433–4.

85 Ibid., 429–30.

86 Justice and Legal Affairs, Marvin Bloos, chair, Canadian Council of Criminal Defence Lawyers, 13 March 1997.

87 Ibid., Bruce Durno, president, Criminal Lawyers' Association.

88 Ibid., Sheila MacIntyre, National Legal Committee, Women's Legal Education and Action Fund, 6 March 1997.

89 Early in the debate, the Reform Party expressed reservations about whether the legislation would unduly restrict access to records, particularly if the alleged victim was not really a victim but was inappropriately influenced by "false memory syndrome." The government was not above taking advantage of the irony of the Party's position in being tough on crime while showing new concern about the rights of criminal suspects. See Kent Roach, *Due Process and Victims' Rights: The New Law and Politics of Criminal Justice* (Toronto: University of Toronto Press 1999), 186.

90 *Dagenais v. Canadian Broadcasting Corp.* [1994] 3 SCR 835 at 877.

91 Justice and Legal Affairs, Jennifer Scott, director of litigation, Women's Legal Education and Action Fund, 6 March 1997.

92 Ibid., Irwin Koziebrocki, treasurer, Criminal Lawyers' Association, 13 March 1997.

93 Ibid., Durno.

94 *R. v. Carosella* [1997] 1 SCR 80.

95 Ibid., 107.

96 Ibid., 113–14.

97 Ibid., 114.
98 Ibid., 120–2, 137–8.
99 Ibid., 142, 146–7.
100 R. *v.* Mills [1999] 3 SCR 668
101 (1997), 56 Alta. LR (3d) 277 (QB)
102 Chief Justice Lamer dissented in part.
103 *R. v. Mills,* 688.
104 Ibid., 748.
105 Ibid., 745.
106 Ibid., 749.
107 Ibid., 712.
108 Ibid., 711.
109 Ibid., 710.

CHAPTER SIX

1 DNA is the acronym for a molecule called Deoxyribonucleic Acid, the genetic material found in the nucleus of cells in the human body. It can be
  viewed as a genetic blueprint of the body that discloses much about a person's life and traits and allows for comparisons of bodily substances re-
  trieved from crime scenes with bodily substances obtained from individual
  suspects.
2 Janet C. Hoeffel, "The Dark Side of DNA Profiling: Unreliable Scientific
  Evidence Meets the Criminal Defendant," *Stanford Law Review,* 42 (1990),
  466.
3 Kent Roach suggests that this emphasis on the potential of DNA to demonstrate factual guilt, and the attendant idea that those who are innocent
  have nothing to hide, explains why DNA testing sits uneasily with other
  due-process values. Kent Roach, *Due Process and Victims' Rights: The New
  Law and Politics of Criminal Justice* (Toronto: University of Toronto Press
  1999), 78.
4 *R. v. Borden* [1994] 3 SCR 145.
5 Ibid., 162.
6 House of Commons *Debates,* 22 June 1995, 14490–1.
7 Standing Committee on Justice and Human Rights, Michael Zigayer, Department of Justice, senior counsel, Criminal Law Policy Section, 11 March
  1998. *http://www.parl.gc.ca/InfoCom/CommitteeEvidence.*asp?
  Language=E&Parliament=2&Joint=0&CommitteeID=65 (Minutes and
  Proceedings and Evidence only available on parliamentary website).
8 House of Commons *Debates,* 22 June 1995, 14490.
9 The legislation also regulates the uses that can be made of the bodily substances and the results of the DNA analysis. For example, where forensic
  analysis establishes that a suspect was not involved in the commission of

the crime, any bodily substances seized under the warrant and the results of the analysis are to be destroyed unless a judge orders otherwise. If the charge is withdrawn, the prosecution is stayed, or an accused is acquitted, any bodily substances seized under the warrant and any information resulting from the analysis must be destroyed.

10 "Government Response to the Ninth Report of the Standing Committee on Justice and Human Rights (Review of the DNA warrant scheme)," 22 Dec. 1998. http://canada.justice.gc.ca/en/dept/pub/dna/report9.html.

11 House of Commons *Debates*, 22 June 1995, 14490.

12 Standing Senate Committee on Legal and Constitutional Affairs, Minutes of Proceedings, 28 June 1995, 46:7–21; 11 July 1995, 49:3–65.

13 House of Commons *Debates*, 22 June 1995, 14490.

14 Justice and Human Rights, Ninth Report to Parliament, 15 May 1998, http://www.parl.gc.ca/InfoComDoc/36/1/JURI/Studies/Reports/jurirp09-e.htm.

15 The associations it was sent to were the Canadian Association of Chiefs of Police, the Canadian Police Association, the Canadian Association of Police Boards, the First Nations Chiefs of Police, and all RCMP detachments, Ontario Provincial Police detachments, and Sûreté du Québec detachments.

16 "Government Response to the Ninth Report."

17 Daniela Bassan, "Bill C-104: Revolutionizing Criminal Investigations or Infringing on *Charter* Rights?" *University of Toronto Faculty of Law Review* 54 (1996), 261–5.

18 Robert E. Astroff, "Identity Crisis: The *Charter* and Forensic DNA Analysis in the Criminal Justice System," *Dalhousie Journal of Legal Studies* 5 (1996), 222.

19 Ian Cram and Clive Walker, "D.N.A. Profiling and Police Powers," *Criminal Law Review* 49 (1990), 486–91.

20 Renee M. Pomerance, " 'Body' of Evidence: Section 487.01 of the Code, Bodily Integrity and the Seizure of Biological Samples," *Crown's Newsletter*, 2 (1995), 43.

21 "Government Response to the Ninth Report."

22 Ibid.

23 *R. v. Stillman* [1997] 1 SCR 607.

24 Ibid., 660–1.

25 Ibid., 744–5. Justice Major dissented on one issue. In his view, the tissue containing the mucous sample was not obtained in violation of section 8 of the *Charter* because the accused voluntarily and intentionally threw the tissue into the washroom wastebasket in full view of the officer. By doing so he lost any expectation of privacy.

26 Ibid., 643–4.

27 Ibid., 644.

28 *R. v. Beare*, [1988] 2 SCR 387 at 413.

29 *R. v. Stillman*, 643.

30 Ibid., 640.

31 Ibid., 705.

32 Ibid.

33 Ibid., 695.

34 Ibid., 684.

35 Ibid., 685–6.

36 Justice and Human Rights, Constable William Donnelly, Canadian Police Association, 24 Feb. 1998.

37 Standing Committee on Legal and Constitutional Affairs, Sergeant Jon Netelenbos, Alberta vice-president, Canadian Police Association, 26 Nov. 1998, 44:7.

38 Ibid., Timothy Danson, legal counsel, Canadian Police Association, 26 Nov. 1998 44:21.

39 Ibid., Grant Obst, president, Canadian Police Association, 26 Nov. 1998, 44:7.

40 Ibid., Detective Sergeant Neale Tweedy, Toronto Police Service, Canadian Police Association, 26 Nov. 1998, 44:9–12.

41 Department of Justice, press release, "Highlights of Bill C-3. A National DNA Data Bank," 1 May 1998. See also Department of Justice, fact sheet, "DNA Sampling: The Federal Government's Position," which stated: "If Bill C-3 were to be amended so that DNA samples could be taken from individuals retroactively for a much broader range of offences and at the time of arrest or charge, it is believed that the legislation would be found to be unconstitutional with very serious consequences for the administration of justice." Found at http://canada.justice.gc.ca/en/news/nr/1998/dnafact.html.

42 Legal and Constitutional Affairs, Stanley Cohen, Department of Justice, senior counsel, Human Rights Law Section, 2 Dec. 1998, 45:39–40.

43 Ibid., Michael Zigayer, senior counsel, Department of Justice, 2 Dec. 1998, 45:30–1.

44 Ibid. See, for example, the testimony of Danson, 26 Nov. 1998, 44:25.

45 Ibid., Netelenbos, 26 Nov. 1998, 44:8.

46 Standing Committee on Justice and Human Rights, as reported by Scott Newark, Canadian Police Association, 24 Feb. 1998.

47 Ibid.

48 Legal and Constitutional Affairs, Danson, 26 Nov. 1998, 44:23.

49 Ibid., 44:18.

50 The legal opinions were requested by Richard G. Mosley, assistant deputy minister, Criminal Law Policy and Community Justice Branch, Department of Justice.

51 News release, "Federal Government Stands Firm on National DNA Data Bank Commitment," Government of Canada, 1 May 1998, http:// canada.justice.gc.ca/en/news/nr/1998/dna.html.

52 "Legal Opinion on the Constitutionality of Taking DNA Samples at Time of Charge, Honourable Charles L Dubin, o.c., q.c., LL.D, April 1998," 32–3. Copy provided by the Department of Justice.

53 Legal Opinion on the Constitutionality of Taking DNA Samples at Time of Charge, Honourable Claude Bisson, q.c., April 1998," 16, referring to the statement made by the Minister of Justice Allan Rock when presenting Bill C-104 to the House of Commons, 22 June 1995, 14490. Copy provided by the Department of Justice.

54 Ibid., 19–20.

55 "Legal Opinion on the Constitutionality of Taking DNA Samples at Time of Charge, Honourable Charles Martin R. Taylor, q.c., April 1998," 15. Copy provided by the Department of Justice.

56 Ibid., 4–5 [emphasis in original, note omitted].

57 "Federal Government Stands Firm on National DNA Data Bank Commitment."

58 Legal and Constitutional Affairs, Danson, 26 Nov. 1998, 44:14.

59 Justice and Human Rights, 26 March 1998.

60 House of Commons *Debates*, 4 May 1998, Peter MacKay, PC. For similar opinions, see Richard Marceau, BQ, Jack Ramsay, Reform, and Peter Mancini, NDP, 4 May 1998, 6451–2.

61 Ibid., Shaughnessy Cohen, Liberal, 4 May 1998, 6452.

62 Ibid., Val Meredith, Reform, 29 Sept. 1998, 8541.

63 Ibid., Jack Ramsay, Reform, 29 Sept. 1998, 8521–2.

64 Ibid., Garry Breitkreuz, Reform, 4 May 1998, 6462.

65 Ibid., Deepak Obhrai, Reform, 29 Sept. 1998, 8504.

66 Ibid., Randy White, Reform, 29 Sept. 1998, 8516.

67 Ibid. See statements by Liberal MPs about why Charter considerations prevented amendments to the bill to satisfy the concerns of police officials and Reform MPs: Lynn Myers, Brenda Chamberlain, Nick Discepola, Paul DeVillers, 29 Sept. 1998, 8500–1, 8506–7, 8514–15.

68 Ibid., Brenda Chamberlain, Liberal, 29 Sept. 1998, 8502.

69 Lawrence MacAulay, solicitor general, Legal and Constitutional Affairs, 7 Dec. 1998, 47:50–1.

70 Legal and Constitutional Affairs, Senator Nolin, 7 Dec. 1998, 47:55.

71 Ibid., Sixteenth Report, 8 Dec. 1998, 48:4–5.

72 News release, Ottawa, solicitor general, "National DNA Data Bank Now in Force," 30 June 2000, http://www.sgc.gc.ca/Releases/e20000630.htm.

73 David M. Paciocco, "Stillman, Disproportion and the Fair Trial Dichotomy under Section 24(2)," *Canadian Criminal Law Review* 2 (1997), 167.

74 Roach, *Due Process and Victims' Rights*, 40–1.

75 Ibid., 41.

76 For a classic treatment of this concept, see Herbert Packer, "Two Models of the Criminal Process," *University of Pennsylvania Law Review* 113 (1964), 1–68.

For analysis of the assumptions, problems, and debates, see Roach, *Due Process and Victims' Rights*, 11–50. Roach argues that this model of the criminal process should be approached with caution because empirical and critical research suggests that the model is counter-productive for most accused and may enable and even legitimize crime control.

77 The Supreme Court made short work of the drafters' intents in *Re B.C. Motor Vehicle Act* [1985] 2 SCR 486 at 497–513. Justice Lamer made it clear that the court did not feel bound by the intent of framers to aspire to a procedural rather than substantive notion of justice. For discussion of the framers' intent in this regard, see Roach, *Due Process and Victims' Rights*, 42–50.

78 *R. v. Brydges* [1990] 1 SCR 190.

79 *Clarkson v. The Queen* [1986] 1 SCR 383.

80 *R. v. Evans* [1991] 1 SCR 869.

81 *R. v. Hebert* [1990] 2 SCR 151.

82 For discussion of differences between Canadian and American approaches, see Robert Harvie and Hamar Foster, "Different Drummers, Different Drums: The Supreme Court of Canada, American Jurisprudence and the Continuing Revision of Criminal Law Under the Charter," *Ottawa Law Review* 24:1 (1992).

83 *R. v. Collins* [1987] 1 SCR 265.

84 Ibid., 283–4.

85 In *R. v. Strachan* [1988] 2 SCR 980, Dickson C.J., for the court, reaffirmed the balancing task at the heart of section 24(2). This approach was affirmed in subsequent cases. For example, see *R. v. Grant* [1993] 3 SCR 223; *R. v. Plant* [1993] 3 SCR 281; *R. v. Wiley* [1993] 3 SCR 263.

86 Although subsequent jurisprudence did not acknowledge that the court was overruling the original balancing approach outlined in *Collins*, factors that relate to the fairness of the trial became, in essence, a foundation for a new and almost automatic exclusionary rule. As a result, evidence is often excluded without further consideration to other factors that might be relevant, such as the seriousness of the Charter violation and its implications for privacy or whether the exclusion of evidence would cause greater disrepute to the administration of justice than its admission.

87 *R. v. Stillman*, 732–3.

88 *R v. Hebert* [1990] 2 SCR 151, as referred to in *R. v. Stillman* at 732.

89 R. v. Elshaw [1991] 3 SCR 24.

90 *R. v. Broyles,* [1991] 3 SCR 595.

91 *R. v. Mellenthin* [1992] 3 SCR 614 at 629.

92 Justice La Forest said of fingerprinting: "A person who is arrested on reasonable and probable grounds that he has committed a serious crime, or a person against whom a case for issuing a summons or warrant, or confirming an appearance notice has been made out, must expect a significant loss

of personal privacy. He must expect that incidental to his being taken in custody he will be subjected to observation, to physical measurement and the like. Fingerprinting is of that nature. While some may find it distasteful, it is insubstantial, of very short duration, and leaves no lasting impression. There is no penetration into the body and no substance is removed from it. I am unable to accept that a provision providing for fingerprinting as an incident of being taken into custody for a serious crime violates the principles of fundamental justice. While a search of one's premises requires a prior authorization based on reasonable and probable grounds to believe both that the offence has been committed and that evidence will be found, the custodial fingerprinting process is entirely different. It involves none of the probing into an individual's private life and effects that mark a search." *R. v Beare* [1998] 2 SCR 387 at 413.

93 The process for taking fingerprints was developed in the late nineteenth century and by 1908 had become the primary method of identification for criminal law enforcement purposes in Canada. Its promise of convenient and reliable identification led to quick acceptance by American, British, and Canadian courts, which recognized fingerprinting as an invaluable tool for criminal investigation because it was virtually infallible, no two persons having identical fingerprints.

94 The significance of familiarity is underscored by the observation of one eminent jurist that perhaps, had the Charter been in place in an earlier era in which fingerprinting was assessed, judgment about whether this procedure is constitutional might have been different. "Legal Opinion on the Constitutionality of Taking DNA Samples at Time of Charge. Honourable Claude Bisson."

95 David Paciocco, "Stillman, Disproportion and the Fair Trial Dichotomy under Section 24(2)," 169–70.

96 Ibid. See also Steven M. Penney, "Unreal Distinctions: The Exclusion of Unfairly Obtained Evidence under s. 24(2) of the Charter," *Alberta Law Review* 32:4 (1994), 808–10.

97 Paciocco, "Stillman, Disproportion and the Fair Trial Dichotomy under Section 24(2)," 170.

98 Alan Young raises this question in "The Charter of Rights as a Murderer's Best Friend," *Canada Watch* (October 1998), 95.

99 Carol A. Brewer, "*Stillman* and Section 24(2): Much to-do about Nothing," *Canadian Criminal Law Review* 2 (1997), 240.

100 Before this rehearing, the following comment by Justice La Forest provided some expectation that the court might be willing to overhaul its approach to remedies: "If the method of approaching s. 24(2) is considered unsatisfactory (and it has not been free from criticism), then we should approach the issue of reformulating it frontally, without creating different approaches for different types of evidence. *R. v. Goldhart* [1996] 2 SCR 463 at 494.

101 Paciocco, "Stillman, Disproportion and the Fair Trial Dichotomy under Section 24(2)," 171.

102 Ibid., See also Tom Goddard, "Stillman: The Majority Could Not Have Intended to Exclude Alternative *Conscriptive* Means from Consideration under the 'Discoverability' Principle," *Criminal Reports* 5 (1997), 110–17.

103 Paciocco, "Stillman, Disproportion and the Fair Trial Dichotomy under Section 24(2)," 171.

104 The majority seemed to exempt breath samples (along with fingerprints) from its treatment of those procedures that may be conscriptive, and therefore to admit evidence derived from these would render the trial unfair. The court did not explain whether this finding overturns the authority of earlier cases in which incriminating evidence from breathalyzer samples was excluded. *R. v. Stillman,* 659.

105 Ibid., 653, emphasis in original.

106 Ibid., 658.

107 Ibid., 659.

108 Young, "The Charter of Rights as a Murderer's Best Friend," 95.

109 *R. v. Stillman,* 699, with reference to *R. v. Burlingham* [1995] 2 SCR 206. Justice McLachlin similarly expressed concern that the majority was not returning to a consideration of "all the circumstances" and the balancing of factors for and against admission required by section 24(2). She characterized the majority's approach, even as revised in *Stillman,* as "a blunt instrument incapable of discriminating between degrees of trial unfairness" because even minor unfairness must necessarily lead to rejection of the evidence, 698.

110 Ibid., 698.

111 For access to reports published by the Department of Justice on the reasons for rejecting proposed amendments, consult (under DNA): http://canada.justice.gc.ca/en/search.html.

112 House of Commons *Debates,* Brenda Chamberlain, Liberal, 29 Sept. 1998, 8503.

113 Ibid., Cohen, Liberal, 29 Sept. 1998, 8545.

114 Don Stuart, *Charter Justice in Canadian Criminal Law* (Scarborough: Carswell Publications 1996), vi.

115 Don Stuart, "An Entrenched Bill of Rights Best Protects against Law and Order Expediency," *South African Journal of Criminal Justice* 11 (1998), 329.

CHAPTER SEVEN

1 *R. v. Feeney* [1997] 2 SCR 13.

2 A representative of the Canadian Association of Chief of Police suggested that the *Feeney* decision was "probably one of the worst decisions from a policing perspective we have ever felt." Brian Ford, chair, Law Amendments

Committee, Canadian Association of Chiefs of Police, Standing Senate Committee on Legal and Constitutional Affairs, 15 Dec. 1997, 11:40.

3 Having ruled that the search violated the suspect's right to be secure against unreasonable search and seizure and his right to privacy in his residence, the majority had to determine what to do with the evidence obtained in the search. The majority excluded factual evidence that is not normally subject to the court's exclusionary rule – evidence that could have been obtained even without violating a suspect's rights. In this case, the evidence of the bloody shirt and shoes, and the money stolen from the murdered victim which was found under the suspect's mattress, were deemed inadmissible. The majority characterized these Charter violations as sufficiently serious that the inclusion of this evidence would cause more harm to the reputation of the justice system than would its exclusion. In its view, the police had "flagrantly disregarded" the suspect's right to privacy and demonstrated a pattern of disregard for the Charter. The majority characterized the police behaviour as "antithetical to the privacy interests protected by the Charter and cannot be condoned." *R v. Feeney*, 58–68.

4 Ibid., 33.

5 Ibid., 38.

6 Ibid., 45.

7 Ibid., 47.

8 Ibid., 51.

9 Ibid. Emphasis added.

10 Stephen G. Coughlan, "Developments in Criminal Procedure: The 1996–97 Term," *Supreme Court Law Review* (2d) 9 (1998), 285.

11 Ibid.

12 Ibid., 285–6.

13 *R. v. Feeney*, 51.

14 Ibid., 49.

15 Ibid., 50.

16 Ibid., 54.

17 These differences went beyond the outcome and included how the majority and minority characterized the conduct of the police. The minority took exception to how the majority had characterized the conduct of the police. Justice L'Heureux-Dubé was critical of the majority's portrayal of police conduct as being akin to "lawless vigilantes, flagrantly and deliberately violating the *Charter* at every turn." In her view, this "litany" of Charter abuses the police were alleged to have perpetrated simply did not stand up to close scrutiny. She stated that, in light of the evidence of brutality at the murder scene and the apparent randomness of the killing, police felt obliged to act quickly in order to prevent any further violence in the community: "For this foresight, they should be commended, not rebuked." *R. v. Feeney*, 116.

18 Then Chief Justice Lamer wrote a separate dissenting judgment indicating that he did not agree with either the majority or the minority opinion. He agreed with the conclusions of Justice L'Heureux-Dubé but for substantially different reasons. Ibid., 24–5.

19 The minority also disagreed with the majority on whether the police had sufficient grounds to make an arrest under the common law. Justice L'Heureux-Dubé offered a different interpretation of the officer's testimony when he responded to the question of whether he had grounds for an arrest with the statement, "Not for an arrest at that time." She was not persuaded that this exchange demonstrated that the officer was aware at the time that he did not have grounds to arrest before entering the dwelling. In her view, police officers should not be held to "the strict exactitude of a lawyer" when assessing a phrase such as "reasonable and probable grounds," particularly when skilful cross-examination may elicit responses that allow for contrary interpretations. Ibid., 40, 84–6. For criticism of the minority's position on this issue, see Coughlan, "Developments in Criminal Procedure: The 1996–97 Term," 276–80.

20 *R. v. Feeney*, 79.

21 Ibid., 97.

22 Ibid., 88.

23 Ibid., 99–100.

24 Ibid., 101–2.

25 *R. v. Feeney* 23 CR (5th) 74.

26 "Canadian Criminal Justice: A Primer," http://www.cjprimer.com/newspub4.htm.

27 Standing Senate Committee on Legal and Constitutional Affairs, Anne McLellan, minister of justice and attorney general, 16 Dec. 1997, 12:21.

28 *Re B.C. Motor Vehicle Act* [1985] 2 SCR 486 at 503.

29 See, for example, *R. v. Swain* [1991] 1 SCR 933. Justice Bertha Wilson suggested: "We are dealing here, not with a rule of law developed through the legislative process, but rather a common law rule created by the judiciary. In such circumstances, there is no room for deference to the legislature: the task of making 'difficult choices' falls squarely on the Court" (at 1033). CJ Lamer stated: "Given that the common law rule was fashioned by judges and not by Parliament or a legislature, judicial deference to elected bodies is not an issue" (at 978).

30 Legal and Constitutional Affairs, Anne McLellan, 16 Dec. 1997, 12:6–7.

31 Renee M. Pomerance, "Parliament's Response to *R. v. Feeney*: New Regime for Entry and Arrest in Dwelling Houses," 13 CR (5th) (1998) 87.

32 Legal and Constitutional Affairs, Anne McLellan, 16 Dec. 1997, 12:7.

33 Ibid., 12:8.

34 Ibid., 12:11.

35 Ibid., 12:8.

36 *R. v. Feeney* [1997] 2 SCR 13 at 49.

37 *R. v. Feeney* [1997] 2 SCR 13 at 50.

38 Legal and Constitutional Affairs, Yvan Roy, Department of Justice, 15 Dec. 1997, 11:17–18.

39 Standing Committee on Justice and Legal Affairs, Anne McLellan, 4 Nov. 1997. *http://www.parl.gc.ca/InfoCom/CommitteeEvidence.*asp?Language=E&Parliament=2&Joint=0&CommitteeID=65 (Minutes and Proceedings and Evidence only available on parliamentary website)

40 Legal and Constitutional Affairs, Yvan Roy, 15 Dec. 1997, 11:17–18, 22.

41 Ibid., 15 Dec. 1997, 11:23. The Quebec Bar Association submitted a letter to the Senate committee expressing concern about Parliament's failure to include a provision in the bill making it necessary to obtain a warrant to enter a house for the purpose of arrest.

42 Ibid., Anne McLellan, 16 Dec. 1997, 12:7–8.

43 Ibid., 12:8.

44 Standing Committee on Justice and Human Rights, Second Report, tabled in the House of Commons 24 Nov.1997, http://www.parl.gc.ca/InfoComDoc/36/1/JURI/Studies/Reports/jurirp02-e.html.

45 Ibid. One of the few groups the Justice Committee heard from, the Criminal Lawyers' Association of Ontario, told the committee that the bill would be vulnerable to a successful Charter challenge for several reasons: the majority's decision in *Feeney* refers to indictable offences whereas the warrant scheme is open-ended and may be interpreted as allowing police officers to enter premises on relatively minor matters; the exigent circumstances exempting a warrant are based on whether a peace officer "suspects" entry is required to prevent bodily harm or death or the destruction of evidence; the criterion of suspicion is too low a threshold; one of the definitions of exigent circumstances is the need to preserve evidence, a circumstance that is inconsistent with the majority's ruling; and the exemption of prior announcement to preserve evidence that "might be there" is not sufficient justification to restrict privacy. A substantially different perspective came from the Canadian Association of Chiefs of Police, which thought that, becaue of the serious safety concerns this Charter ruling created, Parliament should enact the legislative override to exempt the Criminal Code from its effects. Irwin Koziebrocki, vice-president, Criminal Lawyers' Association of Ontario, Brian Ford, chair, Law Amendments Committee, Canadian Association of Chiefs of Police, 5 Nov. 1997.

46 Ibid., Jack Ramsay, Reform, 5 Nov. 1997 (evening meeting).

47 Ibid., Peter Mackay, PC, 5 Nov. 1997.

48 Ibid., Chuck Strahl, Reform, 4 Nov. 1997.

49 Ibid., Derek Lee, Liberal, 5 Nov. 1997 (evening meeting).

50 Justice and Human Rights, Second Report (Bill C-16), tabled 24 Nov. 1997.

51 "Government Response to the Second Report of the Standing Committee on Justice and Human Rights (Circumstances Leading up to and Surrounding its Consideration of Bill C-16)." Copy obtained from committee member.

CHAPTER EIGHT

1 David Rayside, *On the fringe: gays & lesbians in politics* (Ithaca, N.Y.: Cornell University Press 1998), 1–2.
2 For discussion of changes in response to these demands, see "What We Demanded; What We Got," Canadian Lesbian and Gay Archives, http://www.web.net/archives/what/papers/docs/wegot.htm.
3 For discussion of pre-Charter judicial approaches to lesbian and gay rights claims, see Margaret Leopold and Wendy King, "Compulsory Heterosexuality, Lesbians, and the Law: The Case for Constitutional Protection," *Canadian Journal of Women and the Law* 1 (1985); Didi Herman, *Rights of Passage: Struggles for Lesbian and Gay Legal Equality* (Toronto: University of Toronto Press 1994), 20–3.
4 Miriam Smith's study of lesbian and gay liberation movements makes it clear that rights-based claims were part of the strategies used before the adoption of the Charter. Nevertheless, the Charter has influenced decisions of some individuals and groups to use a legal mode of argument to challenge discriminatory treatment. In the process, rights-based arguments take on a different form to comply with the liberal principles of the Charter. Miriam Smith, *Lesbian and Gay Rights in Canada: Social Movements and Equality-Seeking, 1971–1995* (Toronto: University of Toronto Press 1999).
5 This explains the shift from legal strategies of fighting discrimination in the 1970s to greater emphasis on changes to statutory instruments and provincial and federal human rights acts. This change of strategy reflected the assumption that legal recourse was ineffective, particularly in the absence of a supporting statutory basis for arguments. See Herman, *Rights of Passage*, 21–2; Smith, *Lesbian and Gay Rights in Canada*, 41–72.
6 Smith, *Lesbian and Gay Rights in Canada*, 154.
7 The characterization of the difference dimension of lesbian and gay claims has been extremely contested and widely discussed. For a flavour of different perspectives, see Herman, *Rights of Passage;* Carl Stychin, "A Postmodern Constitutionalism: Equality Rights, Identity Politics, and the Canadian National Imagination," *Dalhousie Law Journal* 17 (1994); James E. Jefferson, "Gay Rights and the *Charter,*" *University of Toronto Faculty Law Review* 70 (1985); Leopold and King, "Compulsory Heterosexuality, Lesbians, and the Law"; Didi Herman, "Are We Family? Lesbian Rights and Women's Liberation," *Osgoode Hall Law Journal* 28:4 (1989); Diana

Majury, "Refashioning the Unfashionable: Claiming Lesbian Identities in the Legal Context," *Canadian Journal of Women and the Law* 7 (1994); Shelley A.M. Gavigan, "Paradise Lost, Paradox Revisited," *Osgoode Hall Law Journal* 31:3 (1993).

8 Herman concedes that a rights-based strategy may have been a prudent strategic choice for an earlier generation of early lesbian and gay activists, particularly in their quest to use the liberal paradigm to acknowledge the effects of homophobic assumptions. Yet she believes that the time has come to rethink this strategy, and argues that if lesbians and gay men represented their claims less in terms of *sexual difference* and more in terms of a *political opposition,* then the meaning of "minority" in this context might indeed change. But she considers this unlikely because in North America the mainstream lesbian and gay rights movement has adopted a liberal approach to reform. Herman, *Rights of Passage,* 4, 52 (emphasis in original).

9 Ibid., 51. Herman acknowledges that it is not inevitable that lesbians and gay men, when working within a rights-framework, will adopt this minority paradigm. Nevertheless, legal liberalism tends to favour this approach to discrimination. Lesbian and gay rights activists, if they wish to resist, could reject liberal themes and articulate different rationales, justifications, and arguments.

10 Ibid., 43–4 [notes omitted].

11 Majury, "Refashioning the Unfashionable," 304–7.

12 Carol Smart characterizes legal marriage and family as valid issues for critique and reform. Law "celebrates and sustains a particular family form" and in so doing "privileges marriages above all other relationships." Thus, law constitutes a major obstacle to fundamental change in the reorganization of domestic lives.Carol Smart, *The Ties That Bind: Law, Marriage and the Reproduction of Patriarchal Relations* (London: Routledge and Kegan Paul 1984), 10–11, 221.

13 Ibid., 146.

14 Gavigan, "Paradise Lost, Paradox Revisited," 612.

15 Herman, "Are We Family?" 797.

16 Kathleen A. Lahey, *Are We 'Persons' Yet? Law and Sexuality in Canada* (Toronto: University of Toronto Press 1999), 78–87.

17 Ibid., 28.

18 This occurred in 1977 under the Parti Québécois (PQ) government, which amended the province's then two-year-old human rights legislation, the *Charter of Human Rights and Freedoms.*

19 Special Joint Committee on the Constitution of Canada, November 1980, Minutes of Proceedings, Jean Chrétien, 12 Jan. 1981, 36:14–15.

20 Ibid., 29 Jan. 1981, 48:31–3.

21 A proposal by NDP member Svend Robinson to add sexual orientation as a prohibited ground of discrimination was voted down. Ibid., 29 Jan. 1981, 48:34.

22 Information obtained from interviews with Justice lawyers (who wished to remain anonymous) in the four western provinces and in Ottawa. Interviews were conducted between September and November 1998 and in November 1999.

23 Canada. *Equality for All*, Report of the Sub-committee on Equality Rights of the Standing Committee on Justice and Legal Affairs (Ottawa: 1985), 30.

24 These recommendations included: amend the Canadian Human Rights Act to add sexual orientation as a prohibited ground of discrimination; change the employment practices of the Canadian Armed Forces and the RCMP so that they no longer discriminate on the basis of sexual orientation; change the federal government's security-clearance guidelines covering employees and contractors so that they do not discriminate on the basis of sexual orientation; amend the Criminal Code to provide uniform lawful minimum ages for private consensual sexual activity; support a private member's bill to include sexual orientation in the Canadian Human Rights Act; authorize the Canadian Human Rights Commission to conduct a comprehensive study of all federal legislation and regulations to determine which of these discriminate on the basis of sexual orientation; and require that the minister of justice report back to the House on the steps taken to remove discrimination on the basis of sexual orientation. Ibid., 25–32.

25 Rayside, *on the fringe*, 110.

26 *Toward Equality: Response to the Report of the Parliamentary Committee on Equality Rights* (Ottawa: 1986), 13.

27 Ibid.

28 "The revolt of the Tory right," *Western Report*, 17 March 1986, 12–16.

29 "Gays get break from Crosbie," Calgary Herald, 5 March 1986, A1, A2.

30 This political resistance was reflected in a declaration made in 1985 by then Defence Minister Erik Nielson – that there was no place for gay men and lesbians in the army, navy, or air force because they pose a threat to national security. Forthcoming changes to address sexual discrimination in military policy were announced in 1989, but three years later Defence Minister Marcel Masse indicated that these were being delayed because of caucus resistance. "Rule bars bias against homosexuals," *Globe and Mail*, 6 March 1986, A4; "Gays get break from Crosbie," Calgary Herald, 5 March 1986, A1; "Tory MPs still blocking policy on gays in forces, Masse says," *Globe and Mail*, 25 Jan. 1992, A8; "Ottawa delays decision on gays," *Globe and Mail*, 11 Oct. 1991, A5.

31 An out-of-court settlement with a former lieutenant, who had resigned after admitting to having had a lesbian relationship, included the federal government's consent to a court order declaring that the Forces' policies against

lesbians and gay men violated the Charter. Within hours of the decision, then Chief of Defence Staff General John de Chastelain issued a statement confirming that the Forces would "comply fully" with the ruling."Forces agree to end anti-gay policies," *Globe and Mail,* 28 Oct. 1992, A1.

32 In June 1985 a minority Progressive Conservative government introduced an omnibus bill that was intended to bring Ontario statutes into line with section 15 of the Charter. The Conservative government, which in the 2 May 1985 election had secured a small margin of victory over the Liberal Party, lost its status as the governing party when the Liberals and the NDP reached an "Accord" on governing. Initially, no mention was made of gay rights or of any government intention to address issues of discrimination related to sexual orientation. However, the NDP, holding the balance of power as the junior partner in the Accord, viewed the bill as a logical way to add sexual orientation to the Human Rights Code. For analyses of the political evolution of the bill, see David Rayside, "Gay Rights and Family Values: The Passage of Bill 7 in Ontario," *Studies in Political Economy* 26 (1988); Herman, *Rights of Passage,* chapters 3–4.

33 Ontario, Ontario Human Rights Commission, *Life Together: A Report on Human Rights in Ontario* (Toronto: Ontario Human Rights Commission 1977), 81–2.

34 Rayside, *on the fringe,* 142.

35 *Knodel v. British Columbia (Medical Services Commission)* [1991] 58 BCLR (2d) 356.

36 *Haig v. Canada* [1992], 9 OR (3d) 495.

37 *Layland v. Ontario (Minister of Consumer and Commercial Relations)* [1993] 104 DLR (4th) 214.

38 *Canada (AG) v. Mossop* [1993] 1 SCR 554.

39 Ibid., 577–8, 585–7.

40 Ibid., 617–18.

41 *Haig and Birch v. Canada* 9 OR (3d) 495.

42 *Mossop,* 578–82.

43 According to Rayside, the bill came close to satisfying the demands for comprehensive change that had come from gay activist networks since the NDP formed government in 1990. Rayside, *on the fringe,* 142. However, Kathleen Lahey writes that, despite the wide reach of the bill, as originally drafted, it still would have left unamended many statutes that use the word "spouse". Lahey, *Are We 'Persons' Yet?* 333.

44 Rayside, *on the fringe,* 154.

45 For analysis of the defeat of Bill 167, see Rayside, ibid., 141–77.

46 Lahey, *Are We 'Persons' Yet?* 334.

47 Opposition members presented petitions with hundreds of names opposing the proposed changes. One Liberal MLA, critical of the idea of allowing same-sex partners to adopt children, argued that this change was not in the

best interests of the child. He questioned what rights infants possess under the Charter since they "cannot speak for themselves" and, in legislative debate, remarked "do we think any of them want to be adopted into a same-sex unit?" *Debates* of the Legislative Assembly, Richard Neufeld, Liberal, 26 June 1995, 16128.

48 Ibid., Joy MacPhail, NDP, 26 June 1995, 16123.

49 Justice Sopinka also joined the majority in *Miron v. Trudel* [1995] 2 SCR 418, but he was part of a different majority in *Egan* that upheld legislative distinctions as constitutionally valid. Sopinka died before taking part in any other lesbian and gay equality rights decisions.

50 *Miron v. Trudel* [1995] 2 SCR 418.

51 Lahey argues that it is open to litigants to base their augments on *Miron v. Trudel*. She suggests that Justice McLachlin's emphasis on the effects of legislation on "essential human dignity" provides "an excellent outline within which to particularize how the invisibility, exclusion, and stigmatization of lesbian women and gay men as sexual minorities have affected lesbian and gay relationships and lesbian/gay couples. Lahey, *Are We Persons Yet?* 74–5.

52 *Miron v. Trudel*, 498.

53 Ibid., 494.

54 Ibid., 494–5.

55 Ibid., 497–8.

56 The majority appeared to have little doubt that a definition of spouse applying only to married couples was not a justified restriction of equality under section 1. McLachlin concluded that those defending the married definition of spouse had failed to demonstrate that the exclusion of unmarried members of family units from motor-vehicle accident benefits was justified. Ibid., 502–8.

57 *Mossop*, 634.

58 *Miron v. Trudel*, 501.

59 Ibid., 501–2.

60 Ibid., 457–65.

61 Ibid., 461–2.

62 *Egan v. Canada* [1995] 2 SCR 513.

63 Ibid., 543.

64 Ibid., 604.

65 Ibid., 535.

66 Ibid., 536.

67 Other judges noted that the objective of the act does not support the claim that the spousal allowance should be unique to heterosexual couples or that it is connected to the capacity to have children or produce children or is based on a traditional "male-female" couple or on marriage. Ibid., L'Heureux-Dubé at 569, Cory at 588, and Iacobucci at 607.

68 Justice McIntyre in *Andrews v. Law Society of British Columbia* [1989] 1 SCR 143 at 165.

69 *Egan v. Canada*, 572–6.

70 The preferred remedy of justices Iacobucci and Cory was to reinterpret the act to recognize analogous relationships. This remedy would be subject to a one-year suspension to give Parliament a grace period to determine how it should respond to allow governments at both levels to coordinate their approaches to providing benefits, particularly to low-income households. *Egan v Canada.*, 619–23.

71 Ibid., 618–19.

72 Information obtained from interviews conducted with provincial and federal legal advisers in September 1998 and November 1999.

73 The provinces that had already amended their human rights legislation to prohibit discrimination on the basis of sexual orientation were Quebec (1977), Ontario (1986), Manitoba (1987), Nova Scotia (1991), British Columbia (1992), New Brunswick (1992), and Saskatchewan (1993).

74 "Tories weaken rights, groups say," Winnipeg Free Press, 9 Feb. 1993, A3.

75 The government incurred substantial criticism from Bloc Québécois and NDP members after Max Yalden (outgoing chief commissioner of the Canadian Human Rights Commission) sternly rebuked the government's for failing to amend the CHRA. The commission's annual report called the government's reticence to include sexual orientation in the CHRA "a failure in moral logic and a near-public repudiation of the rights of many law-abiding and tax-paying Canadians." Canadian Human Rights Commission, *Annual Report* (1995), (Ottawa: Minister of Supply and Services Canada 1996), 15.

76 Rayside cites a story in *La Presse* that speculated that the government's vulnerability on the tax issue had influenced its decision to introduce the amendment to the Canadian Human Rights Act. He also quotes an unnamed Liberal member who said, on the morning the legislation was introduced, that the party was "hoping that Reform is going to make a lot of noise about this and sound like the kooks that they are." The day after the bill was introduced, Reform MP Robert Ringma was widely quoted in the media saying that he would fire or move a homosexual employee or a member of an ethnic minority "to the back of the shop" if a customer was offended by his or her presence. The statement provided the context for what has been characterized as a passionate attack on the Reform Party by Prime Minister Chrétien, who described Ringma's controversial statement as "awful" and "just about the worst statement we could hear in Canadian society." Chrétien drew an analogy between discrimination against lesbians and gay men and racism. But the purported passion in his defence of the legislation belied the fact that a significant number of MPs in his own party opposed the bill on grounds similar to those raised by Reform members.

Rayside, *on the fringe,* 127, 329n.54; "Gay would be fired if business hurt: MP," Toronto Star, 30 April 1996, A10; Chrétien on attack over rights for gays," *Globe and Mail,* 1 May 1996, A1, A9.

77 Reform MPs claimed that legislative amendments would provide a "gateway to the agenda of a powerful special interest group" and would provide lesbians and gay men with special rights. They also argued that the amendment was not necessary and challenged the government to demonstrate that lesbians and gay men incur discrimination. House of Commons *Debates,* Sharon Hayes, 9 May 1996, 2539; Darrel Stinson and Mike Scott, 8 May 1996, 2489–93.

78 These assertions were made both in political debate and in a government publication, "Working Against Discrimination: The Amendment to the Canadian Human Rights Act" (Department of Justice, May 1996).

79 Some government members were troubled that, by holding a free vote, the government had sent a message that a vote against protecting lesbians and gays from discrimination is a valid and reasonable position. This concern was reinforced by comments made before the vote by one Liberal member, who suggested that the fact that a free vote was allowed raises the question of whether sexual orientation is in fact a human right at all. "Chrétien on attack over rights for gays," *Globe and Mail,* 1 May 1996, A9; "Free vote doesn't stop gay bill," *Globe and Mail,* 2 May 1996, A1, A8; Rayside, *on the fringe,* 117.

80 *Human Right Commission (Nfld.) et al. v. Newfoundland (Minister of Employment and Labour Relations)* (1995) 134 Nfld. and PEI 66; 417 APR 66.

81 Lahey analyses the effect of the court's section 1 judgment on lower court decisions. See *Are We Persons Yet?* 66–87.

82 *Dwyer v. Toronto* (Metro) [1996] 27 CHRR D/108.

83 *Vogel v. Government of Manitoba* [1995] 126 DLR (4th) 72.

84 *Rosenberg v. Canada (Attorney General)* [1998] 38 OR (3rd) 577.

85 *Vogel,* 74–5.

86 *Rosenberg,* 587.

87 *Vriend v. Alberta* [1998] 1 SCR 493.

88 *M v. H* [1999] 171 DLR (4th) 577. Justice Major dissented in *Vriend* on the question of the appropriate remedy but was part of the unanimous ruling that equality was violated in a manner that was not justified under section 1. He also wrote a separate concurring judgment in *M v. H* indicating that the legislation violated equality and was not justified, 698–9.

89 Justice Bastarache joined the majority in both of these next two cases.

90 Justice Binnie was not appointed when the court reviewed *Vriend* but was part of the majority for *M v. H.*

91 A 1992 ministerial order vetoed a decision by the Alberta Human Rights Commission (AHRC) to investigate complaints based on sexual orientation,

a decision that had been followed by publicized political musings about abolishing the Human Rights Commission. The government appointed a new chief commissioner of the Alberta Human Rights Commission in 1993 and initiated a public review of the *act*. A review panel subsequently recommended that sexual orientation be included as a prohibited ground of discrimination. Its report and recommendations received a "frosty reception" by the Conservative caucus and the chief of the AHRC failed to have his contract renewed.In 1996 the Alberta government introduced amendments to the *IRPA* without including sexual orientation as a prohibited ground of discrimination. The minister responsible offered no explanation or justification for this omission. However, one government member speaking in support of the exclusion suggested that the government should avoid "conjecture and opinion" that individuals face discrimination based on sexual orientation. Alberta Human Rights Commission. *Equality in Dignity and Rights: A Review of Human Rights in Alberta* (Edmonton: Alberta Human Rights Commission 1994), 71, 75; "Mr. Mar meets his unhappy friends: he is caught between the devil and the deep blue Tory caucus," *Western Report*, 28 Nov. 1994, 12; Alberta. Legislative Assembly *Debates*, 18 April 1996, 1232–3.

92 *Vriend*, 550–1.
93 Ibid., 551.
94 Ibid., 530–2.
95 Ibid., 558.
96 Ibid., 559–60.
97 Justice Major dissented on this issue and thought that the Alberta legislature should be free to choose whether it would like to have a Human Rights Act that must include sexual orientated as prohibited grounds of discrimination or no Human Rights Act at all. Furthermore, he ruled that there were numerous ways in which the legislation could be amended to address the issue of under-inclusiveness and that the Alberta government should be given the opportunity to respond as it saw fit. Ibid., 586–8.
98 "One surrender too many: Klein's capitulation on Vriend – and much else – prompts talk of an alternative conservative party," *Alberta Report*, 4 March 1998 (internet edition), http://albertareport.com/home.html.
99 "Rage finds its voice in Alberta," *Globe and Mail*, 12 April 1998.
100 Government of Alberta, news release, 2 April 1998.
101 "Tories gear up for court ruling," Edmonton Journal, 30 March 1998, http://www.edmontonjournal.com.
102 The bill as proposed would have affected legal rights in a number of ways. It would have eliminated legal defences that were otherwise available in respect of these claims; established a maximum cap of $150,000 for damages arising from the sterilization policies; limited the kinds of damages that could awarded by prohibiting courts from making any award in respect of

punitive and related damages; and prevented courts from awarding interest to claimants on damages and limited the amount of legal costs that could be awarded against the province.

103 The United Farmers Alberta government initiated the practice of forcefully sterilizing and/or institutionalizing individuals with certain mental and physical handicaps in 1928, with the intent of sterilizing mentally disabled people "to prevent those individuals from passing mental disabilities to their children." The act was repealed in 1972 when the Progressive Conservative government was elected. In 1996 the province of Alberta was sued by one of the victims of the act who was awarded approximately $1,000,000 in damages, interest, and costs. After the award was granted, approximately 700 individuals filed claims against the province, claiming that they were wrongfully sterilized or wrongfully confined in provincial institutions. Government of Alberta, press release, 10 March 1998.

104 Alberta, Legislative Assembly, *Debates*, Howard Sapers, Liberal, 10 March 1998, 183.

105 Klein retreats in rights scrap," *Globe and Mail*, 12 March 1998, *http://www.Globe*AndMail.CA/docs/news/19980312/GlobeFront/USTERN.html; "Alberta, the notwithstanding Clause and the weak," Vancouver Sun, 12 March 1998, A10; "Klein backs off on sterilization deal," Calgary Herald, 12 March 1998, A1, 3.

106 The definition referred to a person who is married or, alternatively, "either of a man and woman who are not married to each other and have cohabited ... continuously for a period of not less than three years." The term "cohabit" was defined to mean a man and a woman who "live together in a conjugal relationship, whether within or outside marriage."

107 In dissent, Justice Gonthier argued that the law is ameliorative, intended to protect women in failed marriages or opposite-sex relationships, because women in heterosexual relationships incur a dynamic of dependence that is "unique" to opposite sex relationships. To provide a benefit for this group alone is not discriminatory. The legislature, if it wishes, is free to extend this benefit but is not constitutionally obliged to do so. *M v. H*, 647.

108 Justice Bastarache wrote separate reasons.

109 *M v. H*, 611–12. This statement is taken from *Law v. Canada (Minister of Employment and Immigration)*, [1999] 1 SCR 497 at 549.

110 *M v. H*, 618–19.

111 Ibid., 636–7.

112 Ibid., 638.

113 Ibid, 638–640. Justice Iacobucci also stated that, although he did not agree with Justice Sopinka's advocacy of incrementalism in the context of concerns about the financial implications of extending benefits to gay men and lesbians, this issue did not arise. Instead of "increasing the strain on the public coffers," a more inclusive definition of spouse would

help to alleviate financial concerns because same-sex couples would have more responsibilities towards each other and would be less reliant on government welfare.

114 This was a different remedy than the one adopted by the lower court, which had been prepared to "read in" an alternative definition of spouse. The majority's concerns with this approach is that, while the act contains other provisions that allow for opting out of these agreements, through a cohabitation agreement, these apply only to agreements entered between "a man and a woman"; consequently, same-sex partners would be placed in the anomalous position of having no means of opting out of the default system for providing financial support. This judicial approach, as a result, would "remedy one constitutional wrong only to create another." Ibid., 643–4.

115 Ontario *Legislative Debates*, Peter Kormos, NDP justice critic, 27 Oct. 1999, 163–4.

116 "Gay couples win rights" *Globe and Mail*, 21 May 1999, A1.

117 After the *M v. H* ruling, Ontario Premier Mike Harris ruled out using the override clause, saying, "I'm not a fan of the notwithstanding clause at the best of times." "Ontario premier ready to respect same-sex spouses," *National Post*, 21 May 1999, 6.

118 This was underscored by the attorney general's second-reading comments that the legislation was not desired by the government but was forced onto its agenda by the Supreme Court: "This legislation is not part of our Blueprint agenda. We are introducing this bill because of the Supreme Court of Canada decision." Ontario *Legislative Debates*, Jim Flaherty, PC, 27 Oct. 1999, 159.

119 Lahey argues that, because lesbian and gay couples are not permitted to marry, they do not have access to matrimonial-home rules, which give a presumptive half-interest in the value of the family home to each spouse regardless of who purchased the house. They also do not benefit from tax deductions for contributions to Ontario registered home ownership savings, are denied eligibility for the Ontario guaranteed annual income, and are prevented from acting as a trustee of a spouse's estate. Furthermore, lesbian and gay couples do not have the same rights to adopt children. Family-adoption rules apply to people who are "spouses" but exclude same-sex partners. Although there is a new category for adoption for those who do not satisfy the heterosexual definition of spouse, Lahey worries this new category – "any other individuals" – may give rise to judicial interpretations that preclude joint adoptions by lesbian and gay couples. But a year later, the province changed its policy with respect to same-sex adoptions to allow both partners to became patents. Author's correspondence with Kathleen Lahey, 24 Nov. 1999; "Gay adoption breaks new ground," *Globe and Mail*, 9 July 2001, A3.

120 "Ontario bill called 'sexual apartheid,'" *Globe and Mail,* 25 Nov. 1999, A3.

121 *M v. H,* 645. It was this possibility that troubled Gonthier J. (647) in his dissenting judgment. He expressed concern that the majority's ruling that the restricted definition of spouse was unconstitutional would have "far-reaching effects" beyond the particular case at hand.

122 Lahey, *Are We 'Persons' Yet?* 76.

123 Rayside, *on the fringe,* 154.

124 But it also argues that, if benefits are based on partners or couples, these should also be provided for lesbians and gay men. Smith, *Lesbian and Gay Rights in Canada,* 126–7.

125 Bill 32, An Act to Amend Various Legislative Provisions concerning De Facto Spouses, Quebec, Assemblée Nationale, Bills, 36th Legislature, 1st Session, 1999.

126 "Legal Marriage Report – Global Status of Legal Marriage," January 2000: Partners Task Force for Gay and Lesbian Couples, http:www.buddybuddy.com/mar-repo.html.

127 British Columbia, *Legislative Debates,* Ujjal Dosanjh, NDP, 14 July 1997, 5652.

128 "Gay and lesbian parents recognized in BC," 5 Feb. 1998, http://www.groovyannies.com/news/1998/press17.html.

129 The definition of "domestic partner" proposed by the Liberal opposition was any person who has lived with another for at least two years in a "close personal relationship that is of primary importance in both person's lives and which has the attributes of permanence, physical intimacy, sharing and interdependence." British Columbia, Legislative Debates, Geoff Plant, Liberal, 14 July 1997, 5644.

130 Ibid., Ujjal Dosanjh, 15 July 1997, 5745.

131 "Stronger gay rights planned for B.C." http://cbc.ca/cgi-bin/templates/view.cgi?/news/1999/05/20bc_gayrights990520.

132 British Columbia *Legislative Debates,* Geoff Plant, 13 July 1999, 14350–2.

133 It reported that the relevant legislation on same-sex benefits (the Family Relations Amendment Act, the Pension Statutes Amendment Act, the Pension Benefits Standards Amendment Act, and the Definition of Spouse Amendment Act) have each adopted different formulations with respect to the definition of spouse. "Bill 100: The *Definition of Spouse Amendment Act*: The BC Law Institute Comments," http://www.bcli.org/.

134 British Columbia *Legislative Debates,* Andrew Petter, NDP, 26 June 2000, http://www.legis.gov.bc.ca/2000/hansard/H00626p.HTM

135 Ibid.

136 Ibid., 5 July 2000.

137 Bill C-33 would have amended the Family Maintenance Act to define spouse to mean either a person married or a person of the same sex who has lived together in a conjugal relationship continuously for one year.

138 [2000] NSCA 53.

139 Nova Scotia, *Legislative Debates*, Michael Baker, PC, 14 Nov. 2000, 8705.

140 The title of the act reveals the importance of judicial motivation for the legislation. Its short title is the Law Reform (2000) Act. Its long title is An Act Comply with Certain Court Decisions and to Modernize and Reform Laws in the Province.

141 Nova Scotia, *Legislative Debates*, Michael Sampson, Liberal, 14 Nov. 2000, 8706.

142 Government of Saskatchewan, news release, Department of Justice, 30 May 2001.

143 Saskatchewan, *Legislative Debates*, Wayne Elhard, Saskatchewan Party, 20 June 2000, 1986–9.

144 Government of Manitoba, news releace, "Legislation Introduced to Comply with Supreme Court Ruling in M v. H," 30 May 2001.

145 "Manitoba, Sask increase gay rights in line with 1999 Supreme Court ruling," Canadian Press, http://www.travelandtranscendence.com/canada-news.html.

146 "Gay adoption breaks new ground," *Globe and Mail*, 9 July 2001, A3.

147 "Gay couples win Rights," *Globe and Mail*, 21 May 1999 A1.

148 Alberta, *Legislative Debates*, Linda Sloan, Liberal, 9 March 1999, 432–3.

149 Ibid., Gary Dickson, Liberal, 4 March 1999, 357.

150 Opposition members criticized this decision, arguing that the definition of spouse would subject the legislation to litigation where it stood a good chance of being struck down. Alberta, *Legislative Debates*, Hugh MacDonald, Liberal, Linda Sloan, Liberal, Raj Pannu, NDP, 3 May 1999, 1248–9, 1251–2, 1391–2.

151 "Alberta shift on same-sex adoption a ply to head off judges: minister," *National Post*, 23 April 1999, A11.

152 Alberta, *Legislative Debates*, Lyle Oberg, PC, 22 April 1999, 1210. The change was made as part of the Miscellaneous Statutes Amendment Act, described as a "catch-all-process" for allowing the quick passage of legislative changes which have already been vetted by MLAs and which rarely involve issues that are contested or raise debate. In this case, the legislation was introduced and passed the same day (13 May 1999) with virtually no debate; the word adoption did not arise.

153 "Alberta opens door to recognizing same-sex couples," *National Post*, 1 March 2001, A8.

154 "Charter case prompts Alberta to review laws affecting gays," *National Post*, 3 April 2001, A4.

155 "Alberta's estate law ruled unconstitutional," *Globe and Mail*, 4 April 2001, A6.

156 *Rosenberg v. Canada (Attorney General)*. 38 OR (3rd) 577.

157 Lahey, *Are We 'Persons' Yet?* 78–9.

158 *Rosenberg v. Canada (Attorney General).*

159 This would undermine the discretionary power of Revenue Canada to decide how narrowly or expansively it wished to apply the *Rosenberg* ruling on spouse in the Income Tax Act to circumstances other than those specifically involved in this case.

160 Ten days after the *M v. H* decision, the federal government agreed to settle an ongoing dispute over whether same-sex partners could receive survivor benefits under the Canada Pension Plan, conceding that the denial of same-sex survivor benefits was not constitutional. Justice Minister Anne McLellan also indicated that the federal government was working on a strategy to ensure that federal policy is consistent with this ruling. This acknowledgment provoked angry reaction from some caucus members. Not only did some Liberal backbench members criticize the *M v. H* ruling, and suggest that the override should be used to reverse the effects of the decision, but they opposed the government's intent to recognize same-sex partners' pension benefits. "CPP benefits granted to gays for first time," *Globe and Mail,* 1 June 1999, A8; McLellan backs ruling," *Ottawa Citizen,* 21 May 1999, A6.

161 The issue was controversial for a number of reasons. At a general level, many were critical that the federal government wanted ownership of a $30-billion surplus in the pension plan. Ten unions subsequently launched a legal challenge to the government's decision to take over the surplus in the pension funds of federal employees. The unions invoked Charter arguments of equality, alleging that union members are in a uniquely disadvantaged position compared to other employees in Canadian society because their employer, the government, has the power to revoke the terms and conditions of employment. "Public-service workers sue over 'pension grab,'" *Globe and Mail,* 9 Nov. 1999, A4.

162 "Civil service to get same-sex benefits," *Globe and Mail,* 16 March 1999 A1, A8.

163 Government whip Bob Kilger indicated that the pension bill should not be considered, technically, a confidence matter but because a large amount of money was involved, some opposition MPs might try to characterize it as such. Media coverage suggested that some Liberal opponents of the legislation were willing to bring down their own government on its handling of this issue. As one Liberal dissident said of the pressure to support the legislation: "The threat that the issue might become a confidence vote is 'just an excuse to cudgel people into submission.'" However, one report suggested that the political ramifications of the likely defection of the eight Liberal MPs would be negated by the fact that the other political parties did not intend to turn out in full force to try to defeat the bill. "Pension bill granting same-sex benefits appears likely to pass," *Globe and*

Mail, 22 May 1999, A6; "Some Liberal MPs oppose same-sex clause in pension bill," *Globe and Mail*, 24 May 1999, A11.

164 "Pension bill slips through," *Globe and Mail*, 26 May 1999, A2.

165 "Ottawa may draft same-sex omnibus bill," *Globe and Mail*, 27 May 1999, A6.

166 The group indicated that it would be willing to drop the court action if the government introduced legislative changes within a reasonable period of time. Foundation for Equal Families, media release, "Gay Community Launches Historic Federal Omnibus Legal Challenge to Recognize Same-Sex Families," 7 Jan. 1999.

167 Standing Committee on Justice and Human Rights, Lisa Hitch, Department of Justice, 29 Feb. 2000, *http://www.parl.gc.ca/InfoCom/CommitteeEvidence*.asp?Language=E&Parliament=2&Joint=0&CommitteeID=65 (Minutes and Proceedings and Evidence are available only at the parliamentary website).

168 Ibid., Nick Bala and Bruce Ryder, 16 March 2000.

169 Ibid., Andrée Côté, National Association of Women and the Law, 15 March 2000. Another criticism concerned the way the legislation recognized lesbian and gay relationships. Claudine Ouellet from the Coalition gaie et lesbienne du Québec was critical of the government's decision not to use the term "spouse," suggested that it was insulting and offensive because it reduced "our relationships as couples to a simple "partnership." Ibid., 16 March 2000.

170 Ibid., Ted Morton, 15 March 2000.

171 "Gay-rights bill stirring up Liberal caucus: Some MPs threaten to withhold support unless benefits extended to other couples," *Globe and Mail*, 10 Feb. 2000 A3.

172 House of Commons, *Debates*, Peter Goldring, Canadian Alliance, 11 April 2000, 5953.

173 Justice and Human Rights, Anne McLellan, 29 Feb. 2000.

174 Ibid.

175 Ibid., Svend Robinson, NDP, 23 March 2000.

176 In a news release, EGALE indicated that it unequivocally opposes this amendment because it "transforms the message of [Bill 23] from one of acceptance and equality, to one of exclusion and discrimination. "Urgent Action Alert," 22 March 2000.

177 The Reform motion was: "That, in the opinion of this House, it is necessary, in light of public debate around recent court decisions, to state that marriage is and should remain the union of one man and one woman to the exclusion of all others, and that Parliament will take all necessary steps within the jurisdiction of the Parliament Canada to preserve this definition of marriage in Canada." The motion passed with a slight amendment to the wording. A few Liberals who voted against the Reform

motion did so because they believed that the preservation of an exclusively heterosexual definition of legal marriage could be deemed unconstitutional unless the government was prepared to use the override – a course of action they would not support. House of Commons, *Debates*, 8 June 1999, 15960; "Most in poll want gay marriages legalized," *Globe and Mail*, 10 June 1999, A1, A16.

178 Department of Justice, press release, "Government of Canada Proposes Amendment to Bill C-23," 22 March 2000.

179 House of Commons, *Debates*, Eric Lowther, Canadian Alliance, 11 April 2000, 5940.

180 "Liberal backbenchers rebel over same-sex spousal bill," Ottawa Citizen, 12 April 2000, A3.

181 House of Commons, *Debates*, John Bryden, Liberal, 11 April 2000, 5967.

182 "Ottawa introduces same-sex benefits," *Globe and Mail*, 12 Feb. 2000 A4. Some Liberal MPs made similar arguments. "Gay-rights bill stirring up Liberal caucus: Some MPs threaten to withhold support unless benefits extended to other couples," *Globe and Mail*, 10 Feb. 2000, A3.

183 Justice Committee, Anne McLellan, Liberal, 29 Feb. 2000.

184 "Most in poll want gay marriages legalized," *Globe and Mail*, 10 June 1999, A1, A8.

185 *Corbett v. Corbett* [1970] 2 *All ER* 33. In this case, the applicant sought annulment on the basis that his marriage to a transsexual (male-to-female) should be considered valid. The respondent claimed that she was legally female. The court ruled that the wife remained male despite her surgery and granted the annulment.

186 Same-sex marriage challenge begins," *Globe and Mail*, 6 November 2001, A10.

187 Justice and Human Rights, Bruce Ryder, Nick Bala, Claudine Ouelett, and Winifred Holland, 15–16 March 2000.

188 "Same-sex marriage voted a priority policy issue: Youth accused of hijacking meeting," *National Post*, 18 March 2000, A8.

189 British Columbia, Ministry of Attorney General, Press release, "Attorney General's Statement on Same Sex Marriages," 26 May 2000.

190 "B.C. to fight for same-sex marriage rights," *Globe and Mail*, 21 July 2000, A4; "Gays seek recognition for marriage," *Globe and Mail*, 9 November 2001, A6.

191 Justice Minister David Hancock, one of seven Conservative MLA's to vote against the bill, indicated that the legislation would not have any significant legal effect. "New law to ban same-sex marriage," *Calgary Herald*, 16 March 2000, internet edition: www.calgaryherald.com.

192 Alberta, *Legislative Debates*, Gary Dickson, Liberal, 8 March 2000, 321–2.

193 Ibid.

CHAPTER NINE

1 Or, as William Brennan suggests, it provides "a noble expression and shield of human dignity." William J. Brennan, Jr. "Why Have a Bill of Rights?" *Oxford Journal of Legal Studies* 9 (1989), 425.

2 Robert A. Goldwin, *From Parchment to Power: How James Madison Used the Bill of Rights to Save the Constitution* (Washington: AEI Press 1997), 97.

3 Madison wrote that, through the establishment of a "compound republic," the "power surrendered by the people is first divided between two distinct governments, and then the portion allotted to each subdivided among distinct and separate departments," thus providing "a double security" for the rights of the people. "The different governments will control each other, at the same time that each will be controlled by itself." *The Federalist Papers* (New York: New American Library 1961), no. 51, 320–5.

4 Ibid., no. 84, 515.

5 Goldwin, *From Parchment to Power*, 97.

6 Rainer Knopff, "Populism and the Politics of Rights: The Dual Attack on Representative Democracy," *Canadian Journal of Political Science*, 31:4 (1998), 700–1.

7 Ibid., 700. In support of his position, Knopff cites Peter Russell's earlier argument about the political purposes of the Charter. Russell made a distinction between infringements on what he referred to as core rights and infringements of more peripheral rights. About core rights, he suggests there has not been a "serious debate about the *minimum* extent to which each of these values should be realized in the laws and practices of our state." In contrast, more peripheral rights claims will be subject to reasonable differences of opinion. See Peter H. Russell, "Political Purposes of the Canadian Charter of Rights and Freedoms," *Canadian Bar Review* 61 (1983), 43–5.

8 Knopff "Populism and the Politics of Rights," 702.

9 Ibid., 700.

10 My perspective on this issue is setout in Chapters 3 and the Conclusion, where I argue that protection from discrimination on the basis of sexual orientation is a fundamental, core right.

11 Knopff supports the proposal for a sexually indifferent partnership law, under which any two people, regardless of their sexual orientation, and regardless of whether they are sexually involved, can register a partnership, with all the attendant rights and obligations. This model is not specific to same-sex partners, but it does not exclude them. Rainer Knopff, "The Case for Domestic Partnership Laws," *Policy Options* 20:5 (1999), 53–6.

12 This concern to address discrimination in the law is reflected in two public reports that examine forms of discrimination against same-sex partners:

Parliament of Victoria, Equal Opportunity Commission, "Same Sex Relationships and the Law" (March 1998) and Parliament of the Commonwealth of Australia, Senate Legal and Constitutional References
Committee, "Inquiry into Sexuality Discrimination" (December 1997).

13 Robert A. Dahl, "Decision-making in a Democracy: The Supreme Court as
a National Policy-Maker," *Journal of Public Law* 6 (1957), 279–95.

14 Gerald N. Rosenberg, *The Hollow Hope: Can Courts Bring about Social Change?*
(Chicago: University of Chicago Press 1991), 10–21.

15 Ibid., 338.

16 Ibid., 70–1. Emphasis in original.

17 Miriam Smith, *Lesbian and Gay Rights in Canada: Social Movements and Equality-Seeking, 1971–1995* (Toronto: University of Toronto Press 1999), 41–72.

18 Ibid., 135.

19 Charles R. Epp, *The Rights Revolution: Lawyers, Activists, and Supreme Courts
in Comparative Perspective* (Chicago: University of Chicago Press 1998), 23.

20 Ibid., 201 [note omitted].

21 Ibid., 195–6.

22 Ibid.

23 For discussion of the rights obsession of Americans, see Benjamin R. Barber,
"Constitutional Rights – Democratic Instrument or Democratic Obstacle?" in
Robert A. Licht, *The Framers and Fundamental Rights* (Washington: AEI Press
1991), 23–36.

24 Thomas R. Berger, *Fragile Freedoms: Human Rights and Dissent in Canada*
(Toronto: Irwin Publishing 1982). See also Walter Surma Tarnopolsky, *The
Canadian Bill of Rights*, 2nd ed. (Toronto: Macmillan 1978).

25 See the early Supreme Court Charter decisions of *Hunter et al. v. Southam Inc.*
[1984] 2 SCR 145 at 154–7; *R. v. Therens* [1985] 1 SCR 613 at 638–9; *Singh v.
Minister of Employment and Immigration* [1985] 1 SCR 177 at 209; *R. v. Big M
Drug Mart Ltd.* [1985] 1 SCR 295 at 331–2, 344–6.

26 Berend Hovius and Robert Martin, "The Canadian Charter of Rights
and Freedoms in the Supreme Court of Canada," *Canadian Bar Review* 61
(1983), 374.

27 Note the court's different interpretation of freedom of expression in the
context of similar legislation. In *Robertson and Rosetanni v. The Queen*
[1963] 1 SCR 651, the court interpreted freedom of religion in the Bill of
Rights narrowly, considering only the effect and not the purpose of legislation. It ruled that forced closing for businesses on Sundays under the
1906 Lord's Day Act does not restrict religious freedom because it does
not force anyone to adhere to Christian worship. Two decades later, in *R.
v. Big M Drug Mart, Ltd.,* [1985] 1 SCR 295, the court overruled *Robertson,*
concluding that its earlier approach was not appropriate under the Charter. The court adopted a purposive approach to Charter interpretation,

considering not only the effects of legislation on protected rights but also whether the legislation was consistent with the broad purposes of protecting rights, in this case, freedom of religion. It held that a purposive approach would enable courts to scrutinize more vigorously legislation that is challenged under the Charter and would provide a "more vigorous protection of constitutional rights by obviating the individual litigant's need to prove effect violative of Charter rights" (331–2).

28 F.L. Morton and Rainer Knopff, *The Charter Revolution and the Court Party* (Peterborough: Broadview Press 2000), 39.

29 Ibid., 33.

30 Ibid., 34.

31 Ibid., 41.

32 *Little Sisters Book and Art Emporium v. Canada (Minister of Justice)* [2000] 2 SCR 1120.

33 *R. v. Butler* [1992] 1 SCR 452

34 *Little Sisters*, 1155–63. Lawyers for the bookstore argued that erotica plays a different role in gay and lesbian communities than it does in a heterosexual community and that a harm-based approach to obscenity should not apply to gay and lesbian erotica in the same way as it does to heterosexual erotica, if at all. Since gay men and lesbians are defined by their sexuality, they are more vulnerable to sexual censorship. Thus, Little Sisters argued that the Customs legislation violates equality rights and freedom of expression because it operates with disproportionate and discriminatory effects on the gay and lesbian community. In part this is because of the broad discretion it confers on officials who have treated Little Sisters in a prejudicial and unfair way.

35 Ibid., 1162–3. Lawyers for Little Sisters had also argued that the language in *Butler*, which emphasized "degrading or dehumanizing" materials as examples of obscenity, is too subjective and encouraged Customs officials to prohibit depictions of anal intercourse, even after being advised by the Department of Justice that they should not. Nevertheless, the majority was more interested in how it characterized obscenity than in how others interpreted its words, and emphasized that its definition of obscenity, to prevent "degrading or dehumanizing" materials, was qualified by the caveat "if the risk of harm is substantial." The court relied on this qualification to suggest that the obscenity legislation, as the court interpreted it in *Butler*, did not discriminate against lesbian and gay men. Ibid.

36 Ibid., 1194, 1200. The majority did not fault the legislation, even though it did not constrain the discretionary powers of Customs officials. Since Parliament is constitutionally able to confer broad powers on the police and Justice Department officials under the Criminal Code without establishing a specific institutional framework to deal with Charter-sensitive

activities, it is not necessary to legislate special procedures to govern Customs officials. In the majority's view, Parliament has developed an appropriate balance between the restrictive effects of the Customs legislation and the valid legislative objective of prohibiting the entry of socially harmful material.

37 Ibid., 1205. On this issue the majority ruled that section 152(3) of the Customs Act should not be construed and applied so as to place the onus on an importer to establish that goods are not obscene within the meaning of section 163(8) of the Criminal Code. This is because the burden of proving obscenity rests on the crown on others who allege it.

38 Ibid., 1153.

39 Ibid., 1208. In dissent, the minority ruled that the flaws in the Customs regime are not simply because of bad faith or misadministration but flow from the Customs legislation itself. The minority held that the legislation should be invalidated so that Parliament could remedy the constitutional problems.

40 Smith, *Lesbian and Gay Rights in Canada*, 21–2.

41 Ibid., 154.

42 Another criticism of rights-based strategies is that they lead to fragmentation. Smith argues that rights separates law from politics and favours an apolitical approach to litigation, where the goal is to win cases rather than to use rights claiming as a method of mobilizing the grass-roots of the movement. Fragmentation of the lesbian and gay social movement occurs because of the lack of accountability of a legal rights-oriented approach to the diversities of the lesbian and gay communities. Smith, *Lesbian and Gay Rights in Canada*, 73–156.

43 Ibid., 155.

44 *Toward Equality, Response to the Report of the Parliamentary Committee on Equality Rights* (1986), 13.

45 Standing Committee on Justice and Human Rights, Anne McLellan, 29 Feb. 2000. *http://www.parl.gc.ca/InfoCom/CommitteeEvidence.asp?* Language=E&Parliament=2&Joint=0&CommitteeID=65.

46 The Supreme Court enjoys strong political support and its judgments are generally considered authoritative on issues of defining public values. Public opinion surveys conducted in 1987 and 1999 reveal that the Charter is familiar to most Canadians and much admired; a two-to-one majority of Canadians continue to prefer courts rather than legislatures to have the final say on issues of Charter conflicts; and more than 76 per cent of those surveyed are satisfied with the Supreme Court's performance. See Joseph F. Fletcher and Paul Howe, "Canadian Attitudes toward the Charter and the Courts in Comparative Perspective," *Choices: Public Opinion and the Courts* 6:3 (2000), 6–16.

47 This may be less so in Quebec, where memories that the Charter was adopted without the province's consent may, for some, undermine its legitimacy.

CONCLUSION

1 Ronald Dworkin, *Taking Rights Seriously* (Cambridge, Mass.: Harvard University Press 1978).

Index